THE HISTORY OF TEXAS MUSIC

John and Robin Dickson Series in Texas Music

Sponsored by the Center for Texas Music History

Texas State University–San Marcos

Gary Hartman and Gregg Andrews, General Editors

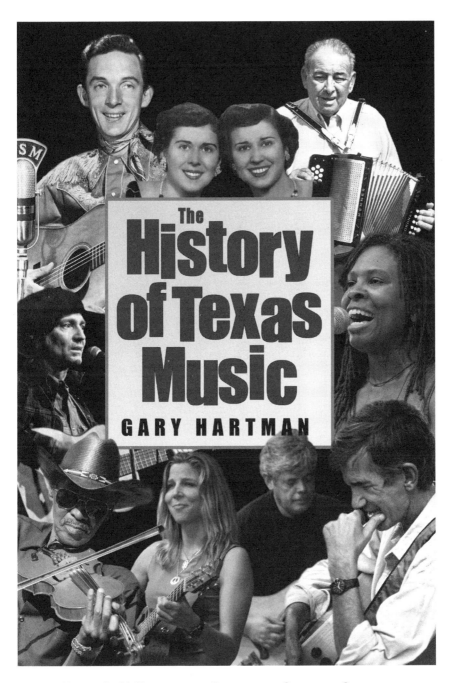

The History of Texas Music

GARY HARTMAN

TEXAS A&M UNIVERSITY PRESS • COLLEGE STATION

Copyright © 2008 by Gary Hartman
Manufactured in the United States of America
All rights reserved
First Edition

This paper meets the requirements
of ANSI/NISO Z39.48–1992
(Permanence of Paper)
Binding materials have been chosen for durability.

Library of Congress Cataloging-in-Publication Data

Hartman, Gary.
The history of Texas music / Gary Hartman. — 1st ed.
    p. cm. — (John and Robin Dickson Series in Texas Music)
Includes bibliographical references (p.) and index.
ISBN-13: 978-1-60344-001-1 (cloth : alk. paper)
ISBN-10: 1-60344-001-1 (cloth : alk. paper)
ISBN-13: 978-1-60344-002-8 (pbk. : alk. paper)
ISBN-10: 1-60344-002-X (pbk. : alk. paper)
1. Popular music—Texas—History and criticism.   I. Title.
ML3477.7.T35H37   2008
780.9764—dc22
2007026611

This book is dedicated to
Clifford Antone,
who loved and supported
all Texas music.

Contents

· ·

Preface

Since I first began teaching courses on the history of music in the Southwest, I often have encountered the same set of questions from students, colleagues, and others: "What exactly is 'Texas' music?" "Is Texas music truly unique compared to other forms of regional American music?" "If Texas music is unique, what makes it so different?" These are not easy questions to answer. Something as broad and complex as Texas music is difficult to define or categorize, and the fact that no single monograph is yet available to provide a comprehensive, scholarly overview of Texas music history has made this even more challenging.[1]

The absence of a broad-based study on Texas music history does not mean that there is a lack of interest in the subject, however. On the contrary, public and scholarly attention focused on Texas music has been growing in recent years.[2] As historians, ethnomusicologists, and others increasingly acknowledge the importance of music in shaping and reflecting the remarkably rich and ethnically diverse culture of the Southwest, several good publications dealing with the state's musical heritage have appeared.[3] In addition, a number of articles, book chapters, unpublished papers, theses, and dissertations deal with a variety of issues related to Texas music.[4]

Although all of these studies are valuable, each tends to focus on a particular genre or aspect of Southwestern music history without providing a broader perspective on this large and complex topic. Consequently, it seemed to me that a real need existed for a more comprehensive historical monograph on Texas music that would tie together the numerous sources of information that are available. I became even more convinced of the need for a more thorough examination of the Southwest's musical heritage after being invited to contribute a chapter to Texas A&M University Press's 2003 book *The Roots of Texas Music*, which deals primarily with Texas music during the first half of the twentieth century. While working on the first chapter (an overview of Texas and Southwestern music history), I realized that I wanted to eventually expand that brief essay into a complete book that would explore in greater detail the long-term musical development of the region.

However, as I began to delve more deeply into the research and writing of the book, the difficulties of taking on a project of this size and scope soon became apparent. How, I wondered, would it be possible to condense into a few hundred pages such a vast and multifaceted topic? I quickly realized that, at best, I could hope to present only a panoramic view of the state's musical history, offer some analysis and insight into certain specific areas, and then refer the reader to other sources for additional information. Consequently, this book is not intended to serve as the definitive study of any particular aspect of Texas music history. Instead, I have tried to present a generalized overview of most of the broader musical developments in the region and to mention, at least briefly, many of the individuals who have played an important role in the evolution of Texas music. Out of necessity, I have had to leave out some of the people, places, and events that others might believe should have been included, and, in some instances, I have made an effort to distill into simpler form some rather large, complex, and abstract issues and concepts. In the end, I take full responsibility for any omissions or errors in fact or interpretation included in this book.

Attempting to produce a comprehensive history of Texas music is indeed a daunting task. Fortunately, I have had available the excellent scholarship and generous guidance of a number of experts who have devoted their careers to researching and writing about specific topics in Southwestern music history. I have also been lucky enough to spend a good deal of time with a number of musicians and others outside of academia who have helped furnish a very important nonacademic perspective on Texas music. As both a historian and musician myself, I believe strongly that the best way to gain a truly complete understanding of the state's remarkable musical heritage is to draw from both academic and nonacademic sources and to take into consideration a variety of viewpoints. In keeping with these principles, I have done my best to combine my scholarly training in ethnic community history with my firsthand knowledge of how important music is as a cultural medium through which human beings communicate information, ideas, emotions, values, and beliefs and bond together as friends, families, and communities.

In an effort to cover the broad and complex topic of Texas music history in a somewhat systematic way, I have organized this book into seven chapters. The first chapter examines the unique social, cultural, economic, and political history of the Southwest, as well as the importance of music to human society. The remaining six chapters focus primarily on individual ethnic communities or sets of communities throughout the region and examine the vital role music has played in their historical and cultural development over the years. I maintain that, as these groups used music to celebrate their history and traditions, communicate their values and beliefs, and articulate their sense of identity and place within society, the Southwest gave rise to a unique, complex, and dynamic cultural environment in which musical influences "cross-pollinated" among various ethnic communities and helped to both shape and reflect the long-term development of the region's history and culture. By examining the rich and diverse musical heritage that grew out of this unique environment, we can gain greater insight into the ways in which certain groups in the Southwest evolved and attempted to reconcile their own sense of history and culture with that of others in the region.

Of course, one of the challenges of writing about the cultural history of specific ethnic groups is that no ethnic community is monolithic. On the contrary, all ethnic groups are complex and continuously evolving as a result of changes taking place both inside and outside of their communities. We can see this quite clearly throughout Texas history, as immigrant groups used music to define and articulate their collective sense of identity while, at the same time, they exchanged musical traditions with others. Today, the music of Texas, which includes Native American, gospel, blues, ragtime, jazz, swing, rhythm and blues, conjunto, Tejano, Cajun, zydeco, Western swing, honky-tonk, polkas, schottisches, rock & roll, rap, hip-hop, and a number of other subgenres, reflects the unique cultural dynamics of the Southwest and the ways in which the musical cultures of various groups have intermingled throughout the region.[5]

Another challenge in writing this book has been to determine whom to include as a "Texas" musician. Most artists discussed here were born and/or raised in Texas. Others were not, but they either spent a substantial amount of time in the state or were strongly influenced by the music of the Southwest. In any case, I have tried to mention, however briefly, most of those who have played a significant role in shaping the region's musical history. At the same time, this book is not meant to be simply a roster of famous Texas musicians. While I certainly have included many prominent artists from the Southwest, I have also examined the important role that music has played in the lives of "ordinary" Texans. In so doing, I have illustrated the way in which music has been vital to the daily fabric of Southwestern culture for virtually everyone living in the region.

Finally, I have tried to write this book in a way that appeals to both scholars and the general public. Although it is grounded in solid research and scholarship, my hope is that this book will be accessible to anyone who is interested in the musical history of the Southwest and will provide readers with an enjoyable and informative guide to this fascinating topic.

As anyone who has written a book knows, a major research and writing project such as this is possible only through the contributions of a number of people. I would like to thank Texas State University–San Marcos and especially my colleagues in the Department of History for their support and encouragement. In particular, I am grateful to Gregg Andrews and Deirdre Lannon at the Center for Texas Music History for shouldering the additional workload necessary to allow me extra time to finish this project. In addition, I would like to express my appreciation to Ron Brown, Vikki Bynum, and their graduate students for their generous help in conducting a number of important interviews through the Texas Music Oral History Program at Texas State University. Thanks also go to my dean, Ann Marie Ellis, and the former and current chairs of the History Department, Ken Margerison, Gene Bourgeois, and Frank de la Teja, for their support and assistance. I am also very grateful to the members of Texas State University's Developmental Leave Committee for granting me time off from teaching in order to undertake additional research.

In addition, I am deeply indebted to numerous other people for their advice, guidance, and assistance. I would especially like to thank the following: Mary Lenn Dixon, Thom Lemmons, and Carol Hoke at Texas A&M University Press, Connie Todd, Steve Davis, and Joel Minor of the Southwestern Writers Collection at Texas State University, John Wheat from the Center for American History at the University of Texas–Austin, Joe Specht in the Jay-Rollins Library at McMurry University in Abilene, John Rumble and Dawn Oberg at the Country Music Hall of Fame and Museum in Nashville, Tennessee, Greg Johnson of the J. D. Williams Library Special Collections at the University of Mississippi–Oxford, Casey Monahan at the Texas Music Office/Office of the Governor, Guadalupe San Miguel Jr. at the University of Houston, Tamara Saviano of American Roots Publishing in Nashville, John and Robin Dickson at Dickson Productions in Austin, Alan Govenar at Documentary Arts in Dallas, Clayton Shorkey at the Texas Music Museum in Austin, David Dennard at Dragon Street Records in Dallas, Marcelo H. Tafoya of the Tejano Artist Music Museum in Austin, Kathleen Hudson at the Texas Heritage Music Foundation in Kerrville, Curtis Peoples and Andy Wilkinson at Texas Tech University, Bill Malone, Dave Oliphant, Kitty Ledbetter, Diana Harrell, Cesar Limón, Mary Brennan, Dwight Watson, Ted and Linda Branson, Susan Roads, Don Anders, James Fraher, Roger Wood, Joe Brown, Claus and Jean Heide, Todd Purifoy, J. Marcus Weekley, Clifford Antone, Rod Kennedy, Dalis Allen, Kent Finlay, Casey Robertson, Lee Ann Womack, Paul Paynter, Enzo DeVincenzo, Robin Devin, Bertie Van der Heijdt and Saskia Zwerver, Arnold Lasseur, Patti Harrison, Georges Carrier, Jacques Bremond, Jacques and Anne Marie Spiry, Julia Hartman, J. B. and Sandra Hartman, Rosetta Wills and Michael Grace, Ramiro Burr, Craig Hillis, Charlie Gallagher, Terry Boothe, Susan Antone, Denise Boudreaux, Kevin Mooney, Laurie Jasinski, Danny Roy Young, Ernie Durawa, Kevin Coffey, Teresa Ward, Gary Mortensen, Art Blondin, Kim Fagerstrom, Dave Seeman, Rod Moag, Jerry Naylor, Burton Wilson, Bill Whitbeck, James White, Barbara Martin, Jim and Alice Niven, and Chris Lehmann. Finally, I would like to thank my wife, Francine Ducharme Hartman, for her love, support, patience, and humor throughout the course of this project.

Gary Hartman,
Austin, Tex.

THE HISTORY OF TEXAS MUSIC

CHAPTER 1

. . . .

Understanding the Music of Texas
and the American Southwest

Perhaps the best place to begin a discussion on the history of Texas music is with the question I have so often heard from students and others: What exactly is "Texas music?" First and foremost, Texas music is extraordinarily diverse. Although many people may think of country music when they think of the Lone Star State, Texas actually encompasses a wide variety of ethnic musical genres and regional styles. These include German and Czech music in Central Texas, conjunto and Tejano radiating northward from the Texas Mexican border region, Western swing and honky-tonk stretching from the grassy prairies of West Texas to the Gulf Coast, the Cajun and zydeco of French-speaking whites and blacks in East Texas, and blues, gospel, ragtime, jazz, rhythm and blues (R&B), country, folk, pop, rock & roll, rap, hip-hop, and many other types of music that can be found in rural and urban communities throughout the state.[1]

This leads us to another important question: Is Texas music truly unique compared to other forms of regional American music? To a certain extent, the answer is yes. Some types of music are native to the Southwest, and Texas has produced a number of artists and musical innovations that are distinct in many ways. However, it would be misleading to suggest that the Lone Star State's music is completely different or somehow separate from other types of regional American music. Quite the opposite is true. Texas music has evolved alongside and in conjunction with other forms of regional music, and it has deep roots extending outward to other parts of North America and around the world. Likewise, Texas music is very much a product of the larger cultural context of the entire American Southwest, which includes New Mexico, Oklahoma, Arkansas, Louisiana, and Mexico. Because of these ties to other outside influences, the music found in Texas has strong symbiotic connections with other regional styles and is most certainly part of the larger mosaic of American and world music.

Nevertheless, there are some aspects of the Lone Star State's history and culture that are truly unique, and this certainly is reflected in Texas music. For one thing, no other region of the country has had quite the same variety and configuration of ethnic cultures coexisting in such proximity and interacting in the same ways that they have in the Southwest. This has resulted in a distinct cultural environment in which a broad array of ethnic genres drawn from Spanish, Mexican, African, Caribbean, English, Irish, German, Czech, French, Jewish, Polish, and other influences have been woven together to create a remarkably eclectic regional music unlike that found anywhere else.

The unique and dynamic musical environment of the Southwest has produced an extraordinary number of influential and innovative musicians who have taken a leading role in shaping American music over the years. Artists such as Scott Joplin (the "father" of ragtime), blues pioneers Blind Lemon Jefferson, Lightnin' Hopkins, Sippie Wallace, and T-Bone Walker, country music stars Bob Wills, Gene Autry, Dale Evans, Tex Ritter, Ernest Tubb, George Jones, Barbara Mandrell, Kris Kristofferson, Kenny Rogers, Willie Nelson, Waylon Jennings, Tanya Tucker, George Strait, Lee Ann Womack, and the Dixie Chicks, piano virtuoso Van Cliburn, jazz giants Charlie Christian and Ornette Coleman, conjunto and Tejano legends Lydia Mendoza, Flaco Jiménez, Selena Quintanilla, and Emilio Navaira, and rock-and-roll icons Buddy Holly, Roy Orbison, Janis Joplin, ZZ Top, Stephen Stills, and Don Henley are just some of the better-known Texas artists who have had a profound impact on the long-term development of American music.

At the same time, Texas has done much more to shape the nation's musical history than simply produce a long list of famous performers. It has also helped introduce important innovations into American music. For example, Scott Joplin's leading role in defining and popularizing ragtime helped set the stage for the emergence of jazz during the early twentieth century. Other Texas musicians, such as Eddie Durham, Charlie Christian, Jack Teagarden, and Ornette Coleman, soon came along to help push jazz in new directions and set standards that others would follow for years to come. Likewise, Blind Lemon Jefferson, Victoria Spivey, Sippie Wallace (along with her brothers George and Hersal Thomas), T-Bone Walker,

Lightnin' Hopkins, Delbert McClinton, Stevie Ray Vaughan, Marcia Ball, Joe Ely, and many other Texans built on earlier African American musical traditions to help bring about important changes in blues, boogie-woogie, R&B, country, and rock & roll.

For generations, conjunto and Tejano artists, especially from the Rio Grande Valley of South Texas, have had a significant influence on the evolution of Latino music throughout North America. Lydia Mendoza, Beto Villa, Flaco Jiménez, Selena Quintanilla, Emilio Navaira, and countless others have borrowed from the centuries-old musical traditions of Spain and Mexico to create a distinct genre known as *música tejana*, or Texas Mexican music, which is now popular throughout the world. In recent years, Texas Mexican performers have kept música tejana evolving in exciting new directions by mixing these older musical traditions with country, R&B, rock & roll, jazz, rap, hip-hop, and other more modern styles.

Texas has also been extraordinarily influential in the development of country music. Beginning in the 1920s, the tremendous commercial success of native sons Vernon Dalhart and Carl T. Sprague, two of the nation's very first country singing stars, prompted major record labels to begin actively promoting country music as a distinct genre. Soon afterward, Gene Autry, Dale Evans, Tex Ritter, and others from the Lone Star State helped popularize this musical style throughout the world and made the Texas cowboy an international icon that would forever be identified with country music. During the 1930s Bob Wills, Milton Brown, and others combined the country, blues, jazz, Cajun, polka, and mariachi sounds they had grown up with in Texas to create a lively new music known as Western swing, which is still quite popular today.

Following World War II, Western swing helped give rise to honky-tonk, a somewhat harder-edged style of country music that reflected the social, economic, and political changes brought about by the mass migration of workers from the countryside into the state's rapidly growing urban centers. Texas artists such as Ernest Tubb, Floyd Tillman, Lefty Frizzell, George Jones, and Hank Thompson were leading pioneers of the honky-tonk sound and helped popularize it world-wide. By the 1970s a new generation of Texans, including Willie Nelson, Waylon Jennings, Kris Kristofferson, Guy Clark, Billy Joe Shaver, Marcia Ball, Michael Martin Murphey, and others, were mixing traditional country with folk, rock & roll, blues, boogie-woogie, and swing to create new musical hybrids known as "progressive country" and "outlaw country."[2] More recently, other Texas-based musicians, including George Strait, Lee Ann Womack, Lee Roy Parnell, Rosie Flores, Robert Earl Keen, Lyle Lovett, Nanci Griffith, the Dixie Chicks, Bruce Robison, Kelly Willis, Charlie Robison, Clint Black, LeAnn Rimes, Cross Canadian

Ragweed, Pat Green, Cory Morrow, Randy Rogers, Kevin Fowler, Jack Ingram, Bonnie Bishop, Todd Snider, Reckless Kelly, Stoney LaRue, and others, have built on the state's rich and varied traditions to continue redefining country music.

Although Cajun and zydeco music trace their roots back to French and African influences in neighboring Louisiana, Texas has played a vital role in the development of these two musical genres as well. During World War II, the Lone Star State's booming petrochemical industry attracted large numbers of French-speaking blacks and whites from Louisiana into East Texas. As Francophone musicians settled in Houston and elsewhere along the Texas Gulf Coast, they blended local musical traditions with their own to help redefine Cajun and zydeco. For example, Harry Choates, a pioneering figure in modern Cajun music who was born in Louisiana but raised in Port Arthur, Texas, helped popularize the Cajun sound throughout the country with his 1946 hit recording of "Jole Blon."[3] Clifton Chenier, the leading architect of modern zydeco, was also born in Louisiana but in the 1940s relocated to Houston, where he made some of the earliest known recordings of zydeco and helped forge the trademark style that future generations of zydeco musicians would follow.[4]

A number of influential pop and rock-and-roll musicians have come from the Southwest, including Buddy Holly, Roy Orbison, J. P. "The Big Bopper" Richardson, Janis Joplin, Don Henley, Seals and Crofts, Stephen Stills, ZZ Top, Doug Sahm, Stevie Ray Vaughan, Christopher Cross, Joe Ely, Los Lonely Boys, and others. All of these artists have blended their own regional influences into the larger musical mainstream to help shape the development of rock & roll worldwide.

Texas has also been important in the long-term development of the nation's recording industry. The Southwest was a favorite destination for major record labels in the 1920s and 1930s, as they sought to fill the growing national demand for "race" records.[5] This interest in marketing regional ethnic music helped lead to the early recording of many prominent Mexican American and African American artists in the state during the early twentieth century, including Blind Lemon Jefferson, Lydia Mendoza, and Huddie "Lead Belly" Ledbetter. The popularity of these and other Texas-based performers helped persuade record companies to expand their catalogs beyond just mainstream popular music to include an array of ethnic and regional styles, such as blues, gospel, jazz, conjunto, and country. This contributed to the emergence of a national market for more ethnically oriented genres, which allowed for the proliferation of blues, jazz, boogie-woogie, conjunto, Tejano, R&B, funk, and other styles over the coming years.[6]

In addition to the state's important role in the development of the commercial recording industry, Texas also produced pioneering musicologists, most notably

John Avery Lomax and his son, Alan Lomax, who traveled throughout the South and Southwest during the 1930s and 1940s recording local musicians in an attempt to document and study the unique ethnic traditions found in the region. The Lomaxes not only helped preserve a vast body of American folk music that might otherwise have been lost but also awakened the public to the rich and diverse musical heritage present throughout the Lone Star State.[7]

The Southwest has also had an important impact on the evolution of radio broadcasting in North America, especially through the enormously popular "border radio" stations of the 1930s, 1940s, and 1950s. These radio stations, which were strategically located in Mexico just across the Rio Grande from Texas as a way to circumvent U.S. broadcasting laws, were able to provide a more freewheeling variety of music, information, advertising, and other forms of entertainment with virtually no governmental regulation. Being exempt from U.S. laws also meant that border radio stations could broadcast their colorful and sometimes controversial programs with much stronger signals, which could reach throughout the United States and well into Canada. Because border radio was such a powerful presence in broadcasting during the first half of the twentieth century, it would continue to have a lasting impact on how other radio stations across the United States structured their formats and marketed music, products, and performers well into the twenty-first century.[8]

In recent years, the impressive growth of the Texas music industry has continued to play a vital role in the development of the state's music. The proliferation of independent and major-label recording studios throughout the Southwest has provided opportunities for musicians of all genres to experiment with a variety of styles and make their music more readily available to the public. A number of popular musical events, such as the Kerrville Folk Festival, Anderson Fair, MusicFest, and others allow up-and-coming performers to work alongside veteran artists, keeping the state's musical legacy alive and evolving for future generations. The critically acclaimed PBS program *Austin City Limits* has helped introduce Texas music to international audiences and, more recently, has spawned one of the largest annual festivals in the country. In 1990 the Texas legislature established the Texas Music Office within the Office of the Governor in order to help promote the music industry, music education, and music-related heritage tourism. Musicians from the Lone Star State now tour regularly throughout Europe, Asia, South America, and the Middle East. Across the state and around the world, Texas music is thriving and continuing to develop as individuals, families, communities, schools, governmental agencies, and others draw on the region's long-standing musical traditions to make Texas music an important part of their daily lives.[9]

With a remarkably varied array of ethnic genres, a long list of influential art-ists, and an impressive record of important contributions to the nation's musical history, there is little doubt that the musical environment found in Texas and the Southwest not only is unique in certain respects but has also had a profound long-term impact on the development of American music in a variety of ways. With this in mind, we can now begin to address another very important ques-tion: If Texas music is unique, what makes it so different? In a word—place. The issue of location or "place" is something that, in recent years, historians and ethnomusicologists have increasingly come to understand is absolutely essential to the development of local and regional culture. Although at first the term "place" may seem only to suggest a specific fixed point on a map, there is actually much more to it than that. In a larger sense, "place" refers to a social and cultural nexus of sorts, in which a variety of factors, including history, geography, climate, demographics, economics, and politics, converge to cre-ate a distinct and dynamic environment unlike that found anywhere else in the world. The Southwest is just such a place where a special set of social, cultural, and historical circumstances has come together to help shape the region, its people, and their music in unique ways.

What is truly at issue in our discussion of place is the question of whether and to what extent our immediate surroundings affect the ways in which we under-stand, process, and communicate culture. In other words, would Buddy Holly have been the same versatile and prolific musician if he had grown up in, say, Bangor, Maine? Did the fact that he spent his formative years in the South Plains of Texas, where the crosscurrents of Western swing, honky-tonk, blues, R&B, pop, and conjunto mixed freely as part of the local cultural landscape, have any meaningful impact on his development as an artist? Would Janis Joplin have been the same raw, gutsy blues singer if she had been raised on a farm in Nebraska instead of in the "Golden Triangle" of the Texas Gulf Coast, where the blues, R&B, Cajun, zydeco, and honky-tonk of English- and French-speaking blacks and whites still blend together in the myriad roadhouses, juke joints, and dance halls?

Of course, it is impossible to know exactly how much these artists' immediate surroundings affected their personalities, musical development, and professional careers. However, the local culture that Holly and Joplin absorbed on a daily basis, beginning in childhood and continuing through their early adult years, undoubtedly had an impact on their musical sensibilities and the ways in which they developed artistically, just as it did for many other Texas musicians.

A number of factors have contributed to the Southwest's distinctive cultural environment and made Texas unique in terms of place. For one thing, the state is so large that it encompasses a stunningly diverse array of climates, topography, ecosystems, and human cultures. From the swamps, bayous, and pine forests of East Texas to the vast deserts of West Texas, and from the wind-blown grasslands of the northern Texas Panhandle to the palm trees, citrus orchards, and beaches of South Texas, the state embraces an extraordinary range of geographic, climactic, agricultural, political, and economic regions.

Even more important than the size, climate, and topography of the Lone Star State is the remarkable ethnic diversity of its people. Largely because it is where the Deep South, the Great Plains, the Southwest, and Mexico intersect, Texas has long been a crossroads for many different ethnic groups, each of which has contributed its own distinct cultural traditions to the region. The number, variety, and placement of the state's ethnic communities are unique in all of North America, and they have allowed for a prolific cross-pollination of musical cultures that has given Texas music its special character. In his seminal study on the history of American country music, *Country Music, U.S.A.*, historian Bill Malone acknowledges the importance of this "cross-cultural matrix," which has allowed for the development of a very ethnically diverse musical environment in the Southwest:

> Young people who grew up in any of the several ethnic communities that extended from Southwest Louisiana to the Texas hill country were torn between . . . the Old Country music of their parents (from France, Mexico, Germany, Poland, Bohemia), and the fashionable music that drifted in from the outside world. Consequently, musical styles became strongly intermeshed, and often in wonderfully exciting ways. Cajun musicians . . . freely mixed their traditional forms with country, blues, and jazz, while over in South Texas it was not at all uncommon to find "Western" bands . . . who played polkas, schottisches, hoedowns, and the latest country hits. Musicians who hoped to prosper playing for dances in the broad territory extending south, east, and west from Austin, Texas, learned quickly that they must be prepared to play anything from "Allá en el Rancho Grande" and "Herr Schmidt" to "Jole Blon" and "Cotton-Eyed Joe."[10]

Ultimately, it is this tremendous ethnic diversity found throughout the Southwest that has had the greatest impact on the region's music. In order to understand how those ethnic dynamics came to be and how they influenced the development of Texas music, it is helpful to first consider the state's unique history.

. . . .

A BRIEF HISTORY OF TEXAS

Long before humans settled there, the Southwest was already developing many of the special characteristics that would help shape the lives of its inhabitants for centuries to come. As early as the Paleozoic era, more than 500 million years ago, the shifting of tectonic plates, along with soil erosion from wind and water, helped create a vast, rolling plain upon which millions of buffalo would eventually graze. Centuries later, longhorn cattle replaced those buffalo and gave rise to one of the state's most important early industries, cattle ranching, which would have a profound impact on the area's economy and culture. Another major development that occurred during prehistoric times involved the decaying of vast amounts of vegetation in the region, forming huge underground reservoirs of oil and natural gas. By the twentieth century, the petroleum extracted from these ancient deposits would become one of the state's most important natural resources, helping fuel its rapid transition to an industrialized economy and attracting a large and diverse human population into the Southwest.

Between 10,000 and 12,000 years ago, the first known humans arrived in the Texas Panhandle. These highly mobile hunter-gatherers adapted well to a harsh environment that presented a variety of challenges ranging from dramatic and unpredictable changes in weather to unreliable supplies of food and shelter. Over the next several thousand years, dozens of other tribal groups migrated into the Southwest, each contributing its own cultural traditions to the region. All of these native communities had to develop the skills and resources necessary to flourish in a remarkably varied environment that ranged from swamps and pine forests in the east to grassy plains and arid mountains in the west.[11]

The human population of the Southwest continued to grow and diversify as Spain became the first European nation to colonize the area. Spanish explorer Álvarez de Pineda ventured into the region as early as 1519 and began mapping the Texas Gulf Coast for the Spanish Crown, but it was not until 1528 that Spaniards finally established direct contact with the area's native inhabitants. It was then that Alvar Núñez Cabeza de Vaca and three other survivors of Pánfilo de Narváez's shipwrecked expedition spent eight years living and traveling among Texas Indians before finally returning to Mexico City, the seat of New Spain's government.[12]

By 1685 the French had begun making inroads into Texas, and Spanish authorities realized that they would have to fortify Spain's presence in the Southwest in order to secure its hold on the region. However, the Spanish government had difficulty persuading its citizens to migrate north from central Mexico into the often inhospitable Texas frontier in order to help populate the area. Consequently,

the northern fringes of Spain's American colonies, including Texas, remained
sparsely inhabited and open to encroachment from other countries.[13]

When Mexico won its independence from Spain in 1821, the newly formed
Mexican government began working in earnest to increase the population of Texas
as a way to solidify its claim on the entire Southwest. As part of this effort, Mexican
authorities agreed to allow a limited number of American immigrants, beginning
with those under the leadership of Moses and Stephen F. Austin, to settle in Texas
during the early 1820s, with the understanding that the newcomers would acquire
Mexican citizenship and abide by all Mexican laws. Soon, however, thousands of
other land-hungry settlers from the United States, especially the American South,
began pouring into Texas. As this growing population of mostly English-speaking "Anglo" Texans became increasingly frustrated with Mexico's restrictions on
slavery, trade, and other issues, they joined with Spanish-speaking Texans, or
Tejanos, to declare independence from Mexico on March 2, 1836. Although the
fighting was sometimes fierce, it only lasted a few weeks, and by late April 1836
a new country, the Republic of Texas, was born.[14]

Texas remained an independent nation from 1836 until 1845, when it was an-
nexed by the United States. During this period of independence and throughout the
remainder of the 1800s, the state's population grew dramatically. The ready avail-
ability of cheap, fertile land attracted a wide range of people from all over Europe,
North America, and Latin America and helped make Texas one of the most ethnically
diverse states in the country. Each of these groups brought its own musical traditions
to add to the region's already complex and dynamic cultural environment.

Of all of the European immigrants to come to the Southwest during the nineteenth century, Germans arrived in the greatest numbers. Aided by organizations
such as the *Adelsverein*, they established several communities, including New
Braunfels and Fredericksburg, in what came to be known as "the German belt,"
which stretched across South Central Texas. In addition to Germans, thousands
of Czechs, Poles, French, Irish, Jews, and other Europeans also came to Texas
during the late nineteenth and early twentieth centuries. Many others migrated
into the state from Mexico, adding to the Spanish-speaking Tejano population,
whose ancestors had already been in the region for centuries. When the Civil War
ended in 1865, a new influx of black and white Southerners began arriving in the
Lone Star State, bringing with them musical traditions that were rooted in both
Africa and the British Isles but had been redefined over generations of living in
the unique environment of the American South.[15]

As the twentieth century dawned, the 1901 discovery of oil at Spindletop, near
Beaumont, helped sweep Texas into a new era during which it transformed from

a predominantly agricultural state into an industrial and economic powerhouse. With the onset of World Wars I and II, the petrochemical industry, which quickly spread along the Upper Gulf Coast, helped make Texas the country's leading oil-producing state, bringing thousands more outsiders into Texas, including French-speaking blacks and whites from neighboring Louisiana who carried with them rich musical traditions extending back to Africa, France, and Eastern Canada. Over time, each of these groups left its own distinct imprint on the state's complex and continuously evolving cultural terrain.[16]

The influx of diverse people and cultures into Texas has continued in recent years. During the 1960s and 1970s hundreds of thousands of Americans from numerous ethnic backgrounds fled the decaying industrial infrastructure of the northern Rust Belt in search of new economic opportunities in Texas and other Sunbelt states. Likewise, immigrants from throughout Europe, Asia, Africa, and Latin America continue to flock to the region. Along with these important demographic developments, Texas has continued its ongoing transformation from a historically rural, agrarian society to a more urban, industrial one. Three of the most important traditional industries that helped fuel the state's economy for decades—oil, cattle, and agriculture—now share the stage with high tech, high finance, and a booming service industry. Today Texas ranks second among the fifty states in both size and population, with 21 million people spread across 261,914 square miles and two time zones. Although it is home to two of the nation's largest cities, Houston and Dallas, most of Texas still is made up of wide open rural spaces interspersed with small to medium-sized towns.[17]

With a large and ethnically diverse population, the cultural landscape of Texas will continue to evolve. According to government estimates, the state's combined population of ethnic minorities will exceed the Anglo population in Texas by 2010, and by 2020 Hispanic Texans could outnumber Anglo Texans.[18] It is unclear exactly what impact this increasingly diverse population will have on Texas culture, including its music. However, it is certain that the state's distinct ethnic, geographic, environmental, demographic, social, political, and economic circumstances have helped give Texas a unique and colorful history that is well represented in the state's remarkable musical heritage.

THE MANY ROLES OF MUSIC

The Southwest is certainly not alone in having a musical culture that reflects that particular region's history. In fact, music and other forms of cultural expression are an essential part of the historical development of virtually all societies, and regional forms of music, no matter where they are found throughout the world, reveal important information about local communities, their history, and their culture. Why, then, is music such an integral part of the human experience? In large part, it is vital because it is one of the most universal means we have for expressing emotions, communicating culture, sharing information and ideas, addressing local issues or concerns, and articulating a sense of collective identity within a family, group, or community. Since music unquestionably influences the way in which individuals and communities conceptualize, communicate, and celebrate their history and culture, it provides us with a powerful lens through which we can observe a particular group's collective experiences over time and better understand how that group has evolved within the larger context of human society.[19]

Music is also significant because it is one of humankind's most democratic forms of cultural expression. Unlike literature and some forms of art, people do not necessarily need an education or formal training in order to participate in music. As a result, throughout human history, music has served as a universally available means of articulating local culture and passing along information, ideas, and traditions from one generation to the next or from one group to another. This has been particularly important in the Southwest since literacy rates were relatively low among most ethnic communities until after World War II. Because it is such a readily accessible and widely used method of human expression, music has also provided historically marginalized groups, such as women and ethnic minorities, a means through which to communicate information, address concerns, and negotiate their positions within society.[20]

Music serves many other purposes as well. For example, it can play a principal role in how we bond with friends, family, colleagues, and others. Our cultural compatibility, including shared tastes in music, food, art, literature, and recreational activities, is an important part of how we select those with whom we associate. At first glance, having compatible tastes in music and other cultural matters may seem somewhat trivial. However, these are important factors in forming what some anthropologists consider "tribal" bonding, a process through which individuals create a collective identity based, in part, on shared cultural interests. As one of the most popular forms of cultural expression, music has long been an integral part of this bonding process among humans. Whether it is a college fight song to rally support for the home team, a national anthem intended to inspire patriotism, or a sentimental tune that reminds friends or lovers of past shared experiences, music fulfills a vital role in bonding groups of people and allowing them to preserve and celebrate their collective experiences.[21]

For most societies, music, especially dance, is also an important part of the courtship and mating process. Whether it be in the form of an ancient tribal ceremony in a remote village or the latest dance moves in a modern, urban singles bar, dance is often part of a larger courting ritual in which people, especially those of a prime mating age, demonstrate their physical agility and emotional sensitivity while looking for the same characteristics in others. In most Western societies, the importance of music and dance in the courtship and mating process has been formally institutionalized through the wedding ceremony, which typically includes a ceremonial first dance, reserved for the newly wed couple, followed by a father-daughter or mother-son dance, in which parents symbolically release their children to begin their married lives. Following these initial rituals, the entire wedding party, made up of friends, family, and others close to the bride and groom, join together for an extended period of music, dancing, and celebration.

As couples move from courtship and marriage into parenthood, music continues to play a central role in their lives, especially as a means of nurturing and communicating with their children. The singing of lullabies and nursery rhymes, along with other musical interaction between parents and offspring, are essential to early childhood nurturing and education. In areas with historically lower literacy rates, such as the Southwest, parents have often relied on oral musical traditions in order to pass along information, social skills, belief systems, and family history to succeeding generations. Music is not only an important part of the life-long developmental process in terms of communicating history, culture, and long-standing traditions; it also serves a vital function in the physical well-being of people. In fact, music triggers certain psychophysiological responses in humans, including the release of endorphins, which contribute to a sense of euphoria and play a crucial role in relieving stress and fatigue and in maintaining good physical and mental health. As a result, music helps promote good social, psychological, and physiological development in human beings.[22]

Music is an integral part of human culture throughout the world precisely because it serves so many important purposes. On the most basic level, it provides emotional and physical stimulation, but in a larger way, music is a fundamental part of the age-old human process of building and maintaining personal and communal relationships. Couples, families, and communities all use music to strengthen bonds, communicate ideas and information, celebrate cultural traditions, pass along customs and beliefs, and articulate a sense of identity and place within society. Because music is such a deep-seated part of the overall human experience, we can better understand how ethnic communities evolve and interact with others by examining the long-term development of their musical culture.

MUSIC: "ORGANIC" OR "SUPERORGANIC?"

While we are looking at the impact of music on our daily lives, it is also important to consider how music originates and evolves within society. According to ethnomusicologist Manuel Peña, music can be divided into two general categories: "organic" and "superorganic." Organic music, Peña says, evolves organically from the grassroots level of local communities over a long period of time. As an important part of the community's cultural vocabulary, organic music is used in a variety of rituals, including births, deaths, courtship, marriage, religious ceremonies, work, planting, harvesting, hunting, warfare, and politics. Because its value is based on its usefulness to the local community, organic music is said to have "use value."[23]

Superorganic music, on the other hand, does not evolve naturally over time as an organic expression of a particular community's culture. Instead, it is most often created and manipulated in order to produce a marketable commodity. An example of this would be a pop song, which is written by professional songwriters, performed by studio musicians, and then mass-marketed to as large an audience as possible through a sophisticated network of advertising and airplay on radio, television, and the Internet. Such music is not generally intended to communicate vital social information or to reinforce community bonds, as is the case with organic music. Instead, superorganic music is calculated to generate financial profits for those who produce it, and there is little, if any, organic relationship between the musicians and their audience. Because its ultimate purpose is to be exchanged for something of economic value, superorganic music has what Peña calls "exchange value."[24]

Thinking of music in terms of organic and superorganic can be very helpful, especially when considering how factors such as race, ethnicity, language, and culture have influenced the development of Texas music over the centuries. However, the organic versus superorganic paradigm also presents some problems, most notably the fact that it is not always possible to clearly differentiate between them since they often overlap in certain ways. In fact, when we start to look more closely at different examples of music, we can see how most of them actually include both organic *and* superorganic characteristics.

A good example of how organic and superorganic music sometimes overlap is the case of traveling troubadours. These were wandering minstrels who could be found in a variety of settings, from the medieval French and Italian countryside to the early twentieth-century Texas Mexican border region. As they traveled from town to town, singing songs, telling stories, and passing along information from one community to the next, troubadours performed an organic function by providing news, entertainment, and social commentary to a remote and mostly illiterate population. Because they borrowed from long-standing organic musical traditions in order to convey information and address the interests and concerns of local communities, these balladeers and their music clearly demonstrated a use value. At the same time, however, since they were performing as a way to earn money, food, and shelter while they traveled the countryside, troubadours also exploited music for commercial purposes, and they often fashioned their songs and stories to maximize their exchange value within the villages in which they performed. Because they played a key role in the local folk culture while also plying their trade for financial profit, troubadours straddled the two worlds of organic and superorganic and freely mixed elements from both.[25]

In other examples of this blurring of boundaries, music sometimes originated as superorganic and transformed over time into what many would now consider essentially organic. For instance, tunes from the great nineteenth-century American songwriter Stephen Foster such as "Oh, Susanna" and "Old Folks at Home," began as commercial compositions. However, as traveling musical shows carried these songs to rural communities throughout the country during the mid- to late-1800s, local musicians adopted them and eventually helped make them part of the nation's folk music repertoire.[26]

During the 1960s, anti–Vietnam War protest songs carried meaningful social messages and often were an important part of articulating political views and mobilizing antiwar activists. At the same time, however, most of these tunes were produced and marketed by commercial record companies with the primary goal of generating revenue. More recently, rap music, which began in the 1970s as an organic expression of the social alienation experienced by mostly black, inner-city youth, was quickly appropriated by record labels that recognized the music's tremendous commercial potential. Although some forms of rap still convey important social messages that resonate in an organic way with audiences, much of rap has been transformed into a superorganic commodity that is commercially marketed as mainstream pop music.[27]

In the end, the organic versus superorganic model can help us to examine the ways in which certain types of music originate and evolve, especially in regard to how ethnic communities in Texas developed their own "homegrown" musical traditions. However, it is important to keep in mind that neither organic nor superorganic music fits neatly within clearly defined parameters. Instead, both overlap in many ways and on many different levels. This will become increasingly clear as we look in more detail at the complex and multidimensional musical environment of the American Southwest.

CHAPTER 2

. . . .

Texas Music Begins

Native American Musical Traditions
of the Southwest

usic has been a part of the story of Texas since the first humans set foot in the region. For thousands of years, American Indians living in the Southwest have made music an integral part of their daily lives through religious ceremonies, tribal gatherings, warfare, family events, and communal activities such as farming, fishing, hunting, and commerce.

Our knowledge of early Native American music in the Southwest is very limited, mainly because it was never recorded or thoroughly documented. Much of what little we do know comes from the writings of Spanish and other European explorers in the region, whose understanding of Indian culture was strongly influenced by their own cultural preconceptions. Although Native Americans themselves have kept many of their musical traditions alive, it is unclear just how closely their modern songs and dances resemble those practiced by their distant ancestors. In fact, because music is such a fluid and continuously changing form of expression, most Native American music performed today may be rooted in ancient traditions but has most likely been significantly altered over the years.[1]

Texas has been home to many Native American communities in the past several centuries. Numerous tribes, many consisting of loosely affiliated bands or family groups, spoke a variety of languages and dialects and operated within a vast, complex network of intertribal trade, migration, and warfare throughout the region.[2] However, few of the Native American groups that lived in the Southwest when the Spanish first began settling in the early 1500s still remain today. These early groups, including the Coahuiltecan, Caddo, Karankawa, Wichita, Atakapan, and Jumano, either died out, were displaced by Europeans or other Indians, or were absorbed into neighboring populations. The only tribes that currently claim permanent residence in Texas are the Kickapoo, Tigua, and Alabama-Coushatta, all three of whom migrated into the state from elsewhere.[3]

Indians of the Southwest adapted to the region's unique environment long before Europeans arrived. In the arid west, native farmers learned to work with limited resources and to cultivate hardy crops that could thrive despite low rainfall and poor soil conditions. To supplement their agricultural endeavors, they developed highly efficient methods of hunting, killing, and preserving smaller game. In some cases, Indians in the western part of Texas had to migrate on a seasonal basis in order to find adequate food, water, and shelter. In the more fertile eastern regions of Texas, groups such as the Caddo built permanent settlements, where they engaged in large-scale crop cultivation and constructed elaborate temple mounds for religious worship. Music was central to the daily lives of all of the Indian communities in the Southwest, helping them to articulate their values and beliefs and pass their history and traditions along from one generation to the next. Singing, chanting, and dancing all were an integral part of communicating information and culture in both secular and religious ceremonies.[4]

Archeologists have found numerous musical artifacts left behind by southwestern Indians, including percussion instruments such as rattles, rasps, drums, and pebble-filled gourds. Animal bones, especially scapulae, or shoulder blades, were used as drumsticks or to strike or rub against other hard objects. These items could be beaten, shaken, scraped, or struck to provide the rhythms needed for the group singing and dancing that were an integral part of many Native American rituals and ceremonies. Wind instruments, including whistles made from wood, bone, or reeds, were also common among southwestern Indian tribes. In addition to using a variety of instruments, some groups enhanced their musical ceremonies with fasting, meditation, or hallucinogenic substances that helped induce a trancelike state among the participants.[5]

Along the Texas Gulf Coast, the Karankawas included music in diverse tribal ceremonies. As a nomadic group whose Spartan lifestyle required significant physical stamina, the Karankawas used dancing as a way to demonstrate both physical agility and intelligence, basic traits that others in the community would certainly seek in a potential mate. The Atakapans, who lived in the marshes and bayous of East Texas, followed a successful hunt with several days of music, singing, and dancing. In South Texas, the Coahuiltecans regularly used singing and dancing in their rituals and apparently incorporated hallucinogens and in some cases cannibalism. The Jumanos, who lived in the southwestern part of the state and traded extensively with other tribes throughout the region, often combined choreographed dancing with singing and vocal mimicking of musical instruments.[6]

The Caddos of East Texas are considered one of the more technologically advanced Native American groups of the Southwest. They developed a sophisticated agrarian society that traded with Europeans and other Indians across a wide region. The Caddos often used music to celebrate the cultivation and harvesting of crops, especially corn, their main food source. The Caddos' technological expertise is evident in their ability to make ceramic utensils, some of which appear to have served as musical instruments. They also acquired metal bells from Spanish traders and may have used these for musical performances as well.[7] Apparently the Caddos made another important contribution to the history and culture of Texas that remains with us today. When Spanish explorers first arrived in East Texas, they took the Hasinai (a subset of the Caddos) word for friend, "techas," and transcribed it as "tejas." Soon the Spaniards began using the term to refer to all of the Caddo Indians in the area. In 1691 Spain officially christened the entire province "Tejas," from which English-speaking settlers eventually derived the name "Texas."[8]

In the nineteenth century, Texas witnessed the arrival of other Indian groups, most of whom had been pushed out of their original homelands elsewhere in the South and Southwest by a rapidly expanding white population. In East Texas the Cherokees included ritual bathing as part of their musical festivities, symbolizing a spiritual purification and the eternal cycle of birth, death, and rebirth. Black Seminoles, who settled along both sides of the Rio Grande in South Texas and Northern Mexico, were the descendants of former slaves and Seminole Indians. Their music reflected a blending of cultural influences from Native American, African American, and Hispanic origins.[9]

During the late nineteenth century, the Wichita and Kiowa Indians living on the North Texas plains became known for their "ghost dances," which were popular rituals practiced by a number of Plains tribes as part of a larger effort to unite Indians culturally and politically against the increasing European American presence in the West. The Comanches, who also arrived in the Southwest after being displaced by American settlers elsewhere, often performed what they called "vision quests." These involved long periods of fasting and music that helped induce a trancelike state and allowed tribal members to communicate with what they considered to be "guardian spirits."[10] The Apaches, who sometimes clashed with the Comanches in West Texas, celebrated the killing of their enemies with ceremonial dancing.[11]

Music was also important to other Indian groups throughout the greater Southwest. For example, the Pueblo, who lived mainly in present-day New Mexico and Colorado but are thought to be related to Texas tribes such as the Tigua, celebrated a mythical figure known as "Kokopelli," whose flute playing was believed to cast an almost magical spell over women. The Pueblo also practiced the *matachines* dance, an old ritual that combines music, dancing, singing, and storytelling through pantomime. Ironically, it may have been Spanish explorers who introduced this type of performance to the region, but over the years the Pueblo adopted the matachines and modified it to include both European and Native American musical instruments, dance steps, and religious and secular themes.[12]

Music is still an important part of daily life for the Kickapoo, Tigua, and Alabama-Coushatta in Texas. Among the many ritual dances performed by the Kickapoo living near Eagle Pass is a celebration in which women dance in unison around cooking pots as a way to honor domestic work. In far West Texas near El Paso, the Tigua have adopted certain Spanish customs, including the annual celebration of Saint Anthony, which combines Catholic rituals with Tigua music, dance, and costumes. Although the Alabama-Coushatta in Northeast Texas were Christianized in the nineteenth century and consequently abandoned some of their traditional practices, many have recently begun to rediscover their ethnic and cultural heritage through celebrations involving native music and dance.[13]

Around sixty thousand American Indians still live in Texas, and music remains an important part of the preservation and perpetuation of their history and culture. Each year thousands gather at powwows throughout the state, where they participate in singing, dancing, religious rituals, and a variety of educational activities in celebration and honor of their Native American heritage.[14] Some organizations, including the American Indian Education Project, based within the Austin Independent School District, work with schools, community centers, libraries, and others throughout the state to provide educational exhibits, performances, and presentations related to Native American history and culture in the region. Groups such as the San Antonio Vocal Arts Ensemble (SAVAE) also research and perform American Indian music from ancient times to the Spanish colonial period. These and other organizations are part of a larger national movement in which Native Americans, many of whom are now urbanized, are not only reconnecting to their ancestral roots but also helping educate others about the rich native cultures found throughout the United States.[15]

Although there is much we will probably never know about the musical customs of early American Indians, music has undoubtedly been an important part of human life in the Southwest since the very first "Texans" arrived.

RECOMMENDED LISTENING

Doc Tate Nevaquaya, *Comanche Flute Music* (Smithsonian Folkways)

Various artists, *Authentic Native American Music* (Delta)

Various artists, *Borderlands: From Conjunto to Chicken Scratch* (Smithsonian Folkways)

Various artists, *Ceremonial and War Dances* (Delta)

Various artists, *Heartbeat: Voices of First Nations Women* (Smithsonian Folkways)

Various artists, *Heartbeat, vol. 2: More Voices of First Nations Women* (Smithsonian Folkways)

Various artists, *Tribal Songs of the American Indians* (Madacy)

CHAPTER 3

. . . .

Música Tejana

Mexican American Music
in the Southwest

Texas Mexican music, known collectively as *música tejana*, has played a major role in the overall musical development of the Southwest. Since Spaniards were the first Europeans to settle in Texas beginning in the 1500s, they gave Spanish culture a strong foothold in the region long before the French, English, Germans, and others began arriving. Today the rapidly growing Mexican American population in Texas, along with the continual flow of people and goods back and forth across the U.S.-Mexican border, ensures that Hispanic culture will always be a significant part of everyday life in the Southwest.[1]

Música tejana is based on older musical traditions from both Europe and Africa, but it has evolved to encompass a rich and diverse variety of subgenres, including *orquesta*, conjunto, *norteño*, corridos, *rancheras, canciónes*, polkas, *cumbias*, mariachi, Chicano country, Tejano, rap, hip-hop, and others. In many ways, música Tejana reflects the remarkable cross-pollination of musical influences that has taken place throughout the Southwest over the years, as Tejanos, or Texans of Mexican descent, combined the older traditions of their ancestors with those of other ethnic communities to create a distinct Texas Mexican musical idiom.[2]

The roots of música tejana extend at least as far back as Spain's occupation by the Moors (711–1492 A.D.). During his period of nearly eight hundred years, much of the Iberian Peninsula, which includes Spain and Portugal, was controlled by Muslims from North Africa. Under Moorish occupation, Spain absorbed a variety of North African cultural traditions and blended them with local Spanish customs, the results of which are still evident today. For example, Flamenco music, for which Spain is universally known, is actually a synthesis of classic Spanish guitar styles and the hand clapping and dance steps of North African nomadic tribes. The Spanish language itself contains many words derived from Arabic dialects, including *ojalá* ("hopefully" or "may God grant it") and *algodón* (cotton). Moreover, Spanish art, architecture, and cuisine all have borrowed from the Islamic cultures of North Africa.[3]

Spain's long history of occupation by Muslim Africans not only had a profound impact on Spanish culture but also influenced the way in which Spain carried out exploration and colonization in the Americas and imposed Spanish culture on the Native Americans living there. During their centuries-long struggle to drive the Moors from the Iberian Peninsula, Spaniards launched what is called the *reconquista*, or reconquest, of their homeland. As part of this reconquista, local Spanish rulers in Castile, Aragón, and other provinces collaborated closely with the Catholic Church in order to consolidate military, political, and religious power throughout Spain. This strong partnership between Spanish political and religious leaders proved very effective in expelling the Moors, so Spain used much the same approach in its conquest of the Americas, where it established military, political, cultural, and religious dominance over the Native American population.[4]

The reconquista finally ended in 1492, when Spain drove out the last of the Moors. In August of that same year, a Genoese Sailor named Cristoforo Colombo (Christopher Columbus in Latinized form) sailed westward under the Spanish flag and established a political, economic, and cultural presence for Spain in the Americas. From the outset, music was an important part of Spanish colonization in the Western hemisphere. Fernal Pérez, a musician in Spain's royal court of King Ferdinand and Queen Isabella, accompanied Columbus on this first voyage to America and entertained crew members with music rooted in both Spanish and Arabic traditions. Soon boatloads of Spaniards began arriving in this "New World," carrying their language, religion, music, food, and other forms of culture with them. As they continued to spread across North and South America over the next two centuries, the Spanish brought their hybridized European African culture along, blending it with the cultures of Native Americans, Africans, and other Europeans with whom they interacted.[5]

While Spain soon grew wealthy from the gold, silver, and other valuable resources it extracted from its newly acquired American territories, other European nations were prompted to establish their own colonies throughout the Western hemisphere. As the Dutch, Portuguese, French, English, and others joined the Spanish in colonizing the Americas, they began importing African slaves to serve as a reliable source of cheap labor in the region. Over the following three centuries, Europeans built an extensive slave-trading network that stretched from West Africa across the Atlantic to the Caribbean Ocean and transported some twelve million African slaves to the Western hemisphere. Slave ships, which often included both black and white musicians who entertained the passengers and crew as a way to ease the drudgery of the long ocean passage, began blending European and African musical traditions to form a complex amalgamation of styles that can still be heard in the Caribbean region and throughout Latin America today.[6]

As the first European country to establish a permanent presence in the Americas, Spain built an extensive political and economic empire that radiated outward from its headquarters in Mexico City and included a vast network of Spanish settlements that stretched from Corpus Christi on the Texas Gulf Coast to Los Angeles and San Francisco on the Pacific Coast. To administer its far-flung territories, Spain built a system of presidio-mission complexes throughout the Southwest, each of which consisted of one or more missions clustered around a nearby presidio, or fort. The presidios helped provide protection for local residents and safe passage for precious minerals and other Spanish trade goods moving through the area. The missions themselves usually included living quarters for the Franciscan priests, a chapel for worship and religious conversion of the native population, and agricultural areas intended to help feed the residents and teach the Indians how to cultivate crops and raise livestock.[7]

As part of Spain's effort to assimilate the Indians and bring them under the social, political, economic, and religious control of the Spanish Crown and the Catholic Church, Franciscan missionaries worked hard to convince the local Native Americans to embrace the Spanish language and other aspects of Spanish culture, especially Christianity.[8] Music became an important tool in this campaign to assimilate and Christianize the Indian population. The Franciscans not only encouraged Native Americans to participate in musical rituals in the church but also taught them secular European music and how to build and play European musical instruments. Apparently the Franciscans' efforts to interest the indigenous population in Spanish music were quite successful. In fact, by 1561 there were so many Indian musicians performing throughout colonial Mexico that Spain's King Philip II placed limits on the number of Native Americans who were allowed to work as professional musicians.[9]

Although the Spanish succeeded in changing Native American culture through-out the Southwest, the Indians managed to retain many of their own folk traditions. Like all ethnic groups, Native Americans selectively assimilated into the more mainstream culture, embraced those customs that suited their needs, and rejected others that did not. Furthermore, the Indians themselves had a significant influence on Spanish culture in the region as well. Perhaps the most obvious example of this is the large number of Spanish men who intermarried with Indian women. This helped give rise to a new mestizo, or mixed-race population, which combined both Native American and Spanish cultures. These mestizos, who soon outnumbered the original Spaniards, dramatically altered the long-term ethnic makeup of the Spanish colonies and contributed to the blending of European, African, and Native American musical cultures that is still evident throughout Latin America today.

THE EARLY DEVELOPMENT OF MÚSICA TEJANA

Music was a vital part of everyday life in virtually all Spanish settlements throughout the Southwest, and by the beginning of the nineteenth century most communities had a number of locations in which different types of music were performed. Much like the rest of Europe, popular musical tastes in Spain and Mexico were defined in large part by class and social status. Colonial Mexico's middle and upper classes generally preferred symphonic or chamber orchestras, while the working class relied more on smaller stringed-instrument groups for musical entertainment. As a simple matter of economics, those with more money could employ larger, more elaborate *orquestas*, or orchestras, while others of more modest means had to make do with whatever local entertainers were available. Ironically, since working-class Mexican bands had fewer musicians than the larger middle-class orquestas, they had to find ways to be more efficient and innovative. This led to their incorporating the accordion and other highly versatile instruments in ways that would allow these smaller groups to produce more music with fewer players. This ability to adapt and innovate served working-class Mexican bands well for generations to come, as they adopted other styles and techniques and modified them to suit their own musical tastes and needs.[10]

Whether middle class or working class, music was central to the daily lives of nearly all Mexicans in the Southwest. Local churches included religious music in their festivals, funerals, baptisms, and weddings, while other locales, such as cantinas, public plazas, theaters, opera houses, and private homes, featured a wide variety of secular music. Although the middle class and working class usually held their events separately, they sometimes shared venues and borrowed from each other's musical customs. For example, working-class musicians often took themes from popular middle-class operettas and worked them into their corridos, or folk ballads, while middle-class Mexican composers sometimes incorporated Native American and working-class folk music into their more formal operas. In addition, Mexicans from all social classes eagerly embraced the latest song styles from Europe during the early 1800s, including waltzes, polkas, schottisches, minuets, and other popular dance steps. Mexicans also created musical hybrids such as the mariachi, a medium-sized ensemble that usually included both brass and stringed instruments. Because the mariachi performed mainly at weddings, its name derived from *mariage*, the French word for "marriage."[11]

In 1821 Mexico won its independence from Spain. Looking for ways to increase the population in the Southwest, the Mexican government soon began allowing English-speaking settlers from the United States to move into the province of Tejas. In both political and cultural terms, this decision would change Mexico's presence in the region forever by accelerating the ethnic diversification of Texas and actually weakening Mexico's hold on the Southwest. By 1836 the bourgeoning Anglo-Hispanic population would rise up and declare independence from Mexico, and the newly sovereign nation of Texas began attracting a flood of English, Irish, German, Czech, French, Polish, and other immigrant groups who would dramatically alter the social, political, and cultural landscape of the region.[12]

Tejanos, who had long been the dominant ethnic group in the region, soon became a marginalized minority that faced a sudden decline in legal, political, social, and economic status. As the Anglo majority grew rapidly throughout the 1800s, authorities began enacting a series of discriminatory laws intended to deprive Mexican Americans (and African Americans) of both property and basic civil rights. Before long, Tejanos found themselves unable to effectively challenge the quickly spreading policies of discrimination. Since they had few other means by which to express their growing concerns, Tejanos relied increasingly on music as both a "voice" through which they could articulate their collective sense of frustration and alienation and a symbol of ethnic pride and cultural defiance against the increasingly dominant Anglo majority.[13]

MÚSICA TEJANA IN THE TWENTIETH CENTURY

By the beginning of the twentieth century, música tejana had evolved to reflect the unique circumstances in which Texas Mexican society found itself. In little more than sixty years, Tejanos had gone from being the majority ethnic group in the region to becoming a marginalized minority that faced widespread discrimination and declining opportunities in employment, education, and political and civil rights. It would take decades of struggle before Tejanos finally began to see significant improvements in these areas during the 1960s and 1970s, mainly as a result of nationwide political activism and federal civil rights legislation. In the meantime, Tejanos continued to be treated as second-class citizens, and música tejana would serve as one of the most popular and effective means of articulating their frustrations and concerns, while also preserving and celebrating their cultural heritage.

Although the increasing marginalization of Mexican Americans had a profound impact on Tejano society and culture, it would be a mistake to think that it was only these difficulties between Tejanos and Anglos that shaped música tejana throughout the twentieth century. On the contrary, música tejana also reflected the many positive experiences of Tejanos as they celebrated life, love, family, friends, and community. In addition, other important changes were also taking place within Texas Mexican society during this time that influenced the development of música tejana. For one thing, Tejanos were going through the long and arduous process of assimilation, which required them to reconcile their dual identity as both Mexicans and Americans. On one level, most Tejanos felt a strong connection to their ancestral roots and wanted to preserve and celebrate certain aspects of their ethnic heritage. However, they also faced growing pressure from both inside and outside their own community to more fully integrate into mainstream society. Just as it had been for all other ethnic groups, this bicultural balancing act of assimilation would not be easy for Tejanos, and the experience had an unmistakable impact on the development of Texas Mexican culture, including música tejana.[14]

Other forces affected Tejano society throughout the twentieth century as well. One chief influence was the nation's rapid transition from a rural, agrarian society to an urban, industrial one during the late 1800s and early 1900s. This shift uprooted many Mexican American families and resulted in dramatic changes in the way Tejanos lived. The widespread devastation wrought by the Great Depression of the 1930s brought additional hardship to many Tejano communities that had already been struggling economically. Following the Depression, World War II brought an economic boom that provided Mexican Americans an unprecedented opportunity for social and economic advancement and helped many Tejanos move from the ranks of the working class into the middle class. At the same time, the deepening of the Cold War during the 1950s and the growing pressure for social conformity, as well as the tremendous social upheaval of the 1960s, ushered in a new era of political activism by ethnic minorities that helped lead to new legal, economic, and civil rights opportunities for Mexican Americans, African Americans, and others.[15]

One other factor that has had an enormous impact on Tejano society throughout the twentieth century is the proximity of Texas to Mexico and the almost continual flow of people, products, and culture back and forth across the U.S.-Mexican border. This has meant that Tejanos, unlike most other ethnic groups, have a culture that is constantly reinforced by direct contact with the ancestral homeland through television, radio, newspapers, commerce, and human migration, especially in the form of thousands of seasonal laborers who enter the United States each year. Although most return home to Mexico, these migrant Mexican workers have become an integral part of the larger U.S. economy, and they help reinforce the presence of Mexican culture throughout the Southwest.[16]

In addition to migrants from Mexico, the native Tejano population, including families whose ancestors came to the area long before English-speaking settlers arrived, has also increased rapidly during the twentieth century. As the twenty-first century began, Texas citizens of Mexican descent made up roughly 32 percent of the state's overall population of more than 22 million (nearly three times the national average of 12.5 percent), while some major Texas cities, especially San Antonio, El Paso, and Corpus Christi, are approaching a Hispanic majority. This growing native Tejano population, along with a significant influx of immigrants from Mexico, promises to keep Mexican culture and a sense of Mexican ethnic identity alive and vibrant throughout the Southwest for the foreseeable future.[17]

ORQUESTA TEJANA VERSUS CONJUNTO

The contrast between orquesta tejana and conjunto provides a good example of how música tejana reflected larger social, economic, political, and generational issues throughout much of the twentieth century. Whereas most middle-class Tejanos had always had the money to hire the larger orquestas—orquestas tejanas, as they were known in Texas—working-class Tejanos still used the smaller, less expensive ensembles, which had come to be known as conjuntos by the early 1900s. The orquesta was based on earlier string orchestras of the nineteenth century and usually included an array of instruments, such as violins, guitars, contrabass, mandolins, horns, and drums. Because they featured a wider variety of instruments and were often led by formally trained conductors, orquestas generally performed more complex musical arrangements and covered a broader range of musical styles.

Johnny Herrera. Courtesy Marcelo H. Tafoya.

Although the core repertoire of most orquestas tejanas was traditional Mexican music, including *canciónes, rancheras, cumbias,* and *boleros,* most also performed the latest pop, jazz, blues, swing, and other mainstream genres.[18]

The ways in which orquestas tejanas evolved during the mid-twentieth century helps illustrate how middle-class Tejanos were trying to selectively assimilate into mainstream American society. In their efforts to achieve an acceptable level of assimilation without completely abandoning their ancestral roots, middle-class Tejanos gravitated toward those orquestas that performed traditional Spanish and Mexican music, as well as other more mainstream styles. By doing so, the Mexican American middle class could reconcile its increasingly bicultural heritage without discarding its deeply rooted ethnic traditions or jeopardizing its quest for greater economic, educational, social, and political integration into American society.[19]

In contrast to the middle class's large and elaborate orquestas tejanas, the smaller conjunto ensembles of working-class Tejanos of the twentieth century typically featured an accordion as the central instrument. If enough money was available, a guitar, contrabass, and *tambora de rancho,* or medium-sized drum, might be included. By the 1930s, most conjunto groups had added the *bajo sexto,* a twelve-string guitar that could either supplement the drums or replace them altogether as a rhythm instrument. Whereas the middle and upper classes hosted more formal *bailes*, or balls, working-class Tejanos generally held less formal public dances known as fandangos, at which conjuntos were often paid by taking up a collection from the audience. In some cases, the conjunto bands adopted musical customs from outside the Texas Mexican community, including polkas, waltzes, and schottisches. However, most conjunto groups generally remained rooted in long-standing Mexican folk traditions and shunned many of the newer, more mainstream styles.[20]

Tejanos sometimes exchanged musical ideas and traditions with other ethnic groups in the Southwest. The schottische, a popular dance step now found in several genres of Texas music, is a good example of how this process of "cultural cross-pollination" worked among immigrant communities. Derived from the German word for "Scottish," the schottische is an adaptation of the traditional Scottish Highland fling and was probably brought to Texas and northern Mexico by German immigrants in the mid-1800s. Similar to a slow polka, in which the participants often dance in a large rotating circle, the schottische quickly gained popularity throughout the Southwest. During the early twentieth century, Tejano musicians adapted the schottische to fit the conjunto style, and it soon became one of the most popular dance steps in the conjunto repertoire. By the mid-twentieth century, the schottische had made its way into the music of other ethnic groups across Texas, including Anglo country bands, who made it a dance hall standard by adding fiddles and steel guitar. Likewise, the polka, which was borrowed from German and Czech cultures, became an important part of the folk music of Tejanos, Anglos, French, and others in the Lone Star State.[21]

The accordion, which is the centerpiece of the conjunto band, is yet another remarkable example of the cultural cross-pollination that took place among ethnic communities in the Southwest. Several variations of the accordion had been patented in Austria, Germany, and Italy by the early 1800s, and by the time German and Czech immigrants brought the instrument to Texas and northern Mexico in the 1840s it was already very popular throughout Europe. As a variety of ethnic groups in the Southwest came to recognize the accordion's tremendous versatility and adaptability to a wide range of musical styles, they quickly added it to their instrumental lineups. In working-class immigrant communities, the accordion was the ideal instrument since it was affordable and easy to transport and could provide a melody, bass line, and rhythm with enough volume to fill a large room or dance hall. Because it was so versatile and practical, the accordion soon became a fixture in conjunto, zydeco, polka, and other types of ethnic folk music in the Southwest.[22]

Narciso Martínez. Photo by Clay Shorkey, courtesy Texas Music Museum.

Bruno Villarreal, José Rodríguez, and Jesús Casiano were among the first Tejano musicians to popularize the accordion throughout Texas and northern Mexico during the early 1900s, and they are largely responsible for helping lay the foundation for the early conjunto style. However, the two men who are most often credited with having forged the modern conjunto sound of the 1930s and 1940s are Narciso Martínez and Santiago Jiménez Sr. Born October 29, 1911, in Reynosa, Mexico, Narciso Martínez grew up as a migrant farm worker in the Rio Grande Valley of South Texas. While still in his twenties, Martínez teamed up with bajo sexto player Santiago Almeida, who was born July 25, 1911, in Skidmore, Texas. In 1935 the two began recording for the Bluebird label, where their polka, "La Chicharronera," became one of the first commercial recordings of conjunto ever made. Martínez and Almeida's groundbreaking work and tremendous popularity throughout the Southwest helped solidify the position of the accordion and the bajo sexto as the core instruments for nearly all future conjunto bands.[23]

Santiago Jiménez Sr., nicknamed "El Flaco" (the Skinny One), was born in San Antonio on April 25, 1913. He learned accordion from his father, Patricio, who played at community dances and church functions throughout South Central Texas and often took young Santiago to hear nearby Texas German bands performing polkas and oompah music. As a teenager, Santiago was already developing his own unique style, which borrowed from Martínez and other Mexican folk musicians but also incorporated the polkas and schottisches he had learned from local German and Czech accordionists. Jiménez, who began recording in 1936 for Decca Records and several other labels in Texas and California, also hosted his own radio show in San Antonio and soon rose to prominence as a pioneer in conjunto music.

Despite his popularity, however, Jiménez never made much money and had to work at times as a janitor to support his family. Nevertheless, he remains one of the most influential and prolific conjunto musicians of the mid-twentieth century, and he epitomizes the blending of ethnic cultures that helped shape música tejana throughout the twentieth century. In 1990, six years after his death, Jiménez finally gained the national recognition he had long deserved when his song "Soy de San Luís" won a Grammy after being recorded by the Texas Tornados, a group that included his eldest son, Leonardo "Flaco" Jiménez.[24]

CANCIÓNES

Although the orquesta and conjunto remained the two most prominent types of musical ensembles in the Tejano community throughout the twentieth century, a number of other important subgenres of música tejana also developed during this period, including *canciónes* and corridos. The canción, which is a type of lyrical song that can be performed as a waltz, polka, or bolero, generally fits into one of two categories—*canciónes romanticas* or *canciónes típicas*. Canciónes romanticas, which are loosely based on the Italian operettas popular among late nineteenth-century middle-class Mexicans, reflect the more urbane characteristics of classic European opera. By contrast, canciónes típicas, also known as *canciónes rancheras*, or simply *rancheras*, were more popular among working-class Mexicans. Rancheras, which tend to be situated in a more rural or "ranchera" setting, often celebrate the lives, loves, and struggles of humble farming folk. For example, some early twentieth-century rancheras described clashes that erupted between rural people and city dwellers as unscrupulous bankers or businessmen from the nearby town tried to swindle the hardworking ranchers and farmers out of their money or land. Occasionally rancheras also offered morality lessons by warning of "inappropriate"

behavior among men and women or lamenting the perceived erosion of the traditional family structure. Of particular concern in some rancheras was the decline
in status of the male authority figure and the growing tendency of women to seek
greater social and economic equality.[25]

The fact that rancheras sometimes addressed such social and moral issues
may be a reflection of the growing concerns many rural Tejanos shared as the
Southwest transformed from agrarian to more urban and industrialized during the early twentieth century. This transition was challenging for rural people
from all ethnic backgrounds, but Mexican Americans faced the added difficulty
of widespread racial discrimination. For many Tejanos who found themselves
increasingly marginalized within the emerging industrial-capitalist economy,
rancheras provided a way to celebrate a supposedly simpler time when common
people were not so much at the mercy of overwhelming outside social, economic,
and political forces. Likewise, those rancheras that offered commentary on "appropriate" social behavior may have reflected the anxiety many rural Tejanos
experienced regarding the relaxing of stringent moral codes and the changing
status of women in society.[26]

Despite the fact that some rancheras celebrated more traditional attitudes and
social mores, they could also be used to promote more progressive themes, including support for greater women's rights. In fact, during the 1930s and 1940s,
a number of Tejana (female Texas Mexican) singers used the ranchera format to
address issues of specific concern to women.[27] For example, Lydia Mendoza, nicknamed the "Lark of the Border," was the most popular Tejana recording artist of
the 1930s and 1940s and sometimes sang about the problems women faced. Born
in Houston on May 13, 1916, Mendoza traveled as a child with her musical family
throughout the United States and Mexico, performing for migrant workers as far
north as Michigan. By 1928 she had landed a recording contract with Okeh Records
and soon became the most commercially successful Tejana singer of the time.

During her career, Mendoza made more than fifty albums, received numerous
regional and national awards, and toured throughout the world. She was also not
afraid to openly address controversial issues of particular concern to Tejanas. Two
of her most popular songs, "Mal Hombre" [Evil Man] and "Dime, Mal Hombre"
[Tell Me, Evil Man], speak candidly about male mistreatment of women. In addition to confronting such matters in a highly public way, Mendoza also helped
create new economic opportunities for women by demonstrating that female artists could achieve substantial commercial success in música tejana. This would
help open the door for dozens of other Tejana performers in the music business
for years to come.[28]

Carmen y Laura. Courtesy Marcelo H. Tafoya.

The sister duo Carmen y Laura, from Kingsville, Texas, also enjoyed tremendous popularity throughout the Southwest during the 1940s and 1950s. Carmen Hernández, born in 1921, and Laura Hernández, born in 1926, not only helped open the traditionally male-dominated recording industry to more women but also worked to bridge the conjunto and orquesta genres by enlarging their own conjunto backup band to include many of the same instruments found in the orquesta tejana. This blending of conjunto and orquesta traditions attracted both working- and middle-class audiences and helped set the stage for the emergence of "Tejano" bands during the 1980s, which combined the conjunto-style accordion with the larger, more elaborate instrumental lineup of the orquesta.[29]

Chelo Silva, born Consuelo Silva on August 25, 1922, in Brownsville, Texas, was another very important Tejana artist of this era. She began by singing radio jingles and performing a variety of song styles, but by the 1950s Silva had come to specialize in boleros and was known as "the Tejana Queen of Boleros" throughout Texas, Mexico, and Latin America. Like Mendoza, Silva's records sold very well not only in the United States but also abroad. Her highly successful career helped lay the groundwork for future generations of Tejana singers to break into the international Spanish-language market.[30]

Another Tejana singer who is rarely recognized as such (mainly because she spent most of her life in Los Angeles, where she established a successful career

Chelo Silva. Courtesy Marcelo H. Tafoya.

in mainstream pop music) is Vikki Carr, born Florencia Bisenta de Casillas Martínez Cordona on April 19, 1942, in El Paso, Texas. As a pop singer in the 1960s
and 1970s, Carr enjoyed tremendous success with hits such as "It Must Be Him"
and "With Pen in Hand." She toured internationally and appeared on stage and
television with Bob Hope, Dean Martin, Jerry Lewis, Ed Sullivan, Carol Burnett,
Johnny Carson, and other major stars of the era. In 1972 Carr returned to her
Mexican American musical roots when she recorded her first Spanish-language
album, *Vikki Carr en Español.* Throughout the 1980s and 1990s she made several
more recordings in Spanish, winning three Grammys and gaining an entirely new
following throughout Latin America.[31]

Several other younger Tejana artists, including Tish Hinojosa, help keep the older canción tradition alive today, while also incorporating other outside influences. Leticia "Tish" Hinojosa, born to immigrant parents on February 6, 1955, in San Antonio, grew up listening to a variety of musical styles, including conjunto, ranchera, pop, rock, swing, jazz, and country. Like so many other young Mexican Americans during the 1950s and 1960s, Hinojosa lived in a bilingual world in which she worked to balance her own ethnic traditions with the dominant Anglo culture around her. Hinojosa's singing and songwriting, which has won widespread critical acclaim, reflect this bicultural upbringing as she remains close to her traditional roots while still blending folk, country, and pop in both English and Spanish.[32]

CORRIDOS

Corridos, or folk ballads, are another integral part of música tejana, and they have been especially important as a means of communicating information, ideas, and culture among working-class Hispanics along the Texas Mexican border. Typically, corridos are epic narratives that tell of actual historical figures or events, although these ballads are often embellished in order to emphasize the heroic exploits of the central character. The corrido tradition reached the height of its popularity in South Texas during the late nineteenth and early twentieth centuries, a time when the Tejano community as a whole felt threatened by the increasingly dominant Anglo majority and the state's swift transition from an agrarian to an industrial economy.[33]

Much like rancheras, corridos served not only as a way to celebrate traditional Mexican American folk culture but also as a symbolic means of resisting assimilation and recalling an earlier time in which Tejanos enjoyed greater power and prestige in the Southwest. As a reflection of this loss of social status experienced by Texas Mexicans since the mid-1800s, corridos often feature as a central character a humble yet courageous Tejano who struggles to overcome the obstacles he faces in an increasingly Anglo-controlled environment. Because working-class Tejanos of the early twentieth century rarely had the opportunity to speak openly about the challenges they faced, corridos provided a format through which they could not only celebrate their folk culture but also symbolically prevail over the systematic discrimination they encountered in their daily lives.[34]

Corridos deal with much more than just conflicts between Anglos and Tejanos, however. They also address important social issues within Mexican American society itself. For example, corridos sometimes reflect prevailing attitudes among

Tejanos regarding gender roles and male-female relationships. In most corridos, the male characters play very active roles that are key to the development of the story line, while the women are generally relegated to more passive, peripheral positions. Likewise, most male figures are portrayed as either brave and trustworthy or cowardly and dishonest, while females are often defined as either virtuous and nurturing or treacherous and evil. In both instances, corridos articulate commonly held notions regarding "appropriate" male and female behavior. Along these same lines, corridos were sometimes used to help define standards of masculinity and femininity, especially in relation to the portrayal of characters as either positive or negative. For instance, the male hero in a corrido might challenge his opponent's manliness by portraying him as weak, cowardly, highly emotional, or even effeminate. By doing so, the protagonist can figuratively emasculate his opponent by calling into question his virility, honor, and, by implication, his very worth as a man.[35]

Perhaps the most famous of all Texas Mexican border ballads, "El Corrido del Gregorio Cortez," includes several examples of this use of gendered imagery to portray characters in either a favorable or an unfavorable light. Many variations on this particular corrido exist, but all of them are based on the true story of Gregorio Cortez, a South Texas ranch hand who, in 1901, killed a white sheriff in self-defense and then eluded authorities for weeks before being arrested, tried, imprisoned, and eventually released. The ballad, which praises Cortez as a hero of his people for triumphing over a discriminatory Anglo-dominated legal system, depicts him as a brave, virile, godlike man whose steadfast courage allows him to prevail against overwhelming odds. By contrast, the Anglo antagonists in the story, especially the Texas Rangers, or *rinches*, are depicted as weak, unscrupulous, and, in a variety of ways, unmanly. The following selected verses translated from the original Spanish highlight the marked difference between Cortez's noble and heroic actions and his pursuers' cowardly behavior:

> *The Americans were coming; they were whiter than a poppy*
>> *From the fear that they had of Cortez and his pistol.*
> *Then the Americans said, and they said it fearfully,*
>> *"Come, let us follow the trail, for the wrongdoer is Cortez."*
> *From Belmont he went to the ranch, where they succeeded in surrounding him,*
>> *Quite a few more than three hundred, but he jumped out of their corral.*
> *Then said Gregorio Cortez, with his pistol in his hand,*
>> *"Don't run, you cowardly rinches, from a single Mexican."*

Gregorio Cortez went out, he went out toward Laredo;
  [The posse] would not follow him because they were afraid of him.
Then said the Major Sheriff, as if he was going to cry,
  "Cortez, hand over your weapons; we do not want to kill you."
Then said Gregorio Cortez, speaking in his godlike voice,
  "I won't surrender my weapons until I'm inside a jail."[36]

In yet another well-known Texas corrido, "El Corrido de Kiansis," Mexican vaqueros, or cowboys, demonstrate their manliness by outperforming their Anglo counterparts on a difficult cattle drive:

Five hundred steers there were, all big and quick;
  Thirty American cowboys could not keep them bunched together.
Then five Mexicans arrive, all of them wearing good chaps;
  And in less than a quarter hour, they had the steers penned up.
Those five Mexicans penned up the steers in a moment,
  And the thirty Americans were left staring in amazement.[37]

The stories of strength and courage demonstrated by Mexican Americans in these ballads are not simply idle boasting. For many Tejanos who felt increasingly powerless in the face of a growing Anglo majority, such corridos provided a sense of empowerment and a chance to celebrate triumph over seemingly insurmountable odds, even if only vicariously through the heroic exploits of the ballad's characters.

Over the years, the corrido tradition has continued to evolve. Some still glorify the exploits of people living on the fringes of society, such as Prohibition-era gangsters who smuggled alcohol and other contraband across the Texas Mexican border during the 1920s and 1930s. In many ways, these "outlaw" corridos are not so different from popular English-language ballads that glamorize notorious criminals such as Frank and Jesse James, Bonnie and Clyde, and Pretty Boy Floyd. During the 1970s, a new type of corrido, known as the narcocorrido, began gaining notoriety as a type of narrative ballad that focuses on drug trafficking between Mexico and the United States. Narcocorridos, which are similar to many earlier corridos in that they often portray social outcasts and other marginalized characters as heroic figures fighting against corrupt and powerful authority figures, are an indication that the corrido tradition remains a popular and enduring musical format.[38]

WORLD WAR II AND MÚSICA TEJANA

World War II brought sweeping changes throughout American society and forever altered the nation's political, economic, and cultural landscape. Even before the United States officially entered the war on December 8, 1941, the Allied demand for U.S. products created an industrial boom that lifted the nation's economy out of the Great Depression and moved millions of Americans from the countryside into the cities to fill factory jobs. Following World War II, a massive population boom, along with a remarkable period of economic growth and technological innovation, ushered in a dramatically higher standard of living for most Americans. Along with these developments came a growing demand for greater civil rights for ethnic minorities and changing attitudes about race relations and the role of women in society.

World War II had a profound impact on Mexican American society and the development of música tejana. Like most Americans, Tejanos emerged from the war with unprecedented opportunities for social, political, and economic advancement. Hundreds of thousands of Mexican Americans who had served in the U.S. Armed Forces learned new skills they could carry into the civilian job market, and the military's G.I. Bill gave many working-class Tejano servicemen their first chance for a college education and the possibility to advance into the ranks of the middle class. In addition to these improvements on the economic front, the newly emerging civil rights movement helped empower Tejanos and other ethnic minorities to push for greater legal and political equality.[39]

Despite these improvements, not all Tejanos benefited equally from the changes that came about in the World War II era.[40] Although the Mexican American middle class grew and prospered, many in the working class continued to languish in low-paying jobs that offered little chance for advancement. This growing social and economic disparity between the working and the middle classes sometimes became a point of contention among Tejanos. While those in the middle class argued that assimilation was the surest way to bring prosperity and greater respectability to the entire Mexican American community, many working-class Tejanos resented being pressured to assimilate, and some even accused middle-class Tejanos of abandoning their ethnic heritage and becoming agringado—"gringo-ized."[41]

The class tensions present within World War II–era Mexican American society are evident in the evolution of música tejana during the 1940s and 1950s, especially in regard to the ongoing rift between the middle-class orquesta and the working-class conjunto. For example, the orquestas of the 1940s and 1950s, which had long included rancheras, cumbias, boleros, waltzes, polkas, and a variety of other styles in their musical repertoires, began incorporating the newer jazz, swing, and pop sounds of Glenn Miller, Benny Goodman, and other non-Hispanic, big-band entertainers. By contrast, most working-class conjunto groups of the World War II–era adhered to the traditional accordion and bajo sexto arrangement that had been popular since the beginning of the century.

Although most Tejanos probably did not consciously choose between orquesta and conjunto to make an overt social or political statement, the schism represented by these two parallel tracks within música tejana nevertheless reveals some important developments within the Texas Mexican community at the time. As middle-class Tejanos continued to advance socially and economically, they em-

Hermanas Gongora. Courtesy Marcelo H. Tafoya.

Eugenio Gutiérrez y Su Orquesta. Courtesy Marcelo H. Tafoya.

braced the more popular musical styles of the day, at least in part, as a reflection of their increasing efforts to assimilate into mainstream society. On the other hand, working-class Tejanos continued to favor the more traditional conjunto, which, for them, had become somewhat of a symbol of cultural defiance not only against Anglo society but also against those in the Mexican American middle class, who seemed far too eager to assimilate.[42]

In spite of such differences, middle- and working-class Tejanos still shared common musical interests in certain areas. For example, even though middle-class audiences enjoyed orquestas that played pop, jazz, and swing, they also expected their favorite bands to continue performing cumbias, boleros, rancheras, and other traditional Texas Mexican music. Likewise, although most working-class conjunto groups resisted adding swing, pop, jazz, and other nontraditional styles to their repertoires, many of them eventually incorporated blues, country, and rock & roll in response to their audiences' changing musical tastes. Furthermore, some in the middle class actually listened to conjunto and more traditional Mexican folk music, while many working-class Tejanos also enjoyed occasionally dressing up on a Saturday night to go hear a formal orquesta perform the latest pop tunes.[43]

Another important factor that helped to shape the evolution of música tejana during the 1940s and 1950s—and one that gave both working- and middle-class Tejanos a greater opportunity to pursue their musical interests—involved the changes that were taking place in the Tejano recording industry. Although major record labels had been sending teams into the Southwest to record Mexican American and African American music since the 1920s, wartime petroleum rationing slowed record production dramatically, and many major labels had pulled out of Texas by the mid-1940s. After the war, several enterprising Tejano businessmen stepped into the void left by the larger companies and launched their own independent record labels in order to fill the growing public demand for new music. In 1946 Armando Marroquín and Paco Betancourt of Alice, Texas, founded Ideal Records (Discos Ideal), the first independent Tejano record company, which was soon followed by other small labels, including Falcon, Corona, Hacienda, and Freddie. Even though these fledgling companies usually had only rudimentary recording equipment and little investment capital with which to work, they generally gave their artists a great deal of creative freedom. This allowed Tejano musicians to innovate and experiment with a variety of styles and instrumental arrangements.

Nash Hernández Orchestra. Courtesy Marcelo H. Tafoya.

Beto Villa. Courtesy Marcelo H. Tafoya.

The result was a very dynamic period in which small, independent-label artists pushed Texas Mexican music in exciting new directions and began attracting a new worldwide audience for música tejana.[44]

One of the most influential architects of post–World War II música tejana was Beto Villa. Born in Falfurrias, Texas, on October 26, 1915, Villa is often considered the "father" of modern orquesta tejana because of his leading role in the development of the 1940s and 1950s-era orquesta. In 1946 Villa began recording for Ideal Records, where he combined traditional rancheras, rumbas, and mambos with big-band swing, fox-trots, and other mainstream dance steps. His skillful blending of these diverse styles brought him widespread popularity, especially among middle-class Tejanos, and provided a model for numerous other modern orquestas to follow.[45]

Isidro López. Courtesy Marcelo H. Tafoya.

Isidro López, born May 17, 1929, in Bishop, Texas, was another prominent orquesta tejana band leader whose innovations helped redefine música tejana during the second half of the twentieth century. Much like Villa, López incorporated pop, blues, swing, jazz, and other styles into his orquesta tejana repertoire but also added some conjunto as a way to attract larger audiences. By modernizing and broadening the scope and sound of orquesta tejana, Villa and López helped pave the way for future variations on the orquesta tradition.[46]

While Villa, López, and others were reshaping orquesta tejana during the postwar period, conjunto artists were also redefining their genre. Although at its core conjunto remained a rather straightforward, accordion-driven dance music, it underwent important changes during the second half of the twentieth century. One of the leading innovators in conjunto during the 1940s and 1950s was accordionist Valerio Longoria. The son of migrant farm workers, Longoria was born in Clarksdale, Mississippi, on March 13, 1924, but grew up in South Texas. Following military service during World War II, he settled in San Antonio and began recording for local labels, including Ideal Records, where he was given considerable latitude to experiment with different styles and instrumental arrangements. While working with Ideal, Longoria introduced modern drums into the conjunto ensemble and expanded the standard conjunto repertoire by incorporating boleros and other dance steps. Perhaps his single most important innovation, however, was the addition of vocal duets to his recordings. Prior to this, conjunto had been primarily an instrumental music, but Longoria's use of vocals opened up an entirely new range of musical possibilities and helped launch the careers of a number of talented singers.[47]

Tony de la Rosa, born October 31, 1931, in Sarita, Texas, was another versatile accordionist who played a major role in reshaping and revitalizing conjunto music during the second half of the twentieth century. De la Rosa grew up listening to both conjunto and country music, especially Western swing, and he even performed in a honky-tonk dance band in the Kingsville area before forming his own conjunto group in 1949. Because of his background in Western swing and honky-tonk, de la Rosa was one of the first to incorporate country music into conjunto, thereby helping set the stage for a multitude of Tejano country bands that would emerge in the 1970s and 1980s. De la Rosa introduced a number of other important

Tony De La Rosa. Courtesy Marcelo H. Tafoya.

innovations as well, such as replacing the *tololoche*, or acoustic upright bass, with an electric bass and making amplifiers and full-sized drum sets a standard part of the modern conjunto ensemble. One of the most significant stylistic changes he brought to conjunto came when he slowed the tempo of the traditionally fast-paced polkas to make them easier for dancing. This new approach proved very popular, and most other conjunto bands soon adopted the slower polka format.[48]

Domingo "Mingo" Saldivar, born May 29, 1936, in Marion, Texas, is another influential accordionist who mixed conjunto with country music. Before launching his own successful career in the 1960s, Saldivar was a sideman in popular bands such as Los Guadalupanos and Los Caminantes. Writing and singing in both English and Spanish, Saldivar has had regional hits with bilingual versions of classic country songs, including Johnny Cash's "Folsom Prison Blues." Well known for his energetic stage performances and his blending of conjunto and country music, Saldivar, nicknamed "the dancing cowboy," continues to perform throughout North America.[49]

During the 1950s and 1960s the group El Conjunto Bernal, founded by brothers Paulino and Eloy Bernal, helped elevate conjunto to a whole new level of technical sophistication. Eloy, born March 11, 1937, and Paulino, born June 22, 1939, began performing as teenagers around Kingsville, Texas, where they recorded for Ideal Records and backed up popular artists such as Carmen y Laura. The brothers' musical proficiency soon surpassed that of most other local conjunto groups as they began experimenting with new and more complex vocal and accordion arrangements. Among other things, they introduced intricate two- and three-part harmonies, thus giving the vocals an even more prominent role in conjunto, and they also crafted more complicated arrangements that brought an unprecedented level of technical challenge and raised the bar for all future conjunto accordion players.[50]

Esteban Jordan (also known as Steve Jordan), sometimes called the "Jimi Hendrix of the accordion," was born February 23, 1939, in Elsa, Texas. Partially blinded as a child, Jordan was unable to work alongside his siblings in the cotton fields, so he stayed home and learned to play the accordion. Although he grew up performing traditional conjunto polkas, waltzes, and schottisches, Jordan expanded his repertoire to include blues, jazz, country, zydeco, and rock & roll. His blending of classic conjunto with rock and other genres has brought criticism from some purists, but Jordan's outstanding technical skills and his commitment to innovation and experimentation have helped broaden the scope of conjunto and enlarge its following.[51]

Leonardo "Flaco" Jiménez and Santiago Jiménez Jr., both sons of conjunto pioneer Santiago Jiménez Sr., have become very influential accordionists in their own right. Flaco Jiménez, born March 11, 1939, in San Antonio, grew up steeped in the older conjunto traditions of his father, but his versatility and innovative skills have brought him widespread acclaim in other genres. He is a multiple Grammy Award–winning artist who played for years with the supergroup the Texas Tornados and helped introduce the conjunto accordion into mainstream country, rock, and pop by recording with well-known artists such as Buck Owens, Bob Dylan, Dwight Yoakam, and the Rolling Stones. Flaco's younger brother, Santiago Jr., born April 8, 1944, in San Antonio, has worked to preserve and promote a more traditional conjunto style along the same lines that his father played. In 1980 Santiago Jr. opened El Chief Studios, where he has worked diligently to document and record an extensive collection of classic conjunto songs.[52]

Eva Ybarra, one of the few prominent Tejana conjunto accordionists, was born March 2, 1945, in San Antonio. Growing up in a very musical family, she began playing accordion at the age of six. Generally considered the best female accordionist in conjunto, Ybarra is adept at a variety of styles, including mariachi, rancheras, waltzes, schottisches, polkas, and corridos. She has toured throughout the United States and Latin America and continues to record, perform, and teach as part of her efforts to pass along the conjunto tradition to younger generations.[53]

Another style that is closely related to conjunto and has had an important impact on the development of música tejana is *música norteña*, commonly called *norteño*. Norteño, which originated in northern Mexico, is very popular along both sides of the Texas Mexican border, and many norteño artists perform and record in Texas. Although conjunto and norteño are similar in many ways, norteño groups tend to sing more corridos, play at a faster tempo, and incorporate additional instruments beyond those used by the traditional accordion and bajo sexto–based conjunto. Because they bring the latest music with them from Mexico, norteño bands are especially popular among recent Mexican immigrants residing in the Southwest and are part of the continual reinforcement of Mexican culture in the region.[54]

LA ONDA CHICANA

During the 1960s, a new subgenre of Mexican American music known as *la onda chicana* (the Chicano wave) appeared. In terms of musical structure, la onda chicana was rooted in the orquesta tradition since it featured larger, multi-instrumental ensembles and combined a variety of musical styles, including Mexican folk music, blues, R&B, country, and rock & roll. However, la onda chicana also included many of the same characteristics found in conjunto, especially its use of the accordion and Spanish-language lyrics. Beyond being simply a new subgenre of música tejana, la onda chicana was also part of a larger campaign of political and social activism known as the Chicano movement, which swept through Mexican American society during the 1960s and 1970s. The Chicano movement, which was made up mainly of young and often college-educated Mexican Americans, sought to honor older Mexican cultural traditions while rallying the Mexican American community to take a more active role in fighting for greater legal, political, and economic rights.

The seeds of la onda chicana in Texas were planted in the 1940s and 1950s, with the birth of a new generation of Tejano baby boomers. As teenagers in the 1960s, young Mexican Americans were coming of age during a tumultuous decade in which minorities, women, youth, and other historically marginalized groups were breaking down long-standing barriers to social, political, and economic equality. Tejanos built on the momentum of older organizations such as the League of United Latin American Citizens (LULAC, founded in 1929), while also establishing newer ones, including la Raza Unida (launched in 1970 by José Angel Gutiérrez and other Chicano activists), in order to preserve and celebrate their Mexican heritage while campaigning for better access to jobs, education, housing, and health care.[55]

As was the case with so many other groups who had struggled to reconcile their dual ethnic identities, Tejanos who were involved in the Chicano movement found themselves caught in a difficult bicultural balancing act. On the one hand, they sought to remain connected to their ancestral roots as a way to rekindle ethnic pride within the Mexican American community. On the other hand, these Tejano baby boomers were already substantially assimilated into mainstream society and were strongly influenced by the cultural and political ideology of their non-Hispanic peers. In many ways, la onda chicana reflected this bicultural ambiguity since it promoted a stronger sense of ethnic identity and political activism within the community while at the same time it borrowed from non-Hispanic musical traditions, such as blues, pop, country, R&B, and rock & roll.[56]

Two musicians who probably best represent the bicultural equilibrium that so many Tejano baby boomers strove to achieve during the 1960s and 1970s are Sunny Ozuna and Joe Hernández. Both were born into the same poverty that many Mexican Americans before them had faced, but as part of the new post–World War II generation, they also had unprecedented access to public education and opportunities for economic advancement. Like many Tejano youngsters in the 1950s, Ozuna and Hernández had grown up listening to Beto Villa, Isidro López,

Valerio Longoria, Santiago Jiménez Sr., and other musicians of their parents' generation. However, they were also drawn to a newly emerging genre known as rock & roll, which was being pioneered by non-Hispanic artists such as Chuck Berry, Bill Haley, Elvis Presley, and Buddy Holly. Ozuna, Hernández, and other young Tejanos of the 1950s and 1960s would end up incorporating these new rock-and-roll influences into música tejana in ways that would reflect the growing trend toward greater assimilation among a new generation of Texas Mexicans.[57]

Sunny Ozuna, born Ildefonso Fraga Ozuna in San Antonio on September 8, 1943, and Joe Hernández, born José María De León Hernández in Temple, Texas, on October 17, 1940, started their own rock-and-roll bands as teenagers and dreamed of making hit records that would propel them out of their working-class neighborhoods and onto the national stage. In 1962 Ozuna and his group, Sunny and the Sunglows, which included two Mexican Americans, two Anglo Americans, and one African American, achieved this dream with the song "Talk to Me," recorded by Houston producer and promoter Huey Meaux. By 1963 "Talk to Me" had become a national hit, charting within the Top Forty for fourteen weeks and earning Ozuna and his new band, Sunny and the Sunliners, a coveted appearance on Dick Clark's popular television show, *American Bandstand.* Although Ozuna was unable to sustain this level of success in mainstream pop for long, he was a major inspiration to other young Texas Mexican artists who also sought to use music as a path to social and economic advancement. Following his short stint in the national limelight, Ozuna went on to build a distinguished and enduring career in the Spanish-language music market that continues today. His musical odyssey from a San Antonio barrio to pop stardom illustrates just how far Tejano musicians of the 1960s had come in terms of succeeding within an increasingly bicultural environment.[58]

Although he never enjoyed the same level of national recognition as Ozuna, in many ways Joe Hernández may have had an even greater long-term impact on música tejana. Hernández's first truly successful group during the early 1960s was Little Joe and the Latinaires, a band that drew on the older orquesta tradition of using multiple instruments and covering a wide range of song styles, including Mexican folk music and mainstream pop. By the late 1960s, however, Hernández had become increasingly involved in the Chicano movement and began to shape a new sound and image that would reflect his growing social activism. Although he adopted the clothing and hairstyle of the more mainstream hippie counterculture, he began to play more ethnically and politically oriented material and even changed the name of his band from Little Joe and the Latinaires to Little Joe y la Familia in tribute to his Spanish-language roots.[59]

Sunny & The Sun Liners. Courtesy Marcelo H. Tafoya.

Little Joe y la Familia performed and recorded in both English and Spanish, often playing songs that focused specifically on issues of concern to the Mexican American community. His 1972 remake of the older tune "Las Nubes" [The Clouds] was a celebration of Mexican American ethnic pride that became an anthem of sorts for the Chicano movement. Hernández continued blending elements of the orquesta tradition with blues, rock & roll, and country throughout the 1970s and helped set the stage for the emergence of a new genre that would come to be known as "Tejano" by the 1980s. Because of his pioneering work in bringing together these diverse influences, Hernández is often considered the "father" of

Little Joe & The Latinaires. Courtesy Marcelo H. Tafoya.

Mel Villareal y Los Unicos. Courtesy Marcelo H. Tafoya.

modern Tejano music. He finally received official recognition for his important role in shaping música tejana when he won a Grammy in 1992 for his album *Diez y Séis de Septiembre*, the first such award ever given to a Tejano artist.[60]

In addition to Sunny Ozuna and Joe Hernández, many other musicians also contributed to the development of música tejana during the 1960s and 1970s and helped lay the foundation for the emergence of Tejano music in the 1980s and 1990s. Rudy (Gonzales) and the Reno Bops played Latin-influenced rock & roll and pop during the 1950s and 1960s. Gonzales, born July 4, 1939, produced the 1967 smash hit "96 Tears" for the Texas-based group ? and the Mysterians and helped pioneer Spanish-language country music in the 1970s. Roberto Pulido, born March 1, 1950, in Edinburg, Texas, helped develop a new style in the 1970s known as *progressive conjunto*. He did so by expanding the traditional four-piece, accordion-based conjunto ensemble to include saxophones and other *pitos* [horns] and by bringing more ballads and country music into the conjunto repertoire.

Another variation on the original conjunto ensemble that appeared in the 1960s and 1970s was known as "Chicano country" and is perhaps best represented by the popular Country Roland Band. Generally these groups did not include accordions or other traditional conjunto instruments but instead featured fiddles and steel guitars and played two-step shuffles and popular country dance tunes such as "Cotton-eyed Joe." Still another offshoot of música tejana during the 1960s and 1970s was the *grupo tejano*. These bands were heavily influenced by pop and rock & roll and usually replaced the traditional accordion with synthesizer keyboards and electric guitars. One of the earliest such groups, Los Fabulosos Cuatro [the Fabulous Four], took its name from the "Fab Four" moniker given to the popular 1960s' British band, the Beatles.[61]

TEJANO MUSIC

By the early 1980s all of these influences, including orquesta, conjunto, la onda chicana, progressive conjunto, Chicano country, and grupo tejano, had given rise to a new style now known as "Tejano." Tejano is undeniably one of the most difficult subgenres of música tejana to define or categorize, in part because it borrows from so many other types of Texas Mexican music. Similar to earlier orquestas, Tejano bands are typically large and feature a variety of instruments, including electric guitars and bass, synthesizer, and full drum sets. Also, much like previous orquestas, most Tejano groups incorporate pop, blues, jazz, rock & roll, and other mainstream influences into their repertoire and often feature elaborate choreographed dance routines, high-tech stage lighting, and other special effects.[62]

However, Tejano also borrows from the more traditional conjunto format in its extensive use of accordions, polkas, and country music, and, like conjunto, Tejano is especially popular among working-class Mexican Americans. Another characteristic that makes Tejano so unique is the fact that, although it is organically connected to older Mexican American cultural traditions, it is the first subgenre of música tejana to have achieved such a remarkable degree of commercial success worldwide. Because it is deeply rooted in older Mexican musical traditions yet has proven to be a highly marketable commodity, Tejano defies categorization as either organic or superorganic and instead provides an extraordinary example of the dynamic blending of diverse musical traditions within Texas Mexican society.[63]

Rubén Ramos, nicknamed "El Gato Negro" [the Black Cat], is a pioneering figure in the development of early Tejano. Born in Sugarland, Texas, on February 9, 1940, Ramos combined traditional Mexican styles with blues, R&B, funk, soul, and country, usually performing with a full-sized orquesta. Since the 1970s Ramos has enjoyed considerable critical and commercial success and helped pave the way for numerous younger Tejano artists. Laura Canales, born August 19, 1954, in Kingsville, Texas, was the most prominent female artist of early Tejano. She first gained national attention singing with the popular group El Conjunto Bernal during the 1970s. By the early 1980s she had helped lay the groundwork for the continued success of Tejano, recording several hits in both English and Spanish and winning the "Best Female Vocalist" category of the Tejano Music Awards four years in a row. Other bands, such as El Grupo Mazz, La Tropa F, and La Mafia, also played leading roles in forging the early Tejano sound with their synthesizer-driven rhythm sections, tight harmonies, and elaborate stage productions.[64]

Although Tejano music was steadily gaining popularity throughout the 1970s and early 1980s, it exploded onto the world stage in the late 1980s with the arrival of a dynamic young singer named Selena Quintanilla. Born in Freeport, Texas, on April 16, 1971, Selena, as she would come to be known, began singing as a child with her family band, Selena y los Dinos, under the guidance of her musician-father, Abraham Quintanilla. With a rich, sultry voice and a commanding stage presence, Selena quickly blossomed into an energetic and charismatic performer who integrated cumbias, rancheras, mariachi, ballads, pop, and rock & roll into her Tejano repertoire. Selena connected easily with a whole new generation of Tejanos who had grown increasingly comfortable balancing their bicultural identities as Mexican Americans. In fact, like many other Tejanos her age, she had grown up speaking mostly English, so she had to learn the Spanish in her songs phonetically.[65]

Selena's career took off in 1987, when she won "Best Female Vocalist" at the Tejano Music Awards. In 1992 her album *Entre a Mi Mundo* soared to the top of the Spanish-language pop charts in the United States and throughout Latin America, generating greater sales than any previous Tejana artist. By the early 1990s Selena was well on her way to a successful career in the mainstream pop market. In 1992 she won a Grammy for her CD *Selena Live*, and her 1994 CD, *Amor Prohibido*, was the first Tejano album to go gold, selling more than five hundred thousand copies.

However, just as Selena was poised to become a major cross-over star, the former president of her fan club, Yolanda Saldivar, fatally shot the young singer on March 31, 1995, following a series of disagreements between Saldivar and the Quintanilla family. Millions of fans worldwide mourned Selena's passing, and some thirty thousand came to pay their respects at her memorial service. Ironically, Selena's tragic murder brought her to the attention of non-Spanish-speaking audiences and led to a huge surge in record sales. Within a month of her death, Selena had five CDs in the *Billboard* Top Two Hundred, a feat previously matched only by artists such as Elvis Presley, the Beatles, and Garth Brooks.[66]

Just as millions of fans considered Selena the "queen" of Tejano music, her closest male counterpart, Emilio Navaira, has often been called the "king" of Tejano music. Navaira, born in San Antonio on August 23, 1962, was influenced by many of his parents' favorite artists, such as Roberto Pulido and Little Joe y la Familia. However, the young Navaira also enjoyed other types of music, including country, pop, and rock & roll. In particular, he was drawn to the smooth singing style of country legend and fellow Texan George Strait. In fact, upon graduating from high school, Navaira earned a choir scholarship to attend Southwest Texas State University (now Texas State University) in San Marcos, the same school from which George Strait had graduated a few years earlier.[67]

Navaira dropped out of Texas State in 1983 in order to replace Ram Herrera as lead singer in the popular group David Lee Garza y los Musicales. Following a brief but successful stint with Los Musicales, Navaira formed his own band, Grupo Río, and made his first CD, *Sensaciones*, which generated several hits in the Tejano market. Navaira soon adopted the stage name "Emilio," and throughout the late 1980s and well into the 1990s he recorded a string of successful CDs, blending both Anglo and Hispanic musical traditions and paying tribute to idols such as Roberto Pulido and George Strait. Emilio's 1995 release, *Life Is Good*, considered his debut country album, sold more than half a million copies. He soon began drawing huge crowds wherever he performed, including at a 1995 appearance with Selena at the Houston Livestock Show and Rodeo, in which the "king" and "queen" of Tejano broke all previous attendance records for a matinee performance. With his seemingly effortless ability to combine a variety of styles in both English and Spanish, Emilio, much like Selena, reflected the strong bicultural influences that he and many other young Tejanos had grown up with in the Southwest during the 1970s and 1980s.[68]

A number of other younger Tejano artists have also enjoyed substantial success in mixing traditional Mexican music with more mainstream genres. Rick Treviño, born in Houston on May 16, 1971, is a talented singer-songwriter who, like Emilio Navaira, released some of his biggest hits first in English and then translated them into Spanish to be distributed throughout Latin America. Shelly Lares, born in San Antonio on November 13, 1971, never reached the superstar status of her friend Selena, but she did build a very successful career combining country and Tejano. More recently, Tejano groups such as Los Kumbia Kings have blended older Texas Mexican traditions with rap and hip-hop, along with the dance steps and multilayered harmonies of mainstream "boy bands" such as NSYNC.[69]

Perhaps the most successful Mexican American band to emerge from Texas in recent years is Los Lonely Boys. This trio from San Angelo, which includes brothers Henry, JoJo, and Ringo Garza Jr., have won international acclaim for blending rock, blues, conjunto, and pop into a spirited yet soulful sound. The trio has been influenced by Stevie Ray Vaughan and a variety of other older artists, including their own father, Ringo Garza Sr., who played conjunto throughout South Texas during the 1970s and 1980s with his own "brother band," the Falcones. After recording backup vocals on some of their father's songs, the three sons formed their own group, whose unique sound soon caught the attention of Texas music legend Willie Nelson. Their debut album, Los Lonely Boys, recorded at Nelson's Pedernales Studios, was released by Epic Records in 2004 and included the song "Heaven," which hit number sixteen on the Billboard Hot One Hundred list. By 2005 Los Lonely Boys was touring with Willie Nelson, Carlos Santana, the Rolling Stones, and Tim McGraw and had won a Grammy for Best Pop Performance by a duo or group with vocals.[70]

Although certainly not a Tejano group, the Texas Tornados deserve to be mentioned here within the larger context of música tejana, primarily because of the ways in which the band combined conjunto, Tejano, blues, R&B, country, and rock & roll to create music with some of the most eclectic roots ever to emerge from the Lone Star State. Well before he joined the others to form the Tornados, Freddie Fender, born Baldemar Huerta on June 4, 1937, in San Benito, Texas, had gained fame in the 1970s with two of the first bilingual country hits, "Wasted Days and Wasted Nights" and "Before the Next Teardrop Falls." Flaco Jiménez, son

Freddy Fender. Courtesy Marcelo H. Tafoya

of conjunto pioneer Santiago Jiménez Sr., had proven his tremendous musical versatility by recording with Buck Owens, Bob Dylan, the Rolling Stones, Linda Ronstadt, Dwight Yoakam, and others. Doug Sahm, born November 6, 1941, in San Antonio, grew up listening to country, pop, and rock & roll as an Anglo Texan, but he was also strongly influenced by conjunto and other types of música tejana. Keyboardist Augie Meyers, born May 31, 1940, played for years in rock, blues, and jazz bands and easily mixed those styles with conjunto, norteño, and country to help fashion the unique Texas Tornado sound. Soon after they formed in 1989 the Tornados won a Grammy for their self-titled 1990 debut album, which mingled Spanish and English lyrics, conjunto, waltzes, polka, country, and rock & roll. Although the group disbanded after Sahm died of heart failure in November 1999, their records continue to sell well throughout the world.[71]

Today, música tejana is more diverse and dynamic than ever. Artists such as Alejandro Escovedo, the Sisters Morales, Patricia Vonne, Rosie Flores, Joel Guzmán, South Park Mexican, Grupo Fantasma, Vallejo, Del Castillo, and many others cover a wide range of styles that represent the remarkable diversity still seen in música tejana. Rooted in older Mexican folk music, música tejana has absorbed a variety of other ethnic influences over the years and developed in ways that reflect the unique history and culture of Texas Mexican society.

RECOMMENDED LISTENING

De la Rosa, Tony, *Así Se Baila en Tejas* (Rounder)
El Conjunto Bernal, *Mi Unico Camino* (Arhoolie)
Emilio, *Life Is Good* (Capitol Nashville)
Fender, Freddy, *Canciónes de Mi Barrio* (Arhoolie)
Hinojosa, Tish, *Culture Swing* (Rounder)
Jiménez, Flaco, *Ay Te Dejo en San Antonio* (Arhoolie)
Jiménez, Flaco (with Los Caminantes), *Flaco's First* (Arhoolie)
Jiménez, Santiago, Jr., *Corridos de la Frontera* (Watermelon)
Jiménez, Santiago, Sr., *Viva Seguín* (Arhoolie)
Jordan, Steve, *Soy de Tejas* (Hacienda)
Kumbia Kings, *Fuego* (EMI International)
Longoria, Valerio, *Texas Conjunto Pioneer* (Arhoolie)
López, Isidro, *El Indio* (Arhoolie)
Los Lonely Boys, *Sacred* (Sony)
Martínez, Narciso, *Father of the Texas-Mexican Conjunto* (Arhoolie)
Mendoza, Lydia, *Mal Hombre* (Arhoolie)
Selena, *Amor Prohibido* (EMI), *Entre a Mi Mundo* (EMI)
Silva, Chelo, *La Reina Tejana del Bolero* (Arhoolie)
Texas Tornados, *Texas Tornados* (Warner Brothers)
Villa, Beto, *Father of Orquesta Tejana* (Arhoolie)
Various artists, *Borderlands: From Conjunto to Chicken Scratch* (Smithsonian Folkways)
Various artists, *Tejano Roots: The Women* (Arhoolie)

CHAPTER 4

. . . .

"See That My Grave Is Kept Clean"

The African Roots of Texas Music

A s one of the largest ethnic minorities in the Southwest, black Americans have had an extraordinary impact on the shaping of Texas music. Just as música tejana reflects the historical and cultural evolution of Tejano society, African American music, which includes blues, gospel, ragtime, jazz, R&B (rhythm and blues), zydeco, soul, funk, rap, hip-hop, and a variety of other styles, mirrors the complexity of the black community in Texas and speaks to the particular experiences of African Americans in the Southwest. Not only have black Texans created a rich musical legacy of their own, but they have also influenced nearly all other genres of music in the region from country to rock & roll.[1]

A number of social, political, and economic factors have contributed to the unique development of African American culture in the United States. Issues such as slavery, racial segregation, and discrimination have had a profound and lasting effect on blacks and their sense of place within society. As recently as the 1960s, African Americans were routinely denied full legal and political rights and equal access to education and employment opportunities. Even now, racial discrimination persists in certain areas of society, creating obstacles to the advancement of many blacks. Over the years, music has been an important means by which African Americans have addressed racism, discrimination, and other challenges. Of course, African American history and culture are not defined merely by negative experiences. On the contrary, black Americans have built on the same positive themes of love, family, and community that have helped shape the musical culture of all other ethnic groups. Nevertheless, the bitter legacy of slavery, segregation, and discrimination has left a lasting imprint on the African American community and its music.[2]

The ancestors of most African Americans came to what is now the United States as slaves, the first arriving in Virginia in 1619. They were followed by hundreds of thousands more before the importation of slaves into the United States became illegal in 1808. By the beginning of the Civil War in 1861, the U.S. slave population stood at around four million, with another half million or so free blacks. Although thousands of black Americans were living throughout New England and the Mid-Atlantic region by the mid-1800s, the spread of labor-intensive tobacco and cotton farming across the South meant that most slaves were concentrated in a swath of Southern states stretching from the Atlantic coastline to Texas.[3]

For us to fully understand the evolution of black music, it is important to place it within the broader cultural context of the American South. Primarily agrarian with a largely rural population, the South developed an economy and a social structure based mainly on nonwage labor, racial segregation, a decentralized government, and a fundamentalist, evangelical orientation to many of its religious institutions. This racially segregated social hierarchy meant that white Southerners clearly controlled most of the official levers of power in the South. At the same time, however, the sheer number of blacks living in the region ensured that African American culture permeated virtually all aspects of daily life and dramatically affected the long-term development of Southern society in a number of ways.

Because Texas is on the western fringes of the Deep South, it evolved somewhat differently from other Southern states politically, socially, and economically. This is particularly evident in the contrasting attitudes regarding slavery and race relations found throughout the Southwest. On the one hand, Texas was indeed a slave state with a large portion of its economy tied to cotton production. It fought on the side of the Confederacy during the Civil War and in fact was one of the last Confederate states to free its slaves. Following the Civil War, Texas implemented many of the same racist policies found throughout the rest of the South, which were designed to marginalize free blacks and deny them equal economic, educational, social, and political opportunities.

On the other hand, Texas had a more diversified population and economy than most Southern states, which tended to undermine broad-based support for slavery in the Southwest. Consequently, the institutions of slavery and post–Civil

War segregation that were more thoroughly entrenched elsewhere in the Deep South never took hold quite so strongly in Texas, especially in the southern, central, and western parts of the state. Because of this, black Texans were generally exposed to a greater variety of other ethnic cultures and faced a somewhat less rigidly structured, race-based social hierarchy. In cultural terms, this may have given blacks in the Southwest more of an opportunity for broad cross-pollination of African American and other ethnic musical traditions.[4]

The first known African to set foot on Texas soil (and probably the first African to come to what is now the United States) was a slave named Estebanico, owned by the Spanish explorer Andrés Dorantes. Estebanico and Dorantes, who were shipwrecked along the Texas Gulf Coast in 1528, joined Alvar Núñez Cabeza de Vaca and one other survivor on an eight-year odyssey across the Southwest. As the men struggled to make their way back to Spanish headquarters in Mexico City, they crisscrossed Texas, interacting with a variety of Indian groups and documenting the flora, fauna, and topography of the region.[5] Not long after arriving safely back in Mexico City, Estebanico returned to Texas temporarily to serve as a guide for other explorers and traders. However, few other Africans would venture into the Southwest over the next three centuries, except for a handful of free blacks and some runaway slaves, who migrated from the American South into Texas to take advantage of Mexico's relatively lenient race laws.[6]

Eventually African Americans began arriving in Texas in large numbers when Moses and Stephen F. Austin's settlers brought them as slaves starting in the 1820s. Most of Austin's colonists were white Southerners who settled in the eastern third of the state, where the soil and climate were well suited to growing cotton. There they worked to reestablish the familiar social, political, and economic institutions of the Deep South, including an agrarian-based economy, a reliance on slave labor, and a clearly stratified social hierarchy defined mainly by race and economic status. By the outbreak of the Civil War in 1861, the continuing influx of white Southerners and their slaves brought the population of Texas to more than 600,000, including nearly 200,000 slaves and some 350 free blacks.[7]

Because the Southwest was inherently different from the Deep South in many respects, early Anglo settlers in Texas faced difficulties in replicating the rather strict system of racial hierarchy that existed throughout much of the rest of the South. One of the most significant obstacles proved to be the dramatic ethnic diversity of the Southwest. Well before slave-holding Anglos began arriving in the 1820s, Texas already had a substantial Hispanic population, which, for the most part, did not relate to or support the institution of slavery. During the 1840s and 1850s, the state's ethnic makeup grew even more varied, as large numbers of

German, Czech, French, Polish, Swedish, Italian, and other immigrants began arriving in the Lone Star State. Most of these groups had little economic interest in supporting slavery, and some, most notably German Texans, openly opposed it on moral grounds.

Although African Americans in the Southwest may have benefited somewhat from the region's wide-ranging ethnic makeup and the lack of uniform endorsement of slavery and segregation, black Texans still faced widespread racial discrimination. Well before the outbreak of the Civil War, Texas had been busy enacting a variety of laws that restricted the rights of slaves and attempted to drive free blacks out of the state. Once it had joined the Confederacy, Texas officially pledged itself to defending and perpetuating the institution of slavery. Even after the Civil War ended on April 9, 1865, some Texas slave owners were so reluctant to admit defeat that they refused to free their slaves until Union troops arrived in the state on June 19, 1865, and forced them to do so. This long-deferred day of liberation is now celebrated by Texas blacks as "Juneteenth."[8]

Following the Civil War and the end of slavery, the black population in Texas continued to grow, as thousands of former slaves migrated from the Deep South into the Lone Star State. By 1890 Texas was the nation's largest cotton-producing state, and many African Americans made their living as sharecroppers, tenant farmers, or hired hands on large cotton farms. However, a series of boll weevil infestations throughout the state during the late 1800s hurt cotton production and drove many black workers off of the farms and into urban areas. As large numbers of African Americans poured into Houston, Dallas, San Antonio, Austin, and other Texas cities, local governments began enacting Jim Crow laws in an effort to regulate the rapidly growing urban black population. These discriminatory laws, which reinforced segregation and denied blacks equal legal, political, and economic status, remained firmly in place throughout the state until the mid-twentieth century, when they were finally overturned by federal civil rights legislation.[9]

The twentieth century brought tremendous growth in the state's black population, as Texas swiftly transitioned toward a more urban, industrialized society. The booming petrochemical industry along the upper Gulf Coast, along with new trade, high tech, and service jobs, have created employment opportunities for thousands of black workers coming into Texas from Louisiana and other neighboring states. As the twenty-first century began, African Americans were the second largest minority group in Texas, making up 11.5 percent of the state's population (as compared to a nationwide average of 12.3 percent). The growing native-born black population, along with the influx of blacks from outside the state, ensure that African Americans will continue making important contributions to Texas' economy, politics, and culture.[10]

EARLY AFRICAN AMERICAN MUSIC

Since most of the slaves who were brought to North America came from West and Central Africa (many by way of the Caribbean Islands), it was the musical traditions of African tribes such as the Ibo, Mandinka, Ashanti, Bantu, and others that formed the basis for most African American music. Although each of these tribes was unique in its own way, they all shared some common cultural traits with other sub–Saharan African groups, especially a strong tradition of oral folklore and group singing and dancing.

Almost immediately upon arriving in North America, African slaves began to blend their musical customs with those of Europeans around them. In many cases, slaves took European instruments, including the fiddle, guitar, piano, and woodwinds, along with European song styles such as hymns, waltzes, reels, jigs, and fiddle breakdowns, and adapted them to fit the musical sensibilities of the African ear. Of course, the slaves also introduced their own instruments and musical traditions to North America, including a lutelike instrument known in different regions of Africa as a "mbanza" or "bangelo," which later served as a model for the banjo. Another device, composed of a row of keys struck with wooden mallets and most commonly called a "balafon," was the predecessor of the modern xylophone. Slaves also took drums and other percussion instruments, which were rarely used in most European music, and made them an integral part of African American music, the results of which are evident in the later development of jazz, R&B, zydeco, country, rock & roll, and pop.[11]

Slaves made many other contributions to the early development of American music as well. One of the most important of these is the "call and response," an old African tradition in which a lead singer calls out verses, while other members of the group respond in unison. The call-and-response format allowed the slaves to engage in a back-and-forth "dialogue" through their songs. This highly interactive type of music not only was very democratic (since it allowed virtually anyone to participate) but also provided numerous opportunities for innovation and improvisation because each singer was free to add or modify the lyrics, phrasing, or rhythm of a song. Call and response also served a much more practical purpose by helping the slaves establish a synchronized work rhythm as they labored in the fields. This allowed them to work more efficiently and helped ease the drudgery of the long hours of back-breaking labor by letting them participate in the ongoing creative process of trading verses and modifying lyrics.[12]

Long after slavery ended, black railroad workers, field hands, and others continued to use call and response in their daily work routine, and it also became important to the development of African American religious music. Beginning with early spirituals and continuing through modern gospel, many black churches have used call and response as a means by which the minister or choir director can communicate back and forth with the congregation while singing. The importance of call and response, with its emphasis on creating an interactive musical dialogue, is evident in other genres of American music as well. Blues, gospel, jazz, R&B, Western swing, rock & roll, and rap all borrow from the call-and-response technique of encouraging musicians to communicate, improvise, and reshape the music as they are performing it.[13]

The blending of African and European musical customs has had a profound and lasting impact on the development of nearly all musical genres in North America. Blacks not only introduced African instruments and stylistic formats into American music but also incorporated European instruments and song styles into their own long-standing African musical traditions. In so doing, they have helped transform music in new and exciting ways, which in turn helped set the stage for the emergence of several uniquely American musical idioms, including blues, gospel, ragtime, jazz, R&B, rock & roll, rap, and hip-hop.[14]

AFRICAN AMERICAN RELIGIOUS MUSIC IN TEXAS

As one of the oldest genres of African American music, religious music provides much of the foundation for other forms of black music that appeared later. African American religious music is deeply rooted in the experiences of slaves, who blended their own African rhythms, dance steps, vocal phrasings, and musical arrangements with the European Christian religious hymns of their white masters. Perhaps ironically, Certain aspects of the Christian religion appealed to the slaves, especially the underlying themes of deliverance and salvation, through which a lifetime of suffering on earth would be rewarded by an eternity of happiness in heaven. While such teachings of the Christian faith resonated with slaves, African Americans also found some very practical reasons to embrace Christianity. Since both free and enslaved blacks were rarely allowed to congregate in public, the local church provided an acceptable venue in which they could gather in large numbers to socialize, share their culture, and exchange ideas and information. The church service not only gave blacks the chance to address their spiritual needs but also provided them with an opportunity to display their musical talents and to bond with others in a setting that was generally acceptable to whites.[15]

During the colonial era, African Americans in the North often attended church alongside whites. Although they normally sat in segregated pews, blacks sang the same hymns as whites and became quite familiar with the lyrics and melodies of European religious music. Over time, African Americans began to reshape these European hymns to suit their own musical sensibilities and make them more relevant to the reality of their daily lives. In 1794 black members of the predominantly white American Methodist Church started their own African Methodist Episcopal Church, which soon included congregations throughout the country. In 1801 one of their leaders, a former slave named Richard Allen, published a hymnal titled *A Collection of Spiritual Songs and Hymns Selected from Various Authors, by Richard Allen, African Minister.* This songbook comprised a number of traditional European hymns that black worshippers had modified over the years. Many of these African Americanized hymns, or spirituals, as they came to be known, emphasized the fundamental Christian belief that hardship and sorrow here on earth will be rewarded with happiness and eternal salvation in heaven. This theme of suffering and redemption, which was prominent in black religious music, also came to be an important part of more secular forms of African American music, especially the blues.[16]

Like all other types of music, African American religious music evolved over time, and by the mid-1900s the hymns and spirituals of the earlier generations had transformed into what came to be known as "gospel." Spirituals, which were often passed along through oral folk traditions rather than being written down, had typically been performed in a more spontaneous manner, with lyrics and melodies continuously changing. Gospel, on the other hand, was somewhat more formalized, and gospel songs were usually published in hymnals that were distributed to an increasingly literate black audience who performed the music in a more structured manner.

In certain ways, this transition from the less formal spirituals to the more formalized gospel format by the mid-twentieth century mirrored some of the more sweeping changes that were taking place within the African American community. Despite the barriers of segregation and discrimination that persisted well into the mid-1900s, blacks, in fact, were becoming better educated and more fully assimilated into mainstream society, and the adoption of a more structured worship service was a reflection of this. Many African Americans, like other minorities, felt compelled to demonstrate that they were a "respectable" ethnic group, and this often meant conforming in certain ways to the expectations of the white majority. This was especially true in the South, where local whites had long pressured black religious leaders to use their churches to encourage obedience and assimilation among their congregations. By adopting a more standardized system of worship akin to that found in many white congregations, African Americans were working to balance the community's needs and desires for assimilation with their commitment to preserving their own long-standing African American traditions.[17]

Religious music has played a central role in the lives of black Texans. Sometimes African Americans performed religious music in public venues for multiracial audiences, as was the case at the 1936 Texas Centennial Exposition in Dallas, where several black groups sang a variety of "Negro spirituals" before a mixed crowd of Anglos, Hispanics, and others. More typically, however, African American religious music was limited to local black congregational churches. The Deep Ellum area of Central Dallas, one of the largest and most dynamic urban African American communities in Texas during the early twentieth century, provides a good example of how essential religious music and the local church have been to black neighborhoods.[18]

Although it became best known for its lively nightclubs and red-light district, Deep Ellum was also a bustling community that included stores, restaurants, schools, barbershops, churches, parks, theaters, and the same types of social organizations and public activities of any other community. Many prominent musicians spent time in Deep Ellum, including Blind Lemon Jefferson, Huddie "Lead Belly" Ledbetter, Aaron Thibeaux "T-Bone" Walker, Charlie Christian, and Bessie Smith. Others such as Duke Ellington and an Oklahoma City–based jazz band known as the Blue Devils, which included Count Basie, Oran "Hot Lips" Page, and Eddie Durham, performed in Deep Ellum as part of their larger national tours. White musicians such as Marvin "Smokey" Montgomery and John "Knocky" Parker from Bob Wills and Milton Brown's Light Crust Doughboys also visited the nightclubs of Deep Ellum, where they learned jazz and blues licks from black musicians and incorporated them into the Western swing that they performed for rural white audiences.[19]

Deep Ellum also had a thriving spiritual community that produced some of the state's most popular religious musicians. One of the best known was Blind Arizona Dranes. Born Arizona Juanita Dranes in Dallas on April 4, 1894, of mixed African American and Mexican American descent, she recorded for Okeh Records in the 1920s and became famous for her "holy blues," which blended lively boogie-woogie piano and ragtime syncopation with traditional spirituals. Dranes spent

Bells of Joy. Courtesy Texas Music Museum.

much of her adult life traveling throughout Texas and Oklahoma, performing her unique blend of religious and secular music, and helping organize new congregations for the black Pentecostal Church of God in Christ.[20]

Blind Willie Johnson, born in Marlin, Texas, in 1902, was another influential holy blues singer in Deep Ellum. An accomplished blues singer and slide guitarist who combined religious and secular themes, Johnson often mixed different musi-

Bright and Early Choir. Courtesy Texas Music Museum.

cal styles to give his gospel songs a more bluesy feel. He recorded for Columbia Records between 1927 and 1930 and released a number of popular tunes, including "Jesus, Make Up My Dying Bed," "Nobody's Fault but Mine," and "I Know His Blood Can Make Me Whole."[21]

In addition to these important religious performers who lived and worked in Deep Ellum, Dallas was also home to the Stamps-Baxter Music and Printing Company. Founded in 1924 by white gospel singer V. O. Stamps, the company became one of the nation's largest and most prolific gospel music publishers, employing dozens of writers and musicians and operating offices throughout the United States.[22] In fact, gospel music has also been popular among Texas whites, giving rise to the Chuck Wagon Gang and other white groups who blended religious music with country and other styles.

Houston has also had its share of prominent black religious musicians, including the Spiritual Gospel Singers and the Soul Stirrers. The latter group, formed in Houston in the early 1920s, eventually became one of the most innovative and influential gospel ensembles in the country. They performed a highly stylized brand of gospel that included choreographed dance steps and intricate harmonies,

Pilgrim Travelers. Photo by Clay Shorkey, courtesy Texas Music Museum.

which later served as a model for popular groups such as the Temptations and the Four Tops. In 1950 a young Sam Cooke joined the Soul Stirrers before going on to become a world-famous soul music singer. As one of the first gospel singers to cross over into mainstream pop, Cooke helped bring greater national attention to this music and paved the way for Aretha Franklin, Lou Rawls, and other gospel singers to succeed in the commercial music market.[23]

Although based in Philadelphia, the Dixie Hummingbirds, one of the nation's most popular gospel groups, recorded nearly fifty songs for Don Robey's Peacock Records in Houston during the 1950s. In addition to winning a Grammy, appearing at the Newport Folk Festival, and earning a large national following, the Dixie Hummingbirds later made their mark in pop music history when they provided backing vocals on Paul Simon's 1973 hit "Loves Me Like a Rock."[24]

Of course, the impact of African American religious music on Texas music extends well beyond Dallas and Houston. San Antonio, Austin, and many other Texas cities boast a number of gospel groups and choirs that have been active for years, including the Bells of Joy, the Bright and Early Choir, and the Pilgrim Travelers. In fact, virtually every black neighborhood throughout the state has long had its own congregational church, which served as its spiritual hub and sponsored a variety of musical activities, including worship services, weddings, baptisms, funerals, and family gatherings. In numerous ways, religious music helped provide the spiritual foundation for most African American communities and became an integral part of the larger mosaic of black music in the Southwest.[25]

THE BLUES

The blues has arguably had a greater overall impact on the development of modern American music than any other single genre. Blues not only forms the foundation for a number of popular musical styles, including jazz, ragtime, swing, R&B, zydeco, rock & roll, hip-hop, and rap but has also strongly influenced country, pop, and many other styles as well. The term "blues" may have come from an old English expression "blue devils," which were widely believed to be malicious spirits that possessed people and made them feel sad. By the late nineteenth century the word "blues" had come to be identified not only with feelings of sadness and melancholy but also with an emerging style of music that often focused on themes of unhappiness and despair.[26]

Blues music itself grew out of a number of older African musical traditions, including call and response, flattening or "bending" notes, and the use of a strong, repetitive rhythm. In the late nineteenth century black Americans would combine these techniques with ballads, reels, shouts, field hollers, work songs, and spirituals to create what we now know as the blues.[27] Perhaps because slaves (and later most free blacks) had limited access to instruments and little or no formal training, early blues evolved as a relatively simple and straightforward musical structure. Today the standard blues format usually conforms to a twelve-bar, three-verse pattern in which the singer repeats the first verse to reiterate the story line and then changes the third verse to make a particularly emphatic point. This basic, repetitive pattern can go on for several stanzas and often includes numerous subtexts within the larger body of the song.[28]

Blind Lemon Jefferson's "Cat Man Blues," recorded in 1929, is a good example of this pattern of repeating rhymed couplets followed by a third verse, which serves as a punch line for the unfolding story. Jefferson's song also demonstrates how the blues format often employs humor, metaphors, symbolism, and implied subtexts in order to address sensitive issues (in this case, infidelity) in a rather indirect way.

> When I come home last night, I heard a noise; asked my wife
>   "What was that?"
> When I come home last night, I heard a noise; asked my wife
>   "What was that?"
> She said, "Don't be so suspicious, that wasn't a thing but a cat."
> I been all through the world, I've taken all kinds of chance.
> I been all over the world, taken all kinds of chance.
> I've never seen a cat come home in a pair of pants.[29]

Ironically, it is the simplicity of the blues format that allows the performer to construct what is often a lyrically or instrumentally complex song. In a very real sense, the basic, uncluttered blues structure provides a framework upon which singers can build intricate and sophisticated storylines and players can continuously improvise. In fact, most blues songs are constructed in such a way as to let the musicians add or change lyrics and instrumental parts spontaneously in the midst of performing. Because the blues format provides the flexibility for lyrical or instrumental improvisation and the incorporation of additional voices or instruments, it allows the performer to explore the full range of human emotions and to innovate and experiment with the music and text.

Blues is also a very interactive form of music, through which performers can exchange verses or musical riffs with each other and sometimes even with the audience. Of course, this process is rooted in the older African tradition of call and response. Because it allows direct participation from other musicians and the audience, the blues is a very democratic art form and one that has become a powerful and effective means of expressing the frustrations and concerns of African Americans over the years. At the same time, however, the blues can also include the kind of satire, humor, and light-hearted commentary on interpersonal relationships that Jefferson's "Cat Man Blues" demonstrates. Whether happy or sad, the raw emotional quality and remarkable adaptability of the blues has given it universal appeal and made it an integral part of a number of musical genres, including jazz, swing, R&B, zydeco, rock & roll, and country.[30]

Texas has been vital to the development of the blues not only because the blues has been a dominant feature of the musical culture of black communities throughout the state but also because the Southwest has produced some of the most important and innovative artists in blues music. Blind Lemon Jefferson, born in Couchman, Texas, on September 24, 1893, was one of the most prolific and influential blues musicians of all time. As a blind, black man with few other opportunities to earn money in a racially segregated society, Jefferson began performing for tips at an early age in and around his hometown.[31] By his twenties, he was spending most of his time in Deep Ellum, where he soon developed a large following playing in churches, brothels, and bars and on street corners. In Deep Ellum Jefferson met and sometimes performed with other pioneering Texas-based blues players, including Huddie "Lead Belly" Ledbetter, Sam "Lightnin' " Hopkins, Aaron Thibeaux "T-Bone" Walker, and Mance Lipscomb. Jefferson got his first big break in 1925, when R. T. Ashford, who owned a record store and shoeshine parlor in Deep Ellum, helped arrange for Jefferson to make some recordings in Chicago for Paramount Records. Paramount was looking for new artists to help it capitalize on the growing "race" records market, and Jefferson seemed to have just the sort of unique sound the label was looking for. Between 1926 and 1929 Jefferson made close to one hundred recordings for Paramount, as well as a handful for Okeh Records in Atlanta, Georgia, and he quickly became the best-selling "race" artist in the country at that time.[32]

Jefferson wrote most of his own material, although, as with many other artists of his day, he also adopted traditional songs or cobbled together parts of tunes he had heard elsewhere. His lyrics could be satirical, humorous, and overtly sexual, but they also were sometimes dark and brooding, filled with images of sadness, anger, and violence. Undoubtedly Jefferson's songs reflected many of the same hopes, fears, joys, and sorrows that most other African Americans experienced, but it is also likely that his blindness had a significant impact on his songwriting. Many of Jefferson's lyrics include references to visual limitations and seem to reflect the anger and frustration he no doubt endured from having a physical impairment in a world that already posed numerous difficulties for a black man.[33]

As remarkable as Blind Lemon Jefferson's career was, it did not last long. On December 22, 1929, he froze to death after apparently becoming lost while walking back to his hotel room in Chicago following a performance. Although the authorities never determined exactly what happened, they returned his body to Texas, where he is buried in Wortham, near his birthplace of Couchman. As the most popular blues singers of his day, Jefferson had a major impact on his contemporaries and also influenced an untold number of younger musicians. His "Matchbox Blues" became a hit for 1950s' rockabilly pioneer Carl Perkins, as well as for the 1960s' pop superstars, the Beatles. Elvis Presley borrowed from Jefferson's "Teddy Bear Blues," with its line "Let me be your teddy bear / tie a string on my neck / I'll follow you everywhere," to produce one of Elvis's earliest hits, "Teddy Bear." Jefferson was also an important influence on folksingers such as Bob Dylan, who included Blind Lemon's "See That My Grave Is Kept Clean" on his debut album. Jefferson's tremendous commercial success also had a major impact on the recording industry itself by persuading dozens of record labels to record and promote other blues artists. This helped bring blues to a worldwide audience, including countless younger musicians who would later use blues as the foundation for rock & roll.[34]

Huddie (pronounced Hugh-dee) Ledbetter, better known as "Lead Belly," was another influential blues pioneer who lived most of his early life in Texas. Lead Belly was born January 21, 1888, near Mooringsport, Louisiana, but his family relocated to Texas when he was still a child. As an adult, Lead Belly worked a variety of jobs, including what may have been a brief stint as a Texas cowboy.[35] However, his true passion was playing music, and he spent a good deal of time in Deep Ellum, where he often performed with Blind Lemon Jefferson and others. During these early years, Lead Belly also served time in prison for various crimes, including assault and murder. In fact, he was in the Louisiana State Penitentiary at Angola in 1934 when Texas folklorist John Lomax and his son, Alan, "discovered" him while traveling the South recording local musicians. The Lomaxes were so impressed with Lead Belly's vast and diverse musical repertoire that they petitioned Louisiana Governor O. K. Allen to release him from prison. After hearing a tune that Lead Belly had composed for him, Governor Allen agreed to pardon the singer, and for the next few years Lead Belly toured the United States with the Lomaxes, performing and recording dozens of songs.[36]

Lead Belly is often referred to as a "country blues" singer, meaning that his repertoire encompassed a broader range of styles than the standard twelve-bar blues so often played by urban blues musicians. In fact, it was Lead Belly's remarkably diverse repertoire, which included ballads, waltzes, reels, and stomps, as well as standard blues, that first attracted the Lomaxes' attention and brought him great popularity among both black and white audiences. Lead Belly's ability to cover a wide range of styles so proficiently earned him tremendous respect among other musicians and made him a major influence on artists from a variety of genres.[37]

Lead Belly died in 1949, but his impact on modern American music can still be heard today. Some of the best-known white folksingers of the 1940s and 1950s, including Woody Guthrie, Pete Seeger, and Burl Ives, recorded Lead Belly songs such as "Goodnight, Irene" and "Cotton Fields at Home." Younger generations of folk, bluegrass, country, and rock-and-roll musicians, including Willie Nelson, Bill Monroe, Eric Burdon, Creedence Clearwater Revival, U2, and Nirvana, have also recorded Lead Belly tunes such as "House of the Rising Sun," "The Midnight Special," "In the Pines," and "Rock Island Line." Because of the tremendous impact he had on a broad and diverse group of musicians and the key role he played in helping to integrate blues into mainstream American music, Lead Belly remains one of the most influential American musicians of the twentieth century.[38]

Lead Belly's relationship with Texas folklorists John and Alan Lomax has been a subject of some controversy among historians. The Lomaxes did much to promote Lead Belly's career, just as they worked hard to preserve American folk music and encourage a greater public appreciation of its importance. However, some critics have accused the Lomaxes of exploiting Lead Belly for commercial profit and altering his music and image to satisfy their own cultural biases as middle-class white men. It is true that the Lomaxes sometimes pressured Lead Belly to "sanitize" certain song lyrics that they thought might be too graphic or sexually explicit for white audiences. At times they also pandered to white stereotypes of black men as being "savage" and "untamed" and had Lead Belly perform in farmer's overalls or in his old prison uniform even though he preferred wearing dress suits. Although such practices can hardly be condoned, the Lomaxes deserve credit for bringing Lead Belly and other important "roots" musicians to national attention and helping to document and preserve a large body of American folk music that might otherwise have been lost forever.[39]

Although not as well known as Lead Belly, Mance Lipscomb, born near Navasota, Texas, on April 9, 1895, was another important African American musician

Mance Lipscomb, 1967. Courtesy Burton Wilson.

who spent time in Deep Ellum. Lipscomb's father, a former slave, was a fiddler who taught his son to play and sometimes took him along to perform at dances and other events held among the black, Czech, and Scots Irish communities scattered throughout rural East Texas around Navasota. Like Lead Belly, Lipscomb was a country blues singer whose broad repertoire included ballads, reels, waltzes, polkas, and other forms of African- and European-based folk music. Lipscomb has also been referred to as a "songster," which is a type of troubadour who traveled among local black communities providing information and entertainment by performing ballads, dance music, and a number of other song styles.[40]

It was not until the 1960s that Lipscomb received national attention after a group of young musicologists, including Chris Strachwitz, Mack McCormick, and Tary Owens, started documenting his life and music and booking him to perform in clubs throughout Texas. Before long, Strachwitz's San Francisco–based Arhoolie Records began issuing recordings of Lipscomb, which led to numerous invitations to perform around the country, including at the 1961 Berkeley Folk Festival. During his career, Lipscomb played with a wide array of musicians, including Earl Scruggs, Doc Watson, Muddy Waters, Lightnin' Hopkins, Robert Shaw, and Howlin' Wolf. Following his belated rise to fame, Lipscomb relocated to Austin at the age of sixty-five, where he continued performing and influencing younger generations of Texas musicians, including Stevie Ray Vaughan, Ian Moore, and others, until his death in 1976.[41]

Another lesser-known Texas blues musician who actually preceded Jefferson, Lead Belly, and Lipscomb is Henry Thomas, nicknamed "Ragtime Texas" Thomas. Born of former slave parents in Big Sandy, Texas, in 1874, Thomas first performed on the quills, a traditional African American folk instrument made from reeds. Later in life he learned to play guitar and made several recordings with both guitar and quills. Like Lipscomb, Thomas is considered a songster because he traveled around to local black communities using his music to entertain, inform, and pass along folk traditions. Thomas's music can also be thought of as country blues since it encompassed a variety of styles, including reels, waltzes, rags, spirituals, square dances, and minstrel songs. Because he used traditional folk instruments and performed a broad repertoire that drew from a number of styles, Thomas was not just an organic part of the local musical culture. He was also an authentic link between African American folk music of the nineteenth century and the emerging blues, ragtime, and jazz of the early twentieth century.[42]

Alger "Texas" Alexander, born September 12, 1900, in Jewett, Texas, is another example of a blues musician who bridged older African American folk traditions with the newly developing styles of the twentieth century. Although he never

learned to play guitar, his powerful voice commanded attention whether performing alone or with other musicians. Alexander traveled throughout the state, singing
in honky-tonks and migrant labor camps and performing alongside prominent
Texas blues men such as Blind Lemon Jefferson and "Lightnin' " Hopkins. In addition to singing blues, ballads, and other styles, Alexander was well known for
his "shouts," which is an African American tradition of hollering out lyrics in a
loud voice. This was used in earlier days by field slaves to communicate over great
distances and, after slavery, by black railroad crews who needed to pass along
information as they labored up and down the railroad lines.[43]

In addition to blues musicians who played guitars, fiddles, quills, and other
instruments, Texas produced a number of important piano-playing blues singers. The adoption of the piano by black musicians was a milestone in the evolution of American music. Because the piano could accommodate more complex
chord structures than the guitar and was ideal for improvising bass, rhythm, and
melody lines, it played a pivotal role in helping transform blues-based rhythms
and progressions into the more technically sophisticated genres of ragtime,
boogie-woogie, and jazz. By taking this European instrument and adapting it to
the unique melodic phrasings and polyrhythms of African and African American
music, black musicians created almost unlimited new possibilities for innovations
in style and technique, many of which continue to impact popular music today.

Texas proved crucial in this monumental transition from blues to jazz during
the early twentieth century not only by producing the so-called father of ragtime,
Scott Joplin, but also by serving as an incubator for the development of the early
boogie-woogie style of piano blues. In fact, one of the first places that boogie-
woogie appeared was in the sawmills and lumber camps of East Texas, Louisiana,
and Arkansas during the early twentieth century. Each evening, black lumber
workers gathered for entertainment in the camp's makeshift tavern, known as a
"barrelhouse" since the bar was made from a long plank placed on top of barrels.
Because the barrelhouses were crowded and noisy, piano players had to develop
a hard-driving, rocking rhythm that was loud enough to be heard throughout the
tavern. The music they created was an up-tempo, rollicking piano style called "barrelhouse," "fast Texas blues," or "boogie-woogie," which was rooted in the basic
twelve-bar blues progression but also included the livelier syncopated flourishes
of ragtime and a strong, repeating bass line that helped make it highly danceable.
A number of Texas pianists would carry this barrelhouse boogie-woogie style
throughout the South and Southwest, where it was picked up by more prominent
musicians and introduced to the general public.[44]

"Whistlin' " Alex Moore, born in Dallas on November 22, 1899, was one of the most influential early Texas piano players. Moore, a self-taught musician who played blues, ragtime, boogie-woogie, and New Orleans Dixieland jazz, performed on radio, in nightclubs, and in "chockhouses," which were makeshift bars that sold homemade alcohol. During his lifetime Moore recorded for Columbia, Decca, and Rounder Records. Despite falling into relative obscurity for a while, Moore made a comeback in the 1960s, when he became quite popular throughout Europe. Although he never again achieved his earlier level of success, he finally gained national recognition in the United States in 1987, when he became the first black Texan to receive the National Heritage Fellowship from the National Endowment for the Arts.[45]

Beulah "Sippie" Wallace was another very popular Texas pianist and singer who mixed boogie-woogie with blues, gospel, and jazz. Wallace was born in Houston on November 1, 1898, and as a child sang spirituals in the Shilo Baptist Church, where her father was a deacon. However, Wallace also loved the ragtime and boogie-woogie she heard from traveling bands that toured through Houston. As a teenager, she joined one of these groups and ended up in New Orleans, where her older brother, pianist George Thomas, lived. Wallace later moved to Chicago to record for Okeh Records and became a much-sought-after singer, working with Louis Armstrong, King Oliver, and another one of her brothers, pianist Hersal Thomas. Despite enjoying tremendous success in the 1920s and 1930s, Wallace took an extended break from performing during the 1940s and 1950s and returned only when her friend and fellow Texas singer, Victoria Spivey, convinced her to start singing publicly again in the 1960s. This helped rekindle Wallace's career, and she went on to record for Atlantic Records and earn a Grammy nomination. With powerful protofeminist songs such as "Woman Be Wise," Wallace also garnered the admiration of numerous younger blues singers, including Bonnie Raitt, with whom Wallace toured and recorded during the 1970s and 1980s.[46]

Sippie Wallace's brothers also played leading roles in shaping Texas piano music, especially boogie-woogie. Her brother George was a successful composer and music publisher in both New Orleans and Chicago between 1914 and 1930. In fact, his 1916 composition, "New Orleans Hop Scop Blues," may have been the first published song to include a boogie-woogie bass line. George and Hersal also cowrote the 1922 song "The Fires," which became a standard among Chicago blues pianists. The brothers' catchy tunes and barrelhouse piano style became very popular and helped inspire nationally renowned performers such as Count Basie and Duke Ellington to incorporate boogie-woogie into their repertoires. Sadly, both of the Thomas brothers died early in their careers—Hersal from food poisoning at the age of sixteen and George in a streetcar accident when he was forty-five. Nevertheless,

Sippie Wallace and her brothers, George and Hersal Thomas, left a lasting imprint on the national music scene with their piano-based blues and boogie-woogie.[47]

Another important blues singer was Sippie Wallace's good friend, Victoria Spivey, who was born in Houston on October 15, 1906. Famous for her hard-edged, moaning vocal style, Spivey began singing and playing piano at an early age in Houston-area bars and bordellos. A talented songwriter, she made her first record, "Black Snake Blues," in 1926 for the Okeh label and went on to write and record many more songs. She performed with Bessie Smith, Memphis Minnie, Louis Armstrong, and others. Although Spivey lapsed into obscurity throughout most of the 1940s and 1950s, she reemerged in the early 1960s, when she started her own record label, Spivey Records, and began performing and touring again. She went on to play at major blues and folk festivals throughout the United States and Europe until her death in 1976.[48]

Robert Shaw, another influential boogie-woogie pianist, was born in Stafford, Texas, on August 9, 1908. Although he dreamed of becoming a jazz musician, Shaw was best known for his barrelhouse piano style, which he first learned to play while living in Houston's predominantly black Fourth Ward. During the 1920s Shaw became part of the so-called Santa Fe Circuit of musicians, which traveled on the Santa Fe Railway to perform as far away as Chicago. By the 1930s he was married and living in Austin, where he ran a grocery store and rarely performed in public. However, in the 1960s, Texas musicologist Mack McCormick sought out Shaw and began recording his music. This helped rekindle Shaw's career by sparking an interest in boogie-woogie piano among a new generation of fans, thereby bringing Shaw invitations to perform at a number of prestigious festivals and events throughout North America and Europe during the 1960s and 1970s.[49]

TEXAS BLUES GOES ELECTRIC

Advances in technology during the 1930s and 1940s helped change the way in which the blues was performed, recorded, and marketed. The introduction of electric guitars, amplifiers, PA (public address) systems, and large drum sets meant that blues bands could play bigger venues without compromising volume or sound quality. Innovations in recording and broadcasting also brought increased radio airplay for blues musicians, and the proliferation of jukeboxes throughout the country helped boost record sales and cultivate a larger national following for the blues, including among white audiences. The new electronic technology of the 1930s and 1940s also changed the very sound of the blues.

Whereas earlier acoustic performers had to work hard just to be heard over the noise of a crowd, amplification gave musicians all of the volume they needed and allowed them to focus on developing more refined playing techniques. With amplified vocals and instruments, blues artists were also able to expand the size of their bands to include electric keyboards, horns, and a larger percussion section, all of which allowed blues groups to perform more elaborate and complex musical arrangements.

As important as the new technology was to the transformation of the blues, changing musical tastes among musicians and their audiences also helped alter the sound and structure of the blues by the mid-twentieth century. During the 1930s and 1940s, while big-band swing was at the height of its popularity, a growing number of black musicians began blending swing with more traditional blues, helping create a new style known first as "jump blues" and later as rhythm and blues, or R&B. For the most part, R&B was a more up-tempo version of blues that featured larger ensembles made up of electric guitars, drums, keyboards, expanded horn sections, and backup singers. During the 1950s, R&B, which was the result of both technological innovation and changing musical tastes, would serve as the foundation for early rock & roll.[50]

Texas musicians played a leading role in this transitional period toward electrified blues and R&B in the 1930s and 1940s. One of the era's most influential electric blues guitarists, Aaron Thibeaux "T-Bone" Walker, was born in Linden, Texas, on May 28, 1910. He grew up in the Dallas suburb of Oak Cliff and often visited Deep Ellum, where he spent time with Blind Lemon Jefferson, Lead Belly, Charlie Christian, and other black Texas musicians. Walker, a multitalented entertainer who could sing, dance, and play guitar and banjo, first gained national attention in 1930 after he won a talent contest sponsored by the popular composer and performer Cab Calloway. Impressed with Walker's versatility, Calloway invited Walker to join him on tour, and before long Walker was performing with Ma Rainey and several other top blues and jazz stars of the era.[51]

In 1935 T-Bone Walker relocated to Los Angeles, where he quickly established a reputation as a superb musician and a dynamic performer. Throughout the 1930s, 1940s, and 1950s he was a leading figure in the development of R&B, and he attracted a huge following with his lively on-stage antics, which included playing the guitar with his teeth and behind his back, leaping in the air, and gyrating his hips. Later generations of performers, including James Brown, Chuck Berry, Elvis Presley, Jimi Hendrix, and Stevie Ray Vaughan, copied Walker's stage moves and made them a standard part of the rock-and-roll repertoire. Walker was also a talented songwriter. His best-known composition, "They Call It Stormy Monday," epitomized the new R&B sound and became a hit among blues, R&B, and pop music fans alike.[52]

Several other important Texas artists contributed substantially to the development of electric blues and R&B during the mid-twentieth century. Sam "Lightnin'" Hopkins, born in Centerville, Texas, on March 15, 1912, was one of the most influential of these modern blues pioneers. He was inspired to play music at an early age by his musician father and brother, as well as by blues greats Blind Lemon Jefferson and Texas Alexander. Hopkins got his nickname "Lightnin' " in 1946, when he recorded with piano player Wilson "Thunder" Smith, and the duo was billed as "Thunder and Lightnin.' " Hopkins went on to record for at least twenty different labels during his lifetime and had five major hits on the R&B charts throughout the 1940s and 1950s. Like so many other African American artists of his era, Hopkins was "discovered" by younger blues and R&B fans in the 1960s, who helped rekindle his career and introduce him to larger mainstream audiences. This resurgence in popularity led to his being invited to perform at Carnegie Hall, the Newport Folk Festival, and elsewhere throughout the United States and Europe, including a command performance for Queen Elizabeth II. Perhaps the most enduring aspect of his legacy came when Hopkins, along with fellow Texan T-Bone Walker and other blues veterans, toured Europe during the early 1960s and helped inspire a new generation of young musicians, including John Lennon, Paul McCartney, Mick Jagger, and Keith Richards, all of whom borrowed from these blues and R&B pioneers to forge their own brand of rock & roll during the mid-1960s.[53]

"Big Mama" Thornton at the Vulcan Gas Company, Austin, 1969. *Courtesy Burton Wilson.*

Willie Mae "Big Mama" Thornton, another influential Texas-based artist of this period, was born in Montgomery, Alabama, on December 11, 1926, but moved to Houston in 1948, where she lived until the 1960s. Her father was a minister, and Thornton's musical influences ran the gamut from church hymns to bawdy songs about drinking, gambling, and spending time in jail. Thornton had a raw, powerful singing style that helped influence a number of younger musicians who were coming of age during the early years of rock & roll, including Elvis Presley and Janis Joplin. In 1951 Thornton signed with Houston-based Peacock Records and soon made her 1953 recording of "(You Ain't Nothin' but a) Hound Dog." Although she earned a total of only five hundred dollars for her version of the Jerry Lieber and Mike Stoller tune, Elvis Presley reworked the song in 1956 and made it one of his first million-selling hits. Janis Joplin, from Port Arthur, Texas, recorded Thornton's "Ball and Chain" in 1968 as a tribute to the veteran blues singer, who had been one of Joplin's biggest musical influences. Because she was a powerful inspiration to many younger artists, Thornton would play a key role in bridging blues and R&B with the rock & roll, pop, and psychedelic rock of the 1960s.[54]

Clarence "Gatemouth" Brown, born in Vinton, Louisiana, on April 18, 1924, but raised in East Texas, was another important R&B performer from the Southwest. His father was an accomplished fiddler, and, Brown grew up listening to blues, country, zydeco, jazz, and a variety of other musical styles found along the Texas-Louisiana border. Brown's tremendous versatility was evident in his eclectic musical tastes and his mastery of several instruments, including guitar, fiddle, drums, mandolin, and viola. In 1947 he began performing in Don Robey's Bronze Peacock nightclub in Houston. When Robey started his Peacock Records label in 1949, he signed Brown, and the two went on to produce dozens of successful R&B tunes. Over the next several decades Brown remained popular, winning a Grammy in 1981 for his album *Alright Again* and continuing to record and tour until his death in 2005. While renowned for his technical expertise, Brown was most notable for his ability to move effortlessly among various musical genres, including blues, country, R&B, Western swing, Cajun, and bluegrass. Perhaps as well as any R&B artist of his day, Gatemouth Brown reflected the unique and diverse folk traditions found among African Americans in the Southwest.[55]

Following World War II, a number of Texas musicians relocated to the West Coast, where they ended up having a major impact on the blues and R&B scene there. Amos Milburn, born in Houston on April 1, 1927, was one such influential singer and piano player who became part of the larger migration of Texas musicians to California during the 1940s. With hits such as "After Midnight," "Let Me Go Home, Whiskey," and "In the Middle of the Night," Milburn became *Billboard*

Clarence "Gatemouth" Brown. Photo by James Fraher.

magazine's top-selling R&B artist of 1949 and helped attract more major record labels to the R&B market. His blending of raw Texas blues and boogie-woogie with the more urbane sounds of West Coast jazz also influenced many younger artists, including Fats Domino and Little Richard.[56]

Ivory Joe Hunter, born October 10, 1914, in Kirbyville, Texas, was another major Texas artist who made his mark in R&B on the West Coast. Hunter, whose father played guitar and mother was a gospel singer, began as a barrelhouse piano player but soon developed into a prolific songwriter and technical innovator who was equally comfortable playing boogie-woogie, R&B, or slow love ballads. In 1942 he moved to California, where he recorded for several record labels, including his own. At times he wove elements of country music into his songs, and in the 1960s he even relocated for a while to Nashville, where he appeared on the Grand Ole Opry. Hunter, whose songs have been recorded by Nat King Cole, Elvis Presley, and many others, had his greatest success with "Since I Met You, Baby," a huge crossover hit that sold well among both black and white audiences and earned him an appearance on the nationally popular Ed Sullivan Show.[57]

"Pee Wee" Crayton, born Connie Curtis Crayton on December 18, 1914, in Rockdale, Texas, also relocated in 1935 to California, where he became another one of the most important architects of the 1940s' and 1950s' West Coast blues and R&B sound. Some of Crayton's biggest influences were fellow Texans Charlie Christian, T-Bone Walker, and Ivory Joe Hunter. In fact, Crayton gained some of his earliest national exposure by performing and recording with Hunter during the 1940s. By 1949 Crayton had his own hit records on the blues and R&B charts, including "Blues after Hours," "Texas Hop," "I Love You So," and "I'm Still in Love with You." He continued to record and perform well into the 1980s, working alongside Big Joe Turner, Gatemouth Brown, Dizzy Gillespie, Johnny Otis, and others.[58]

Another influential Texas artist, "King" Curtis, born Curtis Ousley in Fort Worth, on February 7, 1934, became one of the most sought-after R&B saxophonists of the 1950s and 1960s after he was featured on the Coasters' 1957 hit "Yakety-Yak." His subsequent work with a wide range of artists, including Buddy Holly, Lionel Hampton, Nat King Cole, Wilson Pickett, Andy Williams, Connie Francis, Bobby Darin, Simon and Garfunkel, and the Allman Brothers Band, helped Curtis introduce the R&B sound to a much larger mainstream audience. In addition to working with these established artists, he also helped nurture younger musicians, including a youthful Jimi Hendrix, who played guitar in Curtis's backup band during the early 1960s.[59]

Little Esther Phillips, a very popular female R&B singer, was born in Galveston, Texas, on December 23, 1935, although her family moved to California when she was still a child. In 1949 Los Angeles–based bandleader Johnny Otis hired the fourteen-year-old Phillips as his vocalist. When her recording of "Double Crossing Blues" became a hit in 1950, Phillips earned the distinction of being the youngest R&B musician ever to have a number-one song in the national charts. She went on to record several other hits, including "Ring-a-Ding-Doo" and a popular R&B version of the country song "Please Release Me." During her career, Phillips gained a huge following throughout the United States and Europe. Among her biggest fans were the Beatles, who considered her such a key influence on the early development of their music that they invited her to appear on their 1965 BBC television special.[60]

THE "NEW" TEXAS BLUES

As the second half of the twentieth century unfolded, circumstances for African Americans changed dramatically. Not long after President Harry Truman desegregated the U.S. military in 1948, decades of institutionalized segregation began to give way, and a powerful new civil rights movement helped break down long-standing barriers to racial equality. A growing number of African Americans, like Mexican Americans, made use of the G.I. Bill and the new job skills they had acquired during World War II to advance themselves economically and begin moving into the ranks of the middle class. Although the United States remained a racially divided country in many ways, black and white Americans started coming into more frequent contact with one another at school, in the workplace, and elsewhere.

Just as it had before, music once again served as an essential cultural bridge connecting people of different races and ethnic backgrounds. Although for the most part black and white Americans still lived in separate neighborhoods and moved in different social spheres, the boundaries between African American and Anglo-American culture were becoming increasingly blurred, and more and more people from both sides were starting to share openly in the biracial exchange of musical traditions. Some of the best examples of this growing cultural cross-pollination occurred during the late 1940s and early 1950s, as the electrification of traditional blues and the rapid rise in popularity of R&B help lead to the emergence of rock & roll.

Texas musicians were at the forefront of redefining blues and R&B and helping link them to the early development of rock & roll. One of the most versatile and innovative of these post–World War II blues and R&B pioneers was Albert Collins. Born on October 3, 1932, in Leona, Texas, Collins, a cousin of famed blues man Lightnin' Hopkins, was around seven years old when his family relocated to Houston. There in the city's predominantly African American Third Ward, Collins learned to play the piano. Eventually he switched to guitar and began developing a unique style of playing. Part of what made his sound so different was that Collins often used minor-key tunings, and he played with finger picks instead of a single pick, as most blues guitarists did. He also used a capo, which allowed him to play much higher up the guitar neck, where he could produce sharp, staccato notes that many fans likened to the sound of breaking ice, thereby earning him the nickname "the Iceman."[61]

Until the 1960s Collins was not well known outside of the African American community. However, in 1968, the popular rock band Canned Heat invited "the Iceman" along on tour, introducing him to much larger white audiences. This helped land him a recording contract with Imperial Records, and soon a number of young, white blues and rock-and-roll artists, including Johnny Winter, Janis

Albert Collins. Photo by James Fraher.

Joplin, and David Bowie, began recording with Collins and booking him as their opening act. He continued attracting new fans, both black and white, and went on to win a Grammy in 1983 for his album *Showdown*, which he recorded with blues legends Robert Cray and Johnny Copeland.[62]

Freddie "the Texas Cannonball" King was another dynamic blues guitarist who inspired numerous blues and rock-and-roll musicians. Born in Gilmer, Texas, on September 3, 1934, King moved to Chicago as a teenager, but some of his chief musical influences remained fellow Texans Blind Lemon Jefferson, Lightnin' Hopkins, and T-Bone Walker. During the 1950s and 1960s King performed with a number of groups and recorded on several labels, for whom he produced hits such as "Hideaway," "Going Down," and "Have You Ever Loved a Woman?" In 1963 he moved back to Texas, and by the 1970s he had become one of the most popular performers at Austin's Armadillo World Headquarters, which was re-nowned for its eclectic audiences with wide-ranging musical tastes. Freddie King was an enormous influence on many 1960s' blues and rock musicians, including Jeff Beck, John Mayall, and Eric Clapton, who helped introduce him to worldwide audiences in the mid-1970s by inviting him along on tour. Unfortunately, just as King was reaching the pinnacle of his commercial success, he died in 1976 at the age of forty-two from bleeding ulcers and heart failure.[63]

Barbara Lynn, born in Beaumont, Texas, on January 16, 1942, is a pioneering fe-male figure in Texas blues and R&B. As a talented singer and guitar player, she had the huge 1962 hit "You'll Lose a Good Thing," which gained her an international following and helped earn her appearances with Jackie Wilson, B. B. King, Stevie Wonder, and others. More recently, Lynn has performed several times at Antone's and the Continental Club in Austin, and she continues to tour nationally.[64]

Several other blues and R&B artists from Texas had a notable influence on shaping soul, funk, rock & roll, and the "new" blues sound of the 1970s and 1980s. Archie Bell and the Drells, from Houston, have been one of the most popular and influential groups on the R&B circuit for the past forty years. Their 1968 hit, "Tighten Up," features a skillful blending of soul and R&B that foreshadowed the funk craze of the 1970s. The Drells followed "Tighten Up" with the popular 1970 song "Wrap It Up," which became a hit once again in 1986 for the white Texas R&B band, the Fabulous Thunderbirds.[65]

As blues and R&B grew in popularity outside of the black community, more and more white musicians began to build successful careers in these traditionally African American genres. Delbert McClinton, born in Lubbock, Texas, on Novem-ber 4, 1940, is one such artist who went on to become one of the most popular white R&B singers in the country. As a teenager, he listened to Lightnin' Hopkins,

Jimmy Reed, B. B. King, Howlin' Wolf, and other black blues and R&B artists, but he also loved Hank Williams, Lefty Frizzell, and a variety of white country musicians. During the late 1950s and early 1960s McClinton's band, the Straightjackets, began playing several of Fort Worth's traditionally black R&B dance halls, such as the Skyliner Ballroom and Jack's. In 1962 he found himself catapulted onto the international stage after recording the trademark harmonica lick on Bruce Channel's hit "Hey, Baby." While on tour with Channel in England, McClinton met an aspiring young musician named John Lennon, who would later borrow from McClinton's harmonica riffs for some early Beatles tunes. McClinton went solo in the 1970s and recorded a series of R&B albums that revealed his country, rockabilly, and rock-and-roll roots. He has also enjoyed substantial success as a songwriter. Emmylou Harris had a number-one country hit with his tune "Two More Bottles of Wine," and John Belushi and Dan Akroyd, as the Blues Brothers, recorded McClinton's "B Movie Boxcar Blues." McClinton's 1980 song "Giving It Up for Your Love" reached number eight on the pop charts, and in 1991 he won a Grammy for a duet with Bonnie Raitt. Perhaps more important than awards or record sales, however, is the fact that McClinton helped pave the way for other successful white blues and R&B performers, most notably fellow Texans Jimmie Vaughan and Stevie Ray Vaughan.[66]

The phenomenal careers of Jimmie Vaughan and Stevie Ray Vaughan further exemplify the prolific cross-pollination of the many musical influences found in Texas. Growing up in the Dallas suburb of Oak Cliff, not far from where T-Bone Walker had once lived, the Vaughan brothers absorbed a variety of musical styles, including country, blues, R&B, and rock & roll. As children, they began playing guitars, and by the time they were teenagers the brothers were frequenting the nightclubs of Deep Ellum, where so many earlier generations of musicians had spent time.

The older Jimmie, born on March 20, 1951, moved to Austin in 1970 to immerse himself in the burgeoning live-music scene there. At that time, the blues market in Austin, especially for white teenagers, was quite limited, but Vaughan joined with Clifford Antone, Angela Strehli, Lou Ann Barton, Paul Ray, Doyle Bramhall, and others who were devoted to cultivating a blues scene in the capital city. In 1975 Clifford Antone opened his downtown club, Antone's, which soon became a mecca for young blues and R&B musicians and a place where they could gather to perform with their favorite veteran players.

By 1979 Jimmie Vaughan, Kim Wilson, Keith Ferguson, and Mike Buck had formed the Fabulous Thunderbirds, who became the de facto house band at Antone's. The Thunderbirds soon gained international attention with their rock-

Angela Strehli with James Polk and the Brothers, 1971. Courtesy Burton Wilson.

infused R&B sound, and they went on to record a number of top-selling records, some of which were featured in major motion picture soundtracks. The Fabulous Thunderbirds' widespread popularity throughout the 1980s helped set the stage for Jimmie's younger brother, Stevie, to launch an even more successful career that would make him a true blues-rock superstar.[67]

Stevie Ray Vaughan, born October 3, 1954, followed Jimmie to Austin in the early 1970s and began building a reputation as a dynamic and innovative guitar player. Although he was first and foremost a blues guitarist, "Stevie" Vaughan, as he was known in the early days, also wove the rock guitar stylings of Jimi Hendrix, Johnny Winter, and others into his music. While playing with the Austin-based band the Cobras, Vaughan continued to develop his guitar skills and also began to mature as a vocalist and a songwriter. In 1978 he formed the group Double Trouble, which used Antone's as its home base.

Because his playing was so innovative and technically sophisticated, it appealed to fans across the spectrum of blues, rock, and even heavy metal. Vaughan's

Lavelle White. Photo by Clay Shorkey, courtesy Texas Music Museum.

popularity grew swiftly, and he was soon performing for sellout crowds around the world. His commercial success brought with it critical acclaim, and in 1984 he became the first white person ever to win the prestigious W. C. Handy National Blues Foundation's Entertainer of the Year and Blues Instrumentalist of the Year awards. After releasing a series of top-selling albums throughout the 1980s, Stevie Ray Vaughan was killed in a helicopter crash on August 27, 1990, after finishing a concert with Eric Clapton in Alpine Valley, Wisconsin. Ironically, Vaughan had just undergone a successful drug rehabilitation program to kick the cocaine and alcohol addiction that had plagued him for years. Although some blues purists have complained that he pushed blues too far in the direction of rock, others, including legendary blues pioneer B. B. King, praised Vaughan for helping reinvigorate the blues and introducing it to younger audiences.[68]

A number of other key figures have helped keep the blues and R&B traditions alive in Texas. Clifford Antone, born October 27, 1949, in Port Arthur, Texas,

Ruthie Foster at the Kerrville Folk Festival. Courtesy Susan Roads.

helped launch the careers of the Vaughan brothers and others through his Austin nightclub, and he helped resurrect the dormant careers of many older blues players, while also nurturing young, up-and-coming talent. Veteran artists such as Joe Willie "Pinetop" Perkins, Miss Lavelle White, and W. C. Clark, who mentored the young Stevie Ray Vaughan on guitar, continue to record and perform throughout Texas. Others, many of whom worked alongside the Vaughan brothers in the early days, have also built their own successful careers, including Marcia Ball, Derek O'Brien, Lou Ann Barton, Malford Milligan, Derek Taylor, Angela Strehli, Denny Freeman, and Jon Dee Graham. A new generation of performers, represented by Toni Price, Ruthie Foster, Gary Clark Jr., Sue Foley, Sarah Brown, Carolyn Wonderland, Eve Monsees, Seth Walker, Colin Brooks, and others, is making its own mark on the Texas blues scene and carrying this important genre of American music to new fans around the world.[69]

RAGTIME AND JAZZ

Ragtime and jazz are two other African American musical genres that have had a dramatic impact on mainstream music. Ragtime, which was wildly popular during the late nineteenth and early twentieth centuries, grew out of a variety of earlier musical traditions from Africa, Europe, and North America. While it employed classical European piano techniques, ragtime also featured the polyrhythms of ancient African folk music, along with the innovative phrasing often found in spirituals, minstrel songs, and blues. Originally known as "jig piano," this new style later came to be called "ragged time" or simply "ragtime." Ragtime's most distinctive feature is its strongly syncopated beat, which piano players achieved by setting a steady, repeating rhythm with the left hand while using the right hand to create a more spontaneous melody line that played off of the underlying beat. Ragtime was enormously important in the evolution of American music. For one thing, its complex melodies and energetic rhythms, along with its emphasis on improvisation, helped lay the foundation for the emergence of jazz in the early twentieth century. In addition, as the first black musical genre to achieve widespread commercial success, ragtime brought African American music to a whole new level of national recognition and helped create many new professional opportunities for black musicians and composers.[70]

Texan Scott Joplin, often called the "father" of ragtime, did not invent the genre, but he became ragtime's most famous composer and was a major influence on many younger artists, including Ferdinand "Jelly Roll" Morton, Fats Waller, and

Louis Armstrong, all of whom would become leading architects of early jazz. Joplin was born the child of a former slave near Texarkana, Texas, on November 24, 1868. His parents encouraged their children to play music, and young Scott showed such great promise at an early age that his mother took in extra work in order to pay for his piano lessons. As a child, Joplin studied with several piano teachers, but perhaps the most influential was a local German immigrant named Julius Weiss, who was so impressed with his young student that he agreed to teach Joplin for free. Weiss gave the youngster a thorough training in classical composition and performance, which provided him with the discipline and technical expertise to write and perform complex ragtime pieces as an adult.[71]

Although classical training was very important to Joplin's professional career, he was also strongly influenced by the great variety of African American and European American folk music he heard while growing up in East Texas, including hymns, spirituals, blues, minstrels, marches, polkas, and waltzes. Drawing from these many different styles, Joplin began writing and performing his own songs at an early age. As a young man, he formed a group with some of his brothers, who played throughout East Texas and occasionally ventured as far away as the Midwest and Northeast. During these early years Joplin performed in a variety of venues, from music halls and opera houses to saloons and bordellos, where his eclectic musical background gave him the versatility to play almost any type of music.[72]

Eventually Joplin left Texas and settled in Missouri, where he lived the remainder of his life, composing music and performing with his Texas Medley Quartette. While Joplin was living in Missouri, his reputation as a songwriter continued to grow, and before long he became the most sought-after composer of the ragtime era. Virtually every ragtime artist at the time performed Joplin's tunes, and his sheet music could be found in the piano parlors of countless homes across the country. Although he became best known for his 1899 "Maple Leaf Rag," which has sold millions of copies and become the most famous rag of all time, Joplin wrote many other popular songs, including "Pineapple Rag" and "The Entertainer" (the latter became a pop hit once again some fifty years after Joplin's death as the theme song to *The Sting*, Robert Redford and Paul Newman's 1973 movie). By taking a leading role in defining the ragtime sound and popularizing it among both black and white audiences, Joplin was crucial in laying the groundwork for jazz to emerge during the early twentieth century.[73]

Although less well known than Joplin, Euday L. Bowman was another Texas composer who played a significant role in ragtime and the early development of jazz. Born in Fort Worth on November 9, 1887, Bowman was an accomplished pianist who wrote many songs. His "Twelfth Street Rag," one of the most frequently recorded tunes ever written, was a staple of most ragtime performers and became one of the most popular songs of the early jazz era. Because it has a rather unusual repeating three-note melody, which lends itself well to improvisation, "Twelfth Street Rag" became a musical touchstone for many bands, as each reinterpreted the song by adding new flourishes and innovations that reflected the larger stylistic changes taking place in jazz over the years. First published in 1914, more than 120 versions of "Twelfth Street Rag" have been recorded by several generations of musicians, including Louis Armstrong, Fats Waller, Bennie Moten, Duke Ellington, Count Basie, and Lester Young.[74]

Jazz, which by the 1920s would eclipse ragtime in terms of popularity, exploded onto the national scene during the early twentieth century partly as a result of the dramatic social and cultural changes that were taking place in the United States. For one thing, the outbreak of World War I in 1914 had helped usher in a "Second Industrial Revolution," in which millions of African Americans migrated from rural areas, especially in the South, to fill factory jobs in the larger industrial cities of the North. This massive shift from an agrarian to an urban environment had a profound impact on African American society and helped give rise to a sweeping new cultural movement known as the "Harlem Renaissance," an extraordinary flowering of art, literature, and music in which dozens of African American artists, writers, and musicians brought black culture to national prominence.

Jazz, which is deeply rooted in spirituals, blues, ragtime, and other African American traditions, became the musical "voice" for the Harlem Renaissance. Not only did jazz represent the energy and optimism of a new generation of black Americans, but its uniqueness and spontaneity appealed to millions of others regardless of race, class, or ethnicity. As it grew in popularity across the country and around the world, jazz would undergo numerous changes and spawn a variety of other subgenres, including big-band swing, Western swing, bebop, and fusion jazz.

The Lone Star State's important role in jazz history has not always been widely recognized, in part because so many Texas artists left the Southwest and migrated to the more vibrant jazz scenes that sprang up in New York City, Los Angeles, Chicago, Kansas City, and elsewhere during the 1930s and 1940s. Nevertheless, Texas contributed a number of influential musicians and innovations to the development of jazz.[75] By far one of the most important jazz players ever to come from the Southwest was guitarist Charlie Christian, born in Bonham, near Dallas, on July 29, 1916. His earliest influences included Blind Lemon Jefferson and other Dallas-area musicians, as well as his own father, a blind guitarist and singer whom the young Charlie sometimes escorted to performances.

By his early twenties Christian had developed a remarkable ear for jazz and a unique single-string guitar soloing style that used altered chords and innovative, blues-inflected melody lines. The great clarinetist Benny Goodman, who was the first nationally prominent white bandleader to hire African American musicians into his band, was so impressed with Christian's playing that he recruited him in 1939. As part of Goodman's sextet, Christian quickly gained notoriety in the jazz world and performed with legendary jazz musicians such as Lionel Hampton, Count Basie, Dizzy Gillespie, and Coleman Hawkins. Tragically, Christian's life was cut short when he died of tuberculosis in 1942 at the age of twenty-five. Despite the brevity of his career, many music historians still consider Christian to be the single most influential jazz guitarist of the twentieth century. Over the years numerous musicians have copied Christian's licks on a variety of instruments, and his single-string soloing technique has become the model for countless guitarists in jazz, rock, and country music.[76]

Eddie Durham, born August 19, 1906, in San Marcos, Texas, never achieved the same level of fame as Christian, but Durham was also a towering figure in the development of early jazz, and he may have been partly responsible for Christian's tremendous success. Durham's father, Joe, a fiddler who performed at square dances throughout Central Texas, encouraged his children to play music, and by the time Eddie was a teenager, he was performing professionally with his brothers and cousins. As an adult, Durham made his mark as an instrumentalist, a composer, and an arranger for some of the most popular jazz and swing bands of the 1930s and 1940s. Working with Count Basie, Bennie Moten, Artie Shaw, Glen Miller, and others, Durham arranged and performed classics such as "Moten Swing," "One o'Clock Jump," and "Jumpin' at the Woodside." Durham may also have been the first jazz musician ever to record with an electric guitar when he played on Jimmie Lunceford's 1935 song "Hittin' the Bottle."

In addition to his pioneering studio work, it is possible that Durham was the one who introduced Charlie Christian to the single-string style of playing that became Christian's trademark. An October 1929 recording session with Bennie Moten in the Chicago studios of RCA Victor features Durham laying down some of the first recorded tracks of the single-note lead guitar style that he later demonstrated to Christian when the two finally met in 1937. In recent years Durham has started to receive the recognition he has long deserved with new research into his important role in jazz and an annual celebration honoring him in his hometown of San Marcos.[77]

Another notable Texas jazz musician who has gone largely unrecognized is Gene Ramey. Born in Austin on April 4, 1913, Ramey became one of the most sought-after jazz bass players of the 1930s, 1940s, and 1950s. Like so many other Texas jazz musicians, Ramey left the state early in his professional career to play in the larger and more lucrative jazz scenes elsewhere. Between 1938 and 1944 he lived both in Kansas City, Missouri, and New York City, where he became a key member of the popular Jay McShann Orchestra. During these years Ramey was a close friend of and musical mentor to the young alto saxophonist Charlie "Bird" Parker. Parker would become legendary not only for his brilliant and innovative playing style but also for his drug and alcohol addiction, which ended his life at the age of only thirty-four. Throughout much of their relationship, Ramey struggled unsuccessfully to steer the younger Parker away from drugs and alcohol and to keep him focused on music.[78]

Although he was an important influence on Charlie Parker's life and career, Gene Ramey played perhaps an even bigger role in the evolution of jazz by helping develop the distinctive "Kansas City sound," which featured a rather subdued backing rhythm that allowed instrumentalists, including Charlie Parker, more freedom to improvise. Ramey referred to this unique rhythmic approach as "the Baptist beat," and he claimed that he had learned it as a child in Texas from the hand clapping and call-and-response traditions practiced in his local church. Ramey's Baptist beat provided an understated yet rock-solid background rhythm that freed up soloists to focus more on innovation and experimentation, thereby helping pave the way for bebop and other types of free-form jazz during the second half of the century. During his long and successful career Ramey not only helped change the course of jazz history but also worked with some of the most prominent musicians of his day, including Count Basie, Lester Young, Eartha Kitt, Dizzy Gillespie, and Miles Davis. In 1976 Ramey returned to Texas, where he performed in the Austin area until his death in 1984.[79]

Several other Texas string players have been prominent in the long-term development of jazz. Guitarist Oscar Moore, born in Austin on December 25, 1912, worked with Nat King Cole, Lionel Hampton, Art Tatum, and Lester Young. Herb Ellis, who was born in Farmersville, Texas, on August 4, 1921, took much of his inspiration from fellow Texan Charlie Christian and played guitar with notable artists such as Ella Fitzgerald, Jimmy Dorsey, Joe Pass, and the Oscar Peterson Trio. Jazz-rock guitarist Larry Coryell, born in Galveston on April 2, 1943, was a leader of the 1970s' and 1980s' "fusion jazz" movement, which combined jazz, rock, pop, and R&B. In the 1970s Coryell joined Chick Corea, Billy Cobham, and John McLaughlin to form the highly successful fusion group Eleventh House.[80]

Texas also produced a number of remarkable jazz horn players. Ornette Coleman, born in Fort Worth on March 19, 1930, is one of jazz music's most boldly innovative saxophonists. His diverse musical influences included blues, minstrel, R&B, and Western swing, and he even performed once with the legendary "King of Western Swing," Bob Wills. Coleman's eclectic background led him to develop a unique style known as "harmolodics," in which he abandoned conventional melodies and chord structures and allowed every musician in his band to create new melody lines and rhythmic patterns while performing. This radically different approach alienated some fans and music critics, but it helped launch the "free jazz" movement of the 1950s and was a major influence on jazz innovator Miles Davis, who inspired later generations to experiment with blending jazz and rock.[81]

Saxophonist Henry "Buster" Smith, born in Alsdorf, Texas, on August 24, 1904, performed with several early jazz greats, including Count Basie and Lester Young, and was a key influence on the stylistic development of Charlie Parker. Arnett Cobb, born in Houston on August 10, 1918, played with Lionel Hampton and many other prominent musicians and also had a successful career as a composer, arranger, and producer. Oran "Hot Lips" Page (born January 27, 1908, in Dallas), Kenny Dorham (born near Fairfield, Texas, on August 30, 1924), Leo Wright (born December 14, 1933, in Wichita Falls, Texas), and David "Fathead" Newman (born in Dallas on February 24, 1933) were all top horn players who performed with some of the most influential bands in jazz.[82]

Numerous other Texans have had a significant impact on the development of jazz as well. Tex Beneke, born Gordon Beneke in Fort Worth on February 12, 1914, joined the Glenn Miller Orchestra in 1937 as a vocalist and saxophonist. Beneke, whom Miller affectionately nicknamed "Tex," became one of the band's most popular featured performers, and he sang some of Miller's biggest hits, including "Chattanooga Choo Choo," "I've Got a Gal in Kalamazoo," and "Don't Sit under the Apple Tree." After Miller's death during World War II, Beneke took over leadership of the orchestra until disputes with the band's manager convinced Beneke to leave and form his own group.[83]

Jack Teagarden, born August 20, 1905, in Vernon, Texas, was a white trombonist who was heavily influenced by blues and black gospel and may have been the most creative and innovative jazz trombone player of the big-band era. Before Teagarden, the trombone was considered mainly a background instrument, but he brought it to the forefront with dynamic solos that ranged from slow and bluesy (sometimes described as sounding like a Texas drawl) to exuberant and swinging. He performed and recorded with Bing Crosby, Louis Armstrong, Jimmy and Tommy Dorsey, and many others.[84]

Ernesto "Ernie" Caceres was another significant jazz and swing musician who drew from Mexican American, African American, and Anglo-American influences to become one of the most sought-after multi-instrumentalists of the 1940s and 1950s. Born in Rockport, Texas, on November 22, 1911, Caceres formed a band with his older brother, Emilio, and a cousin, Johnny Gómez, when they were still teenagers. By 1939 Ernie Caceres had joined the Jack Teagarden Orchestra and later went on to play with Glenn Miller, Tommy Dorsey, Benny Goodman, Woody Herman, and Louis Armstrong's All Stars.[85]

In addition to these pioneering horn players, several prominent jazz pianists came from the Lone Star State. Teddy Wilson, born in Austin on November 24, 1912, dropped out of college to play with Art Tatum, Louis Armstrong, and others. As one of the most popular jazz pianists of the 1930s and 1940s big-band swing era, Wilson toured and recorded with Billie Holiday, Ella Fitzgerald, Benny Goodman, Sarah Vaughan, Lena Horne, and Gene Krupa.[86] William "Red" Garland, born in Dallas on May 13, 1923, was a pioneer of bebop during the 1950s and 1960s. In his early career Garland worked with Charlie Parker and Coleman Hawkins, but he probably made his biggest impact after joining the legendary Miles Davis Quintet in 1954. As part of Davis's highly innovative group, Garland became famous for blending delicate piano phrasings with loud, crashing block chords. Another pianist, Joe Sample, born February 1, 1939, in Houston, helped form a band called the Swingsters in the early 1950s, which mingled blues, gospel, jazz, and R&B. By the 1960s the band had changed its name to the Jazz Crusaders, which it later shortened to simply the Crusaders, before going on to enjoy tremendous critical and commercial success during the 1970s by combining jazz, soul, and funk.[87]

Jazz musicians continue to play a vital role in shaping Texas music. Since 1947 the University of North Texas in Denton has been home to one of the most prolific and highly regarded jazz music programs in the country, which trains dozens of talented artists and produces an impressive series of recordings and performances. In addition, there is now a thriving jazz scene in several larger cities throughout the state, which supports a host of inventive jazz musicians, most of whom have drawn inspiration from other Texas pioneers. Trumpeter Roy Hargrove, from Waco, has performed with a number of prominent artists, including Sonny Rollins. Hargrove's repertoire ranges from ballads to bop, and he builds on the work of earlier jazz greats such as Kenny Dorham. Dallas-born pianist Cedar Walton and tenor saxophonist Marchel Ivery, from Ennis, teamed up to record the 1994 album *Marchel's Mode*, an impressive homage to earlier bop in Texas. Critically acclaimed saxophonist Elias Haslanger, who lived for a time in New York City, where he played with Maynard Ferguson and others, is now back in his hometown of Austin, where he is both performing and recording. Veteran keyboardist James Polk was a member of the Ray Charles Orchestra and

Pamela Hart. Photo by Clay Sharkey, courtesy Texas Music Museum.

taught jazz for years at Texas State University in San Marcos. Dennis Dotson, Tony Campise, and Edgar Winter (brother of blues-rock guitarist Johnny Winter) are also very highly regarded Texas-based players who have worked with a number of well-known jazz artists over the years.[88]

Some of the state's best jazz musicians have also found work performing in other musical genres outside of jazz. For example, Austin-based Mitch Watkins, a virtuoso jazz guitarist, plays regularly with singer-songwriter Lyle Lovett, helping to reinforce the jazz and swing nuances of Lovett's country-Americana sound. Violinist Gene Elders, who also plays with Lovett, and guitarist Rick McRae, both outstanding jazz and swing musicians in their own right, form part of country superstar George Strait's Ace in the Hole Band. Paul Glasse, one of the nation's leading jazz mandolinists, began as a bluegrass and Western swing musician but now plays with many different artists who cover every genre from folk and country to blues and swing.

Slim Richey is a veteran guitarist of several Texas jazz bands, but he also founded Ridgerunner Records, one of the first labels to record and market bluegrass in the Southwest. A number of outstanding female artists, including Pamela Hart, Maryann Price, Mady Kaye, Suzi Stern, Lee Ann Atherton, and Kat Edmondson, have demonstrated their talent and versatility by producing top-quality work in a variety of genres. Although not always widely recognized for their contributions, Texas artists have played a major role in jazz since its inception by helping to make it one of the most diverse, dynamic, and vital genres in American music.[89]

TEXAS SOUL, FUNK, DISCO, RAP, AND HIP-HOP

While blues, R&B, ragtime, and jazz have impacted almost all areas of popular music during the past century, other forms of African American music, including soul, funk, disco, hip-hop, and rap, have also emerged in recent years, and Texas artists have been key to the development of these newer genres. Soul music, which is rooted in blues, gospel, and R&B, usually includes deeply emotional or "soulful" vocals that are featured over a supporting instrumental background. Joe Tex, born Joseph Arrington Jr., in Rogers, Texas, on August 8, 1935, pioneered this style of music in the 1950s and 1960s. Tex, who had performed as a teenager at Harlem's legendary Apollo Theater, also popularized a new soul-oriented style of love ballad, in which he slowed the tempo and half-spoke, half-sang the lyrics in a low, husky voice. Years later popular vocalists such as Barry White and Isaac Hayes borrowed from this technique to produce several hits on both the pop and R&B charts. Some of Tex's later recordings also helped lay the foundation for the emergence of funk in the 1970s. During his lifetime Joe Tex performed alongside Otis Redding, Wilson Pickett, and Ben E. King, who also were early soul singers, and he had a successful career as a songwriter, penning hits for James Brown and other top stars.[90]

Barry White, born September 12, 1944, in Galveston, Texas, grew up performing gospel in his church choir but also enjoyed singing blues and soul music. He borrowed from Joe Tex and other earlier artists to develop a soulful, sultry style of singing in which he whispered romantic lyrics over a lushly orchestrated instrumental track. White produced a long string of hits, including "Can't Get Enough of Your Love, Babe," which won him a multitude of fans and made him a pop music icon during the 1970s and 1980s.[91]

Johnny "Guitar" Watson, born in Houston on February 3, 1935, began playing R&B during the 1950s but went on to pioneer the funk and disco sounds of the 1970s. Well known for his energetic live performances, Watson was one of the first guitarists to use electrical feedback, and his wild stage antics, which included playing guitar with his teeth, harkened back to fellow Texan T-Bone Walker's flamboyant style. Throughout his career Watson toured and recorded with a number of major artists, including Little Richard, Frank Zappa, and Herb Alpert. During the 1970s Watson recorded several albums that mixed R&B, funk, and disco and produced songs such as "A Real Mother for Ya" and "Funk beyond the Call of Duty," which became popular with both white and black audiences. Watson died of a heart attack in 1996 while performing on stage in Japan, but he remains a leading figure in the development of R&B, funk, and disco.[92]

Billy Preston, born September 9, 1946, in Houston, also represented a new generation of Texas musicians whose roots in gospel, blues, and R&B helped them reshape pop and rock & roll. His professional career began when, at the age of sixteen, he started playing piano for Little Richard. Preston went on to work with Sam Cooke, Ray Charles, and the Rolling Stones, but perhaps the high point of his career as a sideman occurred when the Beatles invited him to perform on their 1969 songs "Get Back" and "Let It Be." By the mid-1970s Preston had garnered his own number-one hits with "Will It Go Round in Circles?" and "Nothing from Nothing." Following the breakup of the Beatles, he also toured with both George Harrison and Ringo Starr and went on to write the popular Joe Cocker ballad "You Are So Beautiful."[93]

By the 1980s hip-hop and rap had become very popular forms of African American music. First appearing during the mid-1970s in urban black communities throughout the country, rap and hip-hop began as essentially organic musical forms that mixed modern street poetry with intricate dance steps and older African rhythmic traditions. In the beginning, rap and hip-hop provided a format through which disadvantaged inner-city youth could articulate their frustrations and concerns. However, as these two interrelated genres became increasingly popular, various artists and record labels recognized the music's commercial potential and began moving rap and hip-hop more toward mainstream pop music. Today, rap and hip-hop have lost many of their organic qualities and now are largely superorganic commodities used to market everything from toothpaste to automobiles.[94]

Texas musicians played a key role in rap's transformation from street music to mainstream pop. Houston was home to the Geto Boys, one of the most popular and controversial rap bands of the late 1980s and early 1990s. In fact, as pioneers of what later came to be called "gangsta rap," the Geto Boys' lyrics were so graphic and violent that distributors sometimes refused to handle their records. Another important pioneer of early rap was D. J. Screw, a highly innovative rapper, disc jockey, and producer. Born Robert Earl Davis Jr. in Bastrop, Texas, on July 20, 1971, Screw grew up mainly in Houston, where he became best known in the rap music scene for his unique method of "screwing down" music, or slowing songs to half their tempo while mixing in music from other records. This new style caught on among rap artists and producers around the country and helped Houston gain recognition as a major center for rap music in the South. Unfortunately, D. J. Screw's meteoric rise to fame was cut short when he died of a drug overdose in 2000.[95]

Texas artists have also figured prominently in the blending of rap, hip-hop, and pop music in recent years. Tevin Campbell, from Waxahachie, Texas, was only twelve years old when legendary record producer Quincy Jones discovered him and made his first recording, "Tomorrow." Campbell soon had his songs featured in movie soundtracks such as Prince's *Graffiti Bridge*, and he toured with the pop group Boyz II Men. Texas was also home to white rapper Vanilla Ice, born Robert Van Winkle in Miami, Florida, on October 31, 1968. Although Van Winkle was raised in the comfortable Dallas suburb of Carrollton, Texas, he and record executives fabricated an image for him as a tough inner-city rapper, even claiming that he had grown up on the streets of Miami. This marketing ploy worked, and Vanilla Ice's multiplatinum hit "Ice Ice Baby," from the 1990 album *To the Extreme*, helped him surpass the nation's top-selling black rapper at the time, MC Hammer. Another Texas-based group that blended pop, hip-hop, and rap influences was Destiny's Child, from Houston. This African American trio was one of the most popular and widely imitated female bands of the late 1990s. Although the band was together for only a few years, it sold millions of records and toured worldwide. Following the group's breakup, lead vocalist Beyoncé Knowles went on to build a very successful career as a solo artist.[96]

In all its variations, African American music reflects the unique experiences black Americans have undergone over the past several centuries. Whether blues, gospel, ragtime, jazz, R&B, soul, funk, rap, hip-hop, or any other subgenre, this music mirrors the dynamics of African American society and the ways in which black Americans have contributed to the overall cultural development of the nation. Just as they did with so many other genres, Texans have played a vital role in the long-term development of African American music by infusing it with their own distinct Southwestern influences and by making it an integral part of the larger mosaic of American musical culture.

RECOMMENDED LISTENING

Beyoncé, *Dangerously in Love* (Sony International)

Christian, Charlie, *Masters of Jazz*, vols. 1–4 (Média 7)

Dorham, Kenny, *West 42nd Street* (Black Lion)

Dranes, Arizona, *Complete Recorded Works* (Document)

Hopkins, Lightnin,' *The Best of Lightnin' Hopkins* and *The Gold Star Sessions*, vols. 1–2 (Arhoolie)

Jefferson, Blind Lemon, *King of the Country Blues* (Yazoo)

Joplin, Scott, *Scott Joplin: His Complete Works, by Richard Zimmerman, Piano* (Bescol)

Lead Belly, *Where Did You Sleep Last Night? Lead Belly Legacy*, vol. 1 (Smithsonian Folkways)

Lipscomb, Mance, *Texas Songster* (Arhoolie)

Screw, D. J., *Trilogy: A DJ Screw Memorial* (TJ Music/Starz Music)

Shaw, Robert, *The Ma Grinder* (Arhoolie)

Spivey, Victoria, *Complete Recorded Works*, vols. 1–4 (Document)

Thornton, Big Mama, *Ball and Chain* (Arhoolie) and *They Called Me Big Mama* (Proper)

Various artists, *Boogie Woogie Riot* (Arhoolie)

Various artists, *Gospel According to Austin, The*, vols. 1–5 (The Gospel According to Austin)

Various artists, *JSP Jazz Sessions: London, 1980–1985, The*, vol. 2 (JSP)

Various artists, *Texas Blues: The Gold Star Recordings* (Arhoolie)

Vaughan, Stevie Ray, *The Essential Stevie Ray Vaughan and Double Trouble* (Sony)

Vinson, Eddie "Cleanhead," *Kidney Stew Blues* (Proper)

Walker, T-Bone, *The Original Source* (Proper) and *T-Bone Blues* (Atlantic)

Wallace, Sippie, *Complete Recorded Works*, vols. 1–2 (Document)

Watson, Johnny "Guitar," *Space Guitar* (Proper)

White, Barry, *The Ultimate Collection* (Mercury/Universal)

CHAPTER 5

. . . .

From Polkas to Pirogues

The German, Jewish, Czech, Polish, and French Influence on Texas Music

Although they are often overlooked because they were not as large in number as the Anglo-American, Mexican American, and African American populations, German, Jewish, Czech, Polish, and Francophone immigrants into Texas also made a number of notable contributions to the musical development of the Southwest. For each of these groups, music was an essential part of everyday life, and they, like all other ethnic communities throughout the state, used music to celebrate their history, culture, and sense of place within Texas society.

GERMAN MUSIC IN TEXAS

Of the groups just mentioned, ethnic Germans made up the largest influx of Europeans into the Lone Star State during the nineteenth and early twentieth centuries. They began arriving in Texas as early as the 1820s as part of Stephen Austin's colonists. By 1831 Friedrich Ernst and a handful of others had established the first German settlement in what is now Austin County, in East Texas. During the mid-1840s, the influx of Germans increased dramatically, as the *Adelsverein*

(Society for the Protection of German Immigrants in Texas) and other groups began organizing a large-scale resettlement of Germans to the Southwest. In 1910 approximately 110,000 Texans spoke German as their first language, including both immigrants and native-born German Texans, and by the beginning of the twenty-first century, about three million Texans, or one-seventh of the state's population, claimed full or partial German ancestry.[1]

Most German immigration into Texas during the early to mid-1800s was a result of political and economic turmoil throughout the German-speaking states of Central and Eastern Europe. For centuries, a small group of wealthy landowners and other aristocrats had dominated the region's local governments and restricted the legal, political, and economic rights of the vast majority of the population. During the 1830s several disenfranchised groups, including merchants, farmers, intellectuals, and peasants, began agitating for political and economic reforms, but the ruling aristocracy cracked down harshly on the reform movement, and in the mid-1840s thousands of ethnic Germans began fleeing Europe. Continuing political instability, declining economic opportunities, and a shortage of available farmland drove many more Germans to North America during the late 1800s and early 1900s. This massive German exodus, or *Auswanderung*, became a source of concern for the German states, and some of them issued laws restricting emigration. However, with limited possibilities for economic and political advancement in Europe, Germans continued to flock to the United States well into the twentieth century.[2]

Texas was particularly attractive to these displaced Germans because it had an abundance of fertile farmland, a longer growing season than most northern states, and was sparsely populated, so that German-speaking immigrants could establish their own relatively isolated communities in which they could maintain their language and culture. Because the Germans were widely perceived as being industrious, productive, and generally better educated than many other immigrant groups, both government and private promoters in Texas worked hard to recruit them to the region and often collaborated with European organizations that were trying to help the ethnic Germans find new homes in North America.[3]

The Adelsverein, an immigrant aid society led by Prince Karl von Solms-Braunfels and other German noblemen, was one of the largest and most active such organizations, and it helped thousands of displaced Germans settle safely in Texas. Despite some early difficulties, the Adelsverein managed to establish several German communities throughout Central Texas, mainly in Comal, Guadalupe, and Gillespie counties. The first such settlement was New Braunfels, established along the Comal River on March 21, 1845. Prince Karl reportedly selected the site because it had abundant water, arable land, and forests for lumber and was located approximately halfway between Austin and San Antonio, which was ideal for commercial and administrative needs. New Braunfels proved to be quite successful and led to the establishment of the next major German settlement, Fredericksburg, founded on April 23, 1846, some eighty miles to the west. Fredericksburg also flourished and would become an important trading post for American settlers heading west to California during the 1849 gold rush.[4]

Once in Texas, German immigrants tended to remain clustered in their own communities, where they could preserve their language, customs, and kinship networks. Even though most had arrived before the formal establishment of Germany in 1871, they brought with them a deep sense of ethnic pride and a determination to build what some hoped would be a "fortress of German heritage" in their new American homeland.[5] As part of these efforts to keep their folk culture alive, Germans started a number of programs and activities throughout Texas, including crop, livestock, and cooperative societies, as well as fraternal organizations, such as a local chapter of the "Sons of Herman," a national benevolent association that provided insurance and other benefits for its members. German Texans also established schools, German-language newspapers, publishing companies, and a variety of art, literary, athletic, sporting, and educational *Vereine*, or clubs. In addition to these social, cultural, economic, and political organizations, the Texas Germans had dozens of singing societies and musical groups that performed regularly within their local communities and often competed with similar groups from other German settlements throughout the state.[6]

Like all other ethnic groups in the Southwest, Germans had a complex musical culture that encompassed a number of genres, including folk, classical, opera, and religious music. Folk music was especially popular in the Texas German settlements, where songs of love, loneliness, and uprootedness resonated strongly with these immigrants so far from their ancestral homeland. One very popular tune among nineteenth-century Texas Germans was the old Schwäbisch song "Muss I Denn? (Must I Then?)." Later popularized by Elvis Presley, this ballad, which tells of a young man who must leave his sweetheart, friends, and family behind as he ventures out into the world, poignantly captured the feelings of many homesick Germans who left Europe bound for the United States. German Texas bands often performed this and other folk tunes for German immigrants as they arrived at the port of Galveston during the nineteenth century to begin their new lives in the American Southwest.[7]

Along with their love for folk songs, German Texans were also fond of classical music and opera. As early as 1839 popular classically trained German musicians such as vocalist Louise Thieleman and violinist Emil Heerbrugger performed in Austin and Houston. A handful of German operatic troupes also toured through Texas in the 1800s, playing a circuit that included Houston, Galveston, Dallas, Fort Worth, and Waco. In addition to hosting artists from outside the state, German immigrants in San Antonio, Dallas, and other Texas cities established their own classical music societies and opera houses so that they could perform their favorite European music, along with their own compositions.[8]

Several notable German musicians, composers, and conductors lived and worked in Texas during the nineteenth and twentieth centuries. Adolf Fuchs, born on September 19, 1805, in Mecklenburg, Germany, was a Lutheran minister who also served as a music teacher at Baylor Female College in Independence, Texas. Wilhelm Thielepape, born July 10, 1814, in Hessen, Germany, migrated to Indianola, Texas, in 1850 and then relocated to San Antonio in 1854, where he worked as an engineer, surveyor, and musician. He sang in and conducted the San Antonio *Männergesangverein* (men's singing club) and designed the San Antonio Casino, a performance hall and social center used primarily by local Germans. From 1867 to 1872 Thielepape also served as mayor of San Antonio, while he continued composing, conducting, and performing.[9]

Heinrich Guenther, born March 9, 1821, in Saxony, Germany, arrived in Texas in the 1840s and began teaching school in New Braunfels. In 1854 he served as president of the *Staatssängerfest* (state singing festival) and was also one of the earliest directors of the New Braunfels *Gesangverein Germania* (German Singing Club). Julius Schütze, born March 29, 1835, in Dessau, Anhalt, Germany, arrived in Texas in 1852. After founding the Texas *Sängerbund* (Singing Society) in Meyersville, he taught music in San Antonio and Austin, counting Sam Houston's children among his pupils. Carl Venth, born February 16, 1860, in Cologne, Germany, moved to Texas in the early 1900s. He conducted several musical ensembles throughout the state, served as dean of fine arts at Texas Women's College in Fort Worth, was chair of the University of San Antonio's music department, and also published dozens of his own compositions for piano and violin. Fritz Oberdoerffer, born November, 4, 1895, in Hamburg, Germany, was an acclaimed musician, conductor, and teacher who performed throughout Europe before moving to Texas in 1950. With a doctorate from Berlin's Humboldt University, he became a music professor at the University of Texas at Austin, where he taught music theory and performance, published widely, and organized numerous musical events.[10]

One of the most influential yet least well-known German conductors and composers in Texas was Carl Beck. Born April 26, 1850, in Thuringia, Germany, Beck came to San Antonio in 1884 to conduct the *Beethoven Männerchor*, a prominent Texas

German men's chorus. While there, he helped organize some of the biggest and most elaborate musical productions ever held in San Antonio up until that time. Despite his success in San Antonio, Beck was somewhat restless and relocated in 1904 to Odessa, where he directed a medium-sized ensemble that performed throughout West Texas. From Odessa, he moved to Pecos and then on to Kingsville before returning to San Antonio. In the course of his travels Beck helped nurture an appreciation for German folk and classical music and inspired towns throughout West and South Texas to support community music programs.[11]

Composer and conductor Frank van der Stucken was born in Fredericksburg, Texas, on October 15, 1858. In 1866 his family moved to Antwerp, Belgium, where he studied classical music. He soon traveled to Leipzig, Germany, and elsewhere throughout Europe, where he studied with notable composers such as Edvard Grieg, Giuseppe Verde, and Franz Liszt. In 1884 van der Stucken returned to the United States to lead the Arion Society, a men's chorus based in New York. He began directing the North American Sängerbund in Newark, New Jersey, in 1891 before serving as conductor of the Cincinnati Symphony Orchestra from 1895 to 1907 and dean of the Cincinnati College of Music from 1896 to 1901. In 1898 he was elected to the National Institute of Arts and Letters and in 1929 to the American Academy of Arts and Letters.[12]

Olga Samaroff, born Lucie Hickenlooper in San Antonio on August 8, 1882, was perhaps the most famous German Texas pianist of the early twentieth century. Her grandmother Lucie Grünewald, a concert pianist who earlier had helped organize the Houston Philharmonic Singing Society, took her twelve-year-old granddaughter to Paris for classical training. Within a year the thirteen-year-old had become the first American female to win a scholarship to the prestigious Paris Conservatoire. With her worldwide reputation growing, Hickenlooper adopted the stage name of Olga Samaroff in 1904 and hired a professional manager to promote her career. Soon she was performing with the New York Symphony Orchestra, the Boston Symphony, and other well-known groups. Samaroff, who was married for twelve years to famed conductor Leopold Stokowski, was also a pioneer in the early recording of classical music. In 1925 she became one of the first American-born pianists to be offered a teaching position at the Juilliard Graduate School in New York City. During her long and distinguished career Samaroff performed with a variety of orchestras, published instructional materials, and taught at both Juilliard and the Philadelphia Conservatory.[13]

Some of the most acclaimed classical musicians to come from Texas were not German at all, but they were certainly influenced by German composers and performers and benefited from the classical music infrastructure that the

German settlers had helped establish throughout the state.[14] African American baritone Jules Bledsoe, born Julius Bledsoe in Waco, Texas, on December 29, 1897, studied at Bishop College in Marshall, Texas, before enrolling in Columbia University Medical School in 1919. Eventually he left medical school to pursue a professional singing career and appeared in a variety of shows and operas. He became best known for his role as "Joe" in Jerome Kern's 1927 Broadway classic, *Showboat*, in which Bledsoe's rendition of the song "Ol' Man River" became one of the show's highlights. He went on to perform throughout the United States and Europe with the Boston Symphony Chamber Players, London's BBC Symphony, the Chicago Opera Company, and others. In 1942 he appeared in the Hollywood movie *Drums of the Congo*. In addition to his singing and acting career, Bledsoe also was a composer who wrote spirituals, patriotic songs, and operas, including the 1939 *Bondage*, based on Harriet Beecher Stowe's book *Uncle Tom's Cabin*.[15]

The best-known classical musician ever to come from the Southwest, pianist Van Cliburn, was of English and Irish descent. Harvey Lavan "Van" Cliburn Jr. was actually born in Shreveport, Louisiana, on July 12, 1934, but was raised in Kilgore, Texas, where the Cliburn family had lived for generations. A true child prodigy by the age of thirteen, Van Cliburn became a featured soloist with the Houston Symphony Orchestra. He also performed to rave reviews at Carnegie Hall and went on to study at the Juilliard School of Music. The high point of Cliburn's early career came in 1958, when he won the prestigious Tchaikovsky International Piano Competition in Moscow. The Soviet people were enamored of the lanky, young Texan who, according to most critics, was able to perform Tchaikovsky better than any of the native Russian competitors. However, because of the tense relationship between the United States and the Soviet Union at the time, the Russian judges were reluctant to give top honors to an American, and they did so only after Soviet Premier Nikita Khrushchev acknowledged that Cliburn deserved the award. Cliburn continues to perform and has actively supported musical education in Texas by sponsoring scholarships, conservatories, and international competitions.[16]

In addition to their prominent role in promoting folk and classical music throughout the Southwest, German Texans were involved in the development of the state's musical history in other ways as well. The Hauschild Music Company of Victoria is perhaps the best example of how some Texas Germans preserved their cultural traditions while also supporting the music of other ethnic groups across the state. Georg Hermann Hauschild, born on March 12, 1839, in Hannover, Germany, migrated to the United States in 1854. In 1862 he married Adele Luder, a German immigrant from the Alsace-Lorraine region, and the couple moved to Victoria, where in 1866 they opened an inn.

By 1891 Georg and Adele had established the Hauschild Music Company, which began by selling musical instruments and accessories but quickly grew into one of the largest music publishers in the Southwest. Between 1891 and 1922 the company published sheet music in English, Spanish, German, and Czech for a variety of artists and composers throughout the region. The Hauschilds also opened the Hauschild Opera House in Victoria in 1893, where they hosted operas, musical performances, comedies, silent movies, and plays. Facing competition from larger publishers and music companies, the Hauschild Music Company finally shut its doors in 1981, and in 1984 the Texas Historical Commission designated the opera house as an official historical site. Although it is no longer in operation, the Hauschild Music Company played a vital role in preserving and promoting the state's rich and diverse musical heritage for nearly one hundred years.[17]

Germans also contributed to the state's musical culture by establishing an extensive network of singing societies, which performed a wide range of folk, religious, and classical music and met regularly to sing and compete at parades, festivals, and other events. It is not entirely clear who established the first German singing society in Texas, but the Gesangverein Germania, founded in New Braunfels on March 2, 1850, was one of the earliest.[18] As German settlements spread throughout Central Texas, numerous other towns, including San Antonio, Austin, Houston, Dallas, Fredericksburg, Kerrville, Boerne, Sisterdale, and Comfort, also formed their own musical groups. These local German singing societies eventually formed regional leagues such as the West Texas Hill Singers League, the Guadalupe Valley Singers League, and the Comal Singers League, and sponsored festivals, concerts, parades, and other events. On October 15, 1853, several of these organizations met in New Braunfels, where they established the Texas Sängerbund and hosted the first statewide Sängerfest, an annual event in which musical groups from across the state gathered to perform and compete with one another.[19]

San Antonio still has one of the largest and most active German communities in Texas, and some historians believe that is where the first German singing society in the state was founded. Although there is some question as to the exact date, Johann Menger established the Männergesangverein in San Antonio perhaps as early as July 1847. The Männergesangverein went on to become one of the most popular and successful German American singing groups in the Southwest. In 1867 the organization changed its name to the Beethoven Männerchor, and in 1895 constructed its own concert hall, the Beethoven Hall, in San Antonio. After a fire destroyed the structure in 1913, the members built a new Beethoven Hall, which currently stands as a historical landmark in San Antonio's Hemisfair Plaza. The

*Germania Gesangverein (Germanic Singing Club), New Braunfels. Courtesy RABA Studio
and Beethoven Maennerchor Archives.*

Beethoven Männerchor continues to perform today, as do other German musical
groups in the Alamo City. One of the best known is the San Antonio *Liederkranz*
(song circle), which was formed in 1892 and has held numerous performances
throughout North America and Europe, celebrating a unique blend of German
and Texas culture.[20]

Many other Texas cities have established their own German musical organizations as well. The Austin Männerchor, founded in 1852, was the first of several
German singing societies to form in the Capital City. The Austin *Sängerrunde* (singing circle) followed in 1879 and helped spawn a *Damenchor* (women's choir) and
Kinderchor (children's choir), which still perform at the *Sängerrundehalle* (singing
circle hall) on San Jacinto Street in downtown Austin. Germans, Austrians, and
Swiss living in the Dallas area established the Dallas *Frohsinn* (joyful society) in
1877, and Houston is home to the Houston Männerchor, the Houston Liederkranz,
and the Houston Sängerbund, all of which have participated in numerous state
and national German music festivals.[21]

J. M'ALLISTER, JOS. KURTZ, F. M. HALBEDL, F. HENSEL, F. C. KLIEFOTH, WM. DAEHNERT, E. A. TIPS, E. ENGELKE, W. WILKENS,
CASSIRER, BIBLIOTH.
CHAS. HORN, E. STEVES, ALEX ENGELHARDT, M. SUTOR, CARL BECK, S. E. JACOBSON, F. NAGEL, R. SEBBE, WM. M'ALLISTER,
DIRIGENT.
O. STAFFEL, DR. EG. MOECKEL, L. DREISS, F. HERFF, C. H. MUELLER, HY. CLEMENS, A. STEVES, A. LIGHTNER,
VIZE-PRES. PRES.
F. G. WANISZLAEBEN, A. WAHLSTAB, E. RABA, H. DREISS, C. FREY, C. A. R. CAMPBELL
B. BOLTE, C. HARNISCH, H. KARBER, C. H. CLAUSS, WM. SCHUWIRTH, A. DREISS, A. NORDMAN, A. F. BECKMANN.
SEC'Y.

ACTIVE MITGLIEDER DES BEETHOVEN MAENNERCHORS, DECEMBER 25, 1893.

Beethoven Maennerchor, December 25, 1893. Courtesy RABA Studio
and Beethoven Maennerchor Archives.

BEETHOVEN DAMENCHOR
AUSTIN, TEXAS 1952

Beethoven Damenchor, Austin, 1952. Courtesy RABA Studio and Beethoven Maennerchor Archives.

Since Germans tended to remain in fairly close-knit communities where they maintained a well-structured system for cultural preservation through their singing societies and other organizations, they were able to keep many of their traditions intact. Also, because they were one of the most literate of all immigrant groups in Texas, they made extensive use of printed sheet music and published musical literature. This meant that they typically performed both folk and classical music in a standardized, written form, which made them less likely to innovate or to incorporate outside influences.[22]

Nevertheless, German Texans were influenced by the culture of the surrounding ethnic groups and the unique environment of the Texas frontier. This is evident in the changing language of Texas German *Volkslieder* (folk songs). For example, by the early twentieth century German Texas folk music had come to include

Das Deutsche Lied booklet, circa 1921. Courtesy RABA Studio and Beethoven Maennerchor Archives.

numerous English terms and references to the Alamo, Indians, the Texas Rangers, and various Texas place names, such as rivers, counties, and towns. In addition, popular American tunes such as "Dixie," "Oh! Susannah," and "The Yellow Rose of Texas" (which was sometimes performed bilingually as "Die Gelbe Rose von Texas") could be heard alongside traditional German folk songs at German singing festivals throughout the state.[23]

Germans also had a major impact on the music of other ethnic communities in the Southwest by helping popularize the polka, waltz, and schottische and by introducing the accordion to Texas and northern Mexico in the 1840s.[24] Perhaps a less obvious but certainly as important a long-term contribution that Germans made to the development of Texas music was the building of dance halls across the state. Originally constructed by German settlers as community centers for business meetings, dances, festivals, weddings, holiday celebrations, and other local public gatherings, many of these halls eventually became popular venues for country, Tejano, zydeco, blues, rock & roll, and other types of music.[25]

In many ways the story of these old dance halls mirrors the history of the German Texas communities themselves. When first built in the mid- to late-1800s, they served as community centers and were the hubs of social activity in the bustling German settlements. However, by the mid-twentieth century many younger German Texans had left the smaller communities, assimilated into mainstream society, and were less interested in preserving the older ethnic traditions. Furthermore, as World Wars I and II brought widespread public animosity toward Germans, fewer German Texans were willing to celebrate their ancestral heritage so openly. This resulted in a dramatic decline in the use of the original German music halls, and by the 1950s many had fallen into disuse and disrepair, while others closed completely.

Ironically, many of the German halls that survived were able to do so mainly because they opened their doors to the public and began featuring music from other ethnic groups. Beginning in the 1950s and continuing today, several, including Gruene Hall, Luckenbach Dance Hall, Anhalt Hall, Dessau Dance Hall, Fischer Hall, and Club 21 in Uhland, have been transformed into popular live music venues that have hosted nationally known musicians such as Bob Wills, Floyd Tillman, Buck Owens, Merle Haggard, Willie Nelson, George Strait, Jerry Jeff Walker, Lucinda Williams, Flaco Jiménez, Clifton Chenier, Lyle Lovett, Robert Earl Keen, Stevie Ray Vaughan, Tish Hinojosa, Pat Green, Randy Rogers, Cross Canadian Ragweed, and Reckless Kelly. Most of these old German dance halls continue to provide an important organic link with the nearby community by also featuring local, lesser-known musicians. As a result, the musical legacy begun by German Texans during the nineteenth century continues to impact the state's musical culture even today.[26]

JEWISH MUSIC IN TEXAS

Many of the same political and economic problems that uprooted ethnic Germans during the late nineteenth and early twentieth centuries also drove Jewish immigrants out of Central and Eastern Europe to North America, although Jews also fled, in part, to escape religious persecution. Bringing with them a long history of oral folk traditions and musical theater, European Jews quickly established a strong presence in American popular music. Jewish musicians and composers such as Al Jolson, Irving Berlin, Jerome Kern, George Gershwin, and Leonard Bernstein worked on Broadway, Tin Pan Alley, and in Hollywood, blending their musical traditions with those of African Americans and others to create some of the most memorable music of the twentieth century.[27]

Although Jewish immigrants never came to Texas in large numbers, they had an impact on the state's musical culture. There were some Jews among Stephen Austin's earliest settlers, but most Jewish immigrants did not begin arriving in Texas until the mid-1830s. Several fought in the Texas war for independence and helped organize the political and commercial infrastructure of the new republic. Jews continued to arrive in Texas throughout the second half of the nineteenth century and settled mainly in Dallas, Houston, Galveston, and San Antonio, where they established synagogues, schools, community centers, and various cultural preservation societies, including Congregation Beth Israel, the first Jewish congregation in Texas, founded in Houston in 1859, and the Hebrew Benevolent Society of Galveston, formally established in 1866.[28]

Texas Jews celebrated their music in homes, schools, synagogues, and community centers as part of both religious and secular events. Some, such as Anna Hertzberg of San Antonio, were also very active in preserving and promoting European classical music. Hertzberg, who was a founder and president of the San Antonio Symphony Orchestra, also started the city's Tuesday Musical Club in 1901, which organized musical performances and funded scholarships for music students.[29] Years later, Max Reiter, a German Jewish conductor who fled Nazi Germany in the 1930s, came to San Antonio, where he directed the San Antonio Symphony Orchestra and helped transform it into a fully professional, world-class organization by recruiting acclaimed guest performers such as violin virtuoso Jascha Heifetz.[30]

Traditional Jewish music is still performed in Texas today, albeit mostly in private homes and at religious ceremonies. A number of Texas-based Jewish artists have built successful careers in other musical genres as well, sometimes combining older traditions with newer, more mainstream styles. For example, the Best Little Klezmer Band in Texas, based in Houston, mixes Eastern European Jewish folk music with swing and jazz. Austin's Mark Rubin blends country, swing, bluegrass, and other styles with traditional Jewish music. Kinky Friedman and His Texas Jewboys are nationally known for their humorous brand of country music, which pokes fun at a variety of social issues. Ray Benson, founder and leader of the multiple Grammy Award–winning band Asleep at the Wheel, helped lead the 1970s' Western swing revival by introducing a new generation of fans to this unique Texas genre and rekindling the careers of many veteran Western swing artists. Although a relatively small group, Jewish Texans continue to play an important role in shaping the musical culture of the Southwest.[31]

CZECH MUSIC IN TEXAS

Czechs, one of the largest ethnic groups to come to Texas during the 1800s, began arriving in small numbers during the 1840s, and by the end of the nineteenth century numbered more than nine thousand. Many more arrived during the first half of the twentieth century and established some 250 Czech communities throughout the state, thereby making Czech one of the most widely spoken languages in the Southwest, alongside English, Spanish, German, and French. Although most of the Czechs who migrated to Texas during the 1800s came seeking new economic opportunities, they were also fleeing centuries of political instability back home in Europe. Ethnic Czechs, who had lived in the central European provinces of Bohemia and Moravia since the fifth century A.D., had struggled for years against political, economic, and cultural domination from their more powerful neighbors, the Germans, Poles, Russians, and Austrians. After enduring decades of conflict with these other nations, many Czechs began leaving Europe in the early 1800s in search of greater economic and political freedom in the United States and elsewhere.[32]

Although Germans and Czechs are ethnically and linguistically distinct groups, they had lived alongside each other for years in Europe, and their histories and cultures are intertwined in many ways. Because of their long association with Germans, the earliest Czech immigrants to Texas often settled within already-established German communities around the state. However, as Czechs began immigrating in larger numbers in the late 1800s, they founded their own separate settlements in Fayetteville, La Grange, Praha, Rowena, Caldwell, Ennis, Hostyn, Dubina, and elsewhere, as well as their own neighborhoods in larger Texas cities such as Corpus Christi, San Antonio, Temple, and Taylor.[33]

Similar to the Germans, the Czechs established a number of social organizations throughout the state, including the *Československy Ctenarsky Spolek* (Czechoslovakian Reading Club), the *Katolicka Jednota Texaska* (Czech Catholic Union of Texas), and the *Sokol* (Falcon) club, which taught young Czech Texans physical fitness, literature, music, and art. In addition, Czech immigrants founded several Czech-language newspapers, such as *Slovan*, *Svoboda*, *Bratrske Listy*, *Vestnik*, *Hospodar*, and *Nasinec*. Because they successfully replicated many of the cultural institutions they had known back in Europe, the Czechs, like the Germans, were able to preserve many of their artistic, literary, and musical traditions for generations, although they eventually began to assimilate and adopt musical customs from other groups.[34]

Music was very important in the daily lives of most Czech Texans, as is suggested by the old Czech adage "Kazdy Check je musikant" [every Czech is a musician]. Like their German counterparts, virtually every Texas Czech community had singing societies, church choirs, school ensembles, and local bands, which ranged from guitar-fiddle duos to more elaborate orchestras that featured clarinets, saxophones, trumpets, trombones, accordions, piano, and drums. Most Czech groups, whether large or small, usually had a broad repertoire that included polkas, waltzes, schottisches, Czech folk songs, religious music, and other styles. Over time, many Texas Czech bands also combined certain elements of swing, jazz, pop, and country with their more traditional Czech music.[35]

Frederick Limsky, a fifer who arrived in Texas in early 1836 and played in a small band for Sam Houston and his troops at the battle of San Jacinto, may have been the very first Czech musician to perform in the state. Years later, Frank Bača of Fayetteville would become the earliest Texas Czech musician to gain regional fame as a recording and performing artist. The son of Czech immigrants, Bača founded one of the most popular and enduring Czech bands in Texas, the Bača Band, in 1892. The group, which included several of Bača's children, ranged in size from seven to fifteen members and featured a variety of instruments, including dulcimer, guitars, horns, and drums. Over the years, the Bača Band performed at weddings, festivals, parades, and numerous other events around the state. When Frank Bača passed away in 1907, his son Joe took over the group. After Joe died in 1920, his brother John stepped in and led the band through a very successful period in which it performed regularly on radio and recorded for several major labels, including Columbia, Brunswick, and Okeh. Although the Bača Band played many of the more traditional Czech waltzes, polkas, and ballads, it also included jazz, blues, pop, and even Mexican folk songs in its repertoire.[36]

In 1920 John Patek, an immigrant from Czechoslovakia who settled in Shiner, Texas, formed another one of the state's most successful and long-lasting Czech groups, the Patek Band. Much like the Bača Band, the Patek Band was largely a family operation, so, when John's son Joe eventually took over the group, he renamed it the Joe Patek Orchestra. Over the years the Pateks hosted their own radio show, recorded for Decca and other labels, and became one of the most sought-after Czech bands in the Southwest, combining traditional Czech folk music with other styles to give their repertoire a distinctly Texas flavor. One of the group's tunes, "The Shiner Song," which was based on the old Czech ballad "Farewell to Prague," was sung in Czech, but it celebrated the local culture of Shiner and other Texas Czech communities. "The Shiner Song" became so popular among Czech Texans that many consider it to be the unofficial "anthem" of the Texas Czech community. The Pateks also mixed swing, pop, conjunto, and country into their repertoire and even produced one song, "Corrido Rock," which became popular among local Tejanos.[37]

Adolph Hofner was another very versatile and influential Texas Czech musician. Born to a German father and a Czech mother on June 8, 1916, in Moulton, Texas, Hofner moved with his family to San Antonio when he was only twelve. While in San Antonio, Adolph and his younger brother, Emil, were exposed to a wide range of musical influences, including traditional German and Czech music, country, conjunto, blues, and Hawaiian music. The two brothers played together in several polka bands as teenagers, but in the 1930s they found themselves increasingly drawn toward Western swing, which was rapidly gaining popularity throughout the Southwest at the time. As a talented singer, guitarist, fiddler, and accordionist steeped in a variety of ethnic musical influences, Hofner had developed a remarkably diverse repertoire that ranged from Bohemian waltzes and polkas to Mexican ballads and fiddle hoedowns. Western swing, which is a complex amalgamation of country, blues, ragtime, jazz, swing, and other styles, suited Hofner's eclectic tastes perfectly and allowed him to demonstrate his abilities on several instruments. Skillfully blending Western swing with Czech and other influences, Hofner became one of the state's most versatile and dynamic performers during the 1940s and 1950s.[38]

Throughout his long and distinguished career, Hofner recorded for several labels, including RCA, Columbia, Decca, Imperial, and Sarg and worked with a number of prominent musicians, including singer-songwriter Floyd Tillman and fiddler J. R. Chatwell. Hofner's 1941 version of "Cotton-eyed Joe," one of the earliest and most popular recordings of that now classic fiddle tune, earned him a prominent place in Texas music history, and he is also generally credited with having introduced the accordion into Western swing. Over the years Hofner performed and recorded a vast array of songs that demonstrated his ability to synthesize blues, polka, country, pop, big-band swing, and all of the other musical influences he had absorbed from the rich cultural environment of his home state.[39]

"Texas Polka" Sheet Music. Courtesy Center for Texas Music History, Jack Devere Collection.

In addition to Hofner, the Bačas, and the Pateks, there were many other Czechs for whom music played a vital role in their daily lives. One of the best indications of the importance of music to Texas Czech communities is the great number of music venues they established throughout the state, especially their SPJST halls. Czech Texans founded the SPJST (Slavonic Benevolent Order of the State of Texas) on July 1, 1897, as a fraternal organization designed to provide insurance, medical care, and other types of social and economic support for Czech immigrants. As part of an effort to encourage camaraderie and the celebration of Czech culture among its members, the SPJST began building a statewide system of lodges, which doubled as community centers and dance halls. Between 1897 and 1980 the SPJST constructed nearly two hundred of these lodges around the state, each serving as a gathering place for business meetings, political discussions, youth activities, festivals, weddings, and Czech musical events. Although the SPJST halls originated as community centers for the Czech settlers, many were eventually opened to the public and began featuring a broad range of musical styles, including country, big-band swing, blues, and rock & roll. Today the SPJST remains an active organization, and several of its lodges still serve as popular dance halls for rural communities throughout the state.[40]

In recent years Texas Czechs have kept their musical traditions alive through Czech-language radio programs, festivals, and other public events. Thomas Durnin broadcasts traditional and Texas Czech music on Austin's KOOP-FM radio station, and for years KVLG-AM radio in La Grange has featured musical programming and commercial advertising in Czech. Each year, Czechs hold a variety of celebrations throughout Texas, including the "Pražka Prout" in Praha, which features music, dancing, beer, and food. The town of Shiner has an annual Czech folk festival, and Ennis, Texas, southeast of Dallas, hosts the National Polka Festival, which regularly attracts tens of thousands of visitors.[41]

Several Texas Czech musicians, including Kovanda's Czech Band, the Czech Melody Masters, Chris Ryback, Mark Halata, the Czech Harvesters Band, the Czechaholics, the Bobby Jones Czech Band, and Tony Janak's Polka Band, continue to perform around the state, combining traditional Czech music with pop, country, blues, swing, and conjunto.[42] In addition, the Texas Czech Heritage and Cultural Center in La Grange offers a variety of programs and activities aimed at preserving and promoting Czech culture in the state.[43]

POLISH MUSIC IN TEXAS

Although they did not arrive in as large numbers as Germans or Czechs, Poles are another important ethnic group that contributed significantly to the musical development of the Southwest. Like so many other central Europeans, Poles began emigrating to North America after years of political and economic turmoil in their homeland. Among the most serious problems Poles faced in Europe was the repeated partitioning of Poland carried out by Russia, Prussia, and the Austro-Hungarian Empire between 1772 and 1795. After years of repression at the hands of these neighboring countries, the Poles launched an uprising in 1830, which was quickly crushed, prompting thousands to flee to North America. The first Polish immigrants arrived in Texas just in time to join the 1836 war for independence from Mexico. These early settlers also established the first Polish parish and Polish school in the United States at Panna Maria, just southeast of San Antonio. Thousands more Polish immigrants arrived in Texas during the second half of the nineteenth century and settled mainly in Panna Maria, Bandera, Čestohowa, Kościusko, Polonia, Brenham, Marlin, Bremond, Chappell Hill, San Antonio, and Houston.[44]

Because Texas offered abundant and relatively inexpensive land, along with new political, social, and religious freedoms, the Poles thrived in their new surroundings and established a number of social organizations, including a regional chapter of the Polish National Alliance, which sponsored regular gatherings to preserve and celebrate Polish culture. Most Polish Texas communities had at least a few musicians who performed at local events, and those settlements that were sufficiently large and well funded often had more elaborate ensembles that included brass, woodwinds, strings, percussion, and other instruments. Like the Germans and Czechs, the Poles also built community centers, in which they hosted dances, concerts, and a variety of music-related events. Many of these establishments eventually became public dance halls, some of which still operate today, including the Čestohowa Dance Hall and the Kościusko Dance Hall. As important as these public venues were to Polish community culture, Polish Texans also gathered informally in their own homes for music and dancing. Fiddle music was a particularly important part of these get-togethers. Over the years Polish Texas fiddlers came to develop at least two distinct fiddle styles, including the "Washington County" style, which evolved among Polish settlements around Brenham and Chappell Hill and featured a strong, sawing rhythm, and the "Robertson County" style, based in the Polish community of Bremond, which was somewhat more fluid and melodic.[45]

Most Polish Texans today, like most Texans in general, have largely assimilated into the cultural mainstream, but there still are some Polish Texas musicians, including Steve Okonski, Pete Kwiatkowski, and Brian Marshall, who keep the older traditions alive, while also blending them with swing, country, jazz, pop, and other newer styles. In addition, the surviving Polish dance halls, community centers, and churches are a living testament to the continuing importance of music within Polish Texas society, as well as the impact Poles have had on the state's musical heritage.[46]

FRENCH MUSIC IN TEXAS

The French first came to what is now Texas in 1685, when explorer Robert Cavelier, Sieur de la Salle, landed at Matagorda Bay after claiming the Mississippi River and its tributaries for France. He quickly established Fort Saint-Louis, near what is now Vanderbilt, Texas, but the settlement was plagued with problems from the outset, as La Salle and his crew suffered from hunger and frequent clashes with local Indians and Spaniards. Within months, the demoralized expedition left Texas and returned to French headquarters in present-day Canada, although La Salle was murdered by his own men along the way. Despite the limited success of La Salle's incursion into Texas, other French explorers occasionally ventured into the Southwest over the next several years to trade with the native population. Spain's growing concerns about a permanent French presence in the area prompted Spanish authorities to encourage settlers from the interior of Mexico to move northward into Texas in order to populate the area and reinforce Spain's claim to the region.[47]

France eventually established a permanent presence in the Southwest in 1718, when it founded New Orleans at the mouth of the Mississippi River. New Orleans proved to be a very strategically important seaport through which the French could control trade up and down the Mississippi, the main artery connecting the fertile farmlands of the Upper Midwest with the Gulf of Mexico and the Atlantic Ocean. As New Orleans quickly grew into the largest commercial port on the Gulf Coast, thousands more French settlers, most of whom came directly from France, poured into the city and brought with them their art, music, literature, and cuisine. In time they also set up schools, libraries, newspapers, churches, and a variety of literary and musical organizations.

Many of these Frenchmen also brought slaves, who came from different parts of Africa and the Caribbean. Over the years these slaves blended their native dialects with the French of their masters to create a patois, or hybridized Franco-African dialect, remnants of which can still be heard among some Louisiana blacks today. By the late 1800s thousands of these Francophone blacks and whites were migrating from Louisiana westward into Texas, bringing with them a rich blend of French and African traditions, and adding an entirely new dimension to the already diverse cultural landscape of the Lone Star State.[48]

During the nineteenth and twentieth centuries three major groups of French-speaking people migrated to Texas: white creoles, black creoles, and Cajuns. The first group, the white creoles, came more or less directly from France and French Canada in the early to mid-1800s. Among the first of these were several French and French Canadian families who arrived during the 1820s as some of Stephen Austin's colonists. For example, Michel and Pierre Ménard, two French Canadian brothers who fought in the Texas war for independence, went on to establish successful careers in Galveston—Michel as a cotton trader and Pierre as the city's first postmaster. Nicolas Labadie, a French Canadian physician, treated Sam Houston's troops during the Texas revolution and later opened Galveston's first drugstore. As hundreds of other Francophone settlers arrived in the 1830s, French economic and political interest in Texas grew, and in 1839 France became the first sovereign nation to extend formal diplomatic recognition to the new Republic of Texas.[49]

During the 1840s another wave of French immigrants came to Texas and settled mostly in Central and South Texas, but some went as far west as Mineral Wells and Sweetwater. The largest of these groups began arriving in 1842, when Henri Castro, a Frenchman of Jewish Portuguese descent, brought 485 families and 457 single men to an area along the Medina River west of San Antonio, where they founded Castroville and several other small communities. As they spread throughout Texas, the French established farms, businesses, schools, churches, and universities, including Incarnate Word and Saint Mary's in San Antonio. Since many of these early French settlers eventually assimilated into larger Anglo-American communities, not much is known about their musical customs. Nevertheless, Castroville and a few other places with sizeable French populations had their own churches and schools, in which they managed to preserve some vestiges of religious and secular French music. The annual celebration of Saint Louis, one of the patron saints of the Alsace region of France, from which many of Castroville's settlers came, is still held in the town and is a good example of the enduring French cultural legacy in the Southwest.[50]

Black creoles, another major group of Francophones who have had a significant impact on Texas music, came mostly from Louisiana during the nineteenth and twentieth centuries. These French-speaking blacks, who drew from African and

European musical influences, helped create the unique genre known as zydeco. Although zydeco is rooted in the musical traditions of Louisiana, historians have recently come to understand the important role that East Texas, with its substantial population of French-speaking blacks, also played in helping define the zydeco sound and in drawing international attention to this dynamic music.[51]

As mentioned previously, most of the French-speaking black creoles were the descendants of slaves brought to New Orleans by French settlers in the 1700s. Over time, these slaves adopted certain aspects of the French language and culture and blended them with their own African and Caribbean traditions. After France abolished slavery in 1794, many newly freed French-speaking blacks left New Orleans and dispersed throughout southwestern Louisiana, carrying their hybridized Franco-African culture with them.[52]

By the late 1800s some of these black creoles had migrated into Texas, where they found work in a variety of occupations, including farming, fishing, lumbering, and domestic service. Following the discovery of oil at Spindletop near Beaumont in 1901, the state's burgeoning petroleum industry attracted thousands more black creoles from Louisiana into Texas. This influx of French-speaking blacks into the Lone Star State increased even further in the 1940s, as World War II brought an unprecedented global demand for petroleum products. Soon oil refineries began sprouting up all along the Texas Gulf Coast near Houston, Beaumont, and Port Arthur, bringing in a new wave of workers from Louisiana and other surrounding states.[53]

The largest concentration of French-speaking black creoles in Texas was in Houston, especially in the city's predominantly African American Fifth Ward. In 1922 city leaders acknowledged this large Francophone population by officially designating that section of Houston as "Frenchtown." One of the most popular types of music among black creoles in Frenchtown was known as juré, a mostly a cappella form of group singing that often included religious themes and featured hand clapping and foot stomping. Derived from the French word jurer, meaning to "take an oath" or "testify," juré originated among poor, rural, black creoles in Louisiana, who had few musical instruments and only limited exposure to the English language. When black creoles began relocating to Houston and other cities throughout the Texas-Louisiana border region, they brought the juré tradition with them. As they came into increasing contact with English-speaking blacks and whites, black creoles began modifying juré by adding blues inflections, English words, and instruments such as accordion, guitar, and washboard.[54]

As a result of these modifications, juré evolved into a significantly different type of music by the 1930s. This new style, which black creoles began to call French la la, or simply la la, featured a lively syncopated rhythm usually produced by an accordion and a washboard rubbed with spoons or other metal objects. Over time, la la musicians graduated to using double- and triple-row accordions, which were more versatile and better adapted to the bluesy sound that many black creoles had picked up from local English-speaking blacks. At the same time, black creole musicians also began mixing French and English lyrics into their la la songs.[55]

By the 1940s, la la throughout East Texas and southwestern Louisiana had absorbed blues, R&B, and other influences that would further transform this music into a new style that eventually became known as "zydeco." Although it is difficult to know with certainty the true origin of the term "zydeco," it is most likely a phonetic derivation of the French words les haricots (lay-zah-ree-ko), or beans, taken from "Les Haricots Sont Pas Salés" [The Beans Are Not Salty], an old black creole folk song, in which the singer complains about being so poor that he cannot afford even salt meat to flavor his beans. Based on the highly syncopated dance rhythms of juré and la la, zydeco also included blues inflections along with the more complex melodic structures often found in R&B. Even though most zydeco bands would keep the traditional accordion and washboard used in la la, more and more began supplementing these with electric guitars and full drum sets, along with lyrics in both French and English.[56]

The development of black creole music from juré to la la to zydeco during the late nineteenth and early twentieth centuries was part of a larger musical transformation taking place throughout southwest Louisiana and East Texas. Even though these genres originated in Louisiana, places such as Houston's Fifth Ward were also crucial to the overall process because the high concentration of French- and English-speaking African Americans living there in proximity furnished a unique environment in which juré, la la, blues, R&B, and other musical influences could be synthesized into modern zydeco.

In addition to playing a vital role in the early development of zydeco, Texas has also been home to some of the most influential zydeco artists and some of the first known zydeco recordings. In fact, some of the earliest records to feature the zydeco style and references to the term "zydeco" were made in Houston, including Lightnin' Hopkins's 1947 Gold Star record titled "Zolo Go," Clarence Garlow's 1949 "Bon Ton Roula" on the Macy's label, and Clifton Chenier's 1956 "(Zydeco) Haricots et Pas Salés."[57]

Even before these early zydeco records were made, Texas was home to another landmark recording that involved black creole music. On August 8, 1934, the Bluebird/Victor label held what would prove to be a historic recording session for Amédé Ardoin at the Texas Hotel in San Antonio. Ardoin, born in Eunice,

Louisiana, in 1898, had already established himself as an important innovator in black creole music and was probably the first French-speaking black Louisiana musician to record in the 1920s. He performed songs in the traditional la la style but also included Cajun waltzes, one-steps, and blues in his repertoire. At this 1934 recording session in San Antonio, Ardoin performed a total of six tunes, four of which fit the standard la la format, and two of which were blues songs. The fact that fully one-third of the tunes he recorded during this session were blues is a clear indication of the growing influence of African American blues on Ardoin and other French-speaking black creole artists during the early twentieth century.[58]

Ardoin's Texas recordings are noteworthy for another reason as well. More specifically, the six tracks he made in San Antonio are the only ones among his entire catalog of thirty-four recorded songs that feature his use of foot stomping as a rhythmic accompaniment. This traditional method of accentuating the syncopated la la beat was a direct reflection of African rhythmic influences, and it was commonly used by Ardoin and other black creole musicians when they performed live. However, for some reason, foot stomping had been eliminated from all of Ardoin's other recordings, except for those made in San Antonio. This means that his Texas recordings could be considered the most authentic in terms of reproducing the true creole sound in the same way that he and other black creoles would actually have performed it. Even though Ardoin remained a Louisiana-based musician, his travels to Texas and his increasing use of the blues in his repertoire reflect the growing cross-pollination of French, African, and Anglo cultures throughout the Texas-Louisiana border region during the early twentieth century.[59]

Clifton Chenier, born a black creole in Opelousas, Louisiana, on June 25, 1925, is another good example of the important role Texas played in the development of zydeco music. Often called the "king of zydeco" because of his pioneering work in shaping modern zydeco and bringing it to international prominence, Chenier learned to play the accordion from his father and was often accompanied on washboard by his brother, Cleveland, with whom he performed throughout southwestern Louisiana and East Texas.

As they traveled the nightclub circuit between New Orleans and Houston during the early 1940s, Clifton and Cleveland combined the creole music of their ancestors with the blues and R&B that were gaining popularity among black audiences of their own generation. The Chenier brothers experimented with different musical styles and instrumental configurations, adding electric guitars and drums to their lineup and singing in both French and English. One of their most notable innovations was their refashioning of the traditional la la washboard into a sculpted single piece of corrugated metal that could be worn over the chest and strummed with metal thimbles or spoons. This new rubboard vest, known in French as a *frottoir*, caught on quickly with other creole musicians and is now a standard instrument in most zydeco bands.[60]

By 1947 Clifton Chenier had relocated to Houston, where the booming economy provided steady work in local dance clubs. For the next four decades Chenier, along with his Red Hot Louisiana Band, toured throughout Texas, North America, and around the world, helping popularize zydeco among people of all ethnic backgrounds. In addition to being a towering figure in the world of zydeco, Chenier was also a major influence on a number of Francophone artists from other genres, including Cajun and "swamp pop," which was a mixture of creole, Cajun, R&B, and pop.[61]

Clifton Chenier at Soap Creek Saloon, Austin, 1974. Courtesy Burton Wilson.

C. J. Chenier. Photo by James Fraher.

Step Rideau. Photo by James Fraher.

Ponty Bone. Courtesy Susan Roads.

Like all other genres, zydeco continues to evolve, and Texas seems destined to remain part of that ongoing process. Clifton Chenier's son, C. J., based in Houston, now leads the Red Hot Louisiana Band and continues to serve as an international ambassador of zydeco music. The Lone Star State has also been home to many other black creole musicians, including Brian Terry (of Li'l Brian and the Zydeco Travelers), Step Rideau and the Zydeco Outlaws, "Queen Ida" Guillory, Wilfred Chevis, "Little Joe" Doucet, Dora Jenkins, Billy Poullard, and Cedryl Ballou and the Zydeco Trendsetters, who have mixed traditional zydeco with blues, funk, rap, hip-hop, and other styles. A number of white Texas musicians, such as pianist Marcia Ball and accordionists Ponty Bone and Bradley Jaye Williams, also borrow from earlier French and African musical traditions as they blend zydeco with Cajun, country, blues, R&B, and rock.[62]

The third major group of ethnic French to have a key impact on Texas music are the Cajuns, who were originally French-speaking whites from the Acadie (Acadia) region of eastern Canada in modern-day Nova Scotia.[63] Around 1605 French settlers (most of whom came from Normandie and Bretagne in north-western France) first began arriving in Acadie, where their music was rooted in both French and Celtic traditions. Although they quickly established successful farming and fishing communities throughout eastern Canada, by the late 1600s the Acadiens found themselves caught in the middle of a bitter territorial dispute between Great Britain and France for control of Canada. After years of fighting, the British eventually defeated the French and took possession of Acadie and the remainder of French-speaking Canada, including Québec, under the 1713 Treaty of Utrecht.

Angered by the Acadiens' stubborn refusal to submit to British rule and eager to take possession of the region's rich farmland, British authorities began expelling the Acadiens en masse in 1755. Of the approximately eight thousand Acadiens evicted by Great Britain, some returned to France, and others settled in the American colonies, but most fled to Louisiana, where they hoped to find refuge among the local French population. When they arrived in New Orleans, however, authorities feared that these uprooted French Canadians might impose an economic burden on the city, so they redirected the Acadiens to the largely unpopulated bayous, prairies, and swamplands of southwestern Louisiana, where they established their own French-speaking settlements, including Opelousas, Mamou, Lafayette, Abbeville, and Thibodeaux.[64]

The remoteness of rural southwestern Louisiana offered both advantages and disadvantages for the Acadiens, or "Cajuns," as they came to be called. Because they lived in relative isolation, the Cajuns were able to preserve much of their French culture, along with a strong sense of ethnic identity. However, the remote bayous and prairies where the Cajuns had settled also offered little in the way of long-term employment opportunities. For one thing, transportation was difficult; thus they were often required to travel by canoe, or pirogue, which discouraged outside economic investment in the region. As a result, many Cajuns eventually left Louisiana in search of jobs elsewhere.[65]

In the early twentieth century thousands of Cajuns migrated into Texas in search of work in the state's oil fields, lumber camps, and rice farms. As they left behind decades of relative isolation in southwestern Louisiana, the Cajuns underwent the same sort of cultural cross-pollination that so many Anglos, Germans, Czechs, African Americans, Mexican Americans, and others throughout Texas had experienced before. Cajun musicians increasingly absorbed the diverse musical traditions found in the Texas-Louisiana border region, and by the 1940s many Cajun bands throughout East Texas and southwest Louisiana were playing hoedowns, schottisches, polkas, blues, Western swing, and honky-tonk, along with their own Cajun folk music.[66]

Cajuns made music a part of their daily lives in a variety of ways. One of the most popular celebrations among Cajuns in both Louisiana and Texas is the *fais dodo*, in which friends and families gather at private homes or community halls to eat, drink, socialize, and dance. The term *fais dodo*, which means "go to sleep," became the nickname for these events because, in earlier days, babies and small children were placed in a separate room, known as *le parc aux petits*, to sleep while the adults and teenagers danced, drank, ate, and played cards throughout the night. Since parents were ever mindful of their teenaged children's behavior at these events, the young men were sometimes restricted to an area known as *la cage aux chiens*, or dog cage, from which they could emerge only between songs in order to ask a girl to dance. Although the parents tried, it was not always easy to keep a watchful eye over their adolescent children. The old Cajun dance tune "Allons Dancer, Colinda" humorously acknowledges the difficulties of chaperoning teenagers at the fais dodo:

> Colinda was the finest girl in all the bayou land.
> Fellows came from miles around to take Colinda's hand.
> Colinda's mama watched that girl, watched her day and night.
> She didn't want those Cajun boys to hold her daughter tight.[67]

Perhaps the best-known and most influential Cajun musician to reside in Texas was Harry Choates. Born in Vermillion Parish, Louisiana, on December 26, 1922, but raised in Port Arthur, Texas, Choates was regarded by many as the "godfather of Cajun music" for helping bring the genre to national prominence during the 1940s. Playing fiddle, accordion, guitar, and steel guitar, he blended the Cajun style with country, blues, and Western swing. In 1946 Choates recorded a new version of the old Cajun song "Jole Blon" for Gold Star Records of Houston, giving it a more up-tempo, Western swing beat that caught on with audiences and made the tune a regional hit. Soon afterward, Texas piano player Moon Mullican recorded an even more successful version of the song and helped make "Jole Blon" a dance hall standard for Cajun and country bands alike. Although Harry Choates died in Austin at the age of twenty-eight from alcohol-related problems, he made several recordings for Gold Star and other labels, including "Port Arthur Blues," "Baisile Waltz," "Austin Special," "Bayou Pon Pon," and "Allons à Lafayette," all of which reflect the broad range of musical influences from both Texas and Louisiana that he and so many other Cajuns absorbed.[68]

In the end, German, Jewish, Czech, Polish, and French-speaking immigrants, both black and white, all brought their own distinct musical traditions to Texas and blended them with the music of other groups. Today the state's cultural landscape still reflects these diverse influences, which are part of the remarkable musical heritage of the Southwest.

RECOMMENDED LISTENING

Ardoin, Amédé, *I'm Never Comin' Back: The Roots of Zydeco* (Arhoolie)

Chenier, Clifton, *Bon Ton Roulet and More!* and *Zydeco Sont Pas Salé* (Arhoolie)

Choates, Harry, *Fiddle King of Cajun Swing* (Arhoolie)

Halata, Mark, and Texavia, *Moon over Moravia* (Halata Music)

Hofner, Adolph, *South Texas Swing* (Arhoolie)

Li'l Brian and the Zydeco Travelers, *Funky Nation* (Tomorrow Recordings)

Marshall, Brian, and Texas Kapela, *Texas Kapela* (Marszalek)

Rideau, Step, and the Zydeco Outlaws, *Standing Room Only* (Step Rideu-Productions)

Rubin, Mark, *Hill Country Hanukah* (Rubinchick Recordings)

Various artists, *Cajun Honky Tonk* (Arhoolie)

Various artists, *Early Cajun Recordings* (JSP)

Various artists, *J'ai Été au Bal (I Went to the Dance): The Cajun and Zydeco Music of Louisiana*, vols. 1–2 (Arhoolie)

Various artists, *Texas Bohemia: The Texas Bohemian Moravian German Bands* (Indigo)

Various artists, *Texas-Czech Bohemian-Moravian Bands, 1929–1959* (Arhoolie)

CHAPTER 6

"Deep within My Heart Lies a Melody":

Anglo American Music in Texas

Country music is probably the most popular form of Anglo American music to be identified with the Lone Star State. In fact, many people seem to think of country music first when they think of Texas music, even though, as we have seen, the state is home to a remarkably diverse variety of musical genres. This tendency to associate Texas with country music is understandable, though, considering the important role the Southwest has played in the long-term evolution of the genre.

Texas has produced an extraordinary number of influential country musicians, including Vernon Dalhart, Gene Autry, Tex Ritter, Dale Evans, Bob Wills, Cindy Walker, Ernest Tubb, Lefty Frizzell, Hank Thompson, Floyd Tillman, George Jones, Johnny Horton, Barbara Mandrell, Willie Nelson, Waylon Jennings, Kris Kristofferson, Tanya Tucker, Kenny Rogers, George Strait, Lee Ann Womack, Lyle Lovett, Robert Earl Keen, the Dixie Chicks, Pat Green, and many others. Moreover, it has pioneered the development of some of the most important subgenres of country music, such as Western swing, honky-tonk, progressive country, and Americana. In addition, the state has contributed extensively to much of the popular culture often associated with country music, particularly the clothing, cuisine, and musical traditions of the Texas cowboy. Because Texas has played such a vital role in the evolution of country music and because this genre has been an integral part of the Lone Star State's rich musical heritage, country music, in all of its variations, provides substantial insight into the development of Anglo American culture in the Southwest.[1]

When examining Anglo American music in Texas, we need to keep in mind that the term "Anglo" can carry a variety of meanings. In its truest sense "Anglo" denotes someone whose ancestors were English-speaking residents of the British Isles. Over the years, however, the word "Anglo" has come to be used rather generically throughout the Southwest to refer to almost anyone who is not Hispanic, African American, or Asian American. Consequently, many Texans that we might think of today as Anglo actually trace their ancestry back to German, French, Czech, Polish, or a variety of other European ethnic groups. To complicate matters further, many nineteenth-century Anglo immigrants who came from the British Isles originally came from places such as Ireland, Scotland, and Wales, where English was often spoken as a second language.

Nevertheless, the great majority of early Anglo settlers in Texas either were originally of English stock or had been assimilated into the larger English-speaking mainstream elsewhere in the United States before moving to Texas. For our purposes "Anglo" will refer to two main groups of people: those early English-speaking settlers who came to Texas from the British Isles or the American South, as well as the more recent descendants of other European groups who, over time, adopted English as their first language and assimilated fully into mainstream Anglo American culture.

THE SOUTHERN ROOTS OF COUNTRY MUSIC

Country music, which today includes folk, hillbilly, cowboy songs, Western swing, bluegrass, honky-tonk, progressive country, outlaw country, pop country, Americana, and several other subgenres, is rooted mainly in the musical traditions of British Isles immigrants who settled in the American South beginning in the late 1600s. Coming from an island nation with a long seafaring history, these Anglo settlers brought with them a broad musical repertoire that included sea chanteys, hymns, ballads, reels, jigs, and fiddle breakdowns, as well as the waltzes, minuets, square dances, polkas, two-steps, and schottisches they borrowed from their European neighbors.[2]

The music of these Anglo immigrants and their descendants evolved lyrically, thematically, and structurally throughout the eighteenth and nineteenth centuries as a result of social, political, and economic developments taking place around them. For example, the First and Second Great Awakenings, two religious revivalist movements that swept America during the mid-1700s and early 1800s, had a significant impact on Anglo American music. Folk songs that, in the original European version, included references to elves, fairies, and other mythical creatures were often altered by second- and third-generation Anglo Americans who sometimes substituted references to biblical characters or religious themes. Likewise, the Enlightenment, an ideological movement promoting rational thought, representative government, and free expression that began in Europe and spread to the American colonies by the early 1700s, also had an important effect on Anglo American musical culture by making Americans more likely than their European counterparts to politicize popular music and use it to openly address contemporary social and political issues.[3]

Another important influence on Anglo American folk music of the eighteenth and nineteenth centuries was the impact of other ethnic groups and their music. Anglo Americans absorbed a variety of musical traditions from other Europeans and mixed them with their own, often Anglicizing the nomenclature and modifying the song styles to fit their changing musical tastes. For example, *chassé*, a French ballet movement in which dance partners glide across the floor in alternating steps, became "sashay." Allemande, a French interpretation of a German dance, was shortened to "alleman," now a commonly used term in square dancing in the United States. "Do-si-do," another square dance step in which dancers circle with their backs turned toward each other, was derived from the French phrase *dos-à-dos*, meaning "back to back." Cotillon, a type of French folk dance named after a petticoat, was changed to "cotillion," which refers to a complex series of dance steps usually performed by a large group.[4]

Early Anglo Americans drew from other ethnic traditions as well, including guitar stylings from Spain and Mexico, polkas, schottisches, and accordion music from the Germans, Czechs, and Poles, and the steel guitar, which evolved from earlier Filipino and Hawaiian slide guitars. However, the one "outside" ethnic group that probably had the greatest overall impact on the development of Anglo American music was African Americans. Even though American society has been racially segregated throughout much of its history, black and white cultures have always overlapped, and Anglo Americans and African Americans have routinely borrowed from each other's musical traditions. Not only did African Americans adopt European song styles such as hymns, jigs, reels, and waltzes, but Anglo Americans also took blues, ragtime, jazz, swing, boogie-woogie, and other black idioms, along with traditional African instruments such as banjos and drums, and made them an integral part of country, pop, rock & roll, and other mainstream genres.

Examples abound of prominent country artists who have borrowed from African American musical traditions. Bill Monroe, the "father of bluegrass," regularly incorporated blues-based chord progressions, vocal inflections, and instrumental licks into his music. Earl Scruggs, former band mate of Monroe and the single most influential banjo player in bluegrass history, acknowledged country music's debt to African American culture when he said that " 'no musician with ears can leave out the black [influences].'"[5]

Some of the leading pioneers of modern country music, including Jimmie Rodgers, Bob Wills, and Hank Williams, learned many of their singing and playing techniques from African American performers and produced some of their biggest hits, including "Lovesick Blues," "Sitting on Top of the World," "Trouble in Mind," and "Corrine, Corrina," based on the standard twelve-bar blues structure, which features the repeating rhymed couplet commonly found in traditional blues. Many of today's best-known country singers, such as Merle Haggard, George Strait, the Dixie Chicks, and Lyle Lovett, regularly blend blues, jazz, swing, boogie-woogie, and other forms of black music into their repertoires.

The popular song "Corrine, Corrina" is a good example of how the blues became a staple of not only modern country music but other genres as well:

> Corrine, Corrina, where you been so long?
> Corrine, Corrina, where you been so long?
> I ain't had no lovin' since you've been gone.
> Tell me, Corrina, where'd you stay last night?
> Tell me, Corrina, where'd you stay last night?
> You came home this morning, the sun was shining bright.

"Corrine, Corrina" may have started as a slave song long before it was first recorded in 1928 by black Mississippi singer Bo Chatmon. Over the next several decades it became one of the biggest crossover hits of all time and has been adapted to a variety of styles, including country, pop, jazz, R&B, Cajun, and rock & roll. A remarkably diverse array of artists, such as Bob Wills, Art Tatum, Bing Crosby, Lawrence Welk, Muddy Waters, Merle Haggard, Bob Dylan, Steppenwolf, Leo Soileau, Freddy Fender, and Jerry Lee Lewis, have all reinterpreted this song in ways that reflect the broad impact the blues have had on country and nearly all other types of American music.[6]

Country music has not only drawn from a variety of other ethnic genres but has also been strongly influenced by America's urban culture, especially the music composed by professional songwriters living in Hollywood and New York City's

Tin Pan Alley and Broadway. In many cases, songs written by urban composers were introduced to rural audiences by nineteenth-century traveling minstrel shows (or, in later years, through radio, movies, or television) and eventually became a standard part of local folk and country music. However, this exchange of rural and urban musical influences was by no means one sided. Southern music also had a significant impact on popular music in the Northeast and Midwest. For example, traveling minstrel shows sometimes brought Southern songs back to Northern audiences, where they became part of mainstream popular music. Likewise, a number of Southern musicians, including Jimmie Rodgers, Hank Williams, Bob Wills, Elvis Presley, and Jerry Lee Lewis, began their careers performing in traveling shows, which helped carry their Southern musical traditions back to the Northeast and eventually to the rest of the nation.[7]

COUNTRY MUSIC IN TEXAS

Today country music in Texas reflects these diverse influences and also borrows extensively from the same musical traditions brought to the entire southern half of the United States by English, Irish, and other immigrants from the British Isles. The English first arrived in Texas in 1568, when Captain John Hawkins was attacked by Spanish ships while exploring the Gulf of Mexico. After being run aground along the northern coastline of Mexico, Hawkins and a handful of survivors set off on a perilous trek across Texas and eventually arrived safely in present-day Canada, some three thousand miles away. Although he and his men later told of vast tracts of fertile land and abundant wild game throughout the Southwest, few English explorers showed any interest in venturing into the region for the next 250 years.[8]

The first sizeable influx of English-speaking settlers into Texas came after Mexico won its independence from Spain in 1821. It was then that a Connecticut-born businessman named Moses Austin, who was looking for an opportunity to rebuild his lost fortune, negotiated an agreement with the Mexican government to settle some three hundred families in Texas. Moses died before realizing his dream, but his son, Stephen F. Austin, born in Virginia and raised in Missouri, followed through on his father's vision by bringing thousands of land-hungry settlers from the American South into Texas over the following two decades. These immigrants, most of whom were of English descent but also included some Irish, Scottish, Welsh, French, German, Jewish, Czech, and other European stock, soon outnumbered the original Hispanic population by about four to one. In 1836 Texans of all ethnic backgrounds rose up together to declare independence from Mexico and establish the new Republic of Texas. Soon thousands more Anglo settlers from both Europe and the American South began pouring into the region.[9]

Although they are ethnically and linguistically distinct from the English, Irish immigrants made up a large percentage of this rapidly growing Anglo presence in the Southwest. A handful of Irish had been in Texas since the Spanish colonial period, but their numbers increased dramatically throughout the nineteenth century, as Great Britain consolidated its control over Ireland, confiscated Irish farmland, and drove thousands of Irish families from their homes. The great potato famine of 1846 to 1848 only added to the misery of the Irish by bringing widespread starvation and prompting a mass exodus of Irish to North America.[10] Many of these Irish flocked to Texas, where they founded a number of settlements, including San Patricio de Hibernia, Refugio, McGullen, and McGloin, along with sizeable neighborhoods in Victoria, San Antonio, Corpus Christi, and other larger Texas cities. Perhaps the most successful of all the Irish settlements in the state began in 1841, when an Irish American named John Bryan chose a bluff overlooking the Trinity River (currently the site of Dealy Plaza, where President John F. Kennedy was assassinated in 1962) to establish a small trading post that eventually grew to become Dallas.[11]

For the English, Irish, and all of the others who would eventually fall under the heading of Anglo Texan, music played an important role in nearly every aspect of their daily lives, including dances, festivals, church services, weddings, wakes, political rallies, and numerous other events. Over time, the diverse musical traditions these immigrants brought with them from the British Isles and from elsewhere in the American South would blend together with other ethnic influences to create a distinct musical culture that reflected the unique social, political, and economic environment of the Southwest.

EARLY COUNTRY MUSIC AND THE TEXAS COWBOY

During the late 1800s the Texas cowboy would rise to national prominence, capturing the public's imagination and establishing himself as one of the most recognizable and enduring symbols of country music. It was Spanish cowboys who first grazed longhorn cattle on the grassy plains of Texas in the 1600s. By the end of the Civil War in 1865, approximately four million head of cattle roamed throughout the state, about five times the human population. As the northern United States underwent a post–Civil War population boom tied to the rise of a newly industrializing economy, enterprising Texans began herding thousands of cattle to railheads in Kansas, Missouri, and Colorado to be processed and shipped to cities in the Northeast and Midwest, where they would feed the nation's rapidly growing urban population. This boom in the cattle industry created a "gold rush" of sorts that helped make the Texas cowboy an iconic figure in the late nineteenth-century American West. As big as the cattle drives were, however, they did not last long. By the early 1890s most railroads had extended their lines down into Texas, thereby eliminating the need for the massive and arduous trail drives.[12]

Although they lasted only about twenty years, the great cattle drives helped elevate the Texas cowboy to near mythical status in American folklore. A proliferation of romantic novels and popular songs celebrating his life helped feed the public's fascination with the American West, and during the 1920s and 1930s radio programs and Hollywood Western movies further glamorized the cowboy, portraying him as a larger-than-life character who epitomized the pioneering spirit of the West. In many ways the Texas cowboy, who exemplified a rugged yet noble way of life, served as a powerful symbol to millions of Americans who longed for a supposedly simpler time before the onset of twentieth-century urbanization, industrialization, and globalization.[13]

Perhaps because of his near-mythic status, the cowboy remains one of the most misunderstood characters in Texas history, especially in terms of how eclectic his cultural influences were. Even though most cowboys during the late 1800s were white, not all of them were Anglo, and perhaps as many as one-third were Hispanic, African American, or Native American. While cowboys certainly enjoyed the folk ballads and fiddling traditions of the British Isles, they also borrowed from the clothing, cuisine, technology, and music of the Spanish cowboy, or *vaquero* (from which the English word "buckaroo" is derived). Likewise, cowboys adopted banjos and blues music from African Americans, as well as accordions, polkas, waltzes, and schottisches from Germans, Czechs, and others.[14] Texas cowboys also augmented their repertoire with commercially produced tunes, which they heard at local dance halls, saloons, and traveling musical shows. As a result, much of what we might consider today to be authentic cowboy music is actually a combination of many different ethnic influences, along with a mixture of genuine songs of the working ranch hand and pop tunes written by professional songwriters, many of whom had never been out West.[15]

Historians began to document and study the music of the Texas cowboys in the early twentieth century. In 1908 N. Howard "Jack" Thorp, an adventurer and part-time ranch hand, published *Songs of the Cowboys*, a collection of tunes he had gathered from cowboys who had ridden in the great cattle drives of the late 1800s.

In 1910 Texas folklorist John Lomax followed this with his book *Cowboy Songs and Other Frontier Ballads,* which was based on tunes he collected from ranch hands throughout the Southwest. With their publications, Thorp and Lomax helped introduce the American public to the music of working cowboys, and soon tunes such as "A Home on the Range," "The Dying Cowboy (Bury Me Not on the Lone Prairie)," and "The Cowboy's Lament (Streets of Laredo)" found their way into the musical mainstream. By the 1930s these songs and dozens of others patterned after them could be heard in movies and on radios and phonographs across the country.[16]

In large part, early twentieth-century technology, including radio, phonograph records, and movies, helped catapult the Texas cowboy from mere ranch hand to romantic icon of the West. This is particularly ironic since for most people the main appeal of the cowboy was that he symbolized a simpler agrarian past free of such technological advances. Consequently, this widespread infatuation with the cowboy suggests on the one hand a nostalgic longing for older, rural traditions, while at the same time representing the public's eagerness to embrace new technological innovations.

Technology had a dramatic impact on the development of country music in other ways as well. In particular, the advent of radio, which began in earnest during the 1920s, helped break down regional barriers and carry country music beyond its traditional southern borders to places as far away as Canada, the Midwest, and the West Coast. As commercial broadcasting in the United States grew in popularity, radio stations started experimenting with a variety of programming formats designed to attract more listeners and appeal to specific segments of the listening audience. Beginning in 1922, WSB in Atlanta, Georgia, became the first commercial radio station to broadcast country music. By 1923 Fort Worth's WBAP radio had debuted a new format called the "barn dance," which featured square dance music performed by an old-time fiddler named Captain M. J. Bonner, who was backed by Fred Wagner's Hilo Five Hawaiian Orchestra. The barn dance format provided by WBAP proved so successful that other stations throughout the South soon copied it, including Nashville's WSM radio, which launched its "Grand Ole Opry" in 1925, a show that eventually became the best-known country music radio program in the nation.[17]

In their ongoing efforts to find marketable talent for radio, record companies sent scouts into the South and Southwest during the 1920s and 1930s to look for new artists. Because it had such a large and diverse pool of musicians, Texas became one of the most popular destinations for these talent scouts. One of the first Texas country musicians to be discovered by the major record labels during this period was Alexander Campbell "Eck" Robertson. Robertson was born in Delany, Arkansas, on November 20, 1887, but his family moved to the Texas Panhandle near Amarillo when he was only three. By the time he was a teenager, Robertson was steeped in the traditions of Texas-style fiddling, a distinct regional style for which he would become famous. Rooted in older British Isles fiddle traditions, Texas-style fiddling uses a longer bowing technique and carries a distinct inflection of blues and swing not found in most other fiddle music of the South.[18]

Eck Robertson was an accomplished Texas-style fiddler, and he traversed the Southwest performing in musical shows and at dances and fiddle contests. In June 1922 he and his musical partner, Henry C. Gilliland, traveled to the Victor Talking Machine Company in New York City to make what most historians still consider to be the first commercially produced country music recordings. These included the duet's "Arkansas Traveler" and Robertson's solo version of the fiddle tune "Sallie Gooden." Robertson went on to make other recordings, along with several radio appearances, but he was never able to achieve any long-term commercial success. Nevertheless, he remains a very important figure for having introduced Texas fiddle music to a national audience and for having helped launch the commercial country music recording industry.[19]

Prince Albert Hunt, a contemporary of Robertson, was another popular fiddler who helped shape the early country music scene in the Southwest. Born December 20, 1896, in Terrell, Texas, east of Dallas, Hunt played with fiddlers Oscar and Doc Harper, as well as with his own band, the Texas Ramblers. Hunt blended traditional Anglo fiddling techniques with blues and jazz, a practice that became increasingly common by the 1930s with the emergence of Western swing. Hunt did some recording for Okeh Records, but his career was cut short in 1931, when he was shot dead by a jealous husband outside a Dallas nightclub.[20]

Vernon Dalhart, born Marion Try Slaughter II in Jefferson, Texas, on April 6, 1883, was another pioneer in country music who would achieve far greater commercial success than either Robertson or Hunt. As a youngster, Dalhart grew up on his family's ranch riding horses and herding cattle, but by 1907 he had relocated to New York City, where he established a moderately successful career singing light opera and popular music. Looking to broaden his fan base, in 1924 Dalhart recorded the "Wreck of the Old Southern 97," a country ballad about a 1903 train wreck in Virginia. On the B side of this record he included "The Prisoner's Song," a sentimental tale of a convict longing for freedom. The record sold millions of copies and made Dalhart the first true country music star. His success convinced record companies of the tremendous commercial potential for country music and helped launch the careers of many other artists.[21]

One of these new artists was Carl T. Sprague, born near Alvin, Texas, on May 10, 1895. Inspired by Dalhart's success, Sprague traveled to New York City in 1925 to audition for Victor Records. His recording of "When the Work's All Done This Fall" quickly became a hit and persuaded Victor Records to release several more of his songs. Based largely on Dalhart's and Sprague's strong record sales, Victor and other major labels decided to aggressively develop their country music catalogs and started searching for additional artists who could help them capitalize on the growing country music market.[22]

The best-known and most widely imitated performer to benefit from this new national interest in country music was Jimmie Rodgers. Rodgers, often called the "father of modern country music," was born in Meridian, Mississippi, on September 8, 1897, but Texas would play a significant role in his life and career. Rodgers's mother died when he was four, so he followed his father, a railroad gang foreman, back and forth on the railroad lines throughout the South. As a boy, Rodgers carried water to black railroad workers who taught him to play guitar and banjo and to sing the blues. Rodgers, who was also intrigued by the music and folklore of the Texas cowboy, took the blues he had heard as a child and combined it with cowboy ballads and yodeling to create his own unique singing and song-writing style, which included his trademark "blue yodel."[23]

In 1927 Ralph Peer, a Victor Records scout who was traveling the South in search of new talent, heard Rodgers at an open audition in Bristol, Tennessee (along with a little-known singing group called the Carter Family). Victor signed Rodgers to a recording contract, and he soon became the best-selling country artist of the 1920s. His success gave the recording industry a major economic boost and inspired legions of imitators, thereby helping elevate country music from a regional genre to a permanent fixture within mainstream American music.[24]

Although Rodgers lived in Texas for only the final four years of his life, the Lone Star State figured prominently in his musical career. Not only did he borrow from the clothing and musical traditions of the Texas cowboy, but he also traveled and performed throughout the state numerous times, beginning as early as 1916. In November 1927 Rodgers had his first big hit, "Blue Yodel" (also known as "T for Texas"), which was followed by another of his most popular recordings, "Waiting for a Train." In these and other songs Rodgers included themes and anecdotes about Texas, which he called "a place I dearly love." In 1929 Rodgers relocated to Kerrville, Texas, where he hoped the dry climate would slow his advancing tuberculosis. However, by 1933, his condition had worsened, and Rodgers moved to San Antonio for intensive respiratory treatment. He died later that same year at the age of thirty-five while making his final recordings in New York City.[25]

During his short career Jimmie Rodgers was a major influence on hundreds, if not thousands, of other country artists. Gene Autry, Ernest Tubb, and Hank Snow all started as Jimmie Rodgers impersonators, and other country singers from Hank Williams to Merle Haggard borrowed from the "Blue Yodeler's" distinctive, bluesy style, as well as from his lyrical themes of restlessness and longing. Perhaps better than any other country singer of his day, Rodgers helped weave together African American blues, the Anglo hillbilly style of the rural South, and the music of the Texas cowboy. In the process he helped define the parameters of modern country music while introducing this unique American genre to new audiences worldwide. Rodgers was also important in that he represented a new generation of singers who had been raised in a rural environment and learned country music organically as part of the local culture but eventually played a leading role in the growing commercialization of country music during the 1920s and 1930s. As part of this process Rodgers and others were essential to the transition of country music from a mostly organic expression of agrarian folk culture to a superorganic, marketable commodity by the mid-twentieth century.[26]

Because of the success of Rodgers, Dalhart, Sprague, and others, many record labels, radio stations, and movie studios began to look for new ways to capitalize on the popularity of country music. This helped lead to the "singing cowboy" craze, which lasted from the 1930s through the 1950s. During this time movie and television studios churned out full-length films, movie shorts, and TV series featuring a variety of country musicians often billed as "Texas cowboys." In most cases, these artists were not Texans, nor had they actually ever worked as ranch hands. Instead, the majority came from either urban backgrounds or rural areas outside of the Southwest and were more closely connected to the hillbilly style of country music found mainly in the South. However, as the movie studios and record labels increasingly sought to capitalize on the romantic figure of the Texas cowboy, many of these "Southern hillbilly" musicians underwent a wholesale conversion and started trading in their bib overalls and brogan shoes for Stetson hats, Western shirts, and cowboy boots.[27]

The entertainment industry's attempt to cash in on the cowboy's more glamorous image was largely a marketing strategy tied to folk mythology and nostalgia. Movie producers and directors already knew from the phenomenal sales of Western romance novels that the Texas cowboy had both tremendous public appeal and a well-established place within popular culture as a romantic symbol of America's preindustrial past. Because he was already closely linked with the mythology of the West and the characteristics of courage, honesty, and ruggedness that many Americans admired, the entertainment industry seized on the cowboy as a defining symbol for this newly emerging musical style it was marketing as "country." Even though most country music artists and their fans were not from the Southwest, they ultimately embraced Hollywood's version of the Texas cowboy as a folk hero for all rural people, and he soon became the most visible representation of the entire genre of country music. [28]

To meet the growing demand for cowboy movies during the 1930s and 1940s, studios recruited hundreds of actors and musicians to appear in the dozens of Westerns they produced each year. Some of the most famous singing cowboys and cowgirls were from the Lone Star State. Others who were not sometimes claimed to be, apparently hoping to gain greater credibility by associating themselves with Texas. The first Hollywood cowboy to achieve national fame was Ken Maynard, who was born in Vevay, Indiana, in 1895 but sometimes claimed to be from Texas. Although a star in his own right, Maynard is also notable for having helped launch the career of the first true superstar of singing cowboys, Gene Autry. [29]

Orvon "Gene" Autry, born near Tioga, Texas, on September 29, 1907, already had a successful career as a hillbilly singer before he began acting in movies. He had started as a Jimmie Rodgers impersonator and then went on to record several songs, including the 1931 hit "That Silver-haired Daddy of Mine," which sold one million copies and helped earn Autry the first gold album in country music history. Largely because of his popularity as a country singer, Autry landed a minor role in Ken Maynard's 1934 film, In Old Santa Fe. Audiences loved seeing Autry act, and soon he was starring in the first of nearly one hundred feature films, which would help make him the most popular Hollywood cowboy of his era. Comfortable toting both a guitar and a six-shooter, he galloped fearlessly across the screen, crooning ballads, fighting outlaws, romancing damsels, and setting the standard for other Hollywood cowboys to follow. As Autry's film career skyrocketed, he shifted away from his earlier Southern hillbilly persona and started wearing elaborate Western outfits that were better suited to the romantic Texas cowboy image he was now cultivating. He also began expanding his musical repertoire to include more cowboy songs, as well as tunes that featured Spanish lyrics or Texas Mexican borderland themes. [30]

Hollywood recruited several other Texans to appear in its big-screen Westerns, including Dale Evans, Tex Ritter, and Foy Willing. Dale Evans, born Frances Octavia Smith, on October 31, 1912, in Uvalde, Texas, performed in local bands and on various radio stations throughout the country before landing minor roles in several movies. In 1943 Republic Studios paired Evans with singing cowboy Roy Rogers in The Cowboy and the Señorita. The on-screen chemistry between Evans and Rogers worked well, and they soon developed both a personal and a professional,

Gene Autry movie poster. Courtesy Center for Texas Music History, Jack Devere Collection.

relationship. In 1947 the two married and went on to appear together in several successful films, as well as on the popular television series *The Roy Rogers Show.* In addition to singing, acting, and helping promote the couple's career, Dale Evans wrote the duo's most popular song, "Happy Trails," with which they ended each episode of their TV show.[31]

Woodward Maurice "Tex" Ritter, born January 12, 1905, in Murvaul, Texas, attended the University of Texas at Austin, where J. Frank Dobie, John Lomax, and others inspired him to study the music and folklore of the Texas cowboys. Ritter spent several years performing on stage and radio and in musical groups in New York City and elsewhere before signing his first movie contract in 1936. His film career took off quickly, and he became one of Hollywood's most popular singing cowboys. In his movies Ritter sang a combination of authentic cowboy songs, Southern hillbilly tunes, and more mainstream pop material. At the peak of his career Ritter had sold millions of records, was one of the highest-paid actors in

Dale Evans & Roy Rogers movie poster. Courtesy Center for Texas Music History, Jack Devere Collection.

Hollywood, and became one of the very first people to be inducted into the Country Music Hall of Fame.[32]

Foy Willing, born Foy Willingham in Bosque County, Texas, on May 14, 1914, never achieved the same level of fame as Gene Autry, Dale Evans, or Tex Ritter, but he played an important role in defining the music of the singing cowboy era. As a young man, Willing grew up hearing country music within his own family, but he was also influenced by the blues and gospel he heard from local black singers. He worked on radio in Texas and elsewhere for years before moving to California in 1940, where he took over leadership of the musical group the Riders of the Purple Sage. With songs such as "Cool Water" and "Ghost Riders in the Sky," the band became one of the nation's most popular singing cowboy groups, performed on numerous radio shows, and recorded for Columbia, Capitol, Decca, and other labels.

Willing and the Riders of the Purple Sage also had a significant impact on later generations of musicians. One of the first country-rock bands to emerge during the late 1960s, the New Riders of the Purple Sage was named after Willing's original group. The New Riders of the Purple Sage, which evolved out of jam sessions between the Grateful Dead's Jerry Garcia and other musicians who were interested in blending rock and country, soon became a regular opening act for the Grateful Dead and helped inspire the Eagles and several other up-and-coming country-rock acts. More recently, the acoustic trio Riders in the Sky, who pattern much of their music, clothing, and stage persona after the original Riders of the Purple Sage, have helped rekindle a national interest in the singing cowboy tradition.[33]

The image of Hollywood's singing cowboy appealed to Americans of all social, racial, and ethnic backgrounds and had an impact well beyond merely influencing country music. For example, Herb Jeffries, born in Detroit in 1911 of African and Irish descent, was inspired by the early cowboy movies to start his own series of black Westerns, which, he believed, could provide positive role models for young African Americans. Jeffries already had a successful career as a vocalist for great jazz and swing pioneers such as Earl "Fatha" Hines and Erskine Tate. In fact, it was on a concert tour of the South with Hines that Jeffries witnessed the appalling effects of racial segregation and decided that he might be able to offer some hope and inspiration for young blacks by providing more constructive role models through his Western movies. Despite initial reluctance from the film industry, Jeffries eventually found financial backing in Texas and went on to produce several all-black cowboy movies, including *Harlem on the Prairie* (1937) and *The Bronze Buckaroo* (1938).[34]

WESTERN SWING

The Great Depression of the 1930s brought economic suffering, dislocation, and, for many Americans, disillusionment with an economic system that seemed plagued by cycles of boom and bust. However, despite the great difficulties of this era, the decade of the 1930s was also a period of tremendous creativity and innovation in country music, especially with the emergence of a new subgenre known as Texas swing or Western swing. Western swing, which is an eclectic blend of traditional fiddle breakdowns, country ballads, blues, ragtime, jazz, swing, pop, polkas, schottisches, and other musical styles, first appeared in Texas in the early 1930s and soon spread to Oklahoma, California, and elsewhere. For the most part, the pioneers of Western swing were Anglo men and women who were born in the early 1900s and grew up in the Southwest steeped in the traditional rural music of their parents and grandparents. However, as they entered their teen years during the 1920s, these young musicians were also drawn to the exciting new sounds of jazz and swing that were fast becoming the popular music of the day. By the 1930s they had taken the reels, waltzes, fiddle breakdowns, and other styles they had learned from their elders and combined them with blues, rags, jazz, swing, and pop to create a remarkably diverse and dynamic new sound that would come to be known as Western swing.[35]

Although he certainly did not invent this new genre, Bob Wills, often called the "king of Western swing," was its most prominent figure from the 1930s through the 1950s. James Robert Wills, born near Kosse, Texas, on March 6, 1905, moved with his family in 1913 to Hall County in the Texas Panhandle, where they settled near the small town of Turkey.[36] As an adolescent, Wills learned to play fiddle from his father, and they often performed together at dances and other events throughout the area. In addition to his strong family roots in country music, Wills also learned blues from local blacks and heard conjunto and mariachi music from nearby migrant Mexican farm workers. As a teenager during the 1920s, he was drawn to the new sounds of jazz, whose free-spirited, improvisational nature inspired him to innovate and experiment with the more traditional country music on which he had been raised.[37]

As a young man, Wills worked for a time in the small barbershop in Turkey and played fiddle at house parties, barn dances, and fiddling contests in and around Hall County. However, he soon grew restless, and in 1929, just before the onset of the Great Depression, he moved to Fort Worth, where he found work on radio and in blackface minstrel shows. In Fort Worth Wills met fellow musicians Herman Arnspiger, born November 13, 1904, in Van Alstyne, Texas, and Milton Brown, born September 8, 1903, near Stephenville, Texas, and formed the Wills Fiddle Band.[38] By January 1931 Wills, Arnspiger, and Brown were performing on Fort Worth's KFJZ radio as the Light Crust Doughboys, helping to sell Light Crust Flour for their show's sponsor, Burrus Mill and Elevator Company. Because they were versatile and had broad-ranging musical interests, Wills, Brown, and the others could open their radio show with an up-tempo fiddle breakdown, croon a few pop ballads, and then swing into some hot jazz numbers. As Wills admitted, their music was " 'different,' " but the Doughboys soon built a loyal following with their unique and eclectic style.[39]

In addition to their genuine affection for the diverse musical traditions they wove into their music, Wills, Brown, and other Western swing players had a very pragmatic reason to demonstrate such versatility. During the bleak days of the Great Depression, radio stations and their corporate sponsors were eager to hire musicians who could appeal to as large an audience as possible in order to effectively market their products. Since the Doughboys and other Texas swing bands could easily perform country, pop, blues, jazz, swing, and other styles, they attracted a broad and diverse listenership and so were ideal for radio advertisers, who hoped to reach the maximum number of consumers.[40]

Despite these more practical considerations, Wills, Brown, and their peers clearly loved mixing country music with blues, ragtime, jazz, and other black musical idioms. In fact, the first two recordings Wills ever made included "Wills Breakdown," a fiddle tune, and "Gulf Coast Blues," recorded earlier by African American vocalist Bessie Smith, one of his favorite singers. Wills, who once remarked that "'I have always been a blues singer,'" often reworked older blues songs such as "St. Louis Blues," "Milk Cow Blues," "Corrine, Corrina," and "Sitting on Top of the World" to turn them into country hits. He and many other Western swing artists have also acknowledged the influence that the great African American swing fiddler Stuff Smith had on their playing, and some of them, including Marvin "Smokey" Montgomery and John "Knocky" Parker, frequented nightclubs in the Dallas neighborhood of Deep Ellum, where they listened to and learned from black jazz and blues musicians. Wills and his fellow musicians eagerly incorporated these African American influences into their music and then performed it for mostly white rural audiences, who most likely never fully understood the impact black culture had on the Western swing they loved so much.[41]

Despite the initial success the Light Crust Doughboys enjoyed, both Milton Brown and Bob Wills quit the band within a few years, mainly because of disagreements with Burrus Mill's general manager, Wilbert Lee "Pappy" O'Daniel. The flamboyant and outspoken O'Daniel had taken over as emcee of the Doughboys' daily radio broadcast and used the band's growing popularity not only to sell Light Crust Flour but also to promote his own political career (which eventually led to his successful bid for the governorship of Texas). Milton Brown left the Doughboys in 1932 to form his own group, the Musical Brownies, through which he continued to innovate, adding jazz piano and featuring country music's first amplified steel guitar, introduced by Bob Dunn in 1934. Milton Brown and His Musical Brownies played a crucial role in defining early Texas swing, and they were well on their way to spreading the music to a national audience when Brown died in 1936 of complications resulting from a car wreck. Had he lived, Brown would undoubtedly have continued to be one of the major forces shaping Western swing.[42]

In 1933 Wills also quit the Doughboys and formed his own band, Bob Wills and His Texas Playboys, which, over the following forty years, toured throughout the country, sold millions of records, and appeared in eight major motion pictures. Although he had legions of fans across North America, Wills seemed to have little interest in actively promoting himself outside the West and Southwest. Since his musical tastes were so wide ranging and diverse, Nashville record executives had difficulty categorizing and perhaps even understanding him. Wills did not help his reputation in Nashville when, while appearing on the Grand Ole Opry in 1945, he defied official Opry policy and insisted on having a drummer and horn section on stage. Although the show's directors were unhappy, the audience was delighted, and eventually the Grand Ole Opry and other mainstream country music institutions were forced to accept drums as a standard feature in country bands. Despite his somewhat strained relationship with Nashville, the local country music establishment formally recognized Wills and his important overall impact on country music when the Country Music Association Hall of Fame inducted him in 1968.[43]

Bob Wills died in 1975, not long after several of his old band mates had gathered to record a Playboys' reunion album titled *Bob Wills and His Texas Playboys: For the Last Time*. Wills's fame has continued to grow long after his death, and he has been a major influence on many younger artists, including Merle Haggard, Hank Thompson, Mel Tillis, Willie Nelson, Waylon Jennings, George Strait, Lee Ann Womack, Clint Black, Asleep at the Wheel, and numerous others. Along with the Austin-based group Asleep at the Wheel, Haggard has released several Western swing albums over the years, paying tribute to Wills and helping resurrect the careers of many veteran swing artists. Perhaps the most poignant recognition of Wills's importance to mainstream American music came in 1999, when he was inducted into the Rock & Roll Hall of Fame. Although at first this might seem an unlikely honor to bestow upon a country music icon, it was an astute acknowledgement that Wills's blending of diverse musical styles and his willingness to rebel against established musical norms not only symbolized the independent spirit of rock & roll but also helped inspire early pioneers of rock & roll such as Bill Haley and Buddy Holly.[44]

Although Bob Wills generally receives most of the attention when it comes to Western swing, many other musicians, most notably Milton Brown, played important roles in the development of this unique genre. As mentioned previously, Adolph Hofner brought his German and Czech musical influences to Western swing, while Bob Dunn and numerous other Western swing instrumentalists introduced technological innovations that would eventually change most other subgenres of country music.[45] Marvin "Smokey" Montgomery continued performing with the Light Crust Doughboys for seven decades, until his death in 2001. Cliff Bruner, one of the most gifted fiddlers in Western swing, played with many prominent musicians of his generation and inspired countless younger players. Leon Payne, a blind vocalist and musician from Alba, Texas, was also an accomplished songwriter who penned the Hank Williams hits "Lost Highway" and "They'll Never Take Her Love from Me." Oklahoma-born Donell C. "Spade" Cooley, was one of the main architects of West Coast Western swing. Tommy Duncan, Leon McAulliffe, Joe Holley, Tony Sepolio, Al Stricklin, Ocie Stockard, Leon "Pappy" Selph, Johnny Cuviello, Tiny Moore, the McKinney Sisters (Dean and Evelyn), Jesse Ashlock, Keith Coleman, Johnny Gimble, Laura Lee McBride, Eldon Shamblin, Hoyle Nix, Cindy Walker, Herb Remington, Louise Rowe, Leon Rausch, and Bob Boatright are just a few of the hundreds of musicians who were responsible for the tremendous popularity of Western swing.[46]

In recent years Merle Haggard, George Strait, Ray Benson and Asleep at the Wheel, Jody Nix, Billy Mata, Maryann Price, Chris O'Connell, Cornell Hurd, Kenny Frazier, Jim Gough, Jimmy Grabowske, Gene Gimble, Bert Rivera, Richard Gimble, Cindy Cashdollar, Howard Kalish, Alvin Crow, Paul Glasse, Rick McRae, Gene Elders, Randy Elmore, Bobby Flores, Dave Alexander, Al Dressen, Floyd Domino, Rod Moag, Danny Levin, Walt Roberts, Paul Schlesinger, and many others have helped build a loyal base of Western swing fans across the country and around the world. A whole new generation of musicians, including Mark Rubin, Erik Hokkanen, Elana James, Whit Smith, Mike Montgomery, Martin Norgaard, Billy Curtis, Emily Gimble, Ginny Mac, the South Austin Jug Band, and the Sidehill Gougers, are now attracting a large following among younger audiences by combining Western swing with other forms of roots and alternative country music.[47]

HONKY-TONK

World War II, which followed on the heels of the Great Depression, changed American society in profound ways. Not only did it elevate the United States to the status of world superpower, but it also brought greater urbanization and industrialization, increased consumerism, dramatic advances in technology, and changing attitudes toward race relations, the role of women in society, and many other issues. One of the most important consequences of World War II was the massive population shift from rural to urban, as millions of Americans moved from the countryside into the cities to find employment in the rapidly industrializing economy. Although most Americans who followed this path "from farm to factory" generally experienced an overall improvement in their standard of living, it was still difficult for them to abandon their long-standing ties to the land and adjust to living as wage laborers in an unfamiliar urban industrial environment.

During this important period of rural to urban transition in the 1940s and 1950s, a new subgenre of country music known as honky-tonk first appeared. The term "honky-tonk" had been around for decades and was commonly used in a somewhat derogatory way to describe working-class drinking establishments. The adoption of the Eighteenth Amendment in 1918, which prohibited the manufacture and sale of alcohol throughout the country, forced many honky-tonks out of business during the 1920s. However, the repeal of Prohibition in 1933 brought a proliferation of roadside taverns and neighborhood bars that provided newly urbanized working-class Americans a place to drink, socialize, listen to music, and escape the pressures of their daily lives. As these local taverns grew in popularity, country musicians began immortalizing the honky-tonks in song, beginning with Al Dexter's 1936 hit "Honky Tonk Blues." Before long, dozens of other performers from Hank Williams to Kitty Wells were incorporating honky-tonk themes into their music and creating a whole new sound that took the country music world by storm.[48]

The new honky-tonk style grew out of the earlier traditions of Southern hillbilly and Western swing, but it was different in important ways and seemed to reflect many of the recent social, economic, and demographic changes taking place in the lives of World War II–era working-class Americans. For one thing, honky-tonk dealt with certain issues that had not been publicly addressed in country music before, including alcoholism, adultery, divorce, domestic violence, unemployment, and social alienation. Although these problems had plagued American society for years, they took on new significance for families whose lives were disrupted by the dramatic transformation from rural to urban life. Also, because of changing public attitudes regarding sexuality, women's rights, race relations, and other matters, most Americans were now more willing than before to openly address such issues in a public way.

In addition to these thematic changes, honky-tonk was also structurally and instrumentally different from earlier types of country music. Whereas Western swing had borrowed from jazz's more complex chord structures, diverse instrumentation, and emphasis on improvisation, honky-tonk songs typically relied on simple chord progressions with little, if any, improvisation. As a reflection of the music industry's increasingly sophisticated approach to marketing entertainment to a growing consumer base, most honky-tonk tunes were tightly scripted, three-minute productions designed to fit the new and more commercially oriented radio format. Honky-tonk's instrumental lineup also differed from its predecessors in that it featured electric guitars and bass, full drum sets, and pedal steel guitars, which replaced the earlier and technologically simpler lap steel. The fiddle, which had been a mainstay of hillbilly and Western swing music, was optional in honky-tonk, and the banjo was rarely used at all.[49]

Technology has always been a major factor in the evolution of music, and it played a vital role in the development of honky-tonk, especially with the advent of a coin-operated record machine known as the jukebox during the 1930s and 1940s. Named after the juke joints, or illegal clubs that provided dancing and alcohol during Prohibition, jukeboxes spread quickly throughout the country during the postwar era. For smaller clubs that could not afford to hire bands, the jukebox provided patrons with the latest music from the biggest stars and even paid the club owner a percentage of the proceeds. The proliferation of jukeboxes throughout the country meant that fans could hear the same songs performed by their favorite artists in virtually every truck stop, diner, and tavern across North America. The carefully constructed three-minute honky-tonk format suited the jukebox perfectly and ensured that listeners would need to feed coins into the new machines in order to keep the music going. As record companies increasingly linked jukebox playlists with radio station airplay and record distribution, they developed a highly effective marketing system that sold millions of records to a music-hungry public.[50]

The Southwest took a leading role in the development of honky-tonk by contributing some of the earliest and most influential artists to the genre. In fact, several of these performers actually began as Western swing musicians in Texas before going on to play honky-tonk. Ted Daffan, born Theron Eugene Daffan in Beauregard Parish, Louisiana, on September 21, 1912, relocated with his family to Houston when he was still a child. Starting his career in Western swing during the 1930s, Daffan moved increasingly into the newly emerging genre of honky-tonk throughout the 1940s. In addition to singing and playing, he was an accomplished songwriter who penned the first trucker-themed hit, "Truck Driving Blues," as well as one of the first honky-tonk classics, "Born to Lose," which later became a major pop hit for Ray Charles. During his long career, Daffan ran his own record label and worked with many other prominent figures in country music, including Hank Snow, Floyd Tillman, and Cliff Bruner.[51]

Floyd Tillman, who had played with Daffan since the early 1930s, was another influential early honky-tonk singer-songwriter. Born in Ryan, Oklahoma, on December 8, 1914, Tillman and his family moved to Post, Texas, before his first birthday. Eventually he relocated to the Houston area, where he performed with Daffan, Cliff Bruner, and other Western swing and honky-tonk musicians and continued perfecting his guitar playing and song-writing skills. In addition to being one of the first artists in country music to record on electric lead guitar, Tillman also wrote some of honky-tonk's biggest hits, including "Slippin' Around," "Cold War," and "It Makes No Difference Now," all of which epitomized the "drinking, cheating, fighting, and heartbreaking" themes that helped define the entire honky-tonk genre.[52]

"Moon" Mullican was another innovative musician who was active in Western swing, honky-tonk, and a variety of other genres. Born Aubry Wilson Mullican in Polk County, Texas, on March 29, 1909, Moon Mullican developed his piano-playing skills as a teenager performing in Houston bordellos. As an adult, Mullican worked with Cliff Bruner, Ted Daffan, and Floyd Tillman, blending swing, hillbilly, blues, ragtime, and pop into his energetic, piano-pounding performances. In addition to writing some of his own material, Mullican enjoyed remarkable success reworking songs by other artists, such as Lead Belly's "Good Night, Irene." Mullican also had a huge hit with his 1947 "New Jole Blon," an up-tempo rendition of Texas-based fiddler Harry Choates's Cajun classic, "Jole Blon." By the late 1950s Mullican was dabbling in rock & roll, again demonstrating his broad-ranging talents and inspiring a new generation of piano players, including Jerry Lee Lewis and Mickey Gilley.[53]

Although a number of Western swing musicians influenced the development of honky-tonk, the best-known pioneer of Texas honky-tonk did not come from a Western swing background. Ernest Dale Tubb, a sharecropper's son born on a cotton farm near Crisp, Texas, on February 9, 1914, was a devoted Jimmie Rodgers fan and impersonator who had built a modest following by imitating his idol's singing, yodeling, and guitar-playing style. Early in his career, Tubb had befriended Carrie Rodgers, the "Blue Yodeler's" widow, who helped nurture the young singer and introduced him to others in the music industry. Although this helped Tubb break into the music business, his career as a Jimmie Rodgers impersonator ended in 1939, when a tonsillectomy altered Tubb's voice, and he could no longer replicate Rodgers's distinctive yodeling. The change actually proved fortuitous for Tubb since it forced him to begin writing his own material and developing his own singing style. Within just a few years, he would become one of the most successful and influential figures in country music history.[54]

Following his tonsillectomy, Tubb reemerged with a "new" voice and stage persona and started recording for Decca Records in Houston in 1940. By 1941 he had a smash hit with his self-composed "Walkin' the Floor over You." Tubb went on to appear in several Western movies, and he became a regular on the Grand Ole Opry from 1943 to 1982. In 1947 he made music history by being the first major country artist to perform at Carnegie Hall in New York City. Tubb and his band, the Texas Troubadours, toured extensively for nearly five decades and released a long string of honky-tonk classics, including "Soldier's Last Letter," "It's Been So Long, Darling," "Waltz across Texas," and "Filipino Baby." In addition to writing and recording numerous popular tunes, Tubb was a major architect of the early honky-tonk sound. His back-to-basics approach, which used simple chord structures, trademark guitar licks, and a straightforward danceable beat, became the model for countless other honky-tonk bands. Also, because he had received vital assistance early in his career from Carrie Rodgers and others, Tubb became a mentor for other musicians and spent much of his later life working to support and promote younger artists, including Hank Snow, Willie Nelson, Johnny Cash, Loretta Lynn, and perhaps the biggest honky-tonk star of all, King Hiram "Hank" Williams.[55]

Another pioneer of Texas honky-tonk was Henry William "Hank" Thompson, born on September 3, 1925, in Waco, Texas. Thompson showed an early affinity for the music business and even had his own radio show, "Hank the Hired Hand," by the time he graduated from high school. Bob Wills was one of Thompson's biggest influences, and he often mixed older Western swing numbers with more modern Texas two-step shuffles. Another one of Thompson's idols, Tex Ritter, helped him land his first major recording contract with Capitol Records in 1948. This soon led to a series of hit records that included "Humpty Dumpty Heart," "The Wild Side of Life," "A Six Pack to Go," "Smokey the Bar," "On Tap, in the Can, or in the Bottle," and many others. Ironically, many of Thompson's songs celebrated the honky-tonk lifestyle of hard drinking and wild living even though he was born and raised in the socially conservative and, until recently, dry city of Waco. Nevertheless, the tremendous success of Thompson and his Brazos Valley Boys made them Billboard's top-ranked country band from 1953 to 1965, as well as a major influence on future generations of honky-tonk artists.[56]

William Orville "Lefty" Frizzell, born in Corsicana, Texas, on March 31, 1928, was another honky-tonk pioneer who has never been adequately recognized for his remarkable impact on country music. Frizzell, who was inspired to become a singer by listening to Jimmie Rodgers records, developed a unique, almost warbling style of singing, in which he used unconventional phrasing, bluesy notes, and elongated words that often included extra syllables. At first, record companies and music promoters showed little interest in Frizzell's distinctive singing style, so he focused on writing songs for others. However, Don Law at Columbia Records in Nashville was intrigued by Frizzell's unusual voice, as well as his solid songwriting, and arranged to release his first single in 1950. The record included two Frizzell originals, "If You've Got the Money, I've Got the Time" and "I Love You a Thousand Ways," both of which reached number one on the country charts. Frizzell followed these with several other hit records, including "Always Late," "The Long

Lefty Frizzell with Band, 1950. Courtesy David Dennard, Dragon Street Records.

Black Veil," "Saginaw, Michigan," "I Never Go around Mirrors," and "That's the Way Love Goes," the latter two coauthored by fellow Texan Whitey Shafer.[57]

Frizzell's records sold well, and he consistently drew large crowds on his frequent tours, but the most important long-term aspect of his legacy may have been his impact on younger country vocalists. Just as Jimmie Rodgers had been the singer that many up-and-coming artists strove to emulate years earlier, Frizzell became one of the most frequently imitated vocalists for a new generation of country singers. The most notable of these was Merle Haggard, who is arguably the most influential singer-songwriter in country music since Hank Williams. Haggard had long idolized Frizzell and worked hard to copy his singing and song-writing style. As a teenager, Haggard had even made a pilgrimage from his home in Bakersfield, California, to Texas in hopes of meeting Frizzell. Largely because of Haggard's tremendous popularity, Frizzell's influence still resonates throughout country music today. Not only have Haggard and other artists recorded many of Frizzell's songs, but Haggard's singing style, which borrows extensively from Frizzell's unique inflections, has served as a model for numerous country singers of the 1970s, 1980s, and 1990s, including George Strait, Randy Travis, Garth Brooks, Clint Black, Alan Jackson, and others.[58]

George Jones, born September 12, 1931, in a log house near Saratoga, Texas, has been another towering figure in the world of honky-tonk. As a child, Jones sang in the local community church, but by the time he was a teenager he was performing on street corners and in honky-tonks. Jones, whose biggest influences were Gene Autry, Bill Monroe, Roy Acuff, Hank Williams, and Lefty Frizzell, began his professional career in 1954, when he signed with legendary Houston record producer Harold "Pappy" Daily and released his first hit, "Why, Baby, Why?" on Starday Records. Jones then moved on to Mercury Records, where he topped the charts with "White Lightning," "The Window Up Above," and "Tender Years." From there he signed with United Artists, which introduced his next big hit, "She Thinks I Still Care" in 1962, followed by "The Race Is On." He also released popular songs such as "Walk through This World with Me" and "It's Been a Good Year for the Roses" on Musicor Records. Much like Lefty Frizzell, Jones is famous for his unique vocal style, which features an emotional depth and resonance rarely matched by other country singers. During the 1970s and 1980s Jones recorded many other hits, including some with his wife at the time, Tammy Wynette. Despite years of success, his problems with alcohol eventually contributed to the breakup of his marriage to Wynette and to difficulties in his professional career. Nevertheless, Jones has endured, and fans and fellow artists have repeatedly acknowledged him as one of the most respected and influential figures in modern country music.[59]

Johnny Bush, born in Houston on February 17, 1935, has helped keep the honky-tonk tradition alive in Texas dance halls well into the twenty-first century. He grew up playing Western swing and following in the footsteps of one of his idols, Bob Wills. However, Bush quickly established his own unique honky-tonk style, which melded Western swing with a more straightforward Texas two-step dance beat. During the early 1960s he played drums with a relatively unknown singer-songwriter named Willie Nelson, and he also worked for a while in Ray Price's band, the Cherokee Cowboys. By the late 1960s Bush had gained substantial success as a solo artist whose biggest career hit came in 1972 with his self-penned "Whiskey River." Although vocal-chord problems have forced Bush to limit his public singing in recent years, he still performs occasionally and has inspired legions of younger musicians.[60]

A number of other artists in Texas today are helping to keep the honky-tonk tradition alive. Alvin Crow, James White, Dale Watson, Geronimo Treviño, Larry Joe Taylor, Paul Belanger, Wayne Hancock, Doug Moreland, Pauline Reese, Roger Creager, Kevin Fowler, the Derailers, James Hand, Redd Volkaert, Earle Pool Ball, John X. Reed, Cornell Hurd, Bert Rivera, Tommy Alverson, Chaparral, Jesse Dayton, Two Tons of Steel, the Lucky Tomblin Band, Paula Nelson, the Texas Sapphires, and many others build on the work of earlier pioneers to keep the dance halls and beer joints throughout the state echoing with the sounds of honky-tonk.

TEXAS BLUEGRASS

Bluegrass, which is rooted in old-time string band music, burst onto the national scene during the 1940s and has become one of the most popular subgenres of country music in the world. Although the Southwest is better known for its Western swing and honky-tonk traditions, bluegrass has been a vital part of the region's musical history for decades. Bluegrass bands began forming in Texas as early as the 1950s, and by the 1960s the bluegrass scene was thriving throughout the state. With a network of locally organized festivals that featured national and regional groups, bluegrass continued to grow in popularity throughout the 1970s and 1980s as a more roots-oriented alternative to mainstream country music. Even though bluegrass had declined somewhat in national popularity by the 1990s, fans in Texas and elsewhere across the country kept it alive through festivals, backyard "pickin' parties," and a variety of radio programs. In the year 2000, the release of the widely acclaimed Cohen Brothers film *Oh Brother, Where Art Thou?* with its roots music–laden soundtrack helped rekindle a worldwide interest in traditional country music and led to a resurgence in popularity for bluegrass and string band music throughout North America.[61]

Although the state is not often recognized for its contributions to bluegrass music, Texas has been home to a variety of talented bluegrass and string band musicians over the years, including the Mayfield Brothers, Tex Logan, Hank Wilson and the Dixie Drifters, the Country Cut Ups, Alan Munde, Joe Carr, the Stone Mountain Boys, Holly Bond and the Bluegrass Texans, Roanoke, the Grazmatics, the Alfalfa Brothers, Salt Grass, the Lone Star Bluegrass Band, Tennessee Valley Authority, the Double Mountain Boys, the Shady Grove Ramblers, Hickory Hill, Jimmie Don Bates, Robert Pool, Dave Seeman, Rod Moag, Karen Mal, Mike Landschoot, Tom Ellis, Ken Brown, Eddie Collins, Cara Cooke, the Grassy Knoll Boys, Two High String Band, the Siekers, the Blackland Prairie Boys, the Double Eagle String Band, the Gourds, Cooper's Uncle, the Gray Sky Boys, the Asylum Street Spankers, the Boxcar Preachers, White Ghost Shivers, Green Mountain Grass, and many others.

Most of these artists perform traditional bluegrass or string band music, but some have ventured into very nontraditional areas as well. For example, Austin's Waller Creek Boys, who mixed bluegrass with folk and blues, are perhaps best remembered as the band that gave a young Texas singer named Janis Joplin some of her first opportunities to perform in public during the early 1960s. The nationally popular Austin Lounge Lizards not only blend bluegrass, country, and folk music, but they also use wry and sometimes ribald humor in their songs to

South Austin Jug Band at the Kerrville Folk Festival. Courtesy Susan Roads.

poke fun at a variety of social issues. The South Austin Jug Band is another group of talented young players who are as comfortable blazing through a bluegrass fiddle breakdown as they are playing a hot jazz swing tune. Other local bluegrass prodigies include teenage mandolinist Sarah Jarosz, from Wimberley, Texas, who has performed with veteran artists such as Alan Munde and Peter Rowan. Texas has also had an important impact on the development of bluegrass outside of the state. One of the best examples of this can be seen in the influence of non-Texas bluegrass fiddlers such as Kenny Baker and Byron Berline, who have helped incorporate Texas-style fiddling techniques and stylistic flourishes into mainstream bluegrass music.[62]

CROSSOVER COUNTRY

In addition to supporting a very active bluegrass community, Texas has also produced more than its share of artists who helped bridge Western swing, honky-tonk, and other regional styles with more mainstream country and pop during the 1960s, 1970s, and 1980s. Jim Reeves, born James Travis Reeves on August 20, 1923, in Galloway, Texas, was steeped in rural country music traditions but went on to become one of the most successful crossover pop-country singers of the twentieth

Ed McLemore's "Sportatorium," site of the Big "D" Jamboree.
Courtesy David Dennard, Dragon Street Records.

century. Reeves, who attended the University of Texas on a baseball scholarship, began working as a radio announcer shortly after World War II. By the early 1950s he had recorded for the small Macy's label in Houston before moving on to Abbott Records, where his growing popularity earned him appearances on the Louisiana Hayride. In 1955 Reeves joined the Grand Ole Opry and began recording for RCA Records in Nashville, where he worked closely with guitarist and producer Chet Atkins, who was forging a new, more pop-oriented country music style that often featured lavish orchestral arrangements. Soon Reeves began transforming himself from a traditional country singer into a more pop-country crooner and traded in his Western clothing for sport coats and formal wear. His smooth baritone and his new, more sophisticated image helped earn him the nickname "Gentleman" Jim Reeves, which fit perfectly with Atkins's vision of transforming country music from hillbilly to more urbane mainstream pop. Reeves's tremendous success with hits such as "Four Walls," "Am I Losing You?" "He'll Have to Go," and "Welcome to My World" made him a country superstar and helped solidify Nashville's position within the mainstream music market.[63]

In a similar vein, Ray Price, who was born in Perryville, Texas, on January 12, 1926, began as more of a traditional honky-tonk singer but moved increasingly into the pop-country realm during his career. His ability to combine country, pop, and other styles was perhaps a natural outgrowth of his childhood love for many different types of music, which ranged from Jimmie Rodgers and Gene Autry to African American doo-wop groups such as the Ink Spots and the Mills Brothers. As a young man, Price began performing on local radio in Abilene, Texas, but in 1949 he graduated to the nationally popular radio series *The Big "D" Jamboree*, which was broadcast live from Dallas.[64]

Ray Price, Singing on Radio Station WSM. Courtesy David Dennard, Dragon Street Records.

After moving to Nashville in 1951, Price befriended Hank Williams, with whom he sometimes performed. Following Williams's death in 1953, his backup band, the Drifting Cowboys, joined Price to form the Cherokee Cowboys, a band that would include future stars such as Willie Nelson, Johnny Paycheck, and Roger Miller. Although they sometimes incorporated the heavily orchestrated and pop-oriented sound pioneered by Chet Atkins, Price and his Cherokee Cowboys remained rooted in Western swing and honky-tonk and often used a 4/4 shuffle beat that harkened back to the more traditional honky-tonk sound. During his long career Price had a string of hits that have since become country standards, including "Release Me," "Crazy Arms," "City Lights," "Heartaches by the Number," "Make the World Go Away," and "For the Good Times."[65]

One artist who had an even broader impact on country, pop, and rock & roll was Alvis Edgar "Buck" Owens Jr., born a sharecropper's son on August 12, 1929, in Sherman, Texas. Buck was only eight years old when his family fled the great Texas-Oklahoma dust bowl and headed west to Arizona, where he honed his musical skills and began performing on local radio. In 1951 he moved to Bakersfield, California, and began playing country, pop, Western swing, R&B, and rockabilly with a number of different bands. In California Owens met Tommy Collins, Merle Haggard, and others with whom he would create the new "Bakersfield sound." Characterized by twangy electric guitar licks, tight harmonies, and sparse arrangements, the Bakersfield sound was the antithesis of the heavily orchestrated and lavishly produced style that dominated mainstream country music during the 1960s and 1970s.[66]

Audiences loved Buck Owens's sound, and he soon became one of the best-selling country artists ever, with hits such as "Act Naturally" (later recorded by the Beatles), "Together Again," "I've Got a Tiger by the Tail," "It's Crying Time Again," "My Heart Skips a Beat," and "Sam's Place." He also toured internationally and worked for several years as cohost of the popular television show *Hee Haw.* As one of the founders of the Bakersfield sound, Owens had a profound impact on both country music and rock & roll. His melding of traditional country with roots rock not only inspired younger musicians such as Linda Ronstadt, Gram Parsons, and the Eagles as they developed their distinct West Coast country-rock sound during the 1970s but also led to the more recent resurgence of a retro Bakersfield sound as represented by Dwight Yoakam, the Austin-based group, the Derailers, and others. Furthermore, the unique instrumentation pioneered by Owens and other Bakersfield artists, including the trademark Telecaster guitar licks popularized by Haggard's guitarist Roy Nichols, are now a standard part of mainstream country music. In recent years Owens recorded with former Beatle Ringo Starr, Dwight

Yoakam, and others, all of whom readily acknowledge Owens's importance in the development of country, pop, and rock & roll.[67]

Many other musicians from Texas and the Southwest played a key role in the evolution of country music during the 1960s and 1970s. Jimmy Dean, born August 10, 1928, in Plainview, Texas, started working on radio in the late 1940s and then began hosting his own television show, *Town and Country Jamboree*, in the mid-1950s. Dean's career took off in 1961 with the release of his self-composed tune "Big, Bad John" on Columbia Records. "Big, Bad John," which told of a heroic miner who sacrificed his life to save his fellow workers, reached number one on both the pop and country charts and helped fuel a public craze for so-called saga songs. Typically these were ballads that told of larger-than-life characters who performed heroic deeds, often in rustic, outdoor settings. The tremendous popularity of these songs, particularly those that emphasized rural themes, may have reflected a nostalgic longing among many country music fans for the older agrarian way of life that had disappeared during the mass migration of rural families from the countryside to the cities following World War II. Based largely on his success with "Big, Bad John," Dean went on to appear on TV and in movies, and he eventually built a fortune in the food service industry with his Jimmy Dean Meat Company.[68]

Johnny Horton, who was born in Los Angeles on April 30, 1925, but grew up in East Texas near the town of Rusk, also became famous for his saga songs. His ballads "When It's Springtime in Alaska," "North to Alaska," "The Battle of New Orleans," and "Sink the *Bismarck*" were major hits in both country and pop markets. Horton was much more than a ballad singer, however. He also combined classic country with early rock & roll to create a unique style that was part honky-tonk and part rockabilly. His first big hit, "Honky Tonk Man," perfectly captured the image of the honky-tonk lifestyle, but structurally it went well beyond the traditional honky-tonk format by incorporating a rocking boogie-woogie beat that was quite unusual in mainstream country music at the time. Horton's vocal delivery was also very distinct, ranging from a sad and plaintive wail on songs such as "Whispering Pines" to an energetic, Buddy Holly–style yelping on "I'm Ready, If You're Willing." Tragically Horton died in a car wreck near Milano, Texas, on November 5, 1960, but his music remained popular for many years after his death. In the late 1980s Dwight Yoakam paid tribute to Horton with a new hit version of "Honky Tonk Man."[69]

Charline Arthur, born Charline Highsmith in Henrietta, Texas, on September 2, 1929, also blended honky-tonk, blues, pop, and rock & roll with a spirited and sometimes raucous singing style that won her the admiration of Patsy Cline,

Elvis Presley, and others. During the mid-1940s Arthur began performing on local radio in Paris, Texas, and in 1949 she recorded her own composition, "I've Got the Boogie Blues," for Bullet Records. In 1952 legendary promoter Colonel Tom Parker helped bring her to the attention of major label executives, and soon she was recording for RCA. With a unique country boogie sound, Arthur had several hits throughout the early 1950s, including "Leave My Man Alone," "Kiss the Baby Goodnight," "Honey Bun," and "Just Look, Don't Touch, He's Mine," which for a brief time placed her among the ranks of popular contemporary female artists such as Kitty Wells. With her raw, energetic style of boogie-woogie and honky-tonk and her unabashed approach to striving for equality with her male counterparts, Arthur was a pioneer not only in the fields of country and rockabilly music but also in opening doors for other women in the industry.[70]

Roger Miller, born in Fort Worth, Texas, on January 2, 1936, but raised in Oklahoma, was another innovative and multifaceted country musician from the Southwest. He is often considered a storyteller, although his comedic approach was markedly different from the typically serious saga songs performed by Jimmy Dean, Johnny Horton, and others. Miller was a gifted vocalist and an accomplished songwriter who penned hits such as "Invitation to the Blues" for Ray Price and "Half a Mind" for Ernest Tubb. Miller also became a singing star in his own right, topping the country and pop charts in the mid-1960s with "King of the Road," a lighthearted tale of a restless but resourceful vagabond. Although he is probably best remembered for his string of humorous novelty tunes, including "Chug-a-Lug," "Dang Me," "England Swings," and "You Can't Roller Skate in a Buffalo Herd," Miller eventually wrote music for the Broadway production of *Big River: The Adventures of Huckleberry Finn*, for which he won five Tony awards. His remarkable career demonstrated a broad range of singing and song-writing talents seldom equaled by other artists in any genre.[71]

Jeannie C. Riley, born Jeanne Carolyn Stephenson on October 19, 1945, in Anson, Texas, did not have a very successful long-term career in country music, but for a few years during the late 1960s and early 1970s she created a sensation with her rendition of Tom T. Hall's song "Harper Valley P.T.A." This tune was very much in the saga song tradition of Jimmy Dean and Johnny Horton, but it was different in important ways. Rather than celebrating a mythic male hero, "Harper Valley P.T.A." tells of an angry mother who confronts local officials after they accuse her of being an unfit parent. In so doing, she exposes the hypocrisy rampant throughout the community by pointing out the dishonesty, infidelity, and corruption of several of the town's leading figures. Although Riley's country singing career never advanced far beyond this one song, in some ways she served as an important voice for American women at the time by publicly condemning the double standards females often faced. According to Riley, she truly considered "Harper Valley P.T.A." to be a song of social protest and used it to express her unhappiness regarding what she considered gender inequities in American society. In at least a limited way Riley helped expose these problems and made it easier for younger generations of women in country music to openly address social issues through their music.[72]

Charley Pride, an even more iconoclastic figure in modern country music, was born in Sledge, Mississippi, on March 18, 1938, but spent most of his adult life in Texas, where he has managed to parlay his financial success in the music business into a lucrative career in real estate and other investments. Growing up as an African American sharecropper's son in northern Mississippi, Pride regularly listened to radio broadcasts of the Grand Ole Opry and, as a young man, pursued careers in both music and baseball. In 1966 RCA Records signed him to a recording contract but carefully concealed his racial identity since the label was uncertain of how white audiences would respond to a black country singer. Despite initial apprehension on the part of some, most country fans seemed not to care, and Pride quickly became one of the best-selling artists in the history of country music, producing hit after hit, including "The Snakes Crawl at Night," "All I Have to Offer You Is Me," "Kiss an Angel Good Mornin,'" and "Is Anybody Goin' to San Antone?" Although other African Americans had been involved in country music before, Pride was the first black superstar of country music, and he has remained a highly visible symbol of country music's ability to transcend racial and ethnic boundaries.[73]

Johnny Rodríguez is another example of the importance of non-Anglo artists in country music. Rodríguez was born Juan Raúl Davis Rodríguez on December 10, 1951, in Sabinal, Texas, where he absorbed diverse musical influences such as conjunto, Western swing, and rock & roll. Although Rodríguez has recorded some in Spanish during his career, he is first and foremost a traditional country artist who draws from the honky-tonk traditions of Lefty Frizzell and Merle Haggard. Rodríguez released his first Top Ten song, "Pass Me By (If You're Only Passing Through)," in 1972 and soon followed this with hits such as "You Always Come Back to Hurting Me," "Riding My Thumb to Mexico," and the Lefty Frizzell–Whitey Shafer classic, "That's the Way Love Goes." Rodríguez's career has been somewhat up and down over the years, due in part to earlier drug and alcohol problems, as well as an unsuccessful attempt to cross over into country-pop, but he remains a popular and influential performer, as well as a good example of the ongoing cross-pollination of musical cultures in the Southwest.[74]

Johnny Rodríguez. Photo by Clay Shorkey, courtesy Texas Music Museum.

Barbara and Louise Mandrell are also two very successful crossover artists of the 1970s and 1980s. Barbara Mandrell was born December 25, 1948, in Houston, where she grew up singing religious hymns but also listened to country, rockabilly, and rock & roll. By the age of twelve she was proficient on several instruments and began to appear on stage alongside Patsy Cline, Johnny Cash, and other major country artists. Eventually Mandrell became a star in her own right, with hits such as "Woman to Woman," "Married, but Not to Each Other," "Sleeping Single in a Double Bed," and "I Was Country When Country Wasn't Cool," a duet recorded with George Jones. Barbara's younger sister, Louise Mandrell, born in Corpus Christi, Texas, on July 13, 1954, never attained the same level of stardom as her older sibling, but she also had several hit records and appeared regularly on television, where she sang and played banjo, fiddle, and guitar. Although rooted in traditional country music, the Mandrell sisters built their careers on combining country and pop, a fact that has earned them some criticism from country music purists. Nevertheless, both women have proven themselves to be very versatile musicians and energetic performers who helped introduce country music to millions of new fans worldwide.[75]

Tanya Tucker, born in Seminole, Texas, on October 10, 1958, was one of the first child superstars in country music. Actually, it was her older sister, La Costa, whom Tucker's parents first worked to promote as a country singer. Although La Costa would chart with country hits such as "I Wanna Get to You" and "Get on My Love Train," it was the younger Tanya who would have the greatest critical and commercial success after joining with Billy Sherrill at Columbia Records. Tucker had her first hit, "Delta Dawn," in 1972 at the age of thirteen. Others quickly followed, including "What's Your Mama's Name?" "Blood Red and Going Down," "Would You Lay with Me (in a Field of Stone)?" and "San Antonio Stroll." Since some of these songs included rather explicit references to sex, dysfunctional family relations, and psychotic behavior, they caused quite a stir among many country music fans. Although such topics were no longer considered socially taboo by the mid-1970s, the fact that a person of her age was singing these songs brought charges by some that her manager-father and her record company were exploiting her as an underaged sex symbol. However, she brushed aside the controversy and continued to make hit records well into the 1980s. As an adult, Tucker has remained outspoken on matters she considers to be of public concern, including the issue of spousal abuse, especially following her tumultuous relationship with country star Glen Campbell. Since her early days as a teen sensation, Tucker has helped pave the way for other female artists to succeed in the music business while still remaining actively engaged in a variety of outside issues.[76]

Several other Texas musicians have played important roles in crossover country music throughout the 1970s and 1980s. Don Williams, born on May 27, 1939, in Floydada, Texas, started as a folk singer in the 1960s with the Pozo Seco Singers. By the 1970s his folk-country style of songwriting had matured, and he began to climb the charts with hits such as "The Shelter of Your Eyes," "Some Broken Hearts Never Mend," "Tulsa Time," "Lord, I Hope This Day Is Good," and "I Recall a Gypsy Woman." Although Williams is still very popular in the United States, his biggest following may be in Europe, where he has won numerous awards, earned the admiration of British rock stars Eric Clapton and Pete Townshend, and built a huge and loyal fan base.[77]

Johnny Lee, born John Lee Ham in Texas City, Texas, on July 3, 1946, began his rise to stardom playing in Mickey Gilley's Houston-based backup band. When Gilley's namesake honky-tonk was selected as the site for filming the 1980 John Travolta and Debra Winger film *Urban Cowboy*, Lee contributed some of the soundtrack's more memorable songs. His "Looking for Love (in All the Wrong Places)" became a number one country hit and a Top Ten single on the pop charts. He followed this with "Picking Up Strangers," "Cherokee Fiddle," and several other popular songs and became a leading figure in the "urban cowboy" craze of the 1980s. Although some critics consider the urban cowboy phenomenon to be a blatant attempt by the entertainment industry to commercialize country music and market it as mainstream pop, Johnny Lee and others in the urban cowboy genre did much to help promote country music and cowboy culture to a worldwide audience during the 1980s, thereby helping increase the genre's international popularity.[78]

The Gatlin Brothers were another important pop-country group of the 1970s and 1980s. The band's leader, Larry Gatlin, born May 2, 1948, in Seminole, Texas, joined with his brothers, Steve and Rudy, to begin performing gospel on Abilene television while the three were still teenagers. They eventually relocated to Nashville, where the brothers worked as backup singers for Tammy Wynette before scoring several hit records of their own, including "Broken Lady," "All the Gold in California," "Houston (Means I'm Closer to You)," and "The Lady Takes the Cowboy Every Time."[79]

Mac Davis, another West Texas artist who did well in Nashville during the 1970s and 1980s, was born in Lubbock on January 21, 1942, and actually gained prominence first as a songwriter. One of his best-known compositions, "In the Ghetto," which was recorded by Elvis Presley, was a very socially conscious song about the debilitating effects of racism and racial segregation. Davis, who penned several other hit tunes, including "Watching Scotty Grow," "It's Hard to Be Humble," and "Lubbock, Texas, in My Rear View Mirror," also hosted his own TV show and appeared in major motion pictures such as *North Dallas Forty*.[80]

Of all the pop-country crossover artists of the 1970s and 1980s, Kenny Rogers enjoyed the greatest commercial success. Born in Houston on August 21, 1938, Rogers already had a successful career during the 1960s as a folk and pop singer with the New Christy Minstrels and later with the First Edition. By 1977 he was working as a solo artist when his song "Lucille" suddenly skyrocketed up the country and pop charts and made him an international phenomenon almost overnight. Rogers followed this with other huge hits, including "The Gambler," "She Believes in Me," "Coward of the County," and "Lady." He appeared on TV and in movies and made several successful duet recordings with Dottie West, Sheena Easton, Dolly Parton, and Ronnie Milsap. Although Rogers remained popular well into the 1980s, the brand of pop-country that he, the Mandrell Sisters, and others pioneered began losing ground to a resurgence of traditional country by the mid-1980s.[81]

PROGRESSIVE COUNTRY

While several Texas artists played a key role in the crossover-country scene of the 1960s, 1970s, and 1980s, others were moving country music in an entirely different direction by launching a new genre known as "progressive country." Progressive country was a combination of honky-tonk, folk, rock & roll, swing, boogie-woogie, blues, and other styles that would prove to be the most eclectic form of country music to emerge from Texas since Western swing in the 1930s. The progressive movement, which began in the Austin nightclub scene during the early 1970s, was led by Willie Nelson, Jerry Jeff Walker, Ray Wylie Hubbard, Michael Martin Murphey, Marcia Ball, and a number of other artists whose broad musical backgrounds encompassed a number of genres.

For a variety of reasons, Austin became the epicenter of this new progressive country phenomenon. With at least six major colleges and universities in the immediate area, the capital city of Texas had a large population of well-educated, socially and politically progressive young people, many of whom had grown up listening to both their parents' country music and the rock & roll of their own generation. In addition, there were thousands of musicians and music fans who were not students but had simply converged on the city because it provided a cultural oasis of sorts in the midst of a socially and politically conservative state. Since these younger Texans had been raised on both country and rock & roll and were generally more open to other ethnic cultures than previous generations, they readily embraced the blending of musical styles that went into making progressive country.

Unlike most other Texas cities at that time, Austin of the 1960s and 1970s had a vibrant and dynamic live music scene made up of dozens of nightclubs, dance halls, coffee houses, and other venues that hosted a diverse range of performers. The Chequered Flag, the Vulcan Gas Company, Castle Creek, the Armadillo World Headquarters, Soap Creek Saloon, the Split Rail, the Austin Opry House, the One Knight, the Hole in the Wall, Spellman's, the Austin Outhouse, the Broken

Spoke, Antone's, and Cheatham Street Warehouse (in San Marcos), along with a number of local festivals, street dances, and neighborhood concerts, all provided a remarkable mix of country, blues, conjunto, Cajun, zydeco, folk, rock & roll, Western swing, R&B, gospel, jazz, reggae, and other styles. The 1975 debut of the nationally syndicated PBS television series *Austin City Limits* brought even more high-profile attention to the local music scene and helped reinforce Austin's emerging reputation as the "Live Music Capital of the World."[82]

The diversity of both the musicians and the audiences at these Austin venues was a key ingredient in the development of progressive country. On any given night, cowboys, hippies, college students, white- and blue-collar workers, black, white, and Hispanic mingled, eager to hear a broad range of musicians performing almost any type of music, whether traditional honky-tonk, Western swing, blues, jazz, boogie woogie, folk, rock & roll, Cajun, or conjunto. This willingness to embrace such a wide variety of musical styles allowed the Austin club scene to flourish as a hotbed for innovation and experimentation and made possible the emergence of the eclectic progressive country sound.[83]

Of all of the live music venues in Austin during the 1970s, the Armadillo World Headquarters was probably the best known and most popular. Opened in August 1970 by Eddie Wilson, Jim Franklin, and others, the "Dillo" had originally been a National Guard armory located near the intersection of Barton Springs Road and South First Street, just south of the Colorado River. Although the cavernous room, which held around fifteen hundred people, had less than ideal acoustics, the weekly lineup of musical acts was remarkable, featuring a broad range of blues, jazz, gospel, country, rockabilly, conjunto, folk, rock, and other styles. Texas artists, including Willie Nelson, Freddie King, Marcia Ball, Lightnin' Hopkins, ZZ Top, Kinky Friedman, Alvin Crow, Flaco Jiménez, Mance Lipscomb, Asleep at the Wheel, Clifton Chenier, Kenneth Threadgill, Johnny Winter, Doug Sahm, Joe Ely, Stevie Ray Vaughan, Jerry Jeff Walker, and Greezy Wheels, shared the stage with national touring acts such as Bruce Springsteen, the Pointer Sisters, Frank Zappa, Earl Scruggs, Taj Mahal, Leo Kottke, Ravi Shankar, Bill Monroe, Fats Domino, Gram Parsons, Emmylou Harris, Van Morrison, Linda Ronstadt, and the Grateful Dead. Because it helped bring together an eclectic mixture of styles on a grand scale, the Armadillo provided a unique musical environment that helped launch the progressive country movement and pave the way for the diverse and dynamic music scene that continues in Austin today.[84]

Although he did not start the progressive country movement, Willie Nelson became its most visible and influential figure. Nelson, born April 30, 1933, in Abbott, Texas, was raised by his grandparents. He got his first guitar at the age of

Mural inside Armadillo World Headquarters. Courtesy Burton Wilson.

six and was writing songs by the time he was eleven.[85] Even at an early age, Nelson was exposed to a variety of musical influences. Although he listened to Western swing and honky-tonk as a child, he was also fascinated with the blues he heard from black workers in the cotton fields near his home. Nelson sang gospel in his Baptist church, but he also played in local German Czech polka bands and listened to jazz and pop music on the radio. By his early twenties, he was working as a disc jockey at KVAN radio in Vancouver, Washington. There in 1957 he made his first record, "No Place for Me," which was pressed by Pappy Daily's Houston-based D

Records but released on Nelson's own label, Willie Nelson Records. The record, whose flip side included Texas songwriter Leon Payne's "Lumberjack," did well, and Nelson went on to record other songs for D Records. However, when Daily refused to record the Nelson composition "Night Life," claiming that it sounded "too bluesy," the singer secretly released it through another Houston label, RX Records. It was not an immediate hit, so Nelson sold the publishing rights for only $150. Eventually, however, "Night Life" became a best seller, and Nelson was able to reclaim his rights to the tune.[86]

In 1960 Nelson moved to Nashville, where he quickly established himself as a solid musician and a first-rate songwriter. Not only did he play bass for Ray Price's Cherokee Cowboys, but he also began penning hits such as "Crazy," "Hello Walls," "Funny How Time Slips Away," and "Touch Me." Although Nelson was well respected in Nashville as a singer and songwriter and was even invited to become a member of the Grand Ole Opry, he eventually grew frustrated with what he considered the Nashville recording industry's limits on creative freedom. So, when his home in Nashville burned down in 1970, Nelson temporarily relocated to Bandera, Texas, where he easily reintegrated himself into the Texas music scene, playing clubs and dance halls throughout the area. He returned to Nashville after his house was rebuilt but soon realized that he missed the Lone Star State, where he had developed a large and loyal following. By 1972 Nelson had moved back to Texas for good and quickly made himself at home in the laid-back Austin music scene, where an abundance of nightclubs provided Nelson and others a wide-ranging arena in which to perform and try out new material.[87]

In the dynamic musical environment at the Armadillo, Soap Creek Saloon, and other Austin venues, Willie Nelson's writing and performing flourished. By 1973 he had almost completely severed ties with Nashville and RCA Records, and he began working with Atlantic Records and legendary producer Jerry Wexler, who had an immediate appreciation for Nelson's unusual blues and jazz-inflected singing style. Together, Nelson and Wexler released two albums, *Shotgun Willie* and *Phases and Stages*, which reflected Nelson's traditional country roots but also highlighted his broad range of influences. In 1973 Nelson held the first of what would become his legendary Fourth of July picnics in Dripping Springs, just west of Austin, and he invited several of his Nashville-based musician friends to perform. As popular as Nelson had become by 1973, he would gain even greater success with the release of his 1975 breakthrough album, *The Red Headed Stranger*, which included the Fred Rose tune "Blue Eyes Crying in the Rain." The song and the album quickly propelled Nelson to international fame and secured his position as the most recognizable figure in progressive country.[88]

Willie Nelson, 1972. Courtesy Burton Wilson.

Ultimately, Nelson and others in the progressive movement helped change mainstream country by providing an alternative arena in which musicians could have greater artistic freedom while drawing from a wider range of styles. With the tremendous commercial success of Nelson and other progressive country performers, the major record labels now had to acknowledge new, broader boundaries in the country music market. In addition to helping expand the parameters of popular music, progressive country, with its mingling of diverse styles and its emphasis on the singer-songwriter, also helped lay the foundation for the emergence of the "Americana" country movement of the 1990s.

In addition to Willie Nelson, several other artists also played a vital role in the progressive country scene of the 1970s. One of the most important was Jerry Jeff Walker, born Ronald Clyde Crosby in Oneonta, New York, on March 14, 1942. As a young man, Walker had hitchhiked across the South and Southwest and spent time in New Orleans, where a brief stint in jail inspired his best-known song, "Mr. Bojangles." Largely on the success of this one tune, he signed with Atlantic Records in 1968 and began attracting attention as a promising young folk-country songwriter. In 1971 Walker moved to Austin, where he had performed during the 1960s. The city's burgeoning music scene was perfectly suited to Walker's free-wheeling artistic approach, and in 1972 he began recording a string of hits that would make him one of the leading voices of the progressive movement. Some of Walker's better-known songs, penned by Texas-based songwriters, include Guy Clark's "L.A. Freeway" and "Desperados Waiting for a Train," Ray Wylie Hubbard's "Up against the Wall, Redneck Mother," and Gary P. Nunn's "London Homesick Blues (Home with the Armadillo)," which became the theme song for the PBS television series Austin City Limits.[89]

Michael Martin Murphey, born in Dallas on March 13, 1945, had spent time in Los Angeles writing tunes for Kenny Rogers, the Nitty Gritty Dirt Band, the Monkees, and others before moving back to Texas and settling in Austin in 1971. Murphey is primarily a balladeer, and many of his songs focus on the history and mythology of the American West, including his 1972 hit, "Geronimo's Cadillac," a commentary on the federal government's policies toward Native Americans. Another of Murphey's most popular songs, "Cosmic Cowboy," so completely captured the essence of Austin's unique musical culture in the 1970s that the term "cosmic cowboy" became a popular nickname for fans of progressive country music. In addition to playing an important role in defining early progressive country, he went on to have a successful career in mainstream country music and recorded hits such as "Wildfire," "Carolina in the Pines," and "What's Forever For?" Murphey continues to write and perform, and through his

Freda and the Firedogs, 1972. Courtesy Burton Wilson.

ballads and storytelling he has helped repopularize the older "singing cowboy" tradition.[90]

Marcia Ball, born Marcia Mouton in Orange, Texas, on March 20, 1949, is better known today as a popular blues, R&B, and boogie-woogie artist, but during the early 1970s she was a driving force in Austin's progressive country scene. In

1972 Ball formed Freda and the Firedogs, one of the first progressive country bands in Austin, which performed regularly at the Armadillo, the Split Rail, the Broken Spoke, and Soap Creek Saloon. With Ball on piano and vocals, Freda and the Firedogs drew the attention of famed Atlantic Records producer Jerry Wexler. Although the album they recorded with Wexler went unreleased until recently, and the band dissolved completely in 1974, Freda and the Firedogs were key players in helping blend the country, rock, blues, and boogie-woogie styles that defined the progressive country sound.[91]

Steve Fromholz, born June 8, 1945, in Temple, Texas, attended North Texas State University in Denton (now the University of North Texas), where he played in folk bands with fellow student Michael Martin Murphey and others. In 1965 Fromholz and Murphey debuted in Austin at Rod Kennedy's Zilker Park Folk Festival, and for the next several years Fromholz, Murphey, and their circle of musician friends rotated in and out of Austin, leaving their distinct musical imprints on the progressive country scene. Fromholz's affection for the rustic landscape of his home state inspired him to write his well-known "Texas Trilogy," a three-song homage to small-town life and the colorful characters who populate the state's rural communities.[92]

B. W. "Buckwheat" Stevenson, born Louis Charles Stevenson in Dallas on October 5, 1949, also became involved in performing and songwriting while a student at the University of North Texas during the 1960s. By the early 1970s Stevenson had become a regular in the Austin progressive scene, playing at the Armadillo and elsewhere. He appeared poised for a major breakthrough with his 1973 hit "My Maria," but mismanagement by his record label prevented him from realizing his full potential, and in 1988 Stevenson died of complications following heart surgery.[93]

Long-time Texas resident Ray Wylie Hubbard, born in Soper, Oklahoma, on November 13, 1946, is one of the most enduring and adaptable of the progressive country singer-songwriters. He is best known for writing "Up against the Wall, Redneck Mother," a biting parody of Merle Haggard's "Okie from Muskogee." Over the years Hubbard has evolved as a songwriter and has served as a mentor for countless younger Texas-based singer-songwriters. Willis Alan Ramsey, another very influential Austin-based songwriter of the 1970s, was born in Alabama in 1951 but raised in Texas. His 1971 debut album included such a wealth of high-quality songs that he helped inspire the song-writing careers of numerous younger artists, including Lyle Lovett, Shawn Colvin, Robert Earl Keen, and Walter Hyatt.[94]

Ray Wylie Hubbard. Courtesy Susan Roads.

Rusty Wier, from Manchaca, just south of Austin, played drums in a band while attending Texas State University in San Marcos. Although Wier had limited success at the national level, he was a core member of the progressive country scene and had a hit in the late 1970s with "Don't It Make You Wanna Dance?"[95] Richard "Kinky" Friedman, the son of a University of Texas professor, made his mark on the Austin progressive music scene with his wryly humorous songwriting. His provocative stage antics, along with tunes such as "Sold American," "Ride 'Em, Jewboy," "They Ain't Makin' Jews like Jesus Anymore," and "Get Your Biscuits in the Oven (and Your Buns in the Bed)," won him legions of fans but also created controversy and resulted in PBS's decision not to air his 1975 appearance on *Austin*

City Limits. Friedman continues to perform, has written several books, and has campaigned for the governorship of Texas.[96]

Vocalist and piano player Gary P. Nunn, who grew up in Brownfield, Texas, worked for several years as a sideman for Jerry Jeff Walker and wrote one of Walker's biggest hits, "London Homesick Blues (Home with the Armadillo)." With his strong song-writing skills, Nunn went on to have a long and successful career as a solo artist. Bob Livingston, another long-time member of Walker's Lost Gonzo Band, has taken his unique brand of country onto the world stage, performing cowboy songs, progressive country, and original material throughout India, Asia, and the Middle East.[97]

OUTLAW COUNTRY

About the same time that progressive country was gaining national popularity, another genre of country music, known as "outlaw country," was emerging, with three Texans, Willie Nelson, Waylon Jennings, and Kris Kristofferson, leading the way. Nelson and Jennings, in particular, produced several hits during the mid- to late-1970s, including "Good Hearted Woman," "Mommas, Don't Let Your Babies Grow Up to Be Cowboys," and "Luckenbach, Texas (Back to the Basics of Love)," which helped popularize this genre worldwide.[98]

Similar to progressive country, outlaw country represented a rebellion of sorts against the more pop-oriented mainstream country sound, although, with the exception of Nelson, most outlaw artists generally continued to live and record in Nashville. Despite sharing many similarities, progressive country and outlaw country also had some significant differences. For example, progressive country had grown out of a mixture of diverse styles and usually celebrated the more laid-back cosmic cowboy lifestyle, whereas outlaw country was more firmly rooted in traditional blue-collar honky-tonk and generally centered on themes of hard drinking and rowdy living. In fact, the rapid rise in popularity of the grittier, harder-edged outlaw genre suggests that, while many country music fans were disenchanted with mainstream pop country, they were not ready to embrace the more liberal social and political attitudes commonly found among followers of progressive country. In any case, record companies quickly recognized the commercial potential for both progressive country and outlaw country and eagerly sought to exploit them as lucrative niche markets.[99]

Waylon Jennings, born June 15, 1937, near Littlefield, Texas, just outside of Lubbock, was one of the leading figures of the outlaw movement. Jennings had his first job as a DJ by age twelve, and at eighteen was working at Lubbock's KDAV radio, where he befriended another local musician named Buddy Holly. Jennings and Holly worked together on various musical projects, and both saw Elvis Presley during his early appearances in West Texas, an experience that fired their imaginations about the possibility for their own professional careers in music. Jennings eventually joined Holly as his bass player just weeks before the 1959 plane crash that killed Holly, Ritchie Valens, and J. P. "the Big Bopper" Richardson. According to Jennings, he gave up his seat on the doomed plane at the last minute because Richardson was sick and wanted to avoid a long drive on the band's tour bus. Although Jennings was devastated by the loss of Holly and the others, he eventually recovered and went on to build a successful career as a country singer in Nashville during the 1960s. He worked for a while with Chet Atkins at RCA Records, but, like others before him, he grew disenchanted with Atkins's lavish production style and began reverting to a more stripped-down, back-to-basics approach that later became the foundation for the outlaw sound.[100]

Jennings's reputation as an outlaw began to emerge well before the outlaw movement itself became popular. In addition to sometimes using Hell's Angels motorcyclists as bodyguards, he reportedly pulled a gun in a Nashville studio because of a dispute during a recording session. In the 1960s Jennings enjoyed substantial success with more traditional honky-tonk tunes such as "Only Daddy That'll Walk the Line," but he resurfaced in the 1970s with a new look and sound that reflected the more rebellious attitude of progressive country. Sporting long hair, faded jeans, and a black leather vest, he began releasing songs such as "Honky Tonk Heroes" and "Lonesome, Or'nry, and Mean," which glorified a lifestyle of drifting, drinking, fighting, and womanizing. In 1976 Jennings's career took off when he teamed up with Jessi Colter (his wife at the time), Willie Nelson, and Tompall Glaser to release the phenomenally successful album *Wanted: The Outlaws*. As the first country album ever to be certified platinum, *Wanted* included hits such as "Good Hearted Woman" and "My Heroes Have Always Been Cowboys." Jennings remained a country superstar throughout the 1980s and 1990s and played for a time with Willie Nelson, Johnny Cash, and Kris Kristofferson as the Highwaymen until Jennings's death in 2002.[101]

Kris Kristofferson, another important figure in progressive and outlaw country music, was born in Brownsville, Texas, on June 22, 1936. He won a Rhodes scholarship to study at Oxford University in 1958, and, although he stayed at Oxford for only a year, Kristofferson used his time in England to write and perform music under the stage name of Kris Carson. After a stint in the army, which included playing U.S. military bases in Germany, he moved to Nashville. Among his many odd jobs there, he worked as a janitor at Columbia Records, where he managed to plug his songs to other artists. It was fellow Texan Roger Miller who helped jump-start Kristofferson's song-writing career in 1969 by being the first of many to record his tune "Me and Bobby McGee." That same year Johnny Cash released Kristofferson's "Sunday Morning Coming Down." In 1970 Sammi Smith followed with "Help Me Make It through the Night," and Ray Price had a number one hit with "For the Good Times." Soon other artists, including Texas-born rocker Janis Joplin, began clamoring to cover Kristofferson's material.[102]

Kristofferson's writing style was dramatically different from almost anything seen before in country music. Sometimes inviting comparisons to John Steinbeck and other distinguished novelists, Kristofferson wrote lyrics that were Spartan but still complex and highly nuanced in their meaning. He did not hesitate to candidly address controversial contemporary issues such as politics, U.S. foreign policy, drug addiction, alcoholism, poverty, and sexuality, but he never strayed far from a traditional country format. With an unparalleled level of intelligence and sophistication in his work, Kristofferson became one of the most-respected country songwriters of the 1970s, and he also enjoyed success as an actor, appearing in several major motion pictures alongside Bob Dylan, Barbara Streisand, and others. In 1985 Kristofferson joined with his old friends Willie Nelson, Waylon Jennings, and Johnny Cash to make the album *Highwayman*. Although he never promoted himself as an outlaw in the same way that Nelson and Jennings had, Kristofferson's straightforward writing style, his down-to-earth stage persona, and his occasional musical collaborations with Nelson, Jennings, and others helped make him an important part of the larger progressive and outlaw country movements.[103]

RECENT DEVELOPMENTS IN TEXAS COUNTRY MUSIC

In recent years Texas performers have continued to shape the ongoing development of country music. The most notable of these has been George Strait, who has maintained an unrivaled record of critical and commercial success for nearly thirty years. Strait was born in Poteet, Texas, on May 18, 1952, and raised in nearby Pearsall. His parents divorced when he was in the fourth grade, so his father, John Strait, a junior high school math teacher, raised George and his older brother, Buddy. The two boys spent a good deal of time on their grandparents' nearby ranch, where George developed a lifelong passion for horseback riding and calf roping. Strait did not become very interested in country music until his teens, when he discovered the music of Merle Haggard, Bob Wills, George Jones, and Hank Williams. After graduating from high school, he married Norma Voss, went to college for a year at Texas State University in San Marcos, and then joined the army in 1971. While stationed in Hawaii, Strait taught himself to play guitar and began performing locally.[104]

In 1974 George and Norma returned to San Marcos, where he enrolled again at Texas State. At the university Strait met fellow students Mike Daily (grandson of Pappy Daily, famed record producer and founder of D Records), Tommy Foote, Terry Hale, and Ron Cabal, who already had a group but were looking for a new lead singer. Strait auditioned and was hired immediately. Together the five students formed the Ace in the Hole Band and began appearing regularly at Kent Finlay's Cheatham Street Warehouse, just blocks from campus. Eventually the group started playing at other venues in San Marcos and throughout Central Texas, but their weekly appearances at Cheatham Street Warehouse provided a regular opportunity to hone their skills and build a fan base. Unlike most other country dance hall bands at the time, Ace in the Hole showed little interest in performing Top 40 hits. Instead they played almost exclusively classic Western swing and honky-tonk from pioneers such as Bob Wills, Lefty Frizzell, and Merle Haggard. Ironically, their devotion to these more traditional styles made it difficult for them to find bookings in most Austin nightclubs, which were caught up in the progressive country movement of the mid-1970s and had little use for a roots country band. Despite this, Ace in the Hole performed occasionally at several Austin-area venues, including the Split Rail and the Broken Spoke, as well as at Gruene Hall just outside of New Braunfels.[105]

As Ace in the Hole grew more popular, Strait began meeting people who would play a major role in his long-term career. Mike Daily's father, Don Daily, arranged for the band to record several songs for D Records, which he and his brother had taken over from their father, Pappy Daily. Local singer-songwriters, including Darryl Staedtler and Clay Blaker, provided catchy, well-written songs that, combined with Strait's distinctive vocals, would eventually become some of his earliest hits. Kent Finlay gave the group a home base at Cheatham Street Warehouse and even drove Strait and Staedtler to Nashville to meet with record executives. One of these executives in particular, Erv Woolsey, later proved crucial to Strait's phenomenal success. Woolsey, who had previously owned the Prairie Rose nightclub in San Marcos, where Ace in the Hole performed in 1975, was now back in Nashville working for MCA Records. While most other major labels showed little interest in Strait because he was "too traditional," Woolsey believed the young Texan had potential, so he arranged a recording session for Strait with

MCA in 1980. On the strength of Strait's first release, "Unwound," which climbed to number six on the *Billboard* country charts, MCA agreed to release an entire album, titled *Strait Country*, in 1981. The album did very well and helped launch Strait's remarkable record-breaking career. Over the following three decades he has had more number one hits than any other single artist in any musical genre, won numerous awards, starred in a critically and commercially successful major motion picture, has been inducted into the Country Music Hall of Fame, and has received an honorary doctorate from his alma mater, Texas State University.[106]

George Strait's commercial success is well documented. However, his long-term impact on the history of country music has not been adequately examined. Drawing from his rural Texas roots, Strait was committed to playing traditional music in the 1970s at a time when Austin and Nashville had little interest in classic country. Risking exclusion from both markets, Strait refused to compromise his musical integrity and instead proved that modern country audiences would still embrace traditional Western swing and honky-tonk. Once his records started selling in the millions, label executives scrambled to find other artists who could emulate him, and by the mid-1980s Strait was the most widely imitated male vocalist in country music. Just as Jimmie Rodgers, Lefty Frizzell, and Merle Haggard had been the voices of their generations, George Strait became the next country singer whom most younger artists sought to copy.

Strait also had an enormous impact on country music in terms of his image and overall appearance. In sharp contrast to the beards, long hair, and faded jeans that were standard attire in progressive and outlaw country during the 1970s and 1980s, Strait was clean shaven and wore neatly pressed Wrangler jeans and a starched dress shirt, along with a white, broad-brimmed Stetson hat. With his strong, clear baritone, a repertoire of traditional country songs, and an image that helped record executives market him as a sex symbol, Strait attracted legions of fans and imitators. Through both his music and his appearance, Strait helped set in motion a neotraditionalist movement that brought classic country music back into the mainstream and repopularized the image of the traditional Texas cowboy.

Lee Ann Womack, born August 19, 1966, in Jacksonville, Texas, has recorded with George Strait and built a very successful career as both a singer and songwriter in the same neotraditionalist vein as Strait. Much of Womack's early appreciation for country music came from her father, a high school principal and part-time DJ who encouraged his daughter's musical development. As a teenager, she attended South Plains College in Levelland, Texas, where she studied country music before moving to Nashville to enroll in Belmont University's music business program.

George Strait and Lee Ann Womack. Courtesy Lee Ann Womack.

Much like Strait, Womack's love for traditional Western swing and honky-tonk initially put her at odds with mainstream record executives in Nashville. However, she soon attracted the attention of Bill Anderson, Ricky Skaggs, and other prominent local artists, and in 1996 she signed with Decca Records, where her second single, "The Fool," reached the number two spot on the country charts. Working with Erv Woolsey, George Strait's talented manager, Womack has continued to produce strong material rooted in more traditional swing, ballad, and honky-tonk styles, including her 2000 release of "I Hope You Dance," which became a number one hit and solidified her position within the upper echelons of modern country artists. More recently, Womack has demonstrated her broad appeal outside of mainstream country music by winning a whole new generation of fans through her performances with Cross Canadian Ragweed, Drew Womack, Stoney La Rue, Wade Bowen, Randy Rogers, and a number of other young Americana artists.[107]

Clint Black is another important Texas-based singer whose neotraditionalist style has had an important impact on country music. He was born February 4, 1962, in Long Branch, New Jersey, but grew up in Houston, where some of his biggest influences were George Jones, Merle Haggard, and Lefty Frizzell. Black was struggling as a performer in the Houston area when he met Bill Ham, manager of the legendary Texas blues-rock band ZZ Top. Ham helped Black land a contract with RCA Records, and in 1989 he released *Killin' Time*, one of the most successful debut albums in country music history. *Killin' Time* produced four number-one singles, was certified triple platinum, and helped Black win the Country Music Association's 1989 Horizon Award and 1990 Best Male Vocalist. Beyond the awards and impressive record sales, Black has played an important role in cultivating the same appreciation for traditional Western swing and honky-tonk that George Strait did during the 1980s.[108]

Three other Texas singers who have followed in George Strait's footsteps are Mark Chesnutt, Tracy Byrd, and Tracy Lawrence. Chesnutt was born in Beaumont, Texas, on September 6, 1963, and began performing locally as a teenager. By 1990 he had signed with MCA Records and released the hit "Too Cold at Home," followed by "Brother Jukebox" and other songs that were steeped in the older honky-tonk traditions of Lefty Frizzell, George Jones, and George Strait. Tracy Byrd, born on December 18, 1966, in Vidor, Texas, just a few miles from Beaumont, was strongly influenced by Bob Wills and other Western swing artists. After befriending each other in the Beaumont music scene, Chesnutt helped Byrd secure a record deal with MCA. Although his records have sold well, Byrd chose not to relocate to Nashville and decided instead to remain in Texas, where he feels closer to his musical roots.[109] Tracy Lawrence was born in Atlanta, Texas, on January 27, 1968. His 1991 debut single "Sticks and Stones" quickly reached number one, and he followed this with several other hit singles that earned him some of the most frequent airplay of any country artist during the early 1990s. In recent years Lawrence has begun working more behind the scenes in publishing, production, and management.[110]

Other Texas artists have made important contributions to country music in recent years. Lee Roy Parnell, born in Abilene, Texas, on December 21, 1956, is a multitalented singer, songwriter, and guitarist who has built a successful solo career and performed and recorded with many other popular artists, including Patty Loveless and Mary Chapin Carpenter. Growing up with a wide range of musical influences, including Bob Wills, Freddy King, and Muddy Waters, Parnell is a very skilled traditional country guitarist who is also well known for his bluesy slide guitar work. With several hits on the country charts, he has had his own songs recorded by well-known artists such as Delbert McClinton, Collin Raye, and Sweethearts of the Rodeo.[111]

Le Ann Rimes, much like Tanya Tucker before her, was a child prodigy who took the country music world by storm. Rimes was born in Jackson, Mississippi, on August 28, 1982, but moved with her family to Texas at the age of six. In the

Dallas area she began to attract attention by singing in local stage shows and on television. A Fort Worth DJ named Bill Mack was so impressed with Rimes that he gave her a tune to record, which he had originally written for Patsy Cline. The song, titled "Blue," vaulted Rimes to superstardom at the age of fourteen. Soon she had appeared in movies and on TV, won two Grammys, and sold more than $150 million in records. In addition to her remarkable commercial success, Rimes also came to represent a new generation of artists who seem determined to exercise more control over their own professional careers. After years of disagreements, she sued her father, who had been her manager, in order to nullify earlier management and recording contracts.[112]

The Dixie Chicks are the best-known female country artists to come from Texas in recent years, and they are one of the most critically and commercially successful country acts ever. Although they originally began as the Dixie Chickens in 1989, over the years they changed their name, their image, and some of their personnel. The original members all had bluegrass backgrounds, but they also enjoyed performing retro country music, in which they paid tribute to Dale Evans and other female artists from the past. As they struggled to land a major label contract, they toured extensively and got some of their earliest national exposure at Rod Kennedy's Kerrville Folk Festival in 1990. By 1997 two of the founding members, sisters Martie Erwin, born October 12, 1969, in Dallas, and Emily Erwin, born August 16, 1972, in Dallas, had added Natalie Maines, born October 14, 1974, in Lubbock, and the newly reconstituted group released its first major-label album, *Wide Open Spaces*, on Sony Records. Label executives were skeptical at first when the women insisted on doing their own playing rather than using studio musicians, but their powerful vocals and first-rate instrumental work soon quieted those concerns. Fans loved the band's back-to-basics sound overlaid with tight harmonies, and *Wide Open Spaces* sold more than 11 million copies, making it the best-selling album ever by a country group. The Dixie Chicks went on to release more record-breaking albums, including *Fly* and *Home*, and they won numerous awards throughout the music industry.[113]

The Dixie Chicks proved to be iconoclastic in other ways as well. Beginning with their first major-label release, they had already demanded an unprecedented level of artistic control, and, when their albums began selling at a dizzying pace, the group gained even more leverage within the music industry. As their popularity grew, the Dixie Chicks did not shy away from speaking openly about controversial social issues such as spousal abuse, which they addressed in "Goodbye, Earl," a song about a woman who murders her abusive husband. The band also began promoting feminist themes through T-shirts and souvenirs proclaiming "Chicks

Rule!" and "Chicks Kick Ass!" Their outspokenness ruffled some feathers in the country music world and sparked a flood of controversy in March 2003, when lead singer Natalie Maines announced at a London concert her opposition to the impending U.S. invasion of Iraq. Although many Americans supported her position, others were angered and accused the Dixie Chicks of being unpatriotic. Suddenly the band faced a groundswell of criticism from political conservatives, and some radio networks black-listed the group, although most fans remained steadfastly loyal. As a result of this incident, the band came to symbolize a larger ideological rift between conservatives and liberals within country music and, in fact, throughout the entire music industry. Aside from these political controversies, however, the Dixie Chicks have also come to represent a new generation of female country performers who are rooted in traditional music and rural culture but are urbane and sophisticated in their business dealings and their ability to promote and market themselves and their music.[114]

Today the Southwest is home to an abundance of talented country artists, ranging from hardcore neotraditionalists to singer-songwriters to country rockers. Musicians such as Bruce Robison, Kelly Willis, Charlie Robison, Jack Ingram, James Hand, Dale Watson, Gurf Morlix, Wayne Hancock, Larry Joe Taylor, Alvin Crow, Michael Ballew, Tommy Alverson, the Gourds, Pat Green, Kevin Fowler, Pauline Reese, Randy Rogers, Cory Morrow, Susan Gibson, Shooter Jennings, Rodney Hayden, Roger Creager, Jon Emery, Karen Abrahams, KR Wood, Cross Canadian Ragweed, the Texas Sapphires, Heybale, Rosie Flores, John Arthur Martinez, Mike Blakely, Warren Hood, Dierks Bentley, Stoney LaRue, Bonnie Bishop, Todd Snider, Reckless Kelly, Miranda Lambert, Doug Moreland, Hays Carll, Jason Boland, Emily Gimble, Honeybrowne, Brandon Rhyder, Mickey and the Motorcars, Dub Miller, Wade Bowen, Drew Womack, Django Walker, Erin Condo, Houston Marchman, Sunny Sweeney, Bleu Edmonson, Paula Nelson, Ryan Bingham, and many more continue to represent the broad diversity of influences that have made country music in Texas unique and exceptionally dynamic.[115]

THE SINGER-SONGWRITER TRADITION IN TEXAS

Although songwriting is a vital part of all musical genres, the Southwest has been particularly prolific in producing outstanding songwriters in folk and country music. Texas has a strong tradition of songwriting for a number of reasons. For one thing, most ethnic groups in the Southwest had a relatively low level of literacy until after World War II, so oral folk culture, whether in the form of spoken word or song, was a vital part of articulating family and community history, culture, and values. In addition, the long-standing tradition of cultural cross-pollination in the region allowed early Mexican corridos to flourish alongside the ballads and folk music of newly arriving Anglos, African Americans, Germans, Czechs, French, and others. This helped create a vibrant and dynamic song-writing culture in which virtually all ethnic groups used the rich tradition of storytelling through song in order to relate their history and culture.

Another important factor in the development of a strong song-writing tradition in Texas is the abundance of venues and organizations throughout the state that have nurtured and promoted songwriters and given them a chance to hone their skills and earn a living through their music. A number of clubs and events, including the Kerrville Folk Festival, Cheatham Street Warehouse in San Marcos, Threadgill's, the Cactus Café, and the Old Settlers' Music Festival in Austin, as well as Austin-based Dickson Production's MusicFest, Anderson Fair and the Mucky Duck in Houston, the Humble Time Radio Show in Seguin, Gruene Hall near New Braunfels, John T. Floore's Country Store in Helotes, Poor David's Pub in Dallas, and many more, have helped provide an environment in which songwriters are mentored and given the opportunity to practice their craft before live audiences. In addition, a number of organizations, including the Austin Songwriters Group, the Texas Heritage Songwriters Association, and others, provide support and recognition for the song-writing community.[116]

The tradition of songwriting in the Lone Star State goes back at least as far as 1831, when Mary Holley composed "The Brazos Boat Song," perhaps the first English-language folk tune written in Texas. The first Texas-themed song to achieve national fame was "The Yellow Rose of Texas." Although it is unclear whether it began as an authentic folk song shortly after Texas won its independence in 1836 or was written sometime later and then found its way back into the national folk music repertoire, "The Yellow Rose of Texas" became one of the most popular American folk songs of the nineteenth and twentieth centuries and has appeared in several different versions over the years.[117]

David Guion, born in Ballinger, Texas, on December 15, 1892, was perhaps the state's best-known and most prolific early songwriter and is credited with having penned one of the more popular renditions of "The Yellow Rose of Texas" in 1936. Guion had worked as a cowboy but was also a classically trained musician and composer. By the 1920s he had established an international reputation as a first-rate songwriter who wrote folk and pop tunes, as well as complete ballet and orchestral pieces. Many of his best-known songs were his own original compositions, but some were older tunes that he reworked into contemporary hits, including "The Yellow Rose of Texas," "A Home on the Range," "Turkey in the Straw," "and "Arkansas Traveler."[118]

By the 1930s and 1940s other important songwriters from the Southwest were making their mark on the national music scene. Perhaps the best-known folksinger from the region was Woodrow Wilson "Woody" Guthrie, born in Okemah, Oklahoma, on July 14, 1912. In 1929 Guthrie moved to Pampa, Texas, where he lived with his uncle off and on until 1937 and performed with country dance bands throughout the Texas Panhandle. As the Great Depression and the Dust Bowl of the 1930s drove millions of families from their homes in Texas and Oklahoma, Guthrie began writing more politically oriented songs, including "This Land Is Your Land," that reflected the difficulties many working-class Americans faced. Because of his open criticism of the economic disparity present throughout American society, Guthrie became somewhat of a national spokesman for poor and dispossessed people during the Great Depression. Although he died of Huntington's disease in 1967, Guthrie helped inspire the folk music revival of the 1960s and was a major influence on younger folksingers, including Bob Dylan, Joan Baez, Peter, Paul, and Mary, and countless others.[119]

Cindy Walker may be less well known than Woody Guthrie, but she was another very successful songwriter from the Southwest during the 1940s, 1950s, and 1960s. Walker, who was born July 20, 1918, in Mart, Texas, began writing and performing as a child. While on a trip to Los Angeles with her parents in 1941, she visited Bing Crosby's offices and managed to have him record one of her tunes, "Lone Star Trail." She also befriended Bob Wills's manager, O. W. Mayo, who helped turn several of her songs into Western swing hits, including "Dusty Skies," "Cherokee Maiden," "Miss Molly," "Sugar Moon," and "Bubbles in My Beer." Walker was so grateful to Mayo for his assistance that she signed over authorship of her now-classic tune "Blues for Dixie" as a gift to him. She also wrote numerous hit songs for other performers, including "Warm Red Wine," sung by Ernest Tubb, "You Don't Know Me," recorded by Eddy Arnold, Ray Charles, and Mickey Gilley, "In the Misty Moonlight," popularized by both Jerry Wallace and Dean Martin, and "Dream Baby (How Long Must I Dream?)," recorded by Roy Orbison. Although she was a gifted singer and dancer with the sort of natural beauty and stage presence that could have made her a Hollywood star, Walker chose to remain behind the scenes and focus on her songwriting. A pioneering figure in country music at a time when men dominated most areas of the industry, Walker was the first female to be inducted into the Nashville Songwriters Hall of Fame in 1970.[120]

By the 1960s and 1970s folk music was enjoying a resurgence in popularity, and the Southwest produced its share of artists in this genre as well. Carolyn Hester, born in Waco in 1937, was one of the first folksingers from Texas to achieve national prominence in the 1960s. She performed throughout the country and appeared several times at Rod Kennedy's Kerrville Folk Festival. In fact, Hester's early involvement helped the festival gain crucial momentum and go on to become one of the nation's longest-running and most successful annual songwriter events. Another influential folksinger from the Southwest was John Deutschendorf, who performed under the stage name of John Denver. Denver was born in Roswell, New Mexico, on December 31, 1943, but he lived for years in Fort Worth and attended Texas Tech University in Lubbock. He gained national prominence in the Chad Mitchell Trio during the 1960s before launching a phenomenally successful solo career in the 1970s, during which he sold millions of records, starred in several hit movies, and became involved in numerous social and environmental causes.[121]

Shawn Phillips, a contemporary of Denver, was born March 2, 1943, in Fort Worth. He has appeared in films and on Broadway and has cowritten songs with folk-pop star Donovan. Phillips established himself as a successful solo artist in the early 1970s by blending folk, rock, and jazz with lyrics steeped in Eastern mysticism. Another important songwriter, Bobby Bridger, a Houston-based balladeer, has combined his musical talents, his love for historical folklore, and his skills as a teacher to produce narrative folk songs celebrating historical events and characters from the American West of the late 1800s. Bridger has been a fixture at the Kerrville Folk Festival for many years and even wrote what has become the festival's anthem, "Heal in the Wisdom."[122]

In addition to these more folk-oriented songwriters, Texas has produced a number of influential country songwriters in recent years. One of the most popular, Billy Joe Shaver, was born in Corsicana, Texas (Lefty Frizzell's hometown), on August 16, 1939. Raised mostly by his grandmother, Shaver grew up working in the cotton fields near his home and listening to Bob Wills, Roy Acuff, Homer and Jethro, and Hank Williams. As a child, Shaver was also strongly influenced by the church hymns he heard in the local Nazarene church and by the blues and gospel sung by black neighbors. By the late 1960s he had moved to Nashville, where his gritty song-writing style attracted the attention of several established country singers. One of the first to recognize Shaver's talent was fellow Texan Kris Kristofferson, who included Shaver's "Christian Soldier" on his 1971 album *The Silver Tongued Devil and I*. Within months, others in Nashville had begun recording Shaver's tunes, and in 1973 Waylon Jennings released *Honky Tonk Heroes*, an album made up almost entirely of Shaver's compositions. *Honky Tonk Heroes* eventually went multiplatinum and became one of the landmark recordings of the progressive-outlaw country era. Shaver, whose songs have been recorded by Willie Nelson,

Johnny Cash, Bob Dylan, Patty Loveless, Johnny Rodriguez, Ricky Scaggs, Jerry Jeff Walker, the Allman Brothers, Jerry Lee Lewis, and others, remains very active as a songwriter and performer and has gained an entirely new following among younger Americana songwriters.[123]

Guy Clark, born November 6, 1941, in Monahans, Texas, was a pioneer in the progressive-outlaw song-writing movement of the 1970s and 1980s. Raised by his grandmother in the small West Texas town of Monahans, Clark grew up hearing honky-tonk songs, as well as Mexican folk music. He performed throughout Texas and California before moving to Nashville in 1971, where he quickly earned widespread acclaim for his work. By 1973 Jerry Jeff Walker had hits with two of Clark's songs, "L.A. Freeway" and "Desperadoes Waiting for a Train." In 1975 Johnny Cash recorded "Texas, 1947," and Ricky Skaggs scored a number-one hit in 1982 with "Heartbroke." Like Kristofferson's and Shaver's, Clark's songs are more cerebral and introspective than most country fare, but they are still well grounded in older honky-tonk traditions. Clark, who continues to write and tour internationally, has been a major influence on many younger songwriters in both the folk and country genres.[124]

Another good example of a Texas songwriter who straddled the folk and country genres is Townes Van Zandt. Born in Fort Worth on March 7, 1944, Van Zandt grew up in a well-to-do family but was attracted early on to the music and itinerant lifestyle of Woody Guthrie and other Depression-era folksingers. Van Zandt's struggles with alcohol and drugs, along with a variety of emotional and psychological problems, affected him deeply and provided inspiration for some of his best-known songs, including "Pancho and Lefty," recorded by Merle Haggard and Willie Nelson, and "If I Needed You," recorded by Don Williams and Emmylou Harris. Van Zandt died of a heart attack following hip surgery in 1997, but dozens of other artists, including Guy Clark, Lyle Lovett, Robert Earl Keen, Nancy Griffith, Steve Earle, and Rodney Crowell, cite Van Zandt as one of the single most important influences on their songwriting.[125]

Three of the Southwest's most prolific yet underrecognized country songwriters from the 1960s through the 1990s are Whitey Shafer, Sonny Throckmorton, and Freddy Powers. Shafer, born Sanger D. Shafer on October 24, 1934, in Whitney, Texas, cowrote "That's the Way Love Goes" and "I Never Go around Mirrors," recorded by Lefty Frizzell, Merle Haggard, and Johnny Rodriguez, and he wrote "Does Fort Worth Ever Cross Your Mind" and "All My Exes Live in Texas" for George Strait. Throckmorton, who was born in Carlsbad, New Mexico, on April 2, 1941, grew up in Texas and has lived in Brownwood for years. He penned dozens of hit songs for other artists, including "The Way I Am" and "If We're Not

Townes Van Zandt. Courtesy Susan Roads.

Back in Love by Monday" for Merle Haggard, "It's a Cheatin' Situation" for Moe Bandy, "Why Not Me?" for the Judds, and "The Cowboy Rides Away" for George Strait. Freddy Powers has also written hit songs for George Jones, Merle Haggard, Willie Nelson, and others, including "I Always Get Lucky with You," "Let's Chase Each Other around the Room Tonight," "Silver Eagle," and "Looking for a Place to Fall Apart." In addition to his song-writing skills, Powers is an accomplished swing-jazz guitarist.[126]

Lyle Lovett, born November 1, 1957, in Klein, Texas, represents a new generation of highly successful songwriters from the Southwest. Blending country, folk, blues, jazz, Western swing, and pop into a distinct style that has attracted a huge following worldwide, his lyrics are often quirky and humorous, as in songs such as "Creeps like Me" and "She's No Lady (She's My Wife)." Lovett's 1993 marriage to Hollywood superstar Julia Roberts exposed him to a much larger mainstream audience, but his core following remains the more urbane country music fans who appreciate his eclectic musical tastes and clever lyrical work. One of his most significant long-term contributions has been in helping inspire the newer Americana movement, which is rooted in older country and folk styles but emphasizes the singer-songwriter and the time-honored tradition of storytelling through song.[127]

Robert Earl Keen, born in Houston on January 11, 1956, was a college buddy of Lovett's at Texas A&M University. With a degree in English literature, Keen's approach to songwriting reflects his affinity for honing verses into succinct, hard-hitting story lines. He moved to Nashville for a brief period in the 1980s, but most of the major labels did not consider him commercially viable, so Keen returned to Texas in 1987 and began slowly building his fan base. After years of extensive touring and the release of several critically acclaimed albums, he has developed a large following that ranges from college students to middle-aged professionals. Although Lovett may be better known at the national level, in many ways, Keen has done more to contribute to the rise of the Americana movement since he is more popular among college-aged audiences and therefore is a more direct link between the older generation of songwriters, including Townes Van Zandt, Billy Joe Shaver, Ray Wylie Hubbard, and Guy Clark, and younger Americana artists, such as Pat Green, Cory Morrow, Todd Snider, and Randy Rogers.[128]

Nanci Griffith and Tish Hinojosa are two more artists who have drawn on the rich song-writing traditions of the Southwest to build very successful recording careers. Griffith, born in Seguin, Texas, on July 6, 1953, has worked with Lyle Lovett, Guy Clark, and a host of other Texas singer-songwriters to create her own unique sound, which blends folk, country, blues, bluegrass, and pop. Her songs have been recorded by Bette Midler, Kathy Mattea, and others. Although some record labels have had difficulty categorizing and marketing her, Griffith's record sales have been impressive, earning her three gold and two platinum albums.[129] Tish Hinojosa, born February 6, 1955, in San Antonio, absorbed a broad range of musical influences as a child, including conjunto, country, and pop. She began playing local folk clubs as a teen and then spent time in Taos and Nashville before settling in Austin in the late 1980s. Hinojosa, who has made several critically

Nanci Griffith. Courtesy Susan Roads.

acclaimed albums that blend Mexican American folk music with country, pop, and swing, has also written a number of children's songs, along with a bilingual children's book.[130]

Steve Earle is another powerful singer-songwriter who has addressed a variety of social and political issues through his music. Although Earle's family had lived in Texas for generations, he was born January 19, 1955, in Fort Monroe, Virginia, where his father was temporarily stationed in the U.S. Army. Following his father's discharge, the family returned to the Lone Star State, where Steve would spend his youth. In 1974 Earle moved to Nashville and spent time around Jerry Jeff Walker, Guy Clark, Townes Van Zandt, and other songwriters who were involved in Austin's progressive country scene. During the late 1970s Earle relocated to San Antonio for a short time but soon returned to Nashville. In 1986 he scored big with his album *Guitar Town*, a fresh mix of country, rock & roll, and ballads, which won high praise from critics and catapulted him to national prominence. Although he has not been able to replicate the commercial success he achieved with *Guitar Town*, Earle has remained one of the most-respected and consistently high-quality songwriters in the neo-outlaw country vein.[131]

Two Austin-based groups were responsible for providing some of the most unique and dynamic song-writing talent in Texas during the 1980s and 1990s. Uncle Walt's Band, made up of South Carolinians Walter Hyatt, Deschamp "Champ" Hood, and David Ball, performed a combination of swing, blues, folk, and originals that earned them a large and devoted following, as well as appearances on *Austin City Limits* and at other high-profile venues. Uncle Walt's Band also helped nurture younger artists, including Lyle Lovett, who often performed as the group's opening act before he became a star.[132] The Flatlanders, which includes Joe Ely and Jimmie Dale Gilmore from Amarillo and Butch Hancock from Lubbock, have been a formidable song-writing and performing team for four decades. Although each has had a successful solo career, their work as the Flatlanders, blending folk, country, rock, blues, conjunto, honky-tonk, and Western swing, has brought them widespread critical acclaim and a worldwide fan base.[133]

Songwriter Terry Allen is another long-time West Texas resident whose music has been recorded by the Flatlanders and others. Kimmie Rhodes from Lubbock has performed with Willie Nelson and Emmylou Harris and has had her songs recorded by artists such as Wynonna Judd, Trisha Yearwood, Waylon Jennings, and Peter Frampton. Radney Foster, born in Del Rio, Texas, on July 20, 1959, has built a successful career as a performer and a songwriter and penned hit tunes for Keith Urban, the Dixie Chicks, and others. With a deep understanding of and appreciation for the underlying traditions behind country music, Foster has written history-themed ballads such as "Texas in 1880" and hosted the Country Music Television documentary series *Crossroads*.[134]

Several younger Texas singer-songwriters are following in the footsteps of these veteran artists. Michelle Shocked, born Michelle Johnston on February 24, 1962, in Dallas, was "discovered" by British producer Pete Lawrence at the Kerrville Folk Festival in 1986. Although her recordings for Mercury Records sold well, her controversial social and political views put her at odds with label executives, and she eventually left to release her own independent recordings. James McMurtry, born March 18, 1962, in Fort Worth, is the son of famed Texas author Larry McMurtry. With the same gift for lyrical craftsmanship as his father, James McMurtry has won song-writing competitions at the Kerrville Folk Festival and elsewhere and recorded several critically acclaimed albums.[135]

Joe Ely. Courtesy Susan Roads.

   Terri Hendrix, from San Antonio, got her start performing at open mic nights at Cheatham Street Warehouse in San Marcos while a student at Texas State University. She now tours internationally with legendary sideman and record producer Lloyd Maines, and in 2003 she won a Grammy for cowriting the song "Li'l Jack Slade," recorded by the Dixie Chicks. In addition to achieving success as a musician, Hendrix has helped create a business model for other independent artists to follow by managing her own publishing, public relations, and marketing ventures. Ruthie Foster, from College Station, Texas, is another rising star in the Texas songwriter community. She has combined gospel, folk, blues, and reggae to develop a soulful yet energetic folk style that has won her acclaim at festivals worldwide.[136]

A number of other important songwriters are not originally from Texas but have made their homes there in recent years. Shawn Colvin, born January 10, 1956, in Vermillion, South Dakota, but raised in Illinois, came to Texas in 1976 as the vocalist for a Western swing band known as the Dixie Diesels. After relocating to Los Angeles and New York, she became an internationally popular singer-songwriter, won two Grammys, and performed with Joni Mitchell, Tony Bennet, Lyle Lovett, and others. For the past several years Colvin has made Austin her home and continues to work there and support the local music community. Eliza Gilkyson was born and raised in California, where her father, Terry Gilkyson, a well-established, Los Angeles–based songwriter, involved his children in music at an early age. She lived for a while in New Mexico during the 1970s and 1980s but now resides in Austin. Her critically acclaimed work ranges from romantic ballads to songs that include strong social and political commentary.[137]

Dozens of other talented Texas-based writers, including "Red River Dave" McEnery, Darryl Staedtler, Clay Blaker, Aaron Barker, Tom Russell, Bruce Robison, Blaze Foley, Christine Albert, Chris Gage, Shake Russell, Max Stalling, Bob Schneider, Walt Wilkins, Stephen Bruton, Aaron Allan, Susan Gibson, Alan Shamblin, Darden Smith, Sarah Elizabeth Campbell, Alejandro Escovedo, Trish Murphey,

Terri Hendrix and Lloyd Maines. Courtesy Susan Roads.

Cody Canada of Cross Canadian Ragweed. Photo by Todd Purifoy.

Randy Rogers. Photo by Todd Purifoy.

Jimmie LaFave, Todd Snider, Slaid Cleaves, Karen Poston, Monte Montgomery, Wade Bowen, Guy Forsythe, John Dee Graham, George Ensle, Bill Whitbeck, Kent Finlay, Gregg Andrews, Houston Marchman, Adam Carroll, Cody Canada, Randy Rogers, Stoney La Rue, Jason Boland, Seth James, Colin Gilmore, Mike McClure, Shelley King, Stoney La Rue, Dub Miller, Brandon Rhyder, Ryan Bingham, Brennan Leigh, Django Walker, Wade Bowen, Angie McClure, Colin Brooks, Wendy Colonna, Jordan Minor, Darryl Lee Rush, Carley Wolf, Big John Mills, Darren Kozelsky, Erin Condo, and many others have drawn from a variety of musical influences to help keep the state's song-writing scene vibrant and growing.

Whether folk, Western swing, bluegrass, honky-tonk, progressive, outlaw, crossover, Americana, or another subgenre, country music has been an essential part of the state's musical history, just as Texas has played a vital role in the overall development of American country music.

RECOMMENDED LISTENING

Arthur, Charline, *Welcome to the Club* (Bear Family)

Asleep at the Wheel, *Very Best of Asleep at the Wheel* (Big A Entertainment)

Autry, Gene, *Don't Fence Me In* (Proper) and *Back in the Saddle Again* (ASV)

Brown, Milton, and His Musical Brownies, *Daddy of Western Swing* (Proper)

Clark, Guy, *The Essential Guy Clark* (RCA)

Colvin, Shawn, *Polaroids: A Greatest Hits Collection* (Sony)

The Dixie Chicks, *Wide Open Spaces* and *Home* (Sony)

Ely, Joe, *The Best of Joe Ely* (MCA)

Frizzell, Lefty, *Shine, Shave, Shower (It's Saturday Night)* (Proper)

Gilkyson, Eliza, *Hard Times in Babylon* (Red House)

Griffith, Nanci, *From a Distance: The Very Best of Nanci Griffith* (MCA Nashville)

Hendrix, Terri, *The Ring* (Wilory)

Hofner, Adolph, *South Texas Swing* (Arhoolie)

Horton, Johnny, *Honky Tonk Man: The Essential Johnny Horton, 1956–1960* (Sony)

Hubbard, Ray Wylie, *Snake Farm* (Sustain)

Jennings, Waylon, Willie Nelson, Jessi Colter, and Tompall Glaser, *Wanted! The Outlaws* (RCA)

Jones, George, *Jones, by George!* (Proper) and *Greatest Hits* (Mercury)

Keen, Robert Earl, *The Party Never Ends* (Sugar Hill)

Lovett, Lyle, *Anthology, vol. 1: Cowboy Man* (MCA Nashville)

Mandrell, Barbara, *Ultimate Collection* (Hip-O)

Martínez, John Arthur, *Lone Starry Night* (Dualtone)

Moag, Rod, *Ah-Haa! Goes Grass: A Bluegrass Tribute to Bob Wills* (Tex Tracs)

Mullican, Moon, *Moon's Rock* (Bear Family) and *22 Greatest Hits* (Deluxe)

Nelson, Willie, *Redheaded Stranger* (Sony) and *You Don't Know Me: The Songs of Cindy Walker* (Lost Highway)

Owens, Buck, *The Buck Owens Collection 1959–1990* (Rhino)

Pride, Charley, *The Essential Charley Pride* (RCA)

Ritter, Tex, *Sing, Cowboy, Sing* (Proper)

Rodgers, Jimmie, *The Essential Jimmie Rodgers* (RCA)

Shaver, Billy Joe, *The Earth Rolls On* (New West)

Strait, George, *Strait Out of the Box* (MCA Nashville)

Thompson, Hank, *The Wild Side of Life* (Proper)

Tubb, Ernest, *The Texas Troubadour* (Proper)

Tucker, Tanya, *The Upper 48 Hits, 1972–1997* (Raven)

Uncle Walt's Band, *An American in Texas Revisited* (Sugar Hill)

Various artists, *Doughboys, Playboys, and Cowboys: The Golden Years of Western-Swing* (Proper)

Walker, Jerry Jeff, *Viva Terlingua!* (MCA Nashville)

Wills, Bob, and His Texas Playboys, *Take Me Back to Tulsa* (Proper) and *San Antonio Rose* (Bear Family)

Womack, Lee Ann, *I Hope You Dance* (MCA Nashville)

CHAPTER 7

. . . .

"Groover's Paradise"

Texas Rock & Roll

J ust as it has with virtually all other types of American music, Texas played a vital role in the development of rock & roll by contributing some of the most influential musicians and important innovations to the genre. Artists such as Buddy Holly, Roy Orbison, J. P. "the Big Bopper" Richardson, Bruce Channel, Janis Joplin, Trini López, Doug Sahm, B. J. Thomas, Don Henley, Seals and Crofts, Roky Erickson, Stephen Stills, ZZ Top, Steve Miller, Boz Scaggs, Michael Nesmith, Johnny Winter, Stevie Ray Vaughan, Christopher Cross, and many others have drawn from the diverse musical influences of the Southwest to help shape the evolution of rock & roll.[1]

Rock & roll itself is a remarkable example of the ongoing cross-pollination of musical cultures that has taken place throughout North America over the past three centuries. Rooted in the blues and R&B, rock & roll emerged as a distinct genre in the years following World War II, when a number of black and white musicians, including Chuck Berry, Bill Haley, Elvis Presley, Little Richard, and Buddy Holly, began blending blues, R&B, swing, and other African American traditions with country and pop. At first, some white adults denounced rock & roll as "race music," claiming that it was an example of the "negative" influences of black culture on white teenagers. This type of criticism not only was unfair but also may have backfired by making youngsters only that much more intrigued by this "forbidden" music. Despite the controversy (or perhaps partly because of it), rock & roll eventually became so popular that it dominated mainstream music for nearly six decades and impacted, in at least some way, nearly all other forms of popular music.

Cleveland, Ohio, DJ Alan Freed is sometimes credited with having coined the term "rock & roll" in the 1950s, but variations on the phrase had appeared much earlier. In 1929 Tampa Red's Hokum Jug Band recorded "My Daddy Rocks Me (with One Steady Roll)," an up-tempo blues song that some Western swing bands of the 1930s and 1940s also performed. In 1934 a trio known as the Boswell Sisters recorded a tune titled "Rock & Roll," and by the 1940s and early 1950s Louis Jordan, Wynonie Harris, Johnny Ace, Chuck Berry, Bill Haley, and others were referring to "rocking" and "rolling" in several of their songs, often as a euphemism for sex.[2] Regardless of when and how the term originated, rock & roll was the result of a decades-long blending of different musical styles that included blues, jazz, boogie-woogie, swing, R&B, folk, and country. By the late 1950s rock & roll had become a major musical force that would forever redefine American popular culture.

Like so many previous innovations in music, rock & roll came about largely as a result of sweeping social changes taking place in the United States. In this case, it was the onset of the Cold War between the United States and the Soviet Union during the 1950s that helped unleash a host of political and cultural forces and dramatically altered society as a whole. Although Americans and Soviets had been allies during World War II, when the war ended in 1945, relations between their two countries quickly deteriorated, resulting in a tense standoff in which each side struggled to gain military, political, and economic superiority over the other. As these Cold War tensions escalated throughout the 1950s, many Americans became convinced that the communist-led Soviet government was determined to destroy the United States not only through military force but also by undermining the economic, political, social, and cultural foundations of American society. As a growing anti-Communist paranoia gripped the nation, American citizens found themselves under increasing pressure to demonstrate their unwavering loyalty to the United States. Anyone who refused to conform to a vaguely defined notion of "100 percent Americanism" might be suspected of disloyalty and could be subject to social or political persecution.

For many Americans during the 1950s, this Cold War pressure to conform was stifling, and some began to openly rebel. African Americans in particular were unwilling to continue tolerating the long-standing policies of segregation and racial discrimination that they had endured for decades. Having emerged from World War II with a renewed determination to fight for equal rights and greater social and economic opportunities, blacks simply were no longer willing to accept their prewar status as second-class citizens. In the mid-1950s they launched the modern civil rights movement, which shook the foundations of American society and sparked sweeping social and political changes throughout the nation. American women were another traditionally marginalized group who resisted the pressures of Cold War conformity. Because World War II had given them an opportunity to work outside the home and to gain an unprecedented degree of social and economic independence, millions of women began demanding greater legal and political rights and new opportunities for education and employment as part of the modern women's rights movement of the late twentieth century.

American youth also chafed under the yoke of Cold War conformity. Children born in the 1940s and 1950s were raised in circumstances that were very different from those that their parents had known. These post–World War II baby boomers had experienced neither the Great Depression nor the ravages of global warfare. Instead, they grew up in a more prosperous, urbanized, and technologically sophisticated environment and were generally better educated, more mobile, and more consumer oriented than previous generations. Unable to relate to their parents' seemingly irrational fears of Soviet Communism, American youngsters began to resist the overwhelming pressure to conform and instead embraced rock & roll as an antidote to the passé political and cultural mindset of their parents.

Because this rebellious new music would come to play a prominent role in the momentous social changes of the 1950s and 1960s, rock & roll must be understood as more than simply another genre of American popular music. In the larger context of the times, rock & roll symbolizes the emergence of a new post–World War II youth culture that in some ways was more naïve and self-absorbed than that of earlier generations but in other ways was more worldly, altruistic, and tolerant of other ideas and cultures. Rock & roll also reflects the increasingly prominent role that black music had come to play in mainstream American culture by the second half of the twentieth century. Although some parents may have frowned upon the mixing of black and white cultural traditions as represented by rock & roll, most teenagers seemed willing to look beyond earlier racial boundaries and eagerly embraced this new genre. Of course, one of the great ironies of this commingling of ethnic cultures is that, while many white artists gained fame and fortune through rock & roll, most of the black blues, jazz, boogie-woogie, and R&B musicians who laid the foundation for this new music never received adequate public recognition or financial compensation for their contributions.[3]

One of the towering figures of early rock & roll was not from the Southwest, but Texas did play an important role in his life and his music. Bill Haley was born in Highland Park, Michigan, on July 6, 1925, and raised in Chester, Pennsylvania. A devoted fan of Texas artists such as Gene Autry and Bob Wills, Haley was especially drawn to Western swing, with its eclectic blending of country, jazz, blues, and swing. In the late 1940s he formed several country music bands, including one of his more successful early groups, Bill Haley and the Four Aces of Western Swing. By the 1950s he had taken the jazz, blues, and country roots of Western swing, fused them with pop and R&B, and was well on his way to becoming the first international rock-and-roll star. His 1951 hit, "Rocket 88," was originally an R&B number, but in Haley's hands it took on a new level of energy, foreshadowing the rock-and-roll style that Elvis Presley, Buddy Holly, and others would soon follow. By the mid-1950s Haley had released several other rock-and-roll hits, such as "Crazy, Man, Crazy" (the first rock-and-roll song to make the Billboard pop chart in 1953), "Shake, Rattle, and Roll," "See You Later, Alligator," "Rock This Joint," and "Rock around the Clock." Haley, who had struggled with alcoholism and emotional problems for decades, spent the final years of his life in Harlingen, Texas, where he died on February 9, 1981. Although certainly not from Texas, Haley represents an often-overlooked yet important link between the musical traditions of the Southwest, most notably Western swing, and the early development of rock & roll.[4]

Buddy Holly, born Charles Hardin Holley in Lubbock on September 7, 1936, is undoubtedly the most famous and influential early rock-and-roll musician to come from the Lone Star State. Growing up in the Texas Panhandle, Holly absorbed a variety of musical influences, including Baptist church hymns, black blues, gospel, jazz, and R&B, as well as the Western swing, honky-tonk, bluegrass, and other variations on country music that he heard from local white performers. Holly's idols ranged from Hank Williams Sr. and Lefty Frizzell to gospel singer Mahalia Jackson, and he worked hard to imitate the vocal inflections they sometimes used. This became apparent years later, when Holly developed his trademark singing style, which included stuttering and hiccupping his way through lyrics, often adding extra syllables to words in order to make them fit a particular melody.[5]

In 1953 Holly and his high school pals, Bob Montgomery and Larry Welborn, formed the Western and Bop Band and began playing a regular Sunday afternoon country music show on Lubbock's KDAV radio. By 1956 Holly had become popular enough to land a recording contract with Decca Records. However, the label wanted him to perform as a country singer, and by this time he was moving away from his country roots to focus more on rock & roll. Holly's conversion from country to rock & roll had been under way for a couple of years, but it quickly accelerated after he and his band mates saw Elvis Presley play in Lubbock in 1955. As they witnessed Presley's electrifying performance and saw the dramatic effect it had on an audience of screaming girls, Holly and his musician friends concluded that they were ready to switch from country to rock & roll. Holly soon formed a new band, which he called the Crickets, and in 1957 they traveled to Norman Petty's studio in nearby Clovis, New Mexico, to record several songs. These recordings helped launch Holly on a brief but remarkable career in which he produced rock-and-roll classics such as "That'll Be the Day," "Peggy Sue," "Rave On," "Oh Boy," "Maybe, Baby," "Words of Love," "It's So Easy (to Fall in Love)," "Not Fade Away," "Heartbeat," "It Doesn't Matter Anymore," "Well, All Right," and "Slippin' and Slidin.'"[6]

As Holly skyrocketed onto the national charts, he began a rigorous touring schedule that took him across the country and overseas to Europe. One of his best-known U.S. appearances came in August 1957 at the legendary Apollo Theater in Harlem, New York City. Although the Apollo had booked some white entertainers before, the mostly black audience, which had heard the group only on the radio, was surprised to discover that Holly and the Crickets were white. Despite some initial apprehension from the audience members, Holly and the band quickly won over the crowd with their energetic blending of pop, R&B, country, and blues. As Holly grew more popular throughout the United States, he also began performing in Europe. Holly's early tours of Europe, especially England, were very important because he helped inspire a number of young British musicians, including John Lennon, Paul McCartney, Mick Jagger, Keith Richards, and others, to start their own musical careers.[7]

Tragically, Holly's rapid rise to stardom and the continual pressure to tour contributed to his death in a plane crash at the age of twenty-two. In early 1959 he and several other artists were on a Midwestern tour billed as the "Winter Dance Party." Because the schedule was grueling and the tour bus lacked adequate heating, Holly decided to charter a plane rather than drive from a show in Clear Lake, Iowa, to the next evening's performance in Fargo, North Dakota. Joining him on the small plane were fellow singing stars Ritchie Valens ("La Bamba" and "Donna") and J. P. "the Big Bopper" Richardson ("Chantilly Lace"), along with a relatively inexperienced pilot named Roger Peterson. The aircraft crashed shortly after taking off in a snowstorm around 1:00 A.M. on February 3, 1959, and all four men were killed on impact. Holly's bass player at the time, a young Waylon Jennings, was scheduled to have been on the flight but gave up his seat to Richardson, who was too sick to ride on the tour bus.[8]

Although Holly's professional career lasted only a few years, his effect on the long-term development of rock & roll continues even today. He was a major influence on a number of prominent artists, including Bob Dylan, the Byrds, Bruce Springsteen, and Linda Ronstadt, whose covers of Holly songs such as "It Doesn't Matter Anymore," "That'll Be the Day," and "It's So Easy" helped propel her to pop superstardom during the 1970s and early 1980s. Folksinger Don McLean's 1972 hit, "American Pie," which proclaimed the tragic 1959 plane crash as "the day the music died," was a mournful tribute to Holly but also a celebration of the Lubbock rocker's long-term influence on American culture.[9]

In some ways, Holly's impact on European musicians was even more profound. John Lennon, Paul McCartney, George Harrison, and Ringo Starr all considered him to be one of their biggest musical influences and reportedly chose the name "the Beatles" in part as a tribute to Holly's Crickets. Lennon and McCartney have acknowledged that several of the first songs they penned were inspired by Buddy Holly, and they included his tunes in most of their early performances. According to McCartney, the Beatles' very first recording, made in a Liverpool studio, was Holly's classic "That'll Be the Day." Not only did the Beatles count among their earliest hits the Holly tune "Words of Love," but McCartney also considered the Texas singer's music so influential that he bought the entire Buddy Holly song catalog when it became available for purchase in the 1970s.[10]

Other young British musicians idolized Holly and worked to emulate his singing, songwriting, and guitar playing. Mick Jagger and Keith Richards of the Rolling Stones have both acknowledged Holly's effect on them. In fact, the first record the Rolling Stones ever released in the United States was their 1964 rendition of Holly's "Not Fade Away." As a teenager, blues rocker Eric Clapton also admired Holly and went on to perform and record several of his tunes. Graham Nash, who later became part of the folk-rock supergroup Crosby, Stills, and Nash, was so fond of Holly that he named one of his first bands, the Hollies, after the Lubbock singer. The Hollies eventually recorded a tribute album titled *Buddy Holly*, which included sixteen of Holly's songs.[11]

J. P. "the Big Bopper" Richardson, who perished alongside Holly in the plane crash, was another significant figure in early Texas rock & roll and pop. Born Jiles Perry Richardson on October 24, 1930, in Sabine Pass, Texas, he grew up listening to and playing mainly country music. As a teenager, he began working as a DJ on KTRM in Beaumont and in 1955 became the radio station's program director, taking the nickname "the Big Bopper." In 1957 Richardson signed as a country singer with Houston record producer Pappy Daily, but, much like Buddy Holly, Richardson's musical interests were shifting away from country and more toward rock & roll. As a result, he began working with producer Shelby Singleton and in 1958 released the number-one hit "Chantilly Lace." Richardson followed this with "Little Red Riding Hood," which also became a hit in the United States and Great Britain. Ironically, it was his growing popularity that earned him a spot on the ill-fated "Winter Dance Party" tour, in which he, Buddy Holly, and Ritchie Valens were killed. Despite Richardson's tragic death, his influence continued posthumously. "Chantilly Lace" became a rock-and-roll classic, recorded by Jerry Lee Lewis and others, and Richardson's song "Running Bear" became a number-one hit in 1960 for another Texas singer, Johnny Preston.[12]

Johnny Preston, born John Preston Courville in Port Arthur, Texas, on August 18, 1930, started performing in choir and drama groups in high school and college. While attending Lamar Tech (Lamar Institute of Technology) in Beaumont, he joined an R&B band that played throughout the Texas Gulf Coast region. In 1958 Preston met the Big Bopper, who invited him to record one of Richardson's own compositions, "Running Bear." Although Preston was less than impressed with the tune, he recorded it anyway, and "Running Bear" eventually became an international hit. Preston, who followed this with other moderately successful hits, continues to tour throughout North America and Europe.[13]

Second only to Buddy Holly, Roy Orbison is the best-known and most influential early Texas rock & roller. Born April 23, 1936, in Vernon, Texas, Orbison was plagued with poor eyesight from childhood, but he loved music and learned to sing and play guitar from his father. Like so many other white youngsters in the Southwest during the 1930s and 1940s, Orbison was surrounded by the Western swing and honky-tonk music that dominated the airwaves. However, he was also strongly influenced by the pop, R&B, zydeco, classical, and Mexican American music he heard on the family radio. Orbison started his musical career at the age of eight, when he performed in an amateur music show on KVWC radio in Vernon. In 1946 his family relocated to the West Texas oil town of Wink, some forty miles west of Odessa. There Orbison formed a country band called the Wink Westerners, which played throughout the area. After high school, he enrolled at North Texas State College (now the University of North Texas) in Denton, where he met fellow student and future pop idol, Pat Boone. Inspired in part by Boone's budding musical career, Orbison dropped out of college, returned to West Texas, and began leading a new rock-and-roll band, the Teen Kings.[14]

Orbison soon left Texas for Tennessee, where he enjoyed considerably better success as a rock-and-roll musician than he had as a country singer. In 1956 he recorded his first hit, "Ooby Dooby," for Sun Records in Memphis, making him part of Sam Phillips's legendary stable of young artists, which included Elvis Presley, Johnny Cash, Jerry Lee Lewis, and Carl Perkins. Although he recorded a few other tunes for Phillips, Orbison's rather high-pitched, plaintive singing style never truly

Roy Orbison and Charline Arthur. Courtesy David Dennard, Dragon Street Records.

fit the rockabilly sound that Sun Records was promoting, so he eventually moved on to Nashville to focus on songwriting. In 1958 Orbison's tune "Claudette," written for his wife, became a hit for the Everly Brothers and earned him a reputation as a promising young songwriter. He continued to hone his songwriting skills and in 1960 recorded his now classic "Only the Lonely," which helped make him an international star. Over the next several years Orbison produced a string of hits, including "Running Scared," "Dream Baby (How Long Must I Dream?)," "Crying," "In Dreams," "Blue Bayou," "Pretty Paper," "It's Over," and "Oh, Pretty Woman," many of which would be recorded again by future generations of artists.[15]

Orbison, whom Elvis Presley reportedly called "the greatest singer in the world," was a major influence on a number of other musicians and became an important force in blending pop, country, and other styles into rock & roll. In the early 1960s he helped promote relatively unknown acts such as the Beatles, the Rolling Stones, and the Beach Boys, who opened for Orbison on his European,

American, and Australian tours. When the Beatles debuted on BBC Radio in 1962, they sang Orbison's "Dream Baby (How Long Must I Dream?)," which was written by fellow Texan Cindy Walker. Rock superstar Bruce Springsteen has remarked that, as a child, listening to Orbison's soaring falsetto and haunting melodies inspired him to try his hand at singing and songwriting. Although Orbison had fallen into relative obscurity by the late 1960s, his career enjoyed a resurgence in the late 1970s and early 1980s, when Linda Ronstadt, Van Halen, Elvis Costello, the Eagles, Bonnie Raitt, Jackson Brown, Bruce Springsteen, Emmylou Harris, and Tom Petty began performing and recording Orbison's material in tribute to the singer. In 1988 Orbison's career received another boost when he joined George Harrison, Bob Dylan, Tom Petty, and Jeff Lynne to form the supergroup the Traveling Wilburys, which released several hits, including "It's Alright" and "You Got It." Orbison died of a heart attack in 1988, but his legacy in rock & roll and pop music is still evident, as others continue to record his songs and acknowledge his profound influence on American music.[16]

Although less well known, other Texas artists also were helping shape rock & roll and pop during the 1950s and 1960s. Buddy Knox, born July 20, 1933, near Happy, Texas, began performing publicly as a student at West Texas State College (now West Texas A&M University) in Canyon. In 1955 he saw Elvis Presley perform in Amarillo on the same tour of Texas that inspired the young Buddy Holly just down the road in Lubbock. Soon after seeing Presley, Knox took his own band, the Orchids, to Norman Petty's studio in Clovis, New Mexico, and cut an original tune—"(Come Along and Be My) Party Doll"—which became a number-one hit in 1957. Renamed Buddy Knox and the Rhythm Orchids by a record executive who mistakenly thought they were black, Knox and his group released several more hit records, toured internationally, and appeared on the *Ed Sullivan Show*. Trini López, born May 15, 1937, in Dallas, scored several big hits in the mid-1960s, including "Lemon Tree" and "If I Had a Hammer." He also appeared on popular television shows and in major motion pictures such as *The Dirty Dozen* and *Marriage on the Rocks*. Born on August 7, 1942, in Hugo, Oklahoma, but raised in Rosenberg, Texas, B. J. Thomas began his recording career in Houston with producer Huey Meaux. From the mid-1960s through the early 1980s Thomas won six Grammys and released a long string of country, pop, and gospel hits, including "Hooked on a Feeling," "I Just Can't Help Believing," and "Raindrops Keep Falling on My Head," the Academy Award–winning theme song for the Paul Newman and Robert Redford movie *Butch Cassidy and the Sundance Kid*.[17]

Bobby Day, born Robert Byrd in Fort Worth, Texas, on July 1, 1930, had a number two hit in 1958 with "Rockin' Robin," an up-tempo pop tune. In 1972

Michael Jackson and the Jackson Five released their version of the song, and once again it reached number two on the pop charts. Ray Peterson, born April 23, 1939, in Denton, Texas, had a Top Ten hit in 1960 with "Tell Laura I Love Her." Bruce Channel, from Grapevine, Texas, had the 1962 hit "Hey, Baby," on which a young Delbert McClinton from Lubbock played harmonica. Apparently it was McClinton's harmonica riff that inspired John Lennon's memorable harmonica lead on the early Beatles' song "Love Me Do." As the duo Paul and Paula, Ray Hildebrand of Joshua, Texas, and Jill Jackson of McCamey, Texas, had the 1963 million-seller "Hey, Paula." Bobby Fuller, born October 22, 1943, in Goose Creek, Texas, moved with his family to El Paso at the age of fourteen. There he formed the Bobby Fuller Four, which eventually relocated to Los Angeles, where it had a Top Ten hit with "I Fought the Law," a song Fuller had written and recorded years earlier in El Paso.[18]

Two other Texas musicians who enjoyed great success in the 1950s only to re-emerge as even bigger stars in the 1970s were James Seals, born in Sidney, Texas, on October 17, 1941, and Dash Crofts, born in Cisco, Texas, on August 14, 1940. As teenagers, they began playing with a Los Angeles–based group, the Champs, which scored a number-one hit in 1958 with the Latin-flavored instrumental "Tequila." The song was repopularized during the 1980s in comedian Pee Wee Herman's movie *Pee Wee's Big Adventure*. In the early 1970s Seals and Crofts began working as a folk-pop duo and released several multimillion-selling records, including "Hummingbird," "Summer Breeze," "Diamond Girl," and "We May Never Pass This Way Again."[19]

By the mid-1960s American rock & roll began to change dramatically, in large part due to the so-called British Invasion, in which a number of English rock-and-roll bands came to dominate the U.S. pop charts. The British Invasion got its start on February 9, 1964, when the Beatles, who were already very popular throughout Europe, performed for the first time on the *Ed Sullivan Show* before a live television audience of some 73 million American viewers. The response was immediate and overwhelming. "Beatlemania" soon swept the nation, and dozens of British rock-and-roll bands, including the Rolling Stones, the Animals, the Hollies, Herman's Hermits, the Dave Clark Five, and others, began arriving in the United States.[20]

Hoping to capitalize on the sudden popularity of these English groups, many American musicians began to copy their sound, look, and in some cases even their accents. The British Invasion's tremendous impact on American popular music is ironic, of course, because virtually every one of these English rockers had grown up listening to American pop, country, blues, and R&B and had worked for years to emulate their favorite American musicians, including Muddy Waters, Howlin'

Seals and Crofts, 1972. Courtesy Burton Wilson.

Wolf, B. B. King, Bill Haley, Elvis Presley, Buddy Holly, and Roy Orbison. With the British Invasion of the mid-1960s, these English bands were now bringing their own interpretation of American music back to the United States, where it would forever change the nation's popular culture.

The British Invasion certainly affected Texas rock-and-roll bands. Not only did many of them exchange their 1950s-era pompadour haircuts for the new "mop top" style popularized by the Beatles and the Rolling Stones, but they also traded in the softer pop-rock sounds of Bill Haley, Buddy Holly, Roy Orbison, and others for the louder, harder-edged rock & roll played by many of the popular English groups. However, despite their attempts to copy these British musicians, in some ways Texas rock-and-roll bands still reflected the distinct ethnic influences of the Southwest.

One example of the unique Texas-flavored rock & roll that developed during this period is Dallas-born Domingo "Sam" Samudio and his group, Sam the Sham and the Pharaohs. The Pharaohs had one of the best-selling pop songs of the 1960s, "Wooly Bully," which was an unusual blend of conjunto, rock, and pop. "Wooly Bully" began with a Spanish-English count-off of "uno, dos, one, two, tres, quatro" and then launched into a pulsing keyboard, bass, and drum rhythm that was patterned after the traditional conjunto accordion and bajo sexto beat. With its bilingual lyrics, its Latin-based rhythm, and its British rock overtones, "Wooly Bully" was an exotic mix of musical influences from Europe and the Southwest that reached number two on the *Billboard* pop charts and placed this Texas band firmly in the international spotlight. Another group, known as ? and the Mysterians, which included members from both Texas and Mexico, had a number-one hit in 1966 with the pop-rock song "96 Tears." Similar to "Wooly Bully," "96 Tears" had a driving keyboard backbeat that was reminiscent of the traditional conjunto accordion and bajo sexto rhythm but also featured guitars and vocals that were influenced by rock & roll. Although ? and the Mysterians disbanded in 1968, "96 Tears" resurfaced as a hit again in the 1980s, when it became the signature song for Tex-Mex punk rocker Joe "King" Carrasco.[21]

Doug Sahm is one of the best examples of how Texas musicians of the 1960s absorbed certain aspects of the British Invasion but still remained rooted in the musical traditions of the Southwest. Born on November 6, 1941, in San Antonio, Sahm was probably the most original and eclectic of all the rock-and-roll musicians to come from the Lone Star State during the mid-1960s. A true child prodigy, Sahm was performing on the radio by the age of eight and demonstrating his proficiency on the steel guitar, fiddle, and mandolin. As a teenager, he frequented area nightclubs and often sat in with a variety of blues, country, conjunto, jazz, and rock-and-roll groups.[22]

Sahm owed much of his diverse musical tastes to his upbringing in San Antonio, where he was exposed to a remarkable array of musical influences in his youth. In fact, San Antonio is an outstanding example of the importance of place in shaping people's cultural sensibilities. The Alamo City had always been an ethnically diverse community, beginning with the first Spanish settlers in the 1700s and continuing through the 1800s, as large numbers of Anglos, Irish, Germans, French, Czechs, African Americans, and others arrived. Because of its remarkable ethnic mixture, San Antonio was far less rigidly segregated than most other Southern cities in the 1950s, and it became the first major urban area in the South to desegregate its public school system following the Supreme Court's 1954 ruling in *Brown vs. Board of Education of Topeka*. Many of the city's musical venues were also fully integrated and welcomed musicians and patrons from all racial backgrounds, allowing them to mingle freely and exchange musical ideas and traditions. As a result, Sahm and his childhood friends grew up in a social and cultural environment that encouraged musical cross-pollination, and they eagerly absorbed the country, conjunto, blues, jazz, R&B, German polkas, and early rock & roll that filled the dance halls and airwaves throughout South Texas.[23]

In 1964 Sahm formed the Sir Douglas Quintet with his longtime friend Augie Meyers. Working with Houston record producer Huey Meaux, the group released "She's about a Mover" in 1965, which reached the Top Fifteen in both the U.S. and UK pop charts. Hoping to capitalize on the popularity of the British Invasion, Meaux apparently selected the name Sir Douglas Quintet because it sounded "English," and he encouraged Sahm and the others to wear the "mod" clothing and hairstyles of their British counterparts. They may have looked much like the popular British bands of the day (despite the fact that two members of Sahm's group were Mexican American), but the Sir Douglas Quintet's music clearly reflected the band's eclectic Texas-based musical background. Their most popular songs—"She's about a Mover," "Mendocino," and "Dynamite Woman"—featured Meyers's energetic keyboard rhythm that echoed the conjunto accordion and bajo sexto sound, along with Sahm's vocals, which mixed country twang with blues, R&B, and rock influences. By the early 1970s the group had disbanded, but Sahm and Meyers continued to travel back and forth between Texas and California, performing with a variety of musicians, recording songs such as "Texas Me" and "Groover's Paradise," and forging a distinct sound that blended honky-tonk, blues, conjunto, Western swing, R&B, and rock & roll. In the late 1980s their unique and eclectic style would form the foundation for their most successful band, the Grammy Award–winning Texas Tornados, which toured throughout the world during the 1990s until Sahm's death in 1999.[24]

Doug Sahm and Augie Meyers were only two of many Texans who spent time on the West Coast during the mid- to late-1960s. As the epicenter of the hippie counterculture movement, California became a popular destination for numerous young musicians looking to escape the socially and politically conservative climate of the Southwest.[25] Houston's Kenny Rogers, discussed earlier in the chapter on country music, helped form the Los Angeles–based folk group the First Edition in 1967. By early 1968 the band had a number-five hit with "Just Dropped In (to See What Condition My Condition Was In)," a folk-rock song that included veiled references to drug use. The First Edition followed this with several other popular records, including "But You Know I Love You," "Ruby, Don't Take Your Love to Town," "Something's Burning," and "Ruben James," before splitting up in 1974. Rogers continued to work in the folk-rock field until the mid-1970s, when he transformed himself into one of the most commercially successful country artists in history.[26]

Doug Sahm, 1973. Courtesy Burton Wilson.

Without a doubt, the most prominent female rock-and-roll artist ever to come from Texas was Janis Joplin. Born in Port Arthur, on January 19, 1943, Joplin grew up in a comfortable, middle-class family in which her musically gifted mother taught her to play piano. However, Joplin felt constrained by the socially conservative atmosphere in which she was raised and started rebelling at an early age. As a teenager, she began listening to blues and jazz and spent much of her time with a group of high school friends who read the "beat" poetry of Jack Kerouac and frequented the blues, country, zydeco, and Cajun nightclubs scattered along the back roads of East Texas and Southwest Louisiana.[27]

In 1962 Joplin moved to Austin to study art at the University of Texas. There she spent time with other artists and musicians, including Powell St. John, Lanny Wiggins, Juli Paul, and Tary Owens, at a west campus apartment complex affectionately dubbed "the Ghetto." Joplin soon joined St. John and Wiggins to form a band called the Waller Creek Boys, which played folk, country, and blues throughout Austin. Apparently Joplin had no real ambitions at the time to become a professional singer and joined the group mainly "for free beer." However, playing the autoharp and singing folk music with friends helped her develop the self-confidence she would later need to perform before thousands of fans worldwide. One venue in which Joplin truly seemed to flourish as a musician during these early years was Kenneth Threadgill's bar, a converted gas station on North Lamar Boulevard in Austin, where country music fans and college student "folkies" gathered to play songs and drink beer. Because Threadgill welcomed a diverse audience and a variety of musical styles, his club was the ideal environment in which Joplin could develop her vocal skills and stage presence while experimenting with both blues and folk music. Threadgill, himself a singer and yodeler in the style of Jimmie Rodgers, took a special interest in Joplin and gave her guidance and encouragement during this early stage of her career.[28]

After about a year in Austin, Joplin hitchhiked to California, drawn by stories of a more open and progressive music scene on the West Coast. While in San Francisco, she quickly earned a reputation as a promising young singer, although she also became more deeply involved with alcohol and drugs. Joplin returned to Texas in 1965 and began to attract increasing attention around Austin for her unique singing style. Unlike Joan Baez, Judy Collins, Carolyn Hester, and most other female folksingers of the day, Joplin sang in a husky, sometimes bellowing voice, more akin to her blues idols, Big Mama Thornton and Bessie Smith. Although some folk music fans did not care for Joplin's sound, those who were more attuned to blues, R&B, and rock & roll were immediately drawn to her raw and highly emotive style.[29]

In 1966 Joplin returned to San Francisco to front an up-and-coming rock band, Big Brother and the Holding Company. By this time San Francisco had become a mecca for the burgeoning hippie counterculture movement, and Joplin quickly transformed from a folk-blues singer into the premiere female vocalist of the late 1960s' psychedelic rock scene. Big Brother and the Holding Company got its first major break at the 1967 Monterey Pop Festival, where Joplin's blistering vocal performance astonished the crowd and earned the band a recording contract with Columbia Records. Word soon spread about this remarkable young white woman who not only could belt out blues as well as most any black singer but also had a dynamic energy and commanding stage presence that rivaled the most popular male rock stars of the era.[30]

In 1968 Big Brother and the Holding Company recorded the album *Cheap Thrills*, which featured Joplin's powerful, bluesy vocals on tunes such as "Piece of My Heart," "Ball and Chain" (written by Big Mama Thornton), and a soulful yet psychedelic version of the George Gershwin classic "Summertime." Because of her soaring popularity, Columbia Records sidelined the band and began promoting Joplin herself as one of the label's hottest new artists. Over the next two years she worked with other groups, including the Kozmic Blues Band and the Full Tilt Boogie Band, and soon attained the same rock superstar status as Jimi Hendrix and Jim Morrison. Unfortunately, like Hendrix and Morrison, her involvement in drugs and alcohol also led to her early death. While working on her new album, *Pearl*, Joplin died of a heroin overdose in her Los Angeles hotel room on October 4, 1970. *Pearl* was completed from available tracks, and it quickly reached number one on the *Billboard* charts, where it remained for nine weeks. One song from the album, "Me and Bobby McGee," written by her friend and fellow Texan Kris Kristofferson, became the single biggest hit of Joplin's career.[31]

Although Joplin played a vital role in popularizing psychedelic rock, she was fundamentally a blues singer who drew from the traditions of greats such as Bessie Smith, Big Mama Thornton, and Lead Belly. Perhaps without even realizing it, Joplin helped anchor the psychedelic rock of the late 1960s in the earlier blues bedrock of the 1940s and 1950s.[32] In addition to helping bridge older and newer musical traditions, she was also a pioneer for women in the world of rock music. Even though she apparently never considered herself a feminist per se, Joplin clearly served as a progressive role model for millions of women. Although Janis suffered from insecurity and low self-esteem her entire life, her public persona was tough, assertive, and well outside the norm of what many Americans in the late 1960s considered "appropriately feminine." At a time when women still did not have legal, political, and economic equality with men, Joplin was very outspoken about sexuality, drugs, racism, politics, and other controversial issues. Because of her tremendous commercial success and willingness to defy conventional attitudes toward femininity, Joplin also helped break down barriers for other women to succeed on their own terms in the music business.[33]

It is worth considering just how much "place" influenced the direction Joplin took in her personal life and professional career. Growing up in a relatively small Texas town during the 1950s, Joplin endured, with considerable frustration, the overwhelmingly conservative social and political atmosphere that prevailed within the local community, and she began to openly rebel at an early age. Very much against her parents' wishes, she relocated first to Austin and then to the West Coast to try to find the personal freedom and professional fulfillment that had always eluded her in Port Arthur. Although the social limitations of Joplin's hometown may have stifled her and others of her age and background, the local musical environment was rich, and the blues, R&B, zydeco, Cajun, country, and rock & roll that surrounded her unquestionably helped shape her musical sensibilities. It is also quite possible that the conservative social and political environment in which she was raised only made Joplin that much more determined to overcome the barriers she later faced as a woman in the male-dominated world of rock & roll. Although Joplin may have escaped her hometown in order to fulfill her dreams as a performer, the assorted musical traditions from which she began drawing at an early age, along with the particular social challenges she faced, clearly helped lay the foundation for her future development on both a personal and a professional level.

Another important Texan of the psychedelic rock era, and someone with whom Janis Joplin performed in Austin, was Roky Erickson. Erickson, born in Dallas on July 15, 1947, played piano and guitar as a child but later dropped out of high school to become a full-time musician. In 1965 he joined Tommy Hall in the Austin-based band, the 13th Floor Elevators, arguably the Southwest's most influential psychedelic rock band of the late 1960s. While so many other Texas performers, including Joplin, left for the West Coast, the Elevators remained in Austin as the standard bearers for psychedelic rock in the Lone Star State. In 1966 they recorded Erickson's "You're Gonna Miss Me," which not only was a regional hit at the time but also resurfaced during the 1970s as a staple of early Texas punk rock bands. The Elevators released other records as well, including their 1967 album, *The Psychedelic Sounds of the 13th Floor Elevators*, which has become somewhat of a cult classic. As their popularity grew and they toured more extensively throughout the Southwest, the band's reputation for illegal drug use led to repeated encounters with the authorities and several arrests. Erickson spent time in jail, as well as in mental hospitals, but he returned to music in the early 1970s to write protopunk songs such as "Red Temple Prayer (Two-headed Dog)" and "I Walked with a Zombie." Even though he never enjoyed great commercial success, Erickson had a significant impact on other musicians in Texas and elsewhere. During the 1990s several artists, including R.E.M., ZZ Top, Charlie Sexton, the Butthole Surfers, and others recorded tributes to Erickson, acknowledging his impact on their musical careers.[34]

In a somewhat different vein, Michael Nesmith, born December 30, 1942, in Houston and raised in Farmers Branch, outside of Dallas, emerged as one of the most important pop-rock artists of the late 1960s. Nesmith had been playing in folk-country bands since his early twenties and already had substantial performing and recording experience when, in 1965, he joined a newly formed Los Angeles–based band known as the Monkees. The television producers who created the Monkees envisioned the group as America's answer to the Beatles and hoped to capitalize on the British Invasion sweeping the country during the mid-1960s. Because they were far more concerned with the Monkees' looks than their musical abilities, TV executives hired four attractive young men who, with the exception of Nesmith, had very little musical experience. At first, professional songwriters wrote most of the band's material, and studio musicians recorded everything but the vocal tracks. This "packaging" of the Monkees proved tremendously successful in terms of record sales and product marketing, but Nesmith and the others quickly grew frustrated with the artistic limitations placed on them. By 1967 Nesmith had begun writing more of the group's songs, and he insisted that he and the other members be allowed to perform their own instrumental tracks. The Monkees, who for a time were nearly as popular as the Beatles and the Rolling Stones, broke up in 1969, but Nesmith went on to build a successful career as a songwriter and producer of movies, records, and videos.[35]

Stephen Stills, born in Dallas on January 3, 1945, became one of the most prominent figures in the West Coast folk-rock movement of the late 1960s and early 1970s. Like Nesmith, Stills had also auditioned for the Monkees in 1965. Even though he did not get the job, Stills remained in the Los Angeles area and continued to work with other local musicians, including Canadian-born Neil Young. In 1966 Stills and Young formed the group Buffalo Springfield, whose song "For What It's Worth" was one of the first anti–Vietnam War anthems to become a pop hit. Buffalo Springfield disbanded in 1968, so Stills joined David Crosby, formerly of the Byrds, and Graham Nash, from the British group the Hollies, to form the trio Crosby, Stills, and Nash. Their new group continued the country-rock-flavored sound that Buffalo Springfield had helped pioneer and added rich, multilayered harmonies that soon became the band's trademark. Their stunning performance at the 1969 Woodstock festival in upstate New York helped make Crosby, Stills, and Nash one of the most critically and commercially successful folk-rock bands of the time. Neil Young joined the band after the release of its first album but worked only sporadically with the group over the following years. Their folk-country-rock sound, along with their tightly structured harmonies, provided a model for many other West Coast bands, including the Eagles. Stills, who built a successful solo career with hits such as the 1971 "Love the One You're With," occasionally reunites with his former band mates for concert appearances.[36]

Drummer and vocalist Don Henley, born in Gilmer, Texas, on July 22, 1947, was a founding member of the Eagles, the most influential of all the 1970s' West Coast bands and one of the most popular rock groups in history. Henley was raised in Linden, northeast of Gilmer, where he formed several bands, including Felicity and later Shiloh, with childhood friend Richard Bowden, who would go on to play with Linda Ronstadt and others. In 1969 Shiloh relocated to Los Angeles to try to break into the West Coast music scene. There Henley met and began working with

Felicity, 1976. Don Henley, Joey Brown, Richard Bowden, and Jerry Surrat, L. to R.
Courtesy Joey Brown.

Detroit native Glenn Frey. In 1970 Henley and Frey, along with Bernie Leadon and Randy Meisner, served as Linda Ronstadt's backup band on her album *Silk Purse*. By 1971 Henley, Frey, Leadon, and Meisner had formed the Eagles and began recording for Asylum Records. In keeping with their country-rock roots and the emerging West Coast sound, the Eagles combined folk, rock, and country influences with tight harmonies and sophisticated musical arrangements to produce a string of hits that placed them firmly at the top of the 1970s' West Coast country-rock genre. After the Eagles disbanded in 1980 Don Henley went on to have the most critically and commercially successful career of any of the group's former members, releasing several best-selling albums and becoming active in a variety of political and environmental causes. Born in Detroit but raised in Amarillo, Texas, J. D. Souther also played an important role in the early success of the Eagles. Not only was he part of the larger circle of West Coast musicians from which the Eagles emerged, but he also helped write some of the group's biggest hit songs.[37]

Steve Miller, a very popular blues, pop, and rock-and-roll artist of the 1970s and 1980s, was born October 5, 1943, in Milwaukee, Wisconsin, although his family moved to Dallas when he was seven years old. In Texas Miller was first exposed to T-Bone Walker and other blues, R&B, country, and rock-and-roll musicians who would help shape his musical tastes. By the time he was a teenager, Miller had begun forming bands with his Dallas-area friends, including Boz Scaggs, and he started building a loyal following throughout the Southwest with his pop-oriented blues-rock sound. After moving to the West Coast in the late 1960s, Miller began recording for Capitol Records, and in 1973 he released his breakthrough album, The Joker, which vaulted him to the top of the charts. He followed this with several more hit records, including "Space Cowboy," "Living in the U.S.A.," "Fly like an Eagle," "Jet Airliner," and "Abracadabra," which made him one of the most commercially successful pop-rock artists of the 1970s.[38] Miller's close friend William Royce "Boz" Scaggs was born in Ohio on June 8, 1944, but also grew up in Dallas, where he and Miller played music together in high school. During the 1970s Scaggs built a successful career of his own, melding jazz, pop, and disco into his 1976 multimillion-selling album Silk Degrees.[39]

Sylvester "Sly" Stone of Sly and the Family Stone was another Dallas-area musician who helped shape the 1970s' pop-rock scene. Stone was born in Dallas on March 15, 1944, and grew up listening to black gospel, blues, and soul. By the late 1960s he was blending these influences with R&B and rock & roll to help define the newly emerging funk sound. The racially mixed Sly and the Family Stone band, which included several Stone family members, produced a number of hits throughout the late 1960s and 1970s, including "Dance to the Music," "Everyday People," "Hot Fun in the Summertime," "Family Affair," and "Thank You Falletinme Be Mice Elf Again," all of which combined pop, R&B, soul, funk, and rock & roll.[40]

Another influential Texas musician of the 1960s and 1970s was Johnny Winter, who was born February 23, 1944, in Leland, Mississippi, but was raised in Beaumont, Texas, next to Janis Joplin's home town of Port Arthur. Winter's first love was the blues, and he worked hard to emulate his heroes, including Elmore James, Muddy Waters, and B. B. King, but he also infused R&B and rock-and-roll

Tommy Shannon, John Turner, Johnny Winter, 1968. Courtesy Burton Wilson.

sounds into his repertoire. By 1968 Winter had earned a national reputation as one of the hottest young blues-rock guitarists around and was offered an exceptionally generous recording contract with Columbia Records. Because of his remarkable guitar-playing skills, dynamic stage presence, and efforts at bringing the electric guitar to the forefront in rock & roll, Johnny Winter has been compared to 1960s' guitar legend Jimi Hendrix. Similar to Hendrix, Winter was essentially a blues guitarist, although his greatest commercial success came in the rock arena. Winter has remained deeply involved in blues music over the years, working with blues pioneers such as Muddy Waters and producing Waters's 1977 Grammy-winning album *Hard Again*. Johnny Winter's younger brother, Edgar Winter, born in Beaumont on December 28, 1946, played with Johnny frequently in the early days but went on to make his mark with his own band, the Edgar Winter Group, which earned several gold records during the 1970s.[41]

Other Texas musicians also played a significant role in the evolution of rock & roll from the 1960s well into the 1980s. One of the most critically and commercially successful rock-and-roll bands to emerge from Texas during the 1970s was ZZ Top, a group whose music and image clearly reflected its roots in the unique cultural environment of the Southwest. Billy Gibbons, ZZ Top's founder and lead guitarist, was born in Houston on September 16, 1949. The son of a professional musician, he was exposed early on to a wide range of musical traditions, including blues and R&B, from the many black entertainers who performed throughout the Houston area. As a teenager during the mid-1960s, Gibbons was also influenced by the British Invasion, and his high school band, the Coachmen, worked to emulate the look and sound of the English groups that dominated the airwaves at the time. By the late 1960s, as psychedelic rock became more popular, Gibbons formed a new band, the Moving Sidewalks, which featured his hard-driving guitar work, dramatic stage shows, and pyrotechnic displays.[42]

By 1969 Gibbons had hooked up with the talented and ambitious manager Bill Ham, and the pair began assembling the current version of ZZ Top. The two first recruited drummer Frank Beard, born June 11, 1949, in Frankston, Texas, and then bassist Joe Michael "Dusty" Hill, born May 19, 1949, in Dallas. Gibbons, Beard, and Hill had all known each other from previous bands and shared a common vision of building a blues-rock-boogie trio that was rootsier than most other contemporary rock bands and also reflected a distinctive Southwestern identity. In 1970 the

ZZ Top at Armadillo World Headquarters, 1970. Courtesy Burton Wilson.

group debuted with ZZ Top's First Album, which featured its Texas boogie style, a combination of traditional blues, boogie-woogie, and hard-driving rock that the trio delivered with more punch than many bands twice the size. The band's next three albums, Rio Grande Mud, Tres Hombres, and Fandango! produced several hits that covered themes ranging from Texas bordellos to Mexican border culture. In 1976 the group launched "ZZ Top's Worldwide Texas Tour," which sold out venues across North America, Europe, Australia, and Japan. With a long-standing interest in theatrical production and with an obvious pride in their home state, the band took along on its tour a Texas-shaped stage and Lone Star props such as cacti and live cattle. This emphasis on showmanship served the band well over the coming years. Because they were already adept at integrating strong visual imagery into their performances, the group easily adapted to the emergence of MTV in the early 1980s. The group's often lavish costumes, outrageous stage sets, and trademark long, white beards quickly secured their status among the new MTV generation as icons of roots-based blues and rock. With a long list of classic rock hits such as "La Grange," "Tush," "Sharp Dressed Man," and "Cheap Sunglasses," ZZ Top continues to sell out shows and attract fans from all ages and backgrounds.[43]

Several other Texas artists have had successful careers in rock music over the decades. Marvin Lee Aday, better known as "Meatloaf," was born in Dallas on September 27, 1947. His Bat Out of Hell album, released in 1977, was one of the best-selling rock albums of the 1980s. Meatloaf also worked in theater for several years and gained fame as the leather-jacketed biker, Eddie, in the cult movie classic The Rocky Horror Picture Show. Christopher Cross, born Christopher Geppert in San Antonio on May 3, 1951, had a brief but impressive career in the early 1980s. His first album, Christopher Cross, released in 1980, produced four top-twenty hits, including "Sailing" and "Ride like the Wind," and its sales reached quadruple platinum, a remarkable feat for a debut recording. In addition to his commercial success, Cross received critical acclaim for the album, which won five Grammys, including Record of the Year, Album of the Year, and Song of the Year. Cross followed this with other hits, including "Think of Laura" and "Arthur's Theme (the Best That You Can Do)," from the popular Dudley Moore movie Arthur.[44]

Other notable rock musicians from the Lone Star State include guitarists Ian Moore, who has recorded with Carole King, Cat Stevens, and others, and Charlie Sexton, who has worked with Bob Dylan, Don Henley, and the Rolling Stones. Pantera, from Arlington, Texas, transformed from a glam rock band in the 1970s to a popular heavy metal band whose 1994 album, Far beyond Driven, debuted on the Billboard charts at number one. Joe "King" Carrasco, born Joseph Teutsch in

Dumas, Texas, gained an international following in the 1980s and 1990s by merging rock & roll, conjunto, and punk into something he called "nuevo wavo." British-born Ian McLagan, who has worked with Rod Stewart, the Rolling Stones, Bob Dylan, Bruce Springsteen, and others, has lived in Austin for years and performed with a number of local musicians. The Butthole Surfers, formed in San Antonio in 1981, was another popular band that bridged the late punk era with early grunge and developed a national reputation for lewd lyrics and outlandish stage shows. Edie Brickell and the New Bohemians, formed in 1985, got their start playing in the newly restored nightclubs of Dallas's Deep Ellum, the same neighborhood that had once been a thriving and vibrant center for African American music during the early twentieth century. The New Bohemians played a blend of folk, jazz, pop, and rock, and their 1988 debut album, *Shooting Rubberbands at the Stars*, yielded the pop hit "What I Am." Although the band broke up in 1991, Brickell continued as a solo artist and married singer-songwriter Paul Simon, who coproduced her first album. Lisa Loeb, another popular Dallas-born singer, had a number-one hit in 1994 with "Stay" and was featured on the groundbreaking 1997 Lilith Fair tour.[45]

One of the most critically acclaimed and commercially successful Texas-based artists to emerge on the popular music scene in recent years is Norah Jones. Born Geetali Norah Jones Shankar in New York City on March 30, 1979, she moved with her mother to Dallas at the age of four. Norah's father, the well-known Indian sitar player, Ravi Shankar, had already built his own successful solo career, performing with the Beatles and other popular entertainers during the 1960s and 1970s. As a child, Jones started taking piano lessons and singing in church choirs in the Dallas area. She attended the Booker T. Washington High School for the Performing and Visual Arts in Dallas, as well as the University of North Texas in Denton, where she majored in jazz piano. After relocating to New York City, Jones began performing with a variety of jazz and pop artists. Her 2002 debut album, *Come Away with Me*, which combined jazz, pop, country, and soul, reached number one on the *Billboard* Top 200 and won eight Grammy Awards. Jones continues to release hit records, including her 2005 Grammy-winning "Here We Go Again" duet with Ray Charles. She tours internationally and is currently pursuing a part-time acting career.[46]

In a variety of ways, Texas musicians have played an exceptional role in the long-term development of pop and rock & roll. Spanning a remarkable range of styles, these artists represent the culmination of many years of the cross-cultural blending of musical traditions throughout the Southwest.

RECOMMENDED LISTENING

The Big Bopper, *The Best of the Big Bopper* (Universal/Spectrum)

Brickell, Edie, and the New Bohemians, *Ultimate Collection* (Hip-O)

Carrasco, Joe King, *Border Town/Viva San Antone/Bandido Rock* (Last Call)

Cross, Christopher, *The Very Best of Christopher Cross* (Rhino)

Eagles, The, *The Eagles* (Asylum)

Haley, Bill, *The Best of Bill Haley and His Comets, 1951–1954* (Varese Sarabande)

Henley, Don, *Actual Miles: Henley's Greatest Hits* (Geffen)

Holly, Buddy, *A Rock & roll Collection* (MCA)

Jones, Nora, *Come Away with Me* (Blue Note)

Joplin, Janis, *Cheap Thrills and Pearl* (Columbia)

Miller, Steve, *Fly like an Eagle: 30th Anniversary* (Capitol)

Nesmith, Michael, *Magnetic South/Loose Salute* (BMG International)

Orbison, Roy, *The Essential Roy Orbison* (Sony)

Sahm, Doug, *The Best of Doug Sahm and Friends* (Rhino) and *The Best of Doug Sahm and the Sir Douglas Quintet, 1968–1975* (Mercury/Universal)

Seals and Crofts, *Greatest Hits* (Warner Brothers)

Sly and the Family Stone, *The Essential Sly and the Family Stone* (Sony)

Stills, Stephen, *Stephen Stills* (Atlantic)

Thirteenth Floor Elevators, *The Psychedelic Sounds of the 13th Floor Elevators* (Varese Sarabande)

Winter, Edgar, *The Best of Edgar Winter* (Sony)

Winter, Johnny, *The Best of Johnny Winter* (Sony)

ZZ Top, *Rancho Texicano: The Very Best of ZZ Top* (Rhino)

Conclusion

The musical history of Texas and the American Southwest is a broad and complex topic that deserves further study on many different levels. With a wide variety of genres and subgenres, including Native American, gospel, blues, ragtime, jazz, rhythm and blues, conjunto, Tejano, Cajun, zydeco, Western swing, honky-tonk, polkas, schottisches, folk, pop, rock & roll, rap, hip-hop, and many others, Texas music is a living testament to the distinct historical and cultural environment of the Southwest.

A number of important factors have made Texas special in terms of "place" and contributed to the state's unique musical development. In addition to the region's history, geography, climate, demographics, economics, and politics, it is the tremendous ethnic diversity of the Southwest, perhaps more than anything else, that makes Texas music so distinct and multifaceted. For centuries, this area has served as a crossroads for a broad range of ethnic groups whose cultures have mixed and mingled in ways not seen anywhere else. The result has been a remarkable cross-pollination of Spanish, Mexican, African, Caribbean, English, Irish, French, Jewish, German, Czech, Polish, and other influences into a vibrant mosaic of musical traditions.

In many ways, the changes that have taken place in Texas music over the years mirror the larger historical transformation of the American Southwest. The early blending of Indian and Spanish cultures, along with the central role music has played for Mexican Americans, has made música tejana a clear reflection of the complex internal dynamics of the Texas Mexican community as it sought to reconcile its dual identity as both Mexican and American. Likewise, the music of Texas blacks represents the unique situation in which they found themselves, straddling the more rigidly segregated social structure of the Deep South and the somewhat more open and ethnically diverse setting of the Southwest. Of course, music has been essential to all other ethnic groups in the region as well. Germans and Czechs established hundreds of dance halls, singing societies, and local community bands as a way to preserve their cultural heritage. Cajuns celebrated their musical traditions through events such as the *fais dodo*, and Anglo Texans have made music part of their everyday lives in a number of ways from church services to barn dances. For all of these groups, music was both a link to their past and a bridge to the future as they struggled to assimilate into more mainstream society without becoming completely disconnected from their ancestral roots. In this complex and often difficult process of assimilation, music became a principal means through which Texans of all ethnic backgrounds articulated their own sense of identity and left their cultural imprints on the state.

In part because of the region's diverse and dynamic cultural environment, Texas has produced an extraordinary number of influential musicians, and it has had a significant impact on a variety of developments throughout American music. In addition to contributing luminary figures such as the "father of ragtime," Scott Joplin, blues pioneers Blind Lemon Jefferson, Lead Belly, Sippie Wallace, T-Bone Walker, and Lightnin' Hopkins, country music favorites Tex Ritter, Dale Evans, Gene Autry, Bob Wills, Ernest Tubb, George Jones, Willie Nelson, Waylon Jennings, Kenny Rogers, Tanya Tucker, and George Strait, pianist Van Cliburn, jazz legends Charlie Christian and Ornette Coleman, conjunto and Tejano artists Lydia Mendoza, Flaco Jiménez, Emilio Navaira, and Selena Quintanilla, and rock & roll stars Buddy Holly, Roy Orbison, Janis Joplin, ZZ Top, Stephen Stills, and Don Henley, the Southwest has played a crucial role in the long-term evolution of a number of musical genres.

Blind Lemon Jefferson, Sippie Wallace, Lightnin' Hopkins, Stevie Ray Vaughan, and many other Texans blended older African American traditions with newer influences to reshape blues, R&B, country, and rock & roll. As the most popular composer and performer of the ragtime era, Scott Joplin helped lay the foundation for the emergence of jazz in the early twentieth century. Charlie Christian, Eddie Durham, Ornette Coleman, and numerous other Texas artists built on Joplin's earlier work to further develop jazz and help carry it to new audiences worldwide. Lydia Mendoza, Flaco Jiménez, Selena Quintanilla, and many other Tejanos have popularized Latino music throughout North America, mixing older Spanish and Mexican musical traditions with blues, country, rock & roll, jazz, rap, hip-hop, and other styles. As home to thousands of French-speaking blacks and whites, Texas has also been vital to the development of Cajun and zydeco music. Harry Choates, raised in Port Arthur, Texas, introduced Cajun music to the entire country during the 1940s and helped awaken a national interest in Cajun history and culture. Zydeco giant Clifton Chenier tapped into the rich English-French-African musical traditions found in East Texas and southwest Louisiana to forge the modern zydeco sound that now enjoys a global following.

Texans have played leading roles in the stylistic and commercial development of country music as well. Beginning with Vernon Dalhart, Eck Robertson, and Carl T. Sprague in the 1920s and continuing into the 1930s, 1940s, and 1950s, Lone Star artists such as Tex Ritter, Gene Autry, Milton Brown, Bob Wills, Cindy Walker, Ernest Tubb, Lefty Frizzell, Floyd Tillman, Hank Thompson, and George Jones combined traditional fiddle music, cowboys songs, blues, jazz, mariachi, and other styles to help mold Western swing, honky-tonk, and pop country. From the 1960s through the present, Texas musicians such as Willie Nelson, Waylon Jennings, Kris Kristofferson, Guy Clark, Billy Joe Shaver, Barbara Mandrell, Johnny Rodríguez, Tanya Tucker, George Strait, Lee Ann Womack, Robert Earl Keen, Lyle Lovett, the Dixie Chicks, Clint Black, LeAnn Rimes, Cross Canadian Ragweed, Pat Green, Randy Rogers, Kevin Fowler, and Cory Morrow, continue to reshape country music through subgenres such as progressive, outlaw, pop, neotraditional, Americana, and country rock.

The Southwest has also been instrumental in the evolution of musical recording, broadcasting, and marketing. In so doing, Texas has played a key part in changing the very sound of modern American music and in helping make it popular world-wide. Because it was a favorite destination for major record labels seeking "race" musicians during the 1920s and 1930s, the state provided a number of Mexican American and African American artists, including Blind Lemon Jefferson, Lydia Mendoza, and Lead Belly, whose success helped convince record companies to more aggressively promote other ethnic styles, such as blues, gospel, jazz, R&B, conjunto, rancheras, and cumbias.

Because of the work of John and Alan Lomax, Jack Thorp, William Owens, and others, Texas also took a leading role in the development of noncommercial recording and in the preservation and study of regional folk music. As pioneering musicologists of the 1930s and 1940s, the Lomaxes and others traversed the South and Southwest documenting dozens of local performers whose music might otherwise have been lost. This attempt to preserve the state's distinct musical heritage has continued over the years. Due to the efforts of institutions such as the University of Texas, the Institute of Texan Cultures, Texas State University, Texas Tech University, the Texas State Historical Association, the Texas Historical Commission, the Smithsonian Institute, and others, a wealth of recordings, photographs, and archival information related to the history of Texas music has been collected and made available to researchers.

In addition to the many contributions it has made to the development of recording, the Southwest has also had an important impact on the evolution of radio broadcasting in North America. In particular, the proliferation of border radio stations along the Texas Mexican border from the 1930s through the 1950s revolutionized American broadcasting and helped advance the careers of numerous musicians and others in the music industry. Since they were subject to very little government regulation, these border radio stations created an innovative broadcasting format that allowed a more colorful and sometimes controversial mix of music, news, and advertising, which many stations still follow today.

Throughout the twentieth and into the twenty-first centuries, Texas has continued to play a leading role in the music industry and music education. Not only has the state been home to a number of independent and major record labels and recording studios, but it also hosts a variety of notable musical events, including Austin City Limits and the Kerrville Folk Festival, both internationally recognized venues that help promote veteran artists and up-and-coming performers. Through the efforts of the Texas Music Office, the Center for Texas Music History, Texas Folklife Resources, the Center for American History, the Bob Bullock Texas State History Museum, the Texas Heritage Music Foundation, the Texas Music Project, the Texas Music Museum, and a variety of public and private organizations that promote music education and music-related businesses, Texans from all walks of life are taking an active part in the preservation, study, and celebration of the state's unique musical heritage.

At the same time that we recognize the distinct musical environment that has existed for years in the Lone Star State, we must also acknowledge that Texas music has evolved within the larger cultural context of the Southwest and is closely connected to other forms of regional music throughout North America and around the world. As a result, Texas owes a good deal of its rich musical heritage to its neighbors, New Mexico, Oklahoma, Arkansas, Louisiana, and Mexico.

Moreover, the significance of music to the state's history goes well beyond simply contributing a long list of prominent performers and notable innovations to the nation's musical development. Music has also been very important in the daily lives of "ordinary" Texans as well. As a vital part of the cultural vocabulary of the Southwest, music has been one of the region's most democratic means of expressing emotions, communicating culture, sharing information, and articulating a sense of collective identity within families, groups, or communities. In a part of the country that has historically had relatively low literacy rates and where substantial segments of the population have had limited access to other avenues of public expression, music has provided a way for Texans from all walks of life to communicate information, address concerns, and negotiate their positions within society. Because music has been and continues to be a universally accessible and highly adaptable form of cultural expression, we can gain valuable insight into the long-term development of various ethnic groups throughout Texas by studying their musical evolution as they struggled to reconcile their internal conflicts while interacting with others around them.

While considering the impact of music on the development of ethnic groups in the Southwest, it is helpful to examine the ways in which music originates and evolves within human societies. The organic versus superorganic paradigm is useful in this regard since it allows us to better understand how certain types of music arise rather organically from the grassroots level of local communities, while others are created primarily to generate monetary profit or some other type of material compensation. By taking into account the organic and inorganic characteristics of regional culture, this analytical model helps explain how factors such as race, ethnicity, language, economics, and politics have influenced the development of Texas music over the years.

However, it is also important to keep in mind that organic and superorganic music frequently overlap in many areas. Examples of this are evident throughout the Southwest. For instance, the balladeers who traveled among Texas Mexican border communities during the late nineteenth and early twentieth centuries fulfilled an organic function by providing news and information to a relatively isolated and illiterate population, but they also performed as a way to earn money, food, and shelter, thereby using their music for commercial purposes as well. Likewise, Western swing musicians of the 1930s had a genuine affection for the jazz, blues, pop, mariachi, and other styles that they incorporated into their own country music repertoire, but they also understood that this musical diversity made them more marketable to radio audiences during the lean years of the Great Depression.

In a variety of ways, music has always been a vital part of the story of Texas, helping to both shape and reflect the state's rich and colorful history. This history has been guided in large part by the Lone Star State's unique position at the center of the larger cultural crossroads of the American Southwest. Because it is unique in terms of place, Texas has been a crucible of sorts, in which a number of ethnic groups have intermingled and borrowed from each other's musical traditions to reshape their own. Over the centuries, as musicians throughout the Southwest absorbed these diverse influences, they not only redefined the culture of their individual ethnic communities but also altered the long-term musical development of the nation and the entire world.

Notes

* * * * * * * * * * * * * * * * * *

PREFACE

1. The first published study of Texas music was Lota M. Spell's *Music in Texas: A Survey of One Aspect of Cultural Progress*. Years later, Texas-born Columbia University English professor William A. Owens published *Tell Me a Story, Sing Me a Song: A Texas Chronicle*, which is an examination of the folk music of different ethnic communities in the Southwest based on his travels in the region during the 1930s and 1940s. Both of these books are good early attempts at documenting the state's musical culture, but they are now rather outdated.

2. For example, several good publications offer important information on specific topics within this subject. *The Roots of Texas Music*, ed. Lawrence Clayton and Joe Specht, includes a broad collection of essays that address various aspects of Texas music history, although the period it covers extends only up to the mid-twentieth century. *The Handbook of Texas Music*, ed. Roy Barkley et al., is a very useful reference encyclopedia that covers all of the genres of Texas and Southwestern music history. *The Journal of Texas Music History* also features articles on a variety of topics in Texas music history. Larry Willoughby's *Texas Rhythm, Texas Rhyme: A Pictorial History of Texas Music* provides a good, brief introduction to many of the state's most notable musicians and musical genres. Rick Koster's *Texas Music* offers an overview of several genres of Texas music, but it is not a scholarly work and does not always provide adequately researched or documented information.

3. See, for example, Manuel Peña, *Música Tejana: The Cultural Economy of Artistic Transformation*; Guadalupe San Miguel Jr., *Tejano Proud: Tex-Mex Music in the Twentieth Century*; *Puro Conjunto: An Album in Words and Pictures*, ed. Juan Tejeda and Avelardo Valdez; Alan B. Govenar and Jay F. Brakefield, *Deep Ellum and Central Track: Where the Black and White Worlds of Dallas Converged*; Dave Oliphant, *Texan Jazz*; and Roger Wood, *Texas Zydeco*.

4. For the most complete listing of both published and unpublished works related to Texas music history, see the Center for Texas Music History's website (www.txstate.edu/ctmh).

5. For a discussion of the hybridization of ethnic minority cultures within the context of mainstream culture see Roger Wood, "Black Creoles and the Evolution of Zydeco in Southeast Texas: The Beginnings to 1950," p. 195, and David Lloyd, "Adulteration and the Nation: Monologic Nationalism and the Colonial Hybrid," especially pp. 79–82.

CHAPTER 1

1. For a good discussion of some of the popular perceptions regarding Texas music, see Bill C. Malone, "Texas Myth/Texas Music," *Journal of Texas Music History*, 1, no. 1

(Spring 2001): 4–11. Some of the best recorded examples of these many genres of Texas and Southwestern music are available through Arhoolie Records (www.arhoolie.com).

2. Two good sources of information on progressive country are Jan Reid, *The Improbable Rise of Redneck Rock*, and Cory Lock, "Counterculture Cowboys: Progressive Texas Country of the 1970s and 1980s," pp. 14–23.

3. Paul M. Lucko, "Harry Choates," in Barkley et al., *Handbook of Texas Music*, pp. 49–50; Michael Corcoran, *All Over the Map: True Heroes of Texas Music*, pp. 6–9.

4. Paul Oliver, "Clifton Chenier," in H. Wiley Hitchcock and Stanley Sadie, *The New Grove Dictionary of American Music*, vol. 1, p. 414; Roger Wood, "Southeast Texas: Hothouse of Zydeco," *Journal of Texas Music History* 1, no. 2 (Fall 2001): 23–44.

5. Gary Hickinbotham, "A History of the Texas Recording Industry," *Journal of Texas Music History* 4, no. 1 (Spring 2004): 18–32; Bill Wyman, *Blues Odyssey: A Journey to Music's Heart and Soul*, pp. 88–89, 118–19, 174–77, 254–57; Glenn Appell and David Hemphill, *American Popular Music: A Multicultural History*, pp. 40–41, 132–35.

6. For a discussion of Jefferson's recording career, including an examination of some recently discovered recordings, see Luigi Monge and David Evans, "New Songs of Blind Lemon Jefferson," *Journal of Texas Music History* 3, no. 2 (Fall 2003): 8–28.

7. Benjamin Filene, "Our Singing Country: John and Alan Lomax, Leadbelly, and the Construction of the American Past," *American Quarterly* 43, no. 4 (Dec., 1991): 602–24. For more on the life and career of John Lomax's son, Alan, see Ronald D. Cohen, ed., *Alan Lomax: Selected Writings, 1934–1997*.

8. The most complete examination of the border radio phenomenon is the informative and entertaining *Border Radio: Quacks, Yodelers, Pitchmen, Psychics, and Other Amazing Broadcasters of the American Airwaves*, by Gene Fowler and Bill Crawford.

9. See www.governor.state.tx.us/divisions/music; for more on Texas music outside of the United States, see Gary Hartman, "Texas Music in Europe," *Journal of Texas Music History* 4, no. 1 (Spring 2004): 33–41. For the past twenty years, the Festival Country Rendezvous in Craponne-sur-Arzon, France, one of the largest music festivals in Europe, has consistently featured a number of Texas artists in its lineup. For more information, see perso.orange.fr/country.rendez-vous.festival/english.html.

10. Bill C. Malone, *Country Music, U.S.A.*, 2d rev. ed., p. 152.

11. Jesús F. de la Teja, Paula Marks, and Ron Tyler, *Texas: Crossroads of North America*, pp. 7–14.

12. Randolph B. Campbell, *Gone to Texas: A History of the Lone Star State*, pp. 26–32; Cathryn A. Hoyt, "Riches, Religion, and Politics: Early Exploration in Texas," in *Hispanic Texas: A Historical Guide*, ed. Helen Simons and Cathryn A. Hoyt, pp. 13–16.

13. Rupert N. Richardson, Adrian Anderson, Cary D. Wintz, and Ernest Wallace, *Texas: The Lone Star State*, pp. 25–36.

14. See Teja, Marks, and Tyler, *Texas*, 156–217; Campbell, *Gone to Texas*, pp. 106–110. On May 7, 1824, Mexico united the two provinces of Coahuila and Tejas into the single province of Coahuila y Tejas. Since this allowed the more populous state of Coahuila to politically and economically dominate the less populous state of Tejas, most of the

Tejanos and Anglo Texans opposed the move. Their resentment helped set the stage for declaring Texas independence from Mexico in 1836.

15. *The History of Texas*, by Robert A. Calvert and Arnoldo De León, p. 80; Richardson, *Texas*, p. 170; Campbell, *Gone to Texas*, pp. 207–209. The Institute of Texan Cultures at the University of Texas–San Antonio has produced a series of booklets that offer a brief overview of the major ethnic groups that have lived in Texas during the past two centuries.

16. See Teja, Marks, and Tyler, *Texas*, pp. 290–390; Calvert and De León, *History of Texas*, pp. 330–31.

17. *Rand McNally: The Road Atlas of the United States, Canada, and Mexico*, 2002, pp. 96–101. Information is also available at www.randmcnally.com.

18. Campbell, *Gone to Texas*, p. 470.

19. For a broad overview of several important issues in the field of ethnomusicology, see Martin Stokes, "Introduction: Ethnicity, Identity, and Music," in *Ethnicity, Identity, and Music: The Musical Construction of Place*, ed. Martin Stokes, pp. 1–27; Ronald Radano and Philip V. Bohlman, eds., *Music and the Racial Imagination*, pp. 7–10; Kay Kaufman Shelemay, ed., *The Garland Library of Readings in Ethnomusicology*, vol. 1, History, Definitions, and Scope of Ethnomusicology, especially pp. 351–58; Charlotte J. Frisbie, ed., *Explorations in Ethnomusicology: Essays in Honor of David P. McAllester*, pp. 35–44; Kip Lornell and Anne K. Rasmussen, eds., *Musics of Multicultural America: A Study of Twelve Musical Communities*, pp. 16–19; Ron Eyerman and Andrew Jamison, *Music and Social Movements: Mobilizing Traditions in the Twentieth Century*, pp. 6–8, 27–31, 38–41.

20. Kenneth L. Stewart and Arnoldo De León, "Literacy among *Immigrantes* in Texas, 1850–1900," *Latin American Research Review* 20, no. 3 (1985): 180–87; Gary Hartman, "From Yellow Roses to Dixie Chicks: Women and Gender in Texas Music History," in John Storey and Mary Kelly, eds., *Twentieth-century Texas: A Social and Cultural History*; John Koegel, "Crossing Borders: Mexicana, Tejana, and Chicana Musicians in the United States and Mexico," in *From Tejano to Tango: Latin American Popular Music*, ed. Walter Aaron Clark, pp. 97–125; Lomax, *Land Where the Blues Began*, pp. 43–49; Mary A. Bufwack and Robert K. Oermann, *Finding Her Voice: Women in Country Music, 1800–2000*, pp. 92–105.

21. Eyerman, *Music and Social Movements*, pp. 160–63; Cordelia Chávez Candelaria, "*Différance* and the Discourse of 'Community' in Writings by and about the Ethnic Other(s)," in Alfred Arteaga, ed., *An Other Tongue: Nation and Ethnicity in the Linguistic Borderlands*, pp. 185–202, examines the way in which the concept of "community" is represented in literature and popular culture. For a good introduction to the concept of "tribalism" as part of human behavior, see Desmond Morris's classic book *The Naked Ape*.

22. Anne J. Blood and Robert J. Zatorre, "Intensely Pleasurable Responses to Music Correlate with Activity in Brain Regions Implicated in Reward and Emotion," Montreal Neurological Institute, McGill University, Montreal, Quebec, Canada, H3A 2B4 (www.pnas.org/cgi/doi/10.1073/pnas.191355898).

23. Peña, *Música Tejana*, pp. 3–7; San Miguel, *Tejano Proud*, pp. 3–4.

24. Avelardo Valdez and Jeffrey A. Halley, "The Popular in *Conjunto Tejano* Music: Changes in Chicano Class and Identity," in Tejeda and Valdez, *Puro Conjunto*, pp. 199–

201, discuss the organic relationship between performers and audience; Peña, *Música Tejana*, pp. 6–11.

25. For more on medieval troubadours see Elizabeth Aubrey, *The Music of the Troubadours*. For a good discussion of Texas Mexican folksongs and the variety of themes they include, see Américo Paredes, *A Texas-Mexican Cancionero: Folksongs of the Lower Border*. For a more recent look at the importance of the storytelling tradition in Texas music see Kathleen Hudson, *Telling Stories, Writing Songs*.

26. Malone, *Country Music, U.S.A.*, pp. 6–7; Clayton W. Henderson, "Minstrelsy," in Hitchcock and Sadie, *New Grove Dictionary of American Music*, vol. 3, pp. 245–47; Dale Cockrell, "Nineteenth-century Popular Music," in Nicholls, *Cambridge History of American Music*, pp. 165–75. For a good example of how popular Foster's songs remain today, see the Grammy Award–winning tribute CD "Beautiful Dreamer: The Songs of Stephen Foster," produced by American Roots Publishing, Nashville, 2004.

27. For a variety of viewpoints, both positive and negative, regarding rap, see Jared Green, ed., *Rap and Hip Hop: Examining Pop Culture*.

CHAPTER 2

1. Bruno Nettl, Charlotte Heth, and Gertrude Prokosch Kurath, "American Indians," in Hitchcock and Sadie, *New Grove Dictionary of American Music*, vol. 2, pp. 460–79; Lindsay Levine, "American Indian Music, Past and Present," in Nicholls, *Cambridge History of American Music*, pp. 3–29; Appell and Hemphill, *American Popular Music*, pp. 216–29; Frisbie, *Explorations in Ethnomusicology*, pp. 111–26. One of several Native American gatherings occurs in Austin each year. For more information, see www.austinpowwow.org.

2. Solveig A. Turpin, "Native American Music," in Barkley et al., *Handbook of Texas Music*, pp. 225–27; David La Vere, *Life among the Texas Indians: The W.P.A. Narratives*, pp. 4–11; Calvert and De León, *History of Texas*, pp. 3–6.

3. Cecile Elkins Carter, *Caddo Indians: Where We Come From*, pp. 101–24; Thomas F. Schilz, *Lipan Apaches in Texas*, pp. 19–39; Jonathan B. Hook, *The Alabama-Coushatta Indians*, pp. 82–98; "Our Native Spirit" (booklet published by the Texas Music Museum, Austin, 1998), p. 3.

4. Reginald and Gladys Laubin, *Indian Dances of North America: Their Importance to Indian Life*; La Vere, *Life among the Texas Indians*, pp. 131–39.

5. Nettl, Heth, and Kurath, "American Indians," pp. 469–70; Turpin, "Native American Music," pp. 225–28.

6. "Our Native Spirit," p. 4.

7. Carter, *Caddo Indians*, pp. 36–37, 196–98; Turpin, "Native American Music," p. 227.

8. Campbell, *Gone to Texas*, p. 15; Teja, Marks, and Tyler, *Texas*, pp. 55–56.

9. Kevin Mulroy, *Freedom on the Border: The Seminole Maroons in Florida, the Indian Territory, Coahuila, and Texas*, pp. 22–23, 105, 177–79; "Our Native Spirit," p. 3.

10. Nettl, Heth, and Kurath, "American Indians," pp. 471–72; Mildred P. Mayhall, *The Kiowas*, pp. 114, 312–13.

11. Maria F. Wade, *The Native Americans of the Texas Edwards Plateau, 1582–1799*, pp. 196–97; Dianna Everett, *The Texas Cherokees: A People between Two Fires, 1819–1840*, p. 54.

12. Nettl, Heth, and Kurath, "American Indians," pp. 477–78; Turpin, "Native American Music," p. 228. For a good discussion of how the matachines dance represents extensive cross-pollination among Indian and European cultures in the Southwest, see Brenda M. Romero, "Cultural Interaction in New Mexico as Illustrated in the Matachines," in Lornell and Rasmussen, *Musics of Multicultural America*, pp. 155–85.

13. "Our Native Spirit," pp. 8–10; Turpin, "Native American Music," pp. 225, 228.

14. Hook, *Alabama-Coushatta Indians*, pp. 104–107; "Our Native Spirit," pp. 9–11. See also Levine, "American Indian Music, Past and Present." For more information on Native Americans and their musical heritage, visit the following websites: www.isjunction. com/places/indians.htm, www.texasindians.com, and www.indians.org.

15. See www.austinpowwow.org and www.savae.org.

CHAPTER 3

1. Some of the best documentary films on música Tejana have been made by Austin-based director Hector Galán, including *Songs of the Homeland* (1995), *Accordion Dreams* (2001), *Tish Hinojosa: My Heart, My Life* (2005), and *Los Lonely Boys: Cottonfields and Crossroads* (2006). All are available from Hector Galán Productions (www galaninc.com).

2. Ramiro Burr, *The Billboard Guide to Tejano and Regional Mexican Music*, pp. 10–12; Peña, *Música Tejana*, p. xi; Daniel Sheehy, "Mexican Mariachi Music: Made in the U.S.A.," in Lornell and Rasmussen, *Musics of Multicultural America*, pp. 131–54. For a broader overview of Texas Mexican culture see the following: Simons and Hoyt, *Hispanic Texas*; Texas Music Museum, "Música Tejana: History and Development of Tejano Music"; and Richard B. Hughes, "The Mexican Texans."

3. *Britannica Precise Encyclopedia*, pp. 1259, 1750–51; José Angel Gutiérrez, "Chicano Music: Evolution and Politics to 1950," in Clayton and Specht, *Roots of Texas Music*, pp. 149–50; Appell and Hemphill, *American Popular Music*, p. 161.

4. For more on the history of Spain during this period see Henry Kamen, *Spain 1469–1714: A Society of Conflict*; Calvert and De León, *History of Texas*, pp. 7–10.

5. Cathryn A. Hoyt, "Riches, Religion, and Politics: Early Exploration in Texas," in Simons and Hoyt, *Hispanic Texas*, pp. 13–23; Gutiérrez, "Chicano Music," p. 150.

6. Appell and Hemphill, *American Popular Music*, pp. 193–94.

7. Robert S. Weddle, "Cross and Crown: The Spanish Missions in Texas," in Simons and Hoyt, *Hispanic Texas*, pp. 25–35; Teja, Marks, and Tyler, *Texas*, pp. 65–78.

8. For a discussion of the ways in which the Spanish Franciscans worked to assimilate

Pueblo Indians in the Southwest, see Ramón A. Gutiérrez, *When Jesus Came, the Corn Mothers Went Away: Marriage, Sexuality, and Power in New Mexico, 1500–1846.*

9. Nettl, Heth, and Kurath, "American Indians," pp. 470–71; Kate Van Winkle Keller, with John Koegel, "Secular Music to 1800," in Nicholls, *Cambridge History of American Music,* pp. 59–62; Gerard Béhague, *Music in Latin America: An Introduction,* pp. 2–3.

10. Peña, *Música Tejana,* pp. 37–49; Gutiérrez, "Chicano Music," pp. 151–53; San Miguel Jr., *Tejano Proud,* pp. 9–12.

11. Ann Perry, "Tejano Festivals: Celebrations of History and Community," in Simons and Hoyt, *Hispanic Texas,* pp. 123–26; Béhague, *Music in Latin America,* pp. 60–62, 98; Dan W. Dickey, "Música Norteña," in Barkley et al., *Handbook of Texas Music,* pp. 220–22; San Miguel Jr., *Tejano Proud,* pp. 27–28; José R. Reyna, "Notes on Tejano Music," *Aztlán: International Journal of Chicano Studies Research* 13, nos. 1 and 2 (Spring and Fall 1982): 82–83. See also Manuel Peña, *The Texas-Mexican Conjunto: History of a Working-class Music,* pp. 20–24. In *Music in Mexico,* Robert Stevenson provides one of the most thorough accounts of music in colonial Mexico.

12. Dale A. Olsen and Daniel E. Sheehy, eds., *The Garland Handbook of Latin American Music,* pp. 151–52; Appell and Hemphill, *American Popular Music,* pp. 194–98.

13. Manuel Peña, *The Mexican American Orquesta: Music, Culture, and the Dialectic of Conflict,* p. 6; Teja, Marks, and Tyler, *Texas,* pp. 227–50; Carlos Jesús Gómez Flores, "The Accordion on Both Sides of the Border," in Tejeda and Valdez, *Puro Conjunto,* pp. 71–80; Koegel, "Crossing Borders," p. 97; Appell and Hemphill, *American Popular Music,* pp. 193–94. In *Música Tejana,* Peña offers the most complete analysis of the complex internal dynamics of the Texas Mexican community in relation to class structure and music. See also Rafael Pérez-Torres, "Mestizaje in the Mix: Chicano Identity, Cultural Politics, and Postmodern Music," in Radano and Bohlman, *Music and the Racial Imagination,* pp. 206–30, for a discussion of the blending of history, mythology, bilingualism, and ethnic identity in modern Mexican American music.

14. Several good studies discuss discrimination against Mexican Americans in the Southwest. For a concise overview of this subject, see Campbell, *Gone to Texas,* pp. 191–94, 361–86, 402–10, 428–30. See also Arnoldo De León, *They Called Them Greasers: Anglo Attitudes toward Mexicans in Texas, 1821–1900,* pp. 24–28; David Montejano, *Anglos and Mexicans in the Making of Texas, 1836–1986,* pp. 143–48, 179–96, 232–33, 288–92; and Emilio Zamora, Cynthia Orozco, and Rodolfo Rocha, *Mexican Americans in Texas History: Selected Essays.*

15. Avelardo Valdez and Jeffrey A. Halley, "The Popular in Conjunto Tejano Music: Changes in Chicano Class and Identity," in Tejeda and Valdez, *Puro Conjunto,* pp. 199–202.

16. For an interesting look at the symbolic role of this permeable border in Chicano poetry, see Alfred Arteaga, *Chicano Poetics: Heterotexts and Hybridities,* especially pp. 5–19.

17. "Texas Quick Facts," U.S. Bureau of the Census, www.quickfacts.census.gov (accessed Sept. 29, 2004); José R. Reyna, "Tejano Music as an Expression of Cultural Nationalism," and Cathy Ragland, "La Voz del Pueblo Tejano: Conjunto Music and the

Construction of *Tejano* Identity in Texas," both in Tejeda and Valdez, *Puro Conjunto*, pp. 191–98, 211–27.

18. Carlos Guerra, "The Unofficial Conjunto Primer for the Uninitiated Music Lover," in Tejeda and Valdez, *Puro Conjunto*, pp. 4–7; Appell and Hemphill, *American Popular Music*, pp. 193–95; The most complete study of orquestas tejanas is Peña's *Mexican American Orquesta*.

19. Peña, *Música Tejana*, pp. 120–27; Pérez-Torres, "Mestizaje in the Mix," pp. 210–14.

20. Peña, *Texas-Mexican Conjunto*, pp. 29–36; Peña, *Música Tejana*, pp. 27–34; John Dyer, *Conjunto: Voice of the People, Songs from the Heart*, pp. 3, 6–9.

21. See www.thefreedictionary.com (accessed Oct. 24, 2005). I have observed and participated in schottisches performed by German American ensembles, conjunto groups, and country bands. They are all similar and resemble the large, often complex circular group dances I have seen performed in the Scottish Highlands.

22. Peña, *Texas-Mexican Conjunto*, pp. 29–36; Peña, *Música Tejana*, pp. 27–34, 43; Reyna, "Notes on Tejano Music," pp. 82–85. Reyna and Peña acknowledge at least two possible scenarios regarding the accordion's arrival in the Southwest. Either German immigrants introduced it into Mexico during the mid-1800s and traveling musicians brought the instrument northward into Texas, or German and Czech immigrants into Texas at around the same time might have been the first to bring the accordion to Texas Mexican musicians. For more about the accordion in Mexican American music, see Flores, "Accordion on Both Sides of the Border"; Carlos Guerra, "Accordion Menace . . . Just Say Mo'!" and Ramiro Burr, "The Accordion: Passion, Emotion, Musicianship," both in Tejeda and Valdez, *Puro Conjunto*, 115–25; *Britannica Precise Encyclopedia*, p. 8; www.en.wikipedia.org. For a fictional but still enlightening account of the importance of the accordion in the musical culture of many ethnic groups throughout the United States, see E. Annie Proulx, *Accordion Crimes*.

23. Narciso Martínez, interview by Allan Turner, Apr. 24, 1978; Santiago Jiménez Sr., interview by Allan Turner, Mar. 25, 1979; and Fred Zimmerle, interview by Allan Turner and Jay Brakefield, Jan. 14, 1978, all in ATOHC; Teresa Palomo Acosta, "Narciso Martínez," in Barkley et al., *Handbook of Texas Music*, pp. 205–207; Burr, *Billboard Guide*, pp. 147–48.

24. Manuel Peña, "The Emergence of Conjunto Music, 1935–1955" and "Conjunto Music: The First Fifty Years"; Juan Tejeda, "Santiago Jiménez, Sr.," in Tejeda and Valdez, *Puro Conjunto*, pp. 17–19, 62, 255–78; Burr, *Billboard Guide*, pp. 118–19; Jill S. Seber, "Santiago Jiménez, Sr.," in Barkley et al., *Handbook of Texas Music*, pp. 163–64.

25. Appell and Hemphill, *American Popular Music*, pp. 194–96. An older yet still helpful source of information on Texas Mexican folk culture is Mody C. Boatright, *Mexican Border Ballads and Other Lore*; Peña, *Música Tejana*, pp. 37–43; San Miguel, *Tejano Proud*, pp. 21–24.

26. Peña, *Música Tejana*, pp. 50–69.

27. Koegel, "Crossing Borders," provides a good, brief discussion of several important Tejana singers.

28. Lydia Mendoza, interview by Allan Turner, Jay Brakefield, and David Cavasos, Jan. 28, 1978, ATOHC; Carlos B. Gil, "Lydia Mendoza: Houstonian and First Lady of Mexican American Song," *Houston Review* 3 (Summer 1981): 249–57; San Miguel, *Tejano Proud*, pp. 21–22, 39–42; Louis Barbash and Frederick P. Close, "Lydia Mendoza: The Voice of the People," *Texas Humanist* 6 (Nov.–Dec. 1983): 18–20; Burr, *Billboard Guide*, pp. 151–52. *Lydia Mendoza: A Family Autobiography*, comp. and introduced by Chris Strachwitz, with James Nicolopulos, contains an extensive collection of oral interviews with Mendoza and various members of her family, along with a detailed discography of Mendoza's recordings.

29. Koegel, "Crossing Borders," pp. 106–107; San Miguel, *Tejano Proud*, pp. 39–42.

30. Juan Carlos Rodríguez, "Chelo Silva," in Barkley et al., *Handbook of Texas Music*, p. 288; San Miguel, *Tejano Proud*, pp. 42–44; Burr, *Billboard Guide*, pp. 189–90.

31. Robert J. Elster, ed., *International Who's Who in Popular Music 2004*, p. 92; Burr, *Billboard Guide*, p. 73.

32. Tish Hinojosa, conversations with author, Feb. 26, 2002, and Dec. 15, 2005; Tish Hinojosa, email correspondence with author, Jan. 2, 2006; Bill Friskics-Warren, "Tish Hinojosa," in Kingsbury, *Encyclopedia of Country Music*, p. 242. See also Hector Galán's documentary film *Tish Hinojosa: My Heart, My Life* (2005), www.galaninc.com.

33. Dickey, "Corridos," in Barkley et al., *Handbook of Texas Music*, pp. 63–65; John Holmes McDowell, "The Corridos of Greater Mexico as Discourse, Music, and Event," in *And Other Neighborly Names: Social Process and Cultural Image in Texas Folklore*, ed. Richard Bauman and Roger D. Abrahams, pp. 45–75. Corridos are often punctuated by *gritos*, or shouts from the audience. Since audience members often know the basic storyline already, this is a way of involving themselves in the telling of the tale, perhaps in a similar vein to African American call and response; Guadalupe San Miguel Jr., "Música Tejana: Nuestra Música," *Journal of Texas Music History* 1, no. 1 (Spring 2001): 27.

34. Burr, *Billboard Guide*, pp. 75–76. For a discussion of the corrido tradition in neighboring New Mexico, see Aurelio M. Espinosa, *The Folklore of Spain in the American Southwest: Traditional Spanish Folk Literature in Northern New Mexico and Southern Colorado*, ed. J. Manuel Espinosa, especially pp. 126–33.

35. Hartman, "From Yellow Roses to Dixie Chicks"; Paredes, *Texas-Mexican Cancionero*, pp. 64–67; Dan William Dickey, *The Kennedy Corridos: A Study of the Ballads of a Mexican American Hero*, pp. 7–14; Peña, *Música Tejana*, pp. 66–69; Dickey, "Corridos," pp. 63–65. For examples of corridos that address issues of migration, employment, and gender roles, see "Mexican Ballads Justify and Condemn Immigration, 1924" and "Mexican Ballads Ridicule Women's Changing Behavior, 1924," in Jon Gjerde, ed., *Major Problems in American Immigration and Ethnic History*, pp. 182–84, 249–50.

36. See Américo Paredes, *With His Pistol in His Hand*, for the most complete discussion of the facts and folklore surrounding Gregorio Cortez; Peña, *Música Tejana*, pp. 40–41; Paredes, *Texas-Mexican Cancionero*, pp. 64–67.

37. Paredes, *Texas-Mexican Cancionero*, pp. 53–55.

38. Elijah Wald, *Narcocorrido: A Journey into the Music of Drugs, Guns, and Guerillas,* especially pp. 201–10.

39. Montejano, *Anglos and Mexicans,* pp. 264–71, 278–87; Campbell, *Gone to Texas,* pp. 419–21, 428–30.

40. Yolanda Romero, "Trini Gámez, the Texas Farm Workers, and Mexican American Community Empowerment: Toil and Trouble on the South Texas Plains," in Zamora, Orozco, and Rocha, *Mexican Americans in Texas History,* pp. 143–57; Montejano, *Anglos and Mexicans,* pp. 268–81.

41. Pérez-Torres, "Mestizaje in the Mix," especially pp. 212–13, discusses these intraethnic issues of assimilation. Such pressure to conform is common among all ethnic communities. In fact, the greatest pressure on immigrants to assimilate often comes from within their own ethnic community. For a more in-depth discussion of the struggle of immigrant groups to reconcile multiple ethnic or national allegiances and gain "respectability" within mainstream society, see Gary Hartman, "Building the Ideal Immigrant: Reconciling Lithuanianism and 100 Percent Americanism to Create a Respectable Nationalist Movement, 1870–1922," *Journal of American Ethnic History* 18, no. 1 (Fall 1998): 37–76; Peña, "Emergence of Conjunto Music," pp. 286–94.

42. Guadalupe San Miguel Jr., "Música Tejana," *Journal of Texas Music History* 1, no. 1 (Spring 2001): 25–29; Peña, *Mexican-American Orquesta,* pp. 97–108; Dyer, *Conjunto,* pp. 2–9; Peña, *Música Tejana,* pp. 21–22.

43. Guadalupe San Miguel Jr., conversation with author, Mar. 2, 2000; Peña, *Música Tejana,* pp. 106–14; Teresa Palomo Acosta, "Tejano Conjunto Festival," in Barkley et al., *Handbook of Texas Music,* 308–10.

44. Gary Hartman, "Ideal Records," and Teresa Palomo Acosta, "Armando Marroquín," in Barkley et al., *Handbook of Texas Music,* pp. 150, 203–204.

45. Juan Carlos Rodríguez, "Beto Villa," in Barkley et al., *Handbook of Texas Music,* pp. 342–43; Burr, *Billboard Guide,* pp. 214–15; Peña, *Texas-Mexican Conjunto,* pp. 8–15; Appell and Hemphill, *American Popular Music,* pp. 197–98.

46. Peña, *Música Tejana,* pp. 138–42; Burr, *Billboard Guide,* pp. 135–36.

47. Burr, *Billboard Guide,* pp. 134–35; Juan Carlos Rodríguez, "Valerio Longoria," *Handbook of Texas Music,* in Barkley et al., pp. 190–91; San Miguel, *Tejano Proud,* pp. 37–39, 50, 53.

48. Alan B. Govenar, ed., *Masters of Traditional Arts: A Biographical Dictionary,* vol. 1, pp. 164–65; Burr, *Billboard Guide,* pp. 79–80; Peña, *Música Tejana,* pp. 100–101.

49. Mingo Saldivar, conversation with author, Mar. 21, 2006; Dyer, *Conjunto,* pp. 74–75; Burr, *Billboard Guide,* p. 184.

50. Ramón Hernández Jr., "Three of the Greatest Bajo Sexto Players in the History of Conjunto," and Max Martínez, "El Conjunto Bernal: Style and Legacy," both in Tejeda and Valdez, *Puro Conjunto,* pp. 83–84, 97–105; Burr, *Billboard Guide,* p. 75; San Miguel, *Tejano Proud,* p. 55.

51. Michael Corcoran, "The Invisible Genius: Steve Jordan," *Journal of Texas Music His-*

tory 3, no. 1 (Spring 2003): 24–28; Burr, Billboard Guide, p. 124; San Miguel, Tejano Proud, pp. 64–65.

52. Flaco Jiménez, conversation with author, Mar. 25, 2003; Burr, Billboard Guide, pp. 118–23; Juan Tejeda, "Santiago Jiménez, Sr.," and "¡Conjunto! Estilo y Clase: Narciso Martínez, Valerio Longoria, Tony de la Rosa, Paulino Bernal, Flaco Jiménez y Esteban Jordán," in Tejeda and Valdez, Puro Conjunto, pp. 346–48; Govenar, Masters of Traditional Arts, vol. 1, pp. 309–11.

53. Dyer, Conjunto, pp. 14–15; Juan Tejeda, "Eva Ybarra," in Tejeda and Valdez, Puro Conjunto, pp. 295–300; Burr, Billboard Guide, pp. 217–18.

54. Gerard H. Béhague, "Hispanic-American Music," in Hitchcock and Sadie, New Grove Dictionary of American Music, vol. 2, pp. 396–97; San Miguel, Tejano Proud, p. 57.

55. Montejano, Anglos and Mexicans, pp. 278–87; Gutiérrez, "Chicano Music: Evolution and Politics to 1950," in Clayton and Specht, Roots of Texas Music, pp. 167–71; Richardson, Texas, pp. 310–11; Teja, Marks, and Tyler, Texas, pp. 428–30.

56. Pérez-Torres, "Mestizaje in the Mix," pp. 208–17; Arteaga, Chicano Poetics, pp. 68–90; Reyna, "Tejano Music as an Expression of Cultural Nationalism," and Juan Tejeda, "An Odyssey through the Magical Land of Conjunto, el Movimiento Xicano, and the Tejano Conjunto Festival," both in Tejeda and Valdez, Puro Conjunto, pp. 195–98, 364–67; Gutiérrez, "Chicano Music," in Clayton and Specht, Roots of Texas Music, pp. 169–70; Hartman, "Building the Ideal Immigrant," pp. 48–50; Peña, Música Tejana, pp. 150–63. Peña calls the Chicano movement a movement of "romantic nationalism," in which supporters militantly espoused the idealistic notion of "one people, one language, one glorious heritage."

57. Joe Nick Patoski, Selena: Como la Flor, pp. 14–20; Joe Nick Patoski, "Uno, Dos, One, Two, Tres, Quatro," Journal of Texas Music History 1, no. 1 (Spring 2001): 12–14.

58. Huey P. Meaux, correspondence with author, Dec. 5, 2005; San Miguel, Tejano Proud, pp. 69–76; Burr, Billboard Guide, pp. 132–33, 162–63; Peña, Música Tejana, pp. 155–59; Mike Chávez, interview by Joe Nick Patoski, Aug. 29, 1995, Box 589, Folder 1, SQBP.

59. Peña, Música Tejana, pp. 163–69, 176–82.

60. Peña, Mexican American Orquesta, pp. 233–59; Burr, Billboard Guide, pp. 132–33. Gutiérrez, "Chicano Music," p. 170.

61. Burr, Billboard Guide, pp. 171–72; San Miguel, Tejano Proud, pp. 77–84.

62. The rise in popularity of elaborate stage shows in Tejano during the 1980s reflects the influence of MTV (Music Television) and its emphasis on the visual aspects of performance.

63. Larry Star and Christopher Waterman, American Popular Music: The Rock Years, pp. 232–33; San Miguel, "Música Tejana," pp. 24–25.

64. Laura Canales, interview by Joe Nick Patoski, Aug. 18, 1995, Box 588, Folder 8, SQBP; Koegel, "Crossing Borders," p. 108; Burr, Billboard Guide, pp. 71–72, 173–74; Peña, Música Tejana, p. 187.

65. Canales, interview by Patoski, and Ruben García, interview by Joe Nick Patoski, undated, Box 589, Folder 7, SQBP.

66. Burr, *Billboard Guide*, pp. 188–89; Patoski, *Selena*, pp. 34–37, 56, 67, 196–204; San Miguel, *Tejano Proud*, pp. 89–91, 106–12; Corcoran, *All Over the Map*, pp. 131–35.

67. Peña, *Música Tejana*, pp. 207–209; Burr, *Billboard Guide*, pp. 86–87.

68. Patoski, *Selena*, pp. 202–204; San Miguel, *Tejano Proud*, pp. 93–97.

69. Kingsbury, *Encyclopedia of Country Music*, p. 546; Burr, *Billboard Guide*, p. 128; Peña, *Música Tejana*, pp. 213–15; Koster, *Texas Music*, pp. 221–24; Pérez-Torres, "Mestizaje in the Mix," pp. 206–30; San Miguel, *Tejano Proud*, pp. 132–33.

70. Hector Galán's documentary film *Los Lonely Boys: Cottonfields and Crossroads* does an excellent job of placing the band's career within the context of the region's unique social and cultural environment. See also "Los Lonely Boys" at Wikipedia: The Free Encyclopedia, www.wikipedia.org.

71. Allen Olsen, "San Antonio's West Side Sound," *Journal of Texas Music History* 5, no. 1 (Spring 2005): 26–39; James Head, "Douglas Wayne Sahm," in *Handbook of Texas Music*, pp. 280–81; Patricia Romanowski and Holly George-Warren, eds., *The New Rolling Stone Encyclopedia of Rock & Roll*, pp. 903–904, 994.

CHAPTER 4

1. For a brief overview of African American music in Texas, see "Rags to Rap: African-American Contributions to Texas Music" (booklet published by the Texas Music Museum, Austin, 1997).

2. For a good discussion of the evolution of black music and the way in which the issues of race and ethnic identity have affected the long-term development of African American culture, see Guthrie P. Ramsey Jr., *Race Music: Black Cultures from Bebop to Hip-Hop*, pp. 19–22.

3. Even after 1808, smugglers continued to bring some slaves into the United States illegally. For one of the earliest and most important scholarly studies of American slavery, see Eugene Genovese, *Roll, Jordan, Roll: The World the Slaves Made*, especially pp. 4–7, 400–403.

4. Oliphant, *Texan Jazz*, pp. 13–15. By arguing that Texas as a whole had a less rigidly institutionalized system of racial segregation than many other parts of the South, I am in no way trying to minimize the severity of discrimination in the state. Many Anglo Texans supported slavery and a racially segregated society as ardently as other Anglos elsewhere in the South. However, Texas had a more ethnically diverse population and an increasingly diversified economy, both of which undermined more solid support for slavery and full-scale racial segregation. See also Owens, *Tell Me a Story*, pp. 12–16. Owens agrees that greater cross-pollination of ethnic music occurred in the Southwest than in most of the Deep South. Importantly, support for slavery was not uniformly solid throughout the South. In fact, during the Civil War there were pockets of Southern whites and free blacks who refused to support the Confederacy and used a variety of means to resist con-

scription into the Confederate military. For more on this, see Victoria E. Bynum, *The Free State of Jones: Mississippi's Longest Civil War*.

5. Teja, Marks, and Tyler, *Texas*, pp. 35–37. Cabeza de Vaca's journal from these travels, the 1555 *La Relación y Comentarios*, provides detailed information about the sixteenth-century Southwest and is considered to be the earliest written account of Europeans in Texas. The Southwestern Writers Collection at Texas State University–San Marcos has a rare original copy of this journal and has made it available online to researchers in both English and the original Spanish at www.library.txstate.edu/swwc. Because of his skills and knowledge of the region, Estebanico became a highly respected guide for Spanish explorers before he was killed by Zuni Indians in 1539.

6. Alwyn Barr, *Black Texans: A History of African Americans in Texas, 1528–1995*, pp. 1–12.

7. Campbell, *Gone to Texas*, p. 472; Teja, Marks, and Tyler, *Texas*, p. 462; Susan Curtis, *Dancing to a Black Man's Tune: A Life of Scott Joplin*, p. 21.

8. Barr, *Black Texans*, pp. 39–41. See Calvert and De León, *History of Texas*, pp. 35, 54–55, and 59–60, for a discussion of early black migration into Texas; Neil Foley, *The White Scourge: Mexicans, Blacks, and Poor Whites in Texas Cotton Culture*, pp. 1, 64–74, 118–140. Foley provides one of the most thorough examinations of Texas blacks in the context of the state's multiracial makeup and its transition from an almost exclusively agrarian economy to a more diversified, industrial one.

9. Campbell, *Gone to Texas*, pp. 419–29.

10. "Texas Quick Facts," U.S. Bureau of the Census, www.quickfacts.census.gov (accessed Sept. 29, 2004).

11. Radano and Bohlman, *Music and the Racial Imagination*, pp. 6–7; Wyman, *Blues Odyssey*, p. 19, 26–27; Appell and Hemphill, *American Popular Music*, pp. 23–32; Jacqueline Cogdell Djedje, "African American Music to 1900," in Nichols, *Cambridge History of American Music*, pp. 105–112. Rodano argues that notions about the prominent role of rhythm in African and African American music have been exaggerated by Western observers who emphasize the fundamental differences in African and European musical traditions (Ronald Rodano, "Hot Fantasies: American Modernism and the Idea of Black Rhythm," in Radano and Bohlman, *Music and the Racial Imagination*, pp. 459–80).

12. Ramsey, *Race Music*, pp. 19–22.

13. Djedje, "African American Music to 1900," pp. 118–19; Alan Lomax, *The Land Where the Blues Began*, pp. 70–84.

14. Dave Oliphant, *Texan Jazz*, pp. 9–10. See also Bill C. Malone, "Texas Myth/Texas Music," *Journal of Texas Music History* 1, no. 1 (Spring 2001): 4–11, for a brief discussion of the blending of African, Anglo, and other ethnic musical influences in Texas.

15. Lomax, *Land Where the Blues Began*, pp. 104–20; Appell and Hemphill, *American Popular Music*, pp. 87–93.

16. Djedje, "African American Music to 1900," pp. 127–29; Wyman, *Blues Odyssey*, pp. 36–40.

17. Ramsey, *Race Music*, pp. 6–7, 25–34, 44–47; Owens, *Tell Me a Story*, pp. 261–88;

Lomax, *Land Where the Blues Began*, pp. 45–51, 119–20. See also Wyman, *Blues Odyssey*, pp. 226–29, for a good overview of black gospel.

18. Kevin Mooney, "Texas Centennial 1936: African-American Texans and the Third National Folk Festival," *Journal of Texas Music History* 1, no. 1 (Spring 2001): 36–43.

19. Govenar and Brakefield, *Deep Ellum and Central Track*, pp. 22, 126–27, 142–57; Alan B. Govenar, *African American Frontiers: Slave Narratives and Oral Histories*, pp. 167–70, 329–40, 430–34, 439–48. For more on Smokey Montgomery, see John Dempsey, "Marvin 'Smokey' Montgomery: A Life in Texas Music," *Journal of Texas Music History* 1, no. 2 (Fall 2001): 45–57.

20. Corcoran, *All Over the Map*, pp. 48–50; Bradley Shreve, "Blind Arizona Dranes," in Barkley et al., *Handbook of Texas Music*, p. 83.

21. Davis, *History of the Blues*, pp. 33, 118–19; Peggy Hardman, "Blind Willie Johnson," in Barkley et al., *Handbook of Texas Music*, pp. 164–65; Govenar and Brakefield, *Deep Ellum and Central Track*, pp. 100–106.

22. N. D. Giesenschlag, "Virgil Oliver Stamps," and Greg Self, "Stamps-Baxter Music and Printing Company," both in Barkley et al., *Handbook of Texas Music*, pp. 296–97.

23. Paul Petrie, "The History of Gospel Music," www.afgen.com/gospel (accessed Dec. 13, 2004); Govenar and Brakefield, *Deep Ellum and Central Track*, pp. 105–106; Roger Wood, *Down in Houston: Bayou City Blues*, p. 245; Corcoran, *All over the Map*, pp. 2–5.

24. Govenar, "Dixie Hummingbirds: African-American Gospel Singers," in Govenar, *Masters of Traditional Arts*, vol. 1, pp. 170–72. See also Jerry Zolten, *Great God A'Mighty! The Dixie Hummingbirds: Celebrating the Rise of Soul Gospel Music*.

25. See Richard J. Mason, "Gospel Music," in Barkley et al., *Handbook of Texas Music*, pp. 122–24, for a more in-depth discussion of gospel traditions in Texas.

26. Oliphant, *Texan Jazz*, p. 36; Hettie Jones, *Big Star Fallin' Mama: Five Women in Black Music*, pp. 10–11.

27. Robert Santelli, *The Big Book of Blues: A Biographical Encyclopedia*, provides good, brief biographical sketches of more than six hundred blues artists. See also Sheldon Harris, *The Blues Who's Who: A Biographical Dictionary of Blues Singers*, and Bruce Jackson, *Wake Up, Dead Man: Afro-American Work Songs of Texas Prisons*. Another helpful resource for a variety of blues-related topics is www.bluesworld.com.

28. Starr and Waterman, *American Popular Music*, pp. 14–15; Appell and Hemphill, *American Popular Music*, pp. 38–47; Owens, *Tell Me a Story*, pp. 307–11; Lomax, *Land Where the Blues Began*, pp. 266–67.

29. Excerpt from Blind Lemon Jefferson's "Cat Man Blues," in Luigi Monge and David Evans, "New Songs of Blind Lemon Jefferson," *Journal of Texas Music History* 3, no. 2 (Fall 2003): 16.

30. Francis Davis, *The History of the Blues*.

31. See *The B. B. King Companion: Five Decades of Commentary*, ed. Richard Kostelanetz, pp. 19–25, and Alan Govenar, "Blues," in Barkley et al., *Handbook of Texas Music*, pp. 24–28, for a discussion of some of the peculiar characteristics of Texas blues, particularly in

comparison to blues styles found in Kansas City and elsewhere. Also see Alan Govenar, "Blind Lemon Jefferson," in Barkley et al., *Handbook of Texas Music*, pp. 159–61.

32. Govenar and Brakefield, *Deep Ellum and Central Track*, pp. 23, 61–85; Monge and Evans, "New Songs of Blind Lemon Jefferson," pp. 8–28; Wyman, *Blues Odyssey*, p. 108, lists Jefferson's birth date as July 11, 1897.

33. John Lightfoot, "Early Texas Bluesmen," in Clayton and Specht, *Roots of Texas Music*, pp. 98–99. See Monge and Evans, "New Songs of Blind Lemon Jefferson."

34. Govenar, "Blind Lemon Jefferson," p. 161; Govenar and Brakefield, *Deep Ellum and Central Track*, pp. 61–79; Koster, *Texas Music*, pp. 143–14.

35. John A. Lomax Family Papers (JALFP), Center for American History at the University of Texas–Austin, Box 3D200, Folder 5, includes an article from Frank X. Tolbert's column "Tolbert's Texas," in the *Dallas Morning News* (Apr. 27, 1970), p. 21A, titled "Lead Belly's Grave on Caddo Shore," in which he states that several of Lead Belly's acquaintances to whom Tolbert spoke pronounced "Huddie" as "Hugh-dee." Christine Hamm, "Huddie Ledbetter," in Barkley et al., *Handbook of Texas Music*, p. 183. Other sources list Ledbetter's birth year as 1889. *The Leadbelly Songbook*, ed. Moses Asch and Alan Lomax, p. 43, which can be found in the Special Collections, blues archives, at the University of Mississippi–Oxford, includes a Lead Belly composition titled "Come Along, All You Cowboys," a song about riding horses and roping cattle. In a note prefacing the song, Asch says "Leadbelly told me that when he was in the Panhandle (Texarkana) he also did ranch work." Although Texarkana is nowhere near the Texas Panhandle, it is quite possible that Lead Belly, like many other African Americans, did work as a ranch hand. Charles Wolfe and Kip Lornell, *The Life and Legend of Leadbelly*, page xv, discuss the two most common spellings of Ledbetter's stage name, "Lead Belly" and "Leadbelly." I use the former since it was more commonly utilized during Ledbetter's lifetime, whereas the single-word version came into greater usage years after his death.

36. Cohen, ed., *Alan Lomax: Selected Writings*, pp. 51–53; Wyman, *Blues Odyssey*, p. 48; Govenar and Brakefield, *Deep Ellum and Central Track*, pp. 63–65. Although Lead Belly was born in Louisiana, his ties to Texas were extensive. A long-standing dispute over which state can rightfully "claim" the singer made headlines in 1974, when fans and Ledbetter family members argued over whether to have Lead Belly's remains disinterred from the Shiloh Baptist Church cemetery near Blanchard, Louisiana, and moved to Harrison County, Texas. For more on this, see the various newspaper clippings in the "Leadbelly" folder in the Special Collections, University of Mississippi–Oxford.

37. Appell and Hemphill, *American Popular Music*, pp. 42–47; Wyman, *Blues Odyssey*, pp. 178–87. See Malone, *Country Music, U.S.A.*, pp. 86–87, 104–109, 172–73, and 489–94, for a discussion of the influence of blues on country music.

38. Wolfe and Lornell, *Life and Legend of Leadbelly*, pp. 97–99, 200–10.

39. Filene, "Our Singing Country," pp. 602–24. Filene argues that, as important as they were in helping preserve the music of Lead Belly and many other more obscure musicians, in some cases the Lomaxes were guilty of questionable practices in their

selection of artists and material; see Eyerman and Jamison, *Music and Social Movements*, pp. 68–73; Govenar and Brakefield, *Deep Ellum and Central Track*, pp. 63–65; and Wolfe and Lornell, *Life and Legend of Leadbelly*. See also Box 3D200, Folder 5, JALFP, Center for American History, University of Texas–Austin, for a number of newspaper clippings covering Lead Belly's performances in New York City and elsewhere in 1935. Most of the newspaper accounts contain blatantly racist stereotypes of Lead Belly as a black felon, referring to him as a "murderous minstrel," a "homicidal harmonizer," and a "quick tempered knife toting Negro." See also Nolan Porterfield, *Last Cavalier: The Life and Times of John A. Lomax, 1867–1948*, especially pp. 300, 332–34, and 364–67, for more on Lead Belly's relationship with the Lomaxes.

40. Mance Lipscomb, interview by Allan Turner and Jay Brakefield, Nov. 25, 1972, ATOHC; Lipscomb-Alyn Collection, 1960–1995, the Center for American History, University of Texas–Austin, Box 2K197, Folder 5, Transcript of Tape 4 from Alyn interview of Mance Lipscomb, pp. 9–15 and 19–25; John Minton, "Mance Lipscomb," in Barkley et al., *Handbook of Texas Music*, pp. 185–87; Lightfoot, "Early Texas Bluesmen," pp. 107–11.

41. Mack McCormick, "Mance Lipscomb: Texas Sharecropper and Songster," *American Folk Music Occasional* no. 1 (1964), pp. 61–73; Lipscomb-Alyn Collection, 1960–1995, the Center for American History, University of Texas–Austin, Box 2K197, Folder 1, notes regarding Tape 3 of Alyn interview of Mance Lipscomb. In Folder 5, Transcript of Tape 4 from Alyn interview of Mance Lipscomb, p. 66, Lipscomb says he was surprised that McCormick and Strachwitz referred to him as a "sharecropper," when he always just considered himself a farmer. Wood, *Down in Houston*, pp. 48–49; Govenar and Brakefield, *Deep Ellum and Central Track*, p. 66; Glen Alyn, *I Say Me for a Parable: The Oral Autobiography of Mance Lipscomb, Texas Bluesman*, as told to and compiled by Glen Alyn. For one of the most complete online discographies of Lipscomb, see www.wirz.de/music/lipscomb.

42. Santelli, *Big Book of Blues*, p. 399; Dave Oliphant, "Henry Thomas," in Barkley et al., *Handbook of Texas Music*, pp. 321–23.

43. Wyman, *Blues Odyssey*, pp. 121–22; James Head, "Texas Alexander," in Barkley et al., *Handbook of Texas Music*, p. 2; Santelli, *Big Book of Blues*, pp. 5–6.

44. Appell and Hemphill, *American Popular Music*, p. 70; Govenar and Brakefield, *Deep Ellum and Central Track*, pp. 109–110; Wyman, *Blues Odyssey*, pp. 188–93.

45. Randi Sutton, "Alexander Herman Moore," in Barkley et al., *Handbook of Texas Music*, pp. 213–14; Govenar, *Masters of Traditional Arts*, vol. 2, pp. 456–58; Santelli, *Big Book of Blues*, p. 301.

46. Oliphant, *Texan Jazz*, pp. 54–62; Donna P. Parker, "Sippie Wallace," in Barkley et al., *Handbook of Texas Music*, pp. 349–50.

47. James Head, "George Washington Thomas, Jr.," and "Hersal Thomas," in Barkley et al., *Handbook of Texas Music*, pp. 320–21, 323; Wyman, *Blues Odyssey*, p. 188.

48. Donna P. Parker, "Victoria Spivey," in Barkley et al., *Handbook of Texas Music*, pp. 295–96; Santelli, *Big Book of Blues*, pp. 379–80.

49. Robert Shaw, interview by Allan Turner, May 17, 1975, ATOHC; Santelli, *Big Book*

of Blues, p. 362; Teresa Palomo Acosta, "Robert Shaw," in Barkley et al., *Handbook of Texas Music*, pp. 287–88.

50. Appell and Hemphill, *American Popular Music*, pp. 273–78.

51. Davis, *History of the Blues*, pp. 162–63; Helen Oakley Dance, "T-Bone Walker," in Barkley et al., *Handbook of Texas Music*, pp. 348–49; Wyman, *Blues Odyssey*, pp. 236–37.

52. Corcoran, *All Over the Map*, pp. 34–38. For a more in-depth discussion of Walker's life and career, see Helen Oakley Dance, *Stormy Monday: The T-Bone Walker Story*; Govenar and Brakefield, *Deep Ellum and Central Track*, pp. 67–69, 125, 130.

53. In a booklet titled "Lightnin' Hopkins," Frank Scott describes Hopkins's first meeting with Jefferson and the profound impact the older musician had on the young boy. "Lightnin' Hopkins" folder, Special Collections, University of Mississippi–Oxford; Wyman, *Blues Odyssey*, pp. 308, 326–32; Alan Lee Haworth, "Lightnin' Hopkins," in Barkley et al., *Handbook of Texas Music*, p. 142. The Hip-O label has recently issued a series of DVDs titled "The American Folk Blues Festival, 1962–1966," which documents these European tours of Hopkins and Walker, along with Muddy Waters, Sunnyland Slim, and others. See also Sarah Ann West, *Deep Down Hard Blues: A Tribute to Lightnin' Hopkins*.

54. Santelli, *Big Book of Blues*, pp. 404–405; Alan Lee Haworth, "Willie Mae Thornton," in Barkley et al., *Handbook of Texas Music*, pp. 324–25; Wyman, *Blues Odyssey*, p. 268; Wood, *Down in Houston*, pp. 28, 195, 200.

55. Michael Corcoran, "Remembering Gatemouth Brown: This Guitar Genius Went Far, So Far beyond the Blues," *Austin-American Statesman* (Sept. 13, 2005), www.statesman.com/life/content/life/stories/09/13gatemouth; Wood, *Down in Houston*, pp. 49–52; Wyman, *Blues Odyssey*, pp. 256–57, 262; Koster, *Texas Music*, pp. 162–63.

56. Carlyn Copeland, "Amos Milburn," in Barkley et al., *Handbook of Texas Music*, pp. 209–10; Santelli, *Big Book of Blues*, pp. 294–95.

57. Davis, *History of the Blues*, p. 163; Jarad Brown, "Ivory Joe Hunter," in Barkley et al., *Handbook of Texas Music*, p. 147.

58. Santelli, *Big Book of Blues*, p. 108; Alan Govenar, *Living Texas Blues*, p. 51. Govenar lists Crayton's birthplace as Liberty Hill, Texas; Jarad Brown, "Pee Wee Crayton," in Barkley et al., *Handbook of Texas Music*, pp. 69–70.

59. Koster, *Texas Music*, pp. 239–41; James Head, "King Curtis," in Barkley et al., *Handbook of Texas Music*, pp. 178–79; Wyman, *Blues Odyssey*, p. 360.

60. Jim Miller, "Esther Phillips," in Hitchcock and Sadie, *New Grove Dictionary of American Music*, vol. 3, p. 557; James Head, "Esther Mae Phillips," in Barkley et al., *Handbook of Texas Music*, pp. 243–44.

61. Clifford Antone, interview by Joe Moody, June 1, 2005, TMOHP; Santelli, *Big Book of Blues*, pp. 98–99; Wyman, *Blues Odyssey*, p. 354.

62. John G. Johnson, "Albert Collins," in Barkley et al., *Handbook of Texas Music*, p. 62; Wood, *Down in Houston*, pp. 100–104.

63. Romanowski and George-Warren, *New Rolling Stone Encyclopedia*, p. 544; Amy van Beveren, "Freddie King," in Barkley et al., *Handbook of Texas Music*, p. 178.

64. Jay Trachtenberg, "Spotlight: Barbara Lynn," *Austin Chronicle* (Mar. 17, 2006), www.auschron.com; www.nothinbutdablues.bizland.com.

65. Corcoran, *All Over the Map*, pp. 27–29; Romanowski and George-Warren, *New Rolling Stone Encyclopedia*, pp. 66–67; Scott Schinder, "Tighten Up," *Texas Music* 26 (Spring 2006): 24–29.

66. Hudson, *Telling Stories, Writing Songs*, pp. 104–108; Romanowski and George-Warren, *New Rolling Stone Encyclopedia*, pp. 641–42.

67. Clifford Antone, conversation with author, Apr. 10, 2005; Clifford Antone, interview by Moody, June 1, 2005, TMOHP; Bill Crawford and Joe Nick Patoski: Stevie Ray Vaughan Biography Papers, Collection 28, Box 1, Folder 5, "Interview with Clifford Antone and Kim Wilson," May 2, 1992, SWWC, Texas State University–San Marcos; Joe Nick Patoski and Bill Crawford, *Stevie Ray Vaughan: Caught in the Crossfire*, pp. 8–18; Keri Leigh, *Stevie Ray: Soul to Soul*, pp. 28–32.

68. Crawford and Patoski: Stevie Ray Vaughan Biography Papers, Collection 28, Box 1, Folder 18, "Interview with Denny Freeman," undated, SWWC, Texas State University–San Marcos; Robin Dutton, "Stevie Ray Vaughan," in Barkley et al., *Handbook of Texas Music*, p. 340; Patoski and Crawford, *Stevie Ray Vaughan*, pp. 44–46, 89–90, 111–12, 144–51, 180–81, 259.

69. Clifford Antone, interview by Moody, June 1, 2005, TMOHP; Crawford and Patoski, Stevie Ray Vaughan Biography Papers, Collection 28, Box 1, Folder 12, "Interview with W. C. Clark," Jan. 8, 1992, SWWC. For a personal look at the blues music scene in Austin, especially in relationship to Antone's, see Susan Antone, *Picture the Blues*. For an excellent documentary film about the history of Antone's, see Dan Karlok, *Antones: Home of the Blues*.

70. Theodore Albrecht, "Scott Joplin," in Barkley et al., *Handbook of Texas Music*, p. 171; Jeffrey Magee, "Ragtime and Early Jazz," *The Cambridge History of American Music*, pp. 390–92. Texas barrelhouse pianist Robert Shaw is one of the best recent examples of the ragtime influence on boogie-woogie. In addition to Shaw's commercial recordings, his interview by Allan Turner on May 17, 1975 (in the ATOHC), includes samples of Shaw's barrelhouse style, which blends the classic twelve-bar blues format with a strong left-hand ragtime syncopation.

71. Edward A. Berlin, *King of Ragtime: Scott Joplin and His Era*, p. 7; Edward A. Berlin, "Scott Joplin," in Hitchcock and Sadie, *New Grove Dictionary of American Music*, vol. 2, pp. 596–98.

72. Curtis, *Dancing to a Black Man's Tune*, pp. 87, 132–33; Albrecht, "Scott Joplin," pp. 168–71.

73. Oliphant, *Texan Jazz*, pp. 10–35; Berlin, *King of Ragtime*, pp. 6–16, 250–51.

74. Dave Oliphant, *The Early Swing Era, 1930 to 1941*, p. 102; Cheryl Simon, "Euday Louis Bowman," in Barkley et al., *Handbook of Texas Music*, p. 32; Oliphant, *Texan Jazz*, pp. 28–35.

75. For more on this out-migration of Texas jazz musicians, see Joe Bailey, "'The

Texas Shuffle': Lone Star Underpinnings of the Kansas City Sound," and Sterlin Holmesly, "Texas Jazz Veterans: A Collection of Oral Histories," *Journal of Texas Music History* 10 (2006): 8–27, 28–51.

76. Joe B. Frantz, "Charles Christian," in Barkley et al., *Handbook of Texas Music*, pp. 50–51; Govenar and Brakefield, *Deep Ellum and Central Track*, p. 121; Oliphant, *Texan Jazz*, pp. 195–203; Oliphant, *Early Swing Era*, pp. 340–43.

77. Dave Oliphant, "Eddie Durham and the Texas Contribution to Jazz History," *Southwestern Historical Quarterly* (Apr. 1993): 491–525; Oliphant, *Texan Jazz*, pp. 100–101, 195; Dave Oliphant, "Eddie Durham," in Barkley et al., *Handbook of Texas Music*, pp. 86–87; author's conversation with Marcia Durham, Aug. 19, 2005.

78. Kharen Monsho, "Gene Ramey," in Barkley et al., *Handbook of Texas Music*, p. 251. See also Bailey, "'Texas Shuffle,'" and Holmesly, "Texas Jazz Veterans," 8–29, 30–53.

79. Cameron Addis, "The Baptist Beat in Modern Jazz: Texan Gene Ramey in Kansas City and New York," *Journal of Texas Music History* 4, no. 2 (Fall 2004): 8–21.

80. Elster, *International Who's Who in Popular Music 2004*, pp. 123–24; Oliphant, *Texan Jazz*, pp. 405, 425; Dave Oliphant, "Oscar Frederic Moore," in Barkley et al., *Handbook of Texas Music*, p. 215.

81. John Litweiler, *Ornette Coleman: A Harmolodic Life*, p. 21. Litweiler notes that, although most sources list Coleman's birth date as Mar. 19, 1930, Coleman's sister, Truvenza Coleman Leach, claims he was born on Mar. 9, 1931. Raoul Hernandez, "Equality: Harmolodicizing with Ornette Coleman," *Austin Chronicle* (Nov. 12, 2004), p. 70; Oliphant, *Texan Jazz*, pp. 135–39, 225–33, 307–308.

82. Alan Lee Haworth, "Buster Smith," Stephen G. Williams and Kharen Monsho, "Arnett Cobb," and James Head, "Hot Lips Page," all in Barkley et al., *Handbook of Texas Music*, pp. 58, 239, 289–90; Barry Kernfield, "Kenny Dorham," in Hitchcock and Sadie, *New Grove Dictionary of American Music*, vol. 1, p. 647; Dave Oliphant, "Bebop Messengers to the World: Kenny Dorham and Leo Wright," *Journal of Texas Music History* 1, no. 1 (Spring 2001): 15–23.

83. Roy G. Scudday, "Tex Beneke," in Barkley et al., *Handbook of Texas Music*, pp. 19–20; Oliphant, *Early Swing Era*, pp. 138–40.

84. James Lincoln Collier, "Jack Teagarden," in Hitchcock and Sadie, *New Grove Dictionary of American Music*, vol. 4, p. 360; Charles G. Davis, "Jack Teagarden," in Barkley et al., *Handbook of Texas Music*, pp. 306–307; Dave Oliphant, "The Wisconsin-Texas Jazz Nexus," *Journal of Texas Music History* 4, no. 1 (Spring 2004): 8–17.

85. Dave Oliphant, "Emilio Caceres" and "Ernesto Caceres," in Barkley et al., *Handbook of Texas Music*, p. 43.

86. J. Bradford Robinson, "Teddy Wilson," in Hitchcock and Sadie, *New Grove Dictionary of American Music*, vol. 4, p. 540; Vivian Elizabeth Smyrl, "Teddy Wilson," in Barkley et al., *Handbook of Texas Music*, p. 359.

87. Lisa C. Maxwell, "Red Garland," in Barkley et al., *Handbook of Texas Music*, pp. 114–15; Bill Dobbins, "Red Garland," in Hitchcock and Sadie, *New Grove Dictionary of American Music*, vol. 2, pp. 189–90.

88. Oliphant, *Texan Jazz*, pp. 258–64, 314, 431, 434–35; Jay Trachtenberg, "Dream Story: Eli's Coming, Hide Your Horn, Man," *Austin Chronicle* 26, no. 5 (Oct. 6, 2006): 70.

89. Author's conversations with Gene Elders (Nov. 30, 2004), Paul Glasse (Apr. 10, 2005), Rick McRae (Dec. 2, 2006), and Slim Richey (Feb. 11, 2007); Rod Moag, "The History of Early Bluegrass in Texas," *Journal of Texas Music History* 4, no. 2 (Fall 2004): 22–48.

90. Kirvin Tillis, "Joseph Arrington, Jr.," in Barkley et al., *Handbook of Texas Music*, p. 8; Fox, *Showtime at the Apollo*, pp. 105–106; David Brackett, *The Pop, Rock, and Soul Reader: Histories and Debates*, pp. 140–42; Appell and Hemphill, *American Popular Music*, pp. 318–30.

91. Romanowski and George-Warren, *New Rolling Stone Encyclopedia*, pp. 1068–69.

92. Santelli, *Big Book of the Blues*, p. 438; James Head, "Johnny Watson," in Barkley et al., *Handbook of Texas Music*, pp. 350–51.

93. Elster, *International Who's Who in Popular Music*, pp. 458–59; Norman, *Shout!* pp. 359, 392; Romanowski and George-Warren, *New Rolling Stone Encyclopedia*, pp. 786–87.

94. Starr and Waterman, *American Popular Music*, pp. 270–89; Romanowski and George-Warren, *New Rolling Stone Encyclopedia*, p. 814; Appell and Hemphill, *American Popular Music*, pp. 383–94. For a discussion of rap's frequent use of violent, sexist, racist, and homophobic lyrics see Juan Williams, "Fighting Words: Racism, Sexism, and Homophobia in Pop and Rap," and Robin D. G. Kelley, "A Culture of Violence: Gangsta Rap in Context," in Green, *Rap and Hip Hop*, pp. 105–25.

95. Jesse J. Esparza, "D. J. Screw," in Barkley et al., *Handbook of Texas Music*, p. 74; Steven Stancell, *Rap Whoz Who: The World of Rap Music, Performers, Producers, Promoters*, pp. 114–15; Corcoran, *All Over the Map*, pp. 23–26.

96. Matt Diehl, "Pop Rap," in Green, *Rap and Hip Hop*, pp. 57–67; Stancell, *Rap Whoz Who*, pp. 303–304; Koster, *Texas Music*, pp. 254–55; Starr and Waterman, *American Popular Music*, p. 282; Elster, *International Who's Who in Popular Music 2004*, pp. 311–12; www.beyonceonline.com.

CHAPTER 5

1. Rudolph L. Biesele, *The History of the German Settlements in Texas*, pp. 42–82; Campbell, *Gone to Texas*, p. 159; Richardson, *Texas*, p. 346; David Uhler, "University Researchers Are Trying to Record State's Unique, and Dying, German Language," *San Antonio Express-News* (Jan. 30, 2005); Allan O. Kownslar, *The European Texans*, p. 101.

2. For a good, brief overview of German history see Mary Fulbrook, *A Concise History of Germany*. For a discussion of the social, political, and economic instability that helped drive the nineteenth-century German *Auswanderung*, see Mack Walker, *Germany and the Emigration, 1816–1885*. Walker argues that most German immigrants to the United States during this period were not interested in building a more progressive society there. Instead, they actually sought to preserve the older traditions, which they feared German modernization was undermining.

3. Terry G. Jordan, *German Seed in Texas Soil: Immigrant Farmers in Nineteenth-century Texas*, pp. 5–7.

4. Biesele, *History of the German Settlements in Texas*, pp. 118–20, 139–52. See also Glen E. Lich, *The Federal Republic of Germany and Texas: A Sesquicentennial Tribute*.

5. Matthew Lindaman, "Heimat in the Heartland: The Significance of an Ethnic Newspaper," *Journal of American Ethnic History* 23, no. 3 (Spring 2004): 78–98. See also Michael Ermarth, "Hyphenation and Hyper-Americanization: Germans of the Wilhelmine Reich View German-Americans, 1890–1914," *Journal of American Ethnic History* 21, no. 2 (Winter 2002): 33–58, for a good discussion of how some Germans viewed the assimilation of German immigrants in the United States. For a brief, firsthand account of both the opportunities and challenges German immigrants faced in nineteenth-century America, see "Gottfried Duden, a German, Assesses the Possibilities for Immigrants to Missouri, 1827," in Gjerde, *Major Problems*, pp. 98–99; Jean Heide, "Celebrating das Deutsche Lied in Texas," *Journal of Texas Music History* 3, no. 2 (Fall 2003): 37.

6. Jordan, *German Seed in Texas Soil*. See especially pp. 192–203 for a discussion of how the Germans selectively assimilated by combining their own farming traditions with those of other ethnic groups in Texas who had developed new methods more suitable to the frontier environment. For a brief overview of German music in Texas, see "Musikfest: German Contributions to Texas Music" (booklet published by the Texas Music Museum, Austin, 1992). For a more in-depth discussion of German Texas culture see *German Culture in Texas: A Free Earth; Essays from the 1978 Southwest Symposium*, ed. Glen E. Lich and Dona B. Reeves. Also helpful is "The German Texans" (booklet published by the University of Texas, Institute of Texan Cultures at San Antonio, 1987).

7. Michael Broyles, "Immigrant, Folk, and Regional Musics in the Nineteenth Century," in Nicholls, *Cambridge History of American Music*, pp. 145–48; Owens, *Tell Me a Story*, pp. 193–99; Anne Diekmann and Willi Gohl, *Das Grosse Liederbuch*, p. 78.

8. Larry Wolz, "Roots of Classical Music in Texas: The German Contribution," in Clayton and Specht, *Roots of Texas Music*, pp. 120–23.

9. Lota M. Spell, "Adolph Fuchs," and Theodore Albrecht, "Wilhelm Carl August Thielepape," in Barkley et al., *Handbook of Texas Music*, pp. 112–13, 319.

10. Rudolph L. Biesele, "Heinrich Guenther," C. A. Schutze Jr., "Julius Schuetze," and Charles A. Roeckle, "Fritz Oberdoerffer," in Barkley et al., *Handbook of Texas Music*, pp. 127–28, 232, 283–84. See also the Carl Venth Papers at the Center for American History at the University of Texas–Austin and "Carl Venth," in the *Handbook of Texas Online*, www.tsha.utexas.edu/handbook/online/articles/VV.

11. Theodore Albrecht, "Carl Beck," in Barkley et al., *Handbook of Texas Music*, p. 17; Wolz, "Roots of Classical Music in Texas," in Clayton and Specht, *Roots of Texas Music*, pp. 128–29.

12. James Chute, "Frank van der Stucken," in Hitchcock and Sadie, *New Grove Dictionary of American Music*, vol. 4, pp. 444–45; Larry Wolz, "Frank Valentine van der Stucken," in Barkley et al., *Handbook of Texas Music*, pp. 337–38. See also Spell, *Music in Texas*, pp. 38–40.

13. Geoffrey E. McGillen, "Olga Samaroff," in Barkley et al., *Handbook of Texas Music*, pp. 281–82; John G. Doyle, "Olga Samaroff," in Hitchcock and Sadie, *New Grove Dictionary of American Music*, vol. 4, p. 128; Texas Music Museum, "Musikfest."

14. See www.governor.state.tx.us/divisions/music. For more about early classical music in Austin see Mint O. James-Reed, *Music in Austin, 1900–1956.*

15. Dominique-René de Lerma, "Jules Bledsoe," in Hitchcock and Sadie, *New Grove Dictionary of American Music*, vol. 1, p. 233; Lynette Geary, "Jules Bledsoe," in Barkley et al., *Handbook of Texas Music*, p. 23.

16. Howard Reich, *Van Cliburn*, pp. 1–5, 32–33, 40–41, 112–17, 310, 343; "Classical Music," in Barkley et al., *Handbook of Texas Music*, pp. 52–57.

17. Henry Hauschild, conversation with author, Feb. 26, 2002; Henry J. Hauschild, *A Musical Chronicle from the Historical Scrapbooks;* Teresa Palomo Acosta, "Hauschild Music Company," in Barkley et al., *Handbook of Texas Music*, pp. 134–35.

18. The best recent study of German singing societies in Central Texas is Heide's "Celebrating das Deutsche Lied," 29–38. See also Biesele, *History of the German Settlements in Texas*, pp. 208–27, for a discussion of the way in which German Texans integrated politics, culture, and economics in order to address many of the challenges they faced in their new homeland.

19. Heide, "Celebrating das Deutsche Lied," pp. 30–31; Biesele, *History of the German Settlements in Texas*, pp. 222–23; Lota M. Spell, "The Early German Contribution to Music in Texas," *American-German Review* 12, no. 4 (Apr. 1946): 8–10.

20. Theodore Albrecht, "German Music," in Barkley et al., *Handbook of Texas Music*, p. 118; Heide, "Celebrating das Deutsche Lied," pp. 30–33. Albrecht and Heide support Johann Menger's claim that the San Antonio Männergesangverein was founded in July 1847, which would make it the first German singing society in Texas. If, in fact, the Männergesangverein was founded in 1847, it would predate the New Braunfels Gesangverein Germania by about three years; Claus D. Heide, interview by Alberto Coss, TMOHP, June 1, 2005, p. 1.

21. Heide, "Celebrating das Deutsche Lied," pp. 33–37.

22. Lich and Reeves, *German Culture in Texas*, pp. 157–88; Owens, *Tell Me a Story*, pp. 193–208; Uhler, "University Researchers Are Trying to Record State's Unique, and Dying, German Language."

23. Two books in particular provide valuable insight into nineteenth-century Texas German folk music. *Texanische Lieder: Aus mündlicher und schriftlicher Mitteilung deutscher Texaner* includes thirty-one folk songs written in German. Several of these tunes celebrate the "new freedom" that Germans enjoy in Texas and praise the heroism of those who fought for Texas independence at the Alamo. One song, "Ade, Deutschland," tells of the sadness immigrants felt upon leaving Germany but also the happiness they experienced after arriving in Galveston to start a life filled with new opportunities. Also good is Theodore Gish, ed., *Travels in Texas (Texas Fahrten)*. This book is based on Hermann Seele's early nineteenth-century musical, *Texas Fahrten*, the manuscript of which is housed in the

Sophienburg Memorial Association Archives in New Braunfels. This musical traces the adventures of four Texas German friends as they travel throughout the state encountering Indians, Tejanos, Texas Rangers, and others. Gish has translated the original manuscript and added some very helpful commentary and analysis. Copies of both of these books are available at the Center for American History at the University of Texas–Austin. Martha Anne Turner, *The Yellow Rose of Texas: The Story of a Song*, pp. 10–16; Heide, interview by Coss, p. 15, TMOHP. Allan Turner's August 1972 (ATOHC) interview of German Texas bandleader Paul Barsch includes the popular polka "In Heaven There Is No Beer," performed on just a fiddle and a guitar.

24. For a brief history of the waltz see Mosco Carner, *The Waltz*, pp. 9–21; Peña, *Música Tejana*, pp. 43–44. It is difficult to know exactly how such dance steps were introduced to ethnic groups in Texas. Since some of these steps were fashionable across Europe during the late 1700s and early 1800s, it is possible that they were first brought to Mexico by the Spanish or French and then traveled northward into Texas. There is also some debate as to how the accordion first appeared in Texas, but it is most likely that German and Czech immigrants brought it to Texas and northern Mexican during the mid-1800s.

25. For the most complete listing of Texas dance halls, see Geronimo Treviño, *Dance Halls and Last Calls: A History of Texas Country Music*. See also Gail Folkins, "Texas Dance Halls: History, Culture, and Community," *Journal of Texas Music History* (2006): 54–62. Also informative is *The Texas Honky-tonk Trail*, by Tommy Allen, as told to Jack Lane.

26. Brandy Schnautz, "Gruene Hall," p. 126, and Glen E. Lich and Brandy Schnautz, "Luckenbach, Texas," in Barkley et al., *Handbook of Texas Music*, pp. 193–94.

27. William Brooks, "Music in America: An Overview (Part 1)," pp. 45–46, and Stephen Banfield, "Popular Song and Popular Music on Stage and Film," pp. 322–37, in Nichols, *Cambridge History of American Music*; Appell and Hemphill, *American Popular Music*, pp. 101–15.

28. "The Jewish Texans" (booklet published by the University of Texas Institute of Texan Cultures at San Antonio, 1974), pp. 1–8.

29. Kownslar, *European Texans*, pp. 112–13; "Jewish Texans," Institute of Texan Cultures, pp. 14–15.

30. Theodore Albrecht, "San Antonio Symphony Orchestra," in Barkley et al., *Handbook of Texas Music*, pp. 282–83.

31. See www.texasklezmer.com (accessed Mar. 30, 2007); Hinton, *South by Southwest*, p. 102; Reid, *Improbable Rise of Redneck Rock*, pp. 180–92.

32. Clinton Machann and James W. Mendl Jr., trans. and eds., *Czech Voices: Stories from Texas in the Amerikán Národní Kalendář*, pp. xviii–xix; Kownslar, *European Texans*, p. 134; Owens, *Tell Me a Story*, pp. 209–19.

33. "The Czech Texans" (booklet published by the University of Texas Institute of Texan Cultures at San Antonio, 1972), pp. 3–10. See also Clinton Machann and James W. Mendl Jr., *Krasna Amerika: A Study of the Texas Czechs, 1851–1939*, and Victor Greene, *A Passion for Polka: Old-time Ethnic Music in America*.

34. "Czech Texans," pp. 13–23; Kownslar, *European Texans*, p. 143; Owens, *Tell Me a Story*, pp. 212–19.

35. Carolyn F. Griffith, "Czech and Polish Music in Texas before World War II," in Clayton and Specht, *Roots of Texas Music*, pp. 183–87; "Muziky, Muziky: Czech Contributions to Texas Music" (booklet published by the Texas Music Museum, Austin, 1995); Roger H. Kolar, *Early Czech Dance Halls in Texas*; Philip V. Bohlman, "Immigrant, Folk, and Regional Musics in the Twentieth Century," in Nicholls, *Cambridge History of American Music*, pp. 282–83.

36. Spell, *Music in Texas*, pp. 26–27; Ray Ba a, interview by Allan Turner, Mar. 18, 1978, ATOHC; Machann and Mendl, *Czech Voices*, p. xv; "Czech Texans," pp. 1, 3; Andrew Brown, "Bacova Ceska Kapela: A Visit with Clarence Baca," *Taking Off: Musical Journeys in the Southwest and Beyond*, no. 1 (Spring 2005): 42–51; Brandy Schnautz, "Bacas of Fayetteville," in Barkley et al., *Handbook of Texas Music*, p. 14.

37. David DeKunder, "Joe Patek," in Barkley et al., *Handbook of Texas Music*, pp. 239–41; Chris Strachwitz, "Texas Polka Music: Interview with Joe Patek," in Chris Strachwitz and Pete Welding, *The American Folk Music Occasional*, pp. 73–75.

38. Adolph Hofner, interview by Allan Turner, June 8, 1916, ATOHC; Martin Donell Kohout, "Adolph Hofner," in Barkley et al., *Handbook of Texas Music*, p. 137; Malone, *Country Music, U.S.A.*, pp. 152–53.

39. Oliphant, *Early Swing Era*, p. 21; Kohout, "Adolph Hofner," p. 137; Fred Dellar, Alan Cackett, and Roy Thompson, *The Harmony Illustrated Encyclopedia of Country Music*, p. 79.

40. Nick A. Morris, *A History of the S.P.J.S.T: A Texas Chronicle, 1897–1980*, pp. 9–15, 160–285. For more information, see the SPJST website (www.spjst.com).

41. Robert L. Skrabanek, *We're Czechs*, pp. 81–82. See also www.koop.org and www.kvlgkbuk.com (accessed May 30, 2005.). The *Texas Polka News* provides an extensive and updated listing of Czech dances, festivals, and other events. See www.angelfire.com/folk/polka/news (accessed May 30, 2005.)

42. "Czech Texans," pp. 7–22; Koster, *Texas Music*, pp. 229–30. See also www.czechpolka.com/radio/history (accessed Mar. 30, 2007.).

43. See www.czechtexas.org.

44. Kownslar, *European Texans*, pp. 124–30; "The Polish Texans" (booklet published by the University of Texas Institute of Texan Cultures at San Antonio, 1972), pp. 1–3, 5, 9, 17–20, 32; Mr. and Mrs. Felix Mika, interview by Allan Turner, Sept. 23, 1979, ATOHC.

45. Griffith, "Czech and Polish Music," pp. 175–82; Treviño, *Dance Halls and Last Calls*, pp. 83–84, 145–46.

46. See www.markrubin.com/brianmarshall.

47. Richardson, *Texas*, pp. 25–30; Kownslar, *European Texans*, pp. 12–14.

48. Calvert and De León, *History of Texas*, pp. 17–21; "New Orleans History Facts," on the City of New Orleans website, www.new-orleans.la.us (accessed May 17, 2005); John

Joyce, "New Orleans," in Hitchcock and Sadie, *New Grove Dictionary of American Music*, vol. 3, pp. 340–44; Keller, "Secular Music to 1800," pp. 57–58.

49. Campbell, *Gone to Texas*, pp. 94–96; Teja, Marks, and Tyler, *Texas*, pp. 141–45; Kownslar, *European Texans*, p. 14; "The French Texans" (booklet published by the University of Texas Institute of Texan Cultures at San Antonio, 1973), pp. 11–19.

50. "French Texans," pp. 18–23. See also François Lagarde, "Diplomacy, Commerce, and Colonization: Saligny and the Republic," pp. 120–21; Janine Earny, "Grounds for Emigration: Alsace at the Time of Henri Castro," pp. 124–27; Wayne M. Ahr, "Henri Castro and Castroville: Alsatian History and Heritage," 136–39; and Martha Utterback, "French Artists in Texas," pp. 186–87, all in François Lagarde, ed., *The French in Texas: History, Migration, Culture*.

51. Michael Tisserand's *Kingdom of Zydeco* is one of the best sources on the history of zydeco, although it makes only brief mention of zydeco in relation to Texas. Wood, in *Texas Zydeco* and "Southeast Texas: Hothouse of Zydeco," offers the most complete examination of the role of Texas in the development of zydeco.

52. In 1848 France permanently abolished slavery. Mélina Gazsi, "A Tribute to Victor Schoelcher: Down with Slavery!" *Label France*, no. 56 (Oct.–Dec. 2004), www.france.diplomatie.gouv.fr/label_france/56 (accessed May 6, 2005).

53. Roger Wood, "Black Creoles and the Evolution of Zydeco in Southeast Texas: The Beginnings to 1950," in Clayton and Specht, *Roots of Texas Music*, pp. 196–97; Ira Berlin, *Slaves without Masters: The Free Negro in the Antebellum South*, pp. 109–28; Leonard Curry, *The Free Black in Urban America, 1800–1850*, pp. 138–40.

54. Wood, *Down in Houston*, pp. 138–39; Wood, "Southeast Texas: Hothouse of Zydeco," pp. 26–28.

55. Allan Turner's recording of black creoles participating in pre-Lenten festivities in Durald, Louisiana, on Feb. 19, 1980, provides a good example of how modern zydeco borrows from older slave traditions of hand clapping, field hollers, and call and response (ATOHC). See Wood, "Black Creoles and the Evolution of Zydeco in Southeast Texas," in Clayton and Specht, *Roots of Texas Music*, pp. 197–200.

56. Chris Strachwitz, "Zydeco Music, i.e., French Blues," in Strachwitz and Welding, *American Folk Music Occasional*, pp. 22–24. See also Tisserand, *Kingdom of Zydeco*, pp. 9–21.

57. Roger Wood and Andrew Brown, email correspondence with author, Mar. 26 and 27, 2006. According to Wood's *Down in Houston*, pp. 48, 143, "Zolo Go," as a variation on the word "zydeco," may have been a result of white record producer Bill Quinn's misunderstanding of Hopkins's pronunciation of "zydeco."

58. Wood, *Texas Zydeco*, pp. 88–92; Wood, "Black Creoles and the Evolution of Zydeco in Southeast Texas," in Clayton and Specht, *Roots of Texas Music*, pp. 200–202.

59. Wood, "Southeast Texas: Hothouse of Zydeco," pp. 28–29.

60. Strachwitz, "Zydeco Music, i.e., French Blues," pp. 22–29. See also Roger Wood, "Zydeco," in Barkley et al., *Handbook of Texas Music*, pp. 365–66.

61. Alan B. Govenar, "Clifton Chenier: African-American Zydeco Accordionist (Cre-

ole)," *Masters of Traditional Arts*, vol. 1, pp. 126–28; Shane K. Bernard, *Swamp Pop: Cajun and Creole Rhythm and Blues*, pp. 5–6, 60–61, 97, 103; Tisserand, *Kingdom of Zydeco*, pp. 148–56; Santelli, *Big Book of Blues*, pp. 88–89; Romanowski and George-Warren, *New Rolling Stone Encyclopedia*, p. 170.

62. Wood, "Zydeco," in Barkley et al., *Handbook of Texas Music*, p. 366; Bernard, *Swamp Pop*, pp. 75–114; Wood, "Southeast Texas: Hothouse of Zydeco," pp. 41–43.

63. For a good, brief discussion of the differences between zydeco and Cajun music see Rick Olivier and Ben Sandmel, *Zydeco!*, pp. 12–29. For an analysis of the evolution of the word "Cajun," as well as the positive and negative implications of its usage, see Jacques Henry, "From *Acadien* to *Cajun* to *Cadien*: Ethnic Labelization and Construction of Identity," *Journal of American Ethnic History* 17, no. 4 (Summer 1998): 29–62.

64. Barry Jean Ancelet's *Makers of Cajun Music* provides a very good overview of Cajun history and culture in both English and French. See also Charles J. Stivale, *Disenchanting les Bons Temps: Identity and Authenticity in Cajun Music and Dance*, especially pp. 1–3, 40–72, and 132–57, for a discussion of the importance of alienation, displacement, and dispossession in the mythology of Cajun folk culture. The mythology surrounding the forced eviction of the Acadiens from Canada by the British, known in French as *le grand dérangement*, is a critical part of Cajun culture and is retold in Henry Wadsworth Longfellow's poem "Evangeline," as well as in numerous Cajun songs. These centuries-old themes of migration and displacement are still common in Cajun music and can be found in twentieth-century songs such as "Le Grand Texas," which tells of the modern exodus of the Cajuns to the Lone Star State in search of new economic opportunities.

65. See both Paul Tate, "The Cajuns of Louisiana," pp. 8–10, and Harry Oster, "Louisiana Acadians," pp. 18–21, in Strachwitz and Welding, *American Folk Music Occasional*. See also Henry, "From *Acadien* to *Cajun* to *Cadien*," pp. 37–43.

66. Owens, *Tell Me a Story*, pp. 116–20, 127–28; Alan B. Govenar, "Dewey Balfa: Cajun Fiddler," *Masters of Traditional Arts*, vol. 1, pp. 53–55. In this interview Balfa mentions both the importance of World War II in exposing Cajuns to other musical traditions and the influence of Texas musicians such as Bob Wills and Harry Choates on Balfa's playing. Ancelet, *Makers of Cajun Music*, 22–25; Ormonde Plater and Cynthia and Rand Speyrer, *Cajun Dancing*, pp. 21–22, 30–35.

67. Dennis McGee, interview by Allan Turner, Apr. 1, 1978, ATOHC; Oster, "Louisiana Acadians," pp. 20–21; Plater and Speyrer, *Cajun Dancing*, pp. 17–21; "Allons Dancer, Colinda," of which there are many variations, may originally have been sung by black creoles before it became a Cajun standard. This excerpt is from a composite of different versions I have heard throughout Texas and Louisiana.

68. Chris Strachwitz, "Cajun Country," in Strachwitz and Welding, *American Folk Music Occasional*, pp. 13–17; Paul M. Lucko, "Harry H. Choates," in Barkley et al., *Handbook of Texas Music*, pp. 49–50; Ancelet, *Makers of Cajun Music*, 25–26; Corcoran, *All Over the Map*, pp. 6–9.

CHAPTER 6

1. For a brief overview of Texas country music see Gary Hartman, "The Bob Bullock Museum Celebrates Texas Country Music," *Journal of Texas Music History* 2, no. 2 (Fall 2002): 7–15. For a good discussion of Texas country music specifically between 1922 and 1950 see Joe W. Specht, "Put a Nickel in the Jukebox: The Texas Tradition in Country Music, 1922–1950," in Clayton and Specht, *Roots of Texas Music*, pp. 66–94. See Malone, "Texas Myth/Texas Music," regarding the blending of these musical cultures. For examples of the popularity of country music worldwide see Gérard Herzhaft and Jacques Brémond, eds., *Guide de la Country Music et du Folk*; Gary Hartman, "Texas Music in Europe," *Journal of Texas Music History* 4, no. 1 (Spring 2004): 33–41; and Andrei Gorbatov, *Wanted: Country Music in Russia and the Ex-USSR*.

2. Malone's *Country Music, U.S.A.* remains the best and most comprehensive examination of the history of country music. Malone makes it clear that, although the South was the cradle of country music, the genre was also shaped by a variety of other influences from across North America.

3. Keller, "Secular Music to 1800," pp. 75–77. There are many examples of how European folk music was transformed in North America between the seventeenth and twentieth centuries. One of the most interesting ones involves the old Scottish ballad "The Wife of Usher's Well," which is discussed in Owens, *Tell Me a Story*, pp. 28–32.

4. *The Random House College Dictionary* (New York: Random House, Inc., 1979), pp. 36, 395; Malone, *Don't Get above Your Raisin'*, pp. 149–70, includes an in-depth discussion of the development of country music dancing. See also www.dosedo.com.

5. Malone, *Country Music, U.S.A.*, pp 1–6, 466. For a good biography of Bill Monroe see Richard D. Smith, *Can't You Hear Me Callin': The Life of Bill Monroe, Father of Bluegrass*; Henthoff, *Listen to the Stories*, pp. 149–50. For a discussion of how white musicians adopted the banjo from blacks see Robert B. Winans, "The Folk, the Stage, and the Five-string Banjo in the Nineteenth Century," *Journal of American Folklore* 89, no. 354 (Oct. 1976): 407–37. Karen Elizabeth Linn, "The 'Elevation' of the Banjo in Late Nineteenth-century America," *American Music* 8, no. 4 (Winter 1990): 441–64; and Cecilia Conway, *African Banjo Echoes in Appalachia: A Study of Folk Traditions*. For more information about the adaptation of the Hawaiian slide guitar in country music see Dick Spottswood, "Hawaiian Music," in Kingsbury, *Encyclopedia of Country Music*, pp. 231–32, and Richard Carlin, *Country Music: A Biographical Dictionary*, pp. 309–10. Adolph Hofner, Ted Daffan, and Cliff Bruner, all leading figures in Texas country music, state that their interest in Hawaiian guitar was a major factor in their deciding to become musicians. See Adolph Hofner, interview by Allan Turner, Mar. 13, 1980; Ted Daffan, interview by Allan Turner, Oct. 7, 1980; and Cliff Bruner, interview by Allan Turner and Jay Brakefield, June 7, 1981, all in ATOHC.

6. Christopher A. Waterman, "Race Music: Bo Chatmon, 'Corrine, Corrina,' and the Excluded Middle," in Radano and Bohlman, *Music and the Racial Imagination*, pp. 167–205.

7. Dale Cockrell, "Nineteenth-century Popular Music," in Nicholls, *Cambridge History of American Music*, pp. 165–75; Malone, *Country Music, U.S.A*, pp. 6–10. For a very good discussion of how country music has undergone changes regarding terminology and public image see Richard A. Peterson, *Creating Country Music: Fabricating Authenticity*, especially pp. 194–201. See also Cecilia Tichi, *High Lonesome: The American Culture of Country Music*, and Robert K. Oermann, *America's Music: The Roots of Country*.

8. Thomas W. Cutrer, *The English Texans*, pp. 7–10; Richardson, *Texas*, pp. 51–53.

9. Teja, Marks, and Tyler, *Texas*, pp. 158–68; Campbell, *Gone to Texas*, pp. 100–104; Richardson, *Texas*, pp. 75–77.

10. John Brendan Flannery, *The Irish Texans*, pp. 17–20; Kownslar, *European Texans*, pp. 39–46.

11. Govenar and Brakefield, *Deep Ellum*, pp. 1–2; Flannery, *Irish Texans*, pp. 27–53.

12. Richardson, *Texas*, pp. 291–98; Campbell, *Gone to Texas*, p. 472.

13. For a discussion of the mythology surrounding life in the nineteenth-century American West, see Patricia Nelson Limerick, *Legacy of Conquest: The Unbroken Past, of the American West*, and Sarah Deutsch, *No Separate Refuge: Culture, Class, and Gender on an Anglo-Hispanic Frontier in the American Southwest, 1880–1940*. One of the best books available on the mythology of the cowboy and his music, especially in terms of how Hollywood capitalized on this mythology, is Douglas B. Green's *Singing in the Saddle: The History of The Singing Cowboy*.

14. Joe Carr and Alan Munde, *Prairie Nights to Neon Lights: The Story of Country Music in West Texas*, pp. 9–18; Teja, Marks, and Tyler, *Texas*, pp. 306–10; Archie Green, "Austin's Cosmic Cowboys: Words in Collision," in Bauman and Abrahams, *And Other Neighborly Names*, pp. 153–62. For a good sampling of traditional Texas folk and country songs see Francis E. Abernethy, *Singin' Texas*.

15. Owens, *Tell Me a Story*, p. 106; Carr and Munde, *Prairie Nights to Neon Lights*, pp. 23–31.

16. N. Howard Thorp, *Songs of the Cowboys*; Carr and Munde, *Prairie Nights to Neon Lights*, pp. 9–11. See also John A. Lomax, *Cowboy Songs and Other Frontier Ballads*, and John A. Lomax, *Songs of the Cattle Trail and Cow Camp*. In Box 3D177, especially folders 4, 8, and 10, of the John A. Lomax Family Papers at the University of Texas at Austin are a number of typed and handwritten versions of many of these now classic cowboy songs. Of particular note are several variations on "The Dying Cowboy (Bury Me Not on the Lone Prairie)," which is based on an older seafaring song, "The Ocean Burial."

17. For a discussion of the commercialization of country music and the manipulation of regional identity, see Peterson, *Creating Country Music*. Fowler and Crawford's *Border Radio* is still the best account of early radio marketing in the Southwest. Bill C. Malone, *Southern Music/American Music*, pp. 72–73; Malone, *Country Music, U.S.A.*, pp. 33–34.

18. Texas-style fiddling also tends to be more improvisational than most other styles. For example, even today, bluegrass and old-time fiddle contests throughout the country usually emphasize speed and technical ability over innovation, whereas Texas-style

contest fiddling also requires technical proficiency, but it generally rewards players for their improvisational skills. Charles Wolfe, "Eck Robertson," in Kingsbury, *Encyclopedia of Country Music*, pp. 450–51; Govenar and Brakefield, *Deep Ellum*, pp. 152–54. See Neil V. Rosenberg, *Bluegrass: A History*, pp. 240–46, and Charles Gardner, "The Origins of the Texas Style of Traditional Old-time Fiddling," in Frances Edward Abernethy, ed., *2001: A Texas Folklore Odyssey*, pp. 54–73, for a discussion of the unique characteristics of Texas-style fiddling. See also Charles K. Wolfe, *The Devil's Box: Masters of Southern Fiddling*, for more information on regional fiddle styles.

19. Kevin S. Fontenot, "Henry Clay Gilliland," and Jill S. Seeber, "Eck Robertson," in Barkley et al., *Handbook of Texas Music*, pp. 120, 268–69; Ronnie Pugh, "Eck Robertson," in Hitchcock and Sadie, *New Grove Dictionary of American Music*, vol. 4, p. 53.

20. Govenar and Brakefield, *Deep Ellum*, p. 154; Jean Boyd, *The Jazz of the Southwest: An Oral History of Western Swing*, p. 13; Malone, *Country Music, U.S.A.*, p. 159. Malone mentions that a public television documentary about Prince Albert Hunt was made in the 1970s.

21. Jack Palmer, *Vernon Dalhart: First Star of Country Music*, pp. 7–8, 19–55. This book contains a wealth of detailed information and a very helpful discography of Dalhart's recordings. See also "Vernon Dalhart," in Carlin, *Country Music*, p. 94; Jack Palmer, "Vernon Dalhart," in Barkley et al., *Handbook of Texas Music*, pp. 75–77; Malone, *Country Music, U.S.A.*, pp. 60–64.

22. Charlie Seemann, "Carl T. Sprague," in Kingsbury, *Encyclopedia of Country Music*, p. 449; "Carl T. Sprague," in Carlin, *Country Music*, pp. 94, 382; Malone, *Country Music, U.S.A.*, p. 139.

23. "Jimmie Rodgers," in Barkley et al., *Handbook of Texas Music*, pp. 275–76. The definitive biography of Rodgers remains Nolan Porterfield's *Jimmie Rodgers: The Life and Times of America's Blue Yodeler*. Porterfield makes several references to the importance of Texas in Rodgers's life.

24. Wyman, *Blues Odyssey*, pp. 182–83; Dellar, Cackett, and Thompson, *Harmony Illustrated Encyclopedia of Country Music*, pp. 28–29.

25. For a more detailed discussion of Rodgers's time in Texas see Joe Specht, "The Blue Yodeler Is Coming to Town: A Week with Jimmie Rodgers in West Texas," *Journal of Texas Music History* 1, no. 2 (Fall 2001): 17–22.

26. By the end of World War II most country music heard on the radio was highly commercialized and often written, performed, or produced by people who did not have an agrarian background. However, some popular country artists, most notably Merle Haggard, did come from humble rural origins and have consistently produced music that is commercially successful yet still rooted in organic musical traditions. For a discussion of Haggard as a cultural icon in country music see James N. Gregory, *American Exodus: The Dust Bowl Migration and Okie Culture in California*, pp. 238–45. See also Nat Hentoff, *Listen to the Stories: Nat Hentoff on Jazz and Country Music*, pp. 153–64.

27. See Bill C. Malone, *Singing Cowboys and Musical Mountaineers: Southern Culture and the Roots of Country Music*.

28. Green, *Singing in the Saddle*, especially pp. 6–19, provides a good discussion of how popular literature, Wild West shows, and a variety of ethnic influences played a part in creating the culture and mythology of the singing cowboy; see also Peterson, *Creating Country Music*, especially pp. 55–94.

29. See Ken Griffis, "The Ken Maynard Story," *John Edwards Memorial Foundation Quarterly* 9, part 2, no. 30 (Summer 1973): 67–70, as well as the following websites: www hooverarchives.gov/exhibits/HollywoodCowboys and www.cmt.com/artists/az/maynard_ken (accessed July 12, 2005).

30. Jarad Brown, "Gene Autry," in Barkley et al., *Handbook of Texas Music*, pp. 12–13; Bill C. Malone, "Orvon Gene Autry," in Hitchcock and Sadie, *New Grove Dictionary of American Music*, vol. 1, pp. 93–94; Malone, *Country Music, U.S.A.*, pp 142–43; see also www.autry.com.

31. For a very good discussion of the lives, careers, and cultural significance of Dale Evans and Roy Rogers see Raymond E. White, *King of the Cowboys, Queen of the West: Roy Rogers and Dale Evans*; Bufwack and Oermann, *Finding Her Voice*, pp. 118–21; Martin Donell Kohout, "Dale Evans," in Barkley et al., *Handbook of Texas Music*, pp. 95–97.

32. Specht, "Put a Nickel in the Jukebox," pp. 73–75; "Tex Ritter," in Barkley et al., *Handbook of Texas Music*, p. 267; Nancy Toff, "Tex Ritter," in Hitchcock and Sadie, *New Grove Dictionary of American Music*, vol. 4, p. 50.

33. For the most complete discussion of Willing's life and career see Sharon Lee Willing, *No One to Cry To: A Long, Hard Ride into the Sunset with Foy Willing of the Riders of the Purple Sage*. Sharon (Mrs. Foy) Willing, email correspondence with author, July 12, 2005; Foy Willing, interview by Douglas Green, Dec. 17, 1975, Country Music Foundation Oral History Project (CMFOHP); Gary Hartman, "Foy Willing," in Barkley et al., *Handbook of Texas Music*, pp. 355–56; Kevin Coffey, "New Riders of the Purple Sage," and Don Cusic, "Riders in the Sky," in Kingsbury, *Encyclopedia of Country Music*, pp. 377, 444–45. Green, *Singing in the Saddle*, includes a look at the recent revival of interest in the singing cowboy.

34. Govenar, *African American Frontiers*, pp. 217–40. See also www.herbjeffries.com (accessed Mar. 27, 2007).

35. Although most historians agree that Western swing is a remarkably eclectic blend of musical genres, some disagree as to whether Western swing is more country, jazz, or something in between. See, for example, Boyd, *Jazz of the Southwest*, and Specht, "Put a Nickel in the Jukebox."

36. Charles R. Townsend, *San Antonio Rose: The Life and Music of Bob Wills*, pp. 1–7. Townsend has published the most complete biography of Wills. For a more personal account of the life and career of Wills see Rosetta Wills, *The King of Western Swing: Bob Wills Remembered*.

37. Charles Townsend, "Bob Wills," in Barkley et al., *Handbook of Texas Music*, pp. 356–35. See also Rush Evans, "Bob Wills: The King of Western Swing," *Journal of Texas Music History* 2, no. 2 (Fall 2002): 16–29; Hentoff, *Listen to the Stories*, pp. 165–75.

38. John Mark Dempsey, *The Light Crust Doughboys Are on the Air: Celebrating Seventy Years*

of *Texas Music*, pp. 22–25; Townsend, *San Antonio Rose*, pp. 1–52; Duncan Mc Lean, *Lone Star Swing: On the Trail of Bob Wills and His Texas Playboys*, pp. 234–35; Cary Ginell, "Milton Brown," in Kingsbury, *Encyclopedia of Country Music*, pp. 58–59; www.familysearch.org.

39. Jean Boyd, *"We're the Light Crust Doughboys from Burrus Mill": An Oral History*, p. 30.

40. McLean, *Lone Star Swing*, pp. 77–81. According to some of the musicians who played with Wills, the band often had to play more or less nonstop for hours to prevent dancers from pausing long enough to get into fistfights. Johnny Gimble and Johnny Cuviello, conversations with author, Oct. 25 and 26, 2005.

41. Johnny Gimble, conversation with author, Nov. 30, 2006; Stacey Phillips, *Western Swing Fiddle*, pp. 7–20; Townsend, *San Antonio Rose*, pp. 39–46; Govenar and Brakefield, *Deep Ellum*, pp. 138–63.

42. Campbell, *Gone to Texas*, pp. 392–95; Specht, "Put a Nickel in the Jukebox," pp. 76–77. The most complete story of Brown's life and career can be found in *Milton Brown and the Founding of Western Swing*, by Cary Ginell, with special assistance from Roy Lee Brown.

43. Malone, *Country Music, U.S.A*, p. 187. Townsend, *San Antonio Rose*, pp. 102–106, discuss Wills's pioneering role in bringing drums into popular country music.

44. Evans, "Bob Wills," pp. 25–27; Hentoff, *Listen to the Stories*, pp. 165–67.

45. Kevin Coffey, "Steel Colossus: The Bob Dunn Story," *Journal of Country Music* 17, no. 2 (1996): 90–108; William W. Savage Jr., *Singing Cowboys and All That Jazz: A Short History of Popular Music in Oklahoma*, pp. 56–59. Savage says that Bob Dunn recorded with an electrified slide guitar in Chicago in January 1935, eight months before Eddie Durham recorded on electric guitar with Jimmie Lunceford.

46. In this brief segment on Western swing, it would be impossible to adequately cover all of the influential artists of this genre. However, the following sources provide very useful additional information on several of these figures: Bob Dunbar, *From Bob Wills to Ray Benson: A History of Western Swing Music*; Cary Ginell and Kevin Coffey, *Discography of Western Swing and Hot String Bands, 1928–1942*; John Dempsey, "Marvin 'Smokey' Montgomery: A Life in Texas Music," *Journal of Texas Music History* 1, no. 2 (Fall 2001): 45–57; Kevin Coffey, CD liner notes for *Cliff Bruner and His Texas Wanderers*; Cliff Bruner, interview by Turner and Brakefield, June 7, 1981, ATOHC; Richard Carlin, "Leon Payne," *Country Music: A Biographical Dictionary*, p. 308; Charles R. Townsend, "Western Swing," and Jonny Whiteside, "Spade Cooley," in Kingsbury, *Encyclopedia of Country Music*, pp. 109, 579–80; "Spade Cooley," in Dellar, Cackett, and Thompson, *Harmony Illustrated Encyclopedia of Country Music*, p. 37; Leon McAuliffe, interview by Cecil Whaley, Aug. 19, 1969, CMFOHP; Andrew Brown, "Texas Rancher: The Tony Sepolio Interview," and Kevin Coffey, "The Tony Sepolio Discography," in *Taking Off: Musical Journeys in the Southwest and Beyond*, no. 1 (Spring 2005): 2–29; Al Stricklin with Jon McConal, *My Years with Bob Wills*. In Barkley et al., *Handbook of Texas Music*, see Matthew Douglas Moore, "Jesse Ashlock," p. 10; Charles Townsend, "Tommy Duncan," pp. 85–86; Juan Carlos Rodríguez, "Bob Dunn," p. 86; Ryan A. Kashanipour, "Tiny Moore," pp. 215–16; and Joe Specht, "Hoyle Nix," p. 231. Also, Louise Rowe interview by Dee Lannon, May 23, 2005, TMOHP; John E. Perkins Jr., *Leon Rausch: The Voice of the Texas Playboys*.

47. Ray Benson, conversation with author, Mar. 28, 2004; Cindy Cashdollar, conversation with author, Mar. 21, 2006.

48. Specht, "Put a Nickel in the Jukebox," p. 79; Malone, *Don't Get above Your Raisin*,' pp. 161–62. See also Bill Porterfield, *The Greatest Honky Tonks in Texas*, as well as Treviño, *Dance Halls and Last Calls*.

49. See James Rice, *Texas Honky-tonk Music*, and Carr and Munde, *Prairie Nights to Neon Lights*, pp. 60–80, for an overview of the evolution of honky-tonk, especially in relation to Texas. For a colorful and more personal account of performing in Texas honky-tonks and roadhouses, see *The Texas Honky Tonk Trail*, by Tommy Allen, as told to Jack Lane.

50. Bill C. Malone, "Jukeboxes," in Kingsbury, *Encyclopedia of Country Music*, pp. 273–74.

51. Ted Daffan, interview by Allan Turner, Oct. 7, 1980, ATOHC; Ted Daffan, interview by Dorothy Gable, Jan. 31, 1968, CMFOHP; Linc Leifeste, "Ted Daffan," in Barkley et al., *Handbook of Texas Music*, pp. 74–75; Kevin Coffey, "Ted Daffan," in Kingsbury, *Encyclopedia of Country Music*, pp. 130–31.

52. John Rumble, "Floyd Tillman," in Kingsbury, *Encyclopedia of Country Music*, p. 540; Hudson, *Telling Stories, Writing Songs*, pp. 16–21; "Floyd Tillman," in Dellar, Cackett, and Thompson, *Harmony Illustrated Encyclopedia of Country Music*, p. 172; Specht, "Put a Nickel in the Jukebox," pp. 79–82.

53. Paul M. Lucko, "Moon Mullican," in Barkley et al., *Handbook of Texas Music*, pp. 218–19; Carlin, *Country Music*, pp. 274–75.

54. Ronnie Pugh, *Ernest Tubb: The Texas Troubadour*, pp. 4–38, 49–50.

55. Phillip L. Fry, "Ernest Dale Tubb," in Barkley et al., *Handbook of Texas Music*, p. 330; Ronnie Pugh, "Ernest Tubb," in Kingsbury, *Encyclopedia of Country Music*, pp. 547–48.

56. "Hank Thompson," in Dellar, Cackett, and Thompson, *Harmony Illustrated Encyclopedia of Country Music*, pp. 170–71; John Rumble, "Hank Thompson," in Kingsbury, *Encyclopedia of Country Music*, pp. 536–37; Carlin, *Country Music*, p. 398.

57. Phillip L. Fry, "Lefty Frizzell," in Barkley et al., *Handbook of Texas Music*, p. 112; Also helpful is Daniel C. Cooper, *Lefty Frizzell: The Honky Tonk Life of Country Music's Greatest Singer*.

58. Merle Haggard with Peggy Russell, *Sing Me Back Home: My Story*, pp. 27–40; Malone, *Country Music, U.S.A.*, pp. 231–32; Daniel Cooper, "Lefty Frizzell," in Kingsbury, *Encyclopedia of Country Music*, pp. 184–86.

59. George Jones, with Tom Carter, *I Lived to Tell It All*, pp. 16–22, 50–53, 176–84. The Pappy Daily Collection in the Southwestern Writers Collection at Texas State University–San Marcos includes numerous newspaper and magazine clippings regarding George Jones's difficulties. Of particular note is a letter from Pappy's son, Don Daily, to fellow Texas record producer Huey P. Meaux, thanking Meaux for his positive comments about Pappy in an interview conducted by Nick Tosches for an article in the July 1994 issue of *Texas Monthly* magazine. Carlin, *Country Music*, pp. 207–208; Bob Allen, "George Jones," in Kingsbury, *Encyclopedia of Country Music*, pp. 268–69.

60. Herzhaft and Brémond, *Guide de la Country Music et du Folk*, p. 83; "Johnny Bush," in Dellar, Cackett, and Thompson, *Harmony Illustrated Encyclopedia of Country Music*, p. 25.

61. The most complete history of bluegrass is Rosenberg's *Bluegrass.* One of the longest-running and most popular bluegrass radio shows in Central Texas is KOOP-FM's "Strictly Bluegrass," which airs every Sunday morning on FM 91.7.

62. For the most complete coverage of bluegrass music in Texas, see Moag, "The History of Early Bluegrass in Texas," pp. 22–48. For bluegrass in West Texas, see Carr and Munde, *Prairie Nights to Neon Lights,* pp. 97–117. See Rosenberg, *Bluegrass,* pp. 241–45, for a discussion of the impact of Texas-style fiddling on bluegrass.

63. Bill C. Malone, "Jim Reeves," in Barkley et al., *Handbook of Texas Music,* pp. 262–63; John Rumble, "Jim Reeves," in Kingsbury, *Encyclopedia of Country Music,* pp. 435–36; Peterson, *Creating Country Music,* p. 154. Also helpful is Pansy Cook, *The Saga of Jim Reeves: Country and Western Singer and Musician.*

64. For the most complete account of the Big D Jamboree and its impact on country music see Kevin Coffey, "The Story of the Big 'D' Jamboree," liner notes for the CD *The Big "D" Jamboree Live!* vols. 1–2, produced by David Dennard and Dragon Street Productions, 2000.

65. Ray Price, interview by Hugh Cherry, Mar. 10, 1967, Frist Library and Archive, Country Music Hall of Fame and Museum; Carlin, *Country Music,* pp. 317–18; Daniel Cooper, "Ray Price," in Kingsbury, *Encyclopedia of Country Music,* pp. 422–23.

66. See Gerald Haslam, *Working Man Blues: Country Music in California,* for a good discussion of the Bakersfield sound and other West Coast country music trends. "Buck Owens," in Dellar, Cackett, and Thompson, *Harmony Illustrated Encyclopedia of Country Music,* pp. 126–27; Gregory, *American Exodus,* p. 241.

67. Tad Richards and Melvin B. Shestack, *The New Country Music Encyclopedia,* pp. 175–76; Elster, *International Who's Who in Popular Music 2004,* p. 433; Mark Fenster, "Buck Owens," in Kingsbury, *Encyclopedia of Country Music,* pp. 399–400; Greg Risling, "Country Music Superstar Buck Owens Dies at 76," from *Associated Press* (Mar. 25, 2006), www Austin360.com (accessed Mar. 26, 2006).

68. Margaret Jones, "Jimmy Dean," in Kingsbury, *Encyclopedia of Country Music,* p. 140.

69. Michael LeVine, *Johnny Horton: Your Singing Fisherman,* pp. 9–16, 111–17; Malone, *Country Music, U.S.A.,* pp. 283–85; Jill S. Seeber, "Johnny Horton," in Barkley et al., *Handbook of Texas Music,* pp. 142–43.

70. Bob Allen, "Charline Arthur," in Kingsbury, *Encyclopedia of Country Music,* p. 17; Bufwack and Oermann, *Finding Her Voice,* pp. 147–50; Carlin, *Country Music,* p. 11.

71. Richards and Shestack, *New Country Music Encyclopedia,* pp. 151–53; Carlin, *Country Music,* p. 265; Phillip L. Fry, "Roger Dean Miller," in Barkley et al., *Handbook of Texas Music,* p. 210. For a collection of insightful interviews with a variety of musicians who knew Miller, see Lyle E. Style, *Ain't Got No Cigarettes: Memories of Music Legend Roger Miller.*

72. Bufwack and Oermann, *Finding Her Voice,* pp. 278–79; Carlin, *Country Music,* p. 342; Don Rhodes, "Jeannie C. Riley," in Kingsbury, *Encyclopedia of Country Music,* p. 446.

73. Charley Pride with Jim Henderson, *The Charley Pride Story;* Bob Millard, "Charley Pride," in Kingsbury, *Encyclopedia of Country Music,* pp. 423–24; Carlin, *Country Music,* pp. 318–19.

74. Burr, *Billboard Guide*, pp. 180–81; Malone, *Country Music, U.S.A.*, pp. 312–13; Hudson, *Telling Stories, Writing Songs*, pp. 238–44.

75. Charles Paul Conn, *The Barbara Mandrell Story*, pp. 7–11, 20–21, 112–19; Bufwack and Oermann, *Finding Her Voice*, pp. 208, 338–43, 353–54. Perhaps ironically, Barbara Mandrell cofounded the Association of Country Entertainers (ACE) in 1974 in protest of the Country Music Association's selection of pop singer Olivia Newton-John as that year's CMA Female Vocalist of the Year. Although Mandrell was a pop-country artist herself, she and others believed that the CMA had betrayed country fans and performers by so honoring Newton-John, who was clearly outside the realm of what many considered country music; Carlin, *Country Music*, pp. 249–50.

76. Tanya Tucker, telephone interview by Paul Kingsbury, Feb. 21, 1992, CMFOHP; Tanya Tucker and Patsi Bale Cox, *Nickel Dreams: My Life*, pp. 8, 20–26; Bob Allen, "Tanya Tucker," in Russell D. Barnard, ed., *The Comprehensive Country Music Encyclopedia*, pp. 399–400; Irwin Stambler and Grelun Landon, eds., *Country Music: The Encyclopedia*, pp. 504–506; Daniel Cooper, "Tanya Tucker," in Kingsbury, *Encyclopedia of Country Music*, pp. 549–50; Bufwack and Oermann, *Finding Her Voice*, pp. 348, 386–89; Hudson, *Telling Stories, Writing Songs*, pp. 199–202.

77. "Don Williams," in Dellar, Cackett, and Thompson, *Harmony Illustrated Encyclopedia of Country Music*, p. 187; John Lomax III, "Don Williams," in Kingsbury, *Encyclopedia of Country Music*, p. 589.

78. Bob Millard, "Johnny Lee," in Kingsbury, *Encyclopedia of Country Music*, p. 295; Carlin, *Country Music*, p. 229.

79. Richards and Shestack, *New Country Music Encyclopedia*, pp. 92–93; Carlin, *Country Music*, p. 147.

80. Chet Flippo, "Mac Davis," in Kingsbury, *Encyclopedia of Country Music*, p. 137.

81. Peterson, *Creating Country*, pp. 137, 150–55. See especially Peterson's discussion of Rogers as a member of the "soft shell" contingency of country music. Although Peterson's method of categorization seems somewhat flawed, it provides insight into the relationship among artists in terms of their styles and approach to their music and public persona. Thomas Goldsmith, "Kenny Rogers," in Kingsbury, *Encyclopedia of Country Music*, pp. 455–56.

82. Although it is not a scholarly work, the most thorough account of the development of progressive country is Jan Reid's *Improbable Rise of Redneck Rock*. For a brief but very good examination of the culture, politics, and social issues involved in the progressive country phenomenon see Cory Lock, "Counterculture Cowboys: Progressive Texas Country of the 1970s and 1980s," *Journal of Texas Music History* 3, no. 1 (Spring 2003): 14–23.

83. Reid, *Improbable Rise of Redneck Rock*, pp. 3–10. On a personal note, I moved to Austin after graduating from high school in 1974 and frequented all of these clubs. Although I do not know of anyone who fully comprehended the magnitude of the progressive country phenomenon at the time, it was clear to me and to many with whom I have spoken that Austin in the 1970s truly was home to a unique and vibrant music scene.

84. Burton Wilson, interview by Rosebud Kuntz and Jack Kinslow, May 23, 2005, TMOHP; John Wheat, "Armadillo World Headquarters," in Barkley et al., *Handbook of Texas Music*, pp. 6–7; Reid, *Improbable Rise of Redneck Rock*, pp. 64–66. Long-time Austin resident Burton Wilson became the unofficial house photographer at the Armadillo during this period, and his vast collection of photographs from there and other Austin venues documents the remarkable live music in Austin. The best sampling of Wilson's work is *The Austin Music Scene through the Lens of Burton Wilson, 1965–1994*, by Burton Wilson, with Jack Ortman.

85. The Southwestern Writers Collection (SWWC) at Texas State University–San Marcos has the original copy of Willie Nelson's personal songbook, in which he was composing songs at the age of eleven. For more information regarding the Nelson songbook, see the SWWC's website (www.library.txstate.edu/swwc); Willie Nelson with Bud Shrake, *Willie: An Autobiography*, pp. 39–41, 47–48, 50–53.

86. Willie Nelson, interview by Tamara Saviano, Apr. 9, 2000, TSTMA; Brian Hinton, *South by Southwest: A Road Map to Alternative Country*, pp. 100–10; Steven Opdyke, *Willie Nelson Sings America*, pp. 1–10.

87. Willie Nelson, interview by Lou Staples, Dec. 1974, Frist Library and Archives, Country Music Hall of Fame and Museum, CMFOHP; Aaron Allan, interview by Jack Kinslow, May 24, 2005, TMOHP; Bob Allen, "Willie Nelson," in Kingsbury, *Encyclopedia of Country Music*, pp. 374–76.

88. Jerry Wexler, telephone conversation with author, June 2, 2004; Nelson, interview by Staples, Dec. 1974, CMFOHP; Opdyke, *Willie Nelson Sings America*, pp. xii–xiii; Allen, "Willie Nelson," in Kingsbury, *Encyclopedia of Country Music*, pp. 374–76.

89. Daniel Cooper, "Jerry Jeff Walker," in Kingsbury, *Encyclopedia of Country Music*, p. 569.

90. Michael Martin Murphey, conversation with author, Oct. 24, 2003; Richards and Shestack, *New Country Music Encyclopedia*, pp. 158–59; Reid, *Improbable Rise of Redneck Rock*, pp. 193–214; Carlin, *Country Music*, pp. 275–76.

91. Jerry Wexler, telephone conversation with author, June 2, 2004; Marcia Ball, conversation with author, Mar. 20, 2001; Hudson, *Telling Stories, Writing Songs*, pp. 141–46; Wheat, "Armadillo World Headquarters," in Barkley et al., *Handbook of Texas Music*, pp. 6–7.

92. Craig Hillis, *Texas Trilogy: Life in a Small Texas Town*, provides an outstanding look not only at Fromholz's songs but also at daily life in the rural communities of Bosque County, Texas. See also Rod Kennedy, *Music from the Heart: The Fifty-year Chronicle of His Life in Music (with a Few Sidetrips!)*, p. 37.

93. Reid, *Improbable Rise of Redneck Rock*, pp. 129–40; Gary Hickinbotham, "B. W. Stevenson," in Barkley et al., *Handbook of Texas Music*, pp. 297–98.

94. Herzhaft and Brémond, *Guide de la Country Music et du Folk*, pp. 265, 403; Lock, "Counterculture Cowboys," p. 19; Paul Kingsbury, "Willis Alan Ramsey," in Kingsbury, *Encyclopedia of Country Music*, p. 428.

95. Reid, *Improbable Rise of Redneck Rock*, pp. 169–77, 280.

96. Stephen R. Tucker, "Kinky Friedman," in Kingsbury, *Encyclopedia of Country Music*, p. 184; Reid, *Improbable Rise of Redneck Rock*, pp. 169–92; Hudson, *Telling Stories, Writing Songs*, pp. 147–57.

97. Reid, *Improbable Rise of Redneck Rock*, pp. 99, 106–107; Hudson, *Telling Stories, Writing Songs*, pp. 187–93; Craig Hillis, "Cowboys and Indians: The International Stage," *Journal of Texas Music History* 2, no. 1 (Spring 2002): 17–30.

98. Herzhaft and Brémond, *Guide de la Country Music et du Folk*, pp. 377–78; Carlin, *Country Music*, pp. 285–86; Michael Bane's *Outlaws: Revolution in Country Music* offers a very informative behind-the-scenes account of the development of outlaw country. On pp. 4–8 Bane explains how the term "outlaw" derived from the 1972 Lee Clayton song "Ladies Love Outlaws," which was popularized by one of the genre's biggest stars, Waylon Jennings.

99. Malone, *Country Music, U.S.A.*, pp. 398–99; Reid, *Improbable Rise of Redneck Rock*, pp. 273–75.

100. Cathy Brigham, "Waylon Jennings," in Barkley et al., *Handbook of Texas Music*, pp. 161–62; Joe W. Specht, "I Forgot to Remember to Forget: Elvis Presley in Texas, 1955," *Journal of Texas Music History* 3, no. 1 (Spring 2003): 7–13; Bane, in *Outlaws*, pp. 66–69, discuss Jennings's preference for a rawer, more rootsy country sound.

101. Chet Flippo, "Waylon Jennings," in Kingsbury, *Encyclopedia of Country Music*, pp. 263–64. For a more complete look at Jennings's life and career see R. Serge Denisoff, *Waylon: A Biography*. Pages 66–70 offer a detailed account of the night Jennings gave up his seat on the ill-fated plane.

102. Richards and Shestack, *New Country Music Encyclopedia*, pp. 128–30; "Kris Kristofferson," in Dellar, Cackett, and Thompson, *Harmony Illustrated Encyclopedia of Country Music*, p. 91; Carlin, *Country Music*, pp. 220–21.

103. Malone, *Country Music, U.S.A.*, pp. 305–306; Jack Bernhardt, "Kris Kristofferson," in Kingsbury, *Encyclopedia of Country Music*, pp. 286–87.

104. Mark Bego, *The Story of Country's Living Legend: George Strait*, pp. 7–14; Mike Daily, email correspondence with author, June 29, 2006.

105. Tommy Foote, interview by Jeannene Herber, May 24, 2005, TMOHP; Mike Daily, interview by Amy Cockreham, Mar. 31, 2005, TMHOP; Ron Cabal, *A Honky Tonk Odyssey: My Eight Years with George Strait*, pp. 4–6, 8–11. According to Cabal, the band's first public performance was at the Split Rail in Austin, although he acknowledges that "it was more of an audition than a real paying gig." Their first official appearance was at Kent Finlay's Cheatham Street Warehouse in San Marcos on Oct. 13, 1975, where they quickly developed a large following among college students and secured a regular weekly gig.

106. Gregg Andrews, "It's the Music: Kent Finlay's Cheatham Street Warehouse in San Marcos, Texas," *Journal of Texas Music History* 5, no. 1 (Spring 2005): 12–15; Darryl Staedtler, interview by Jeannene Herber, May 25, 2005; Chris Dickinson, "George Strait," in Kingsbury, *Encyclopedia of Country Music*, pp. 513–14.

107. Lee Ann Womack, conversation with author, Jan. 8, 2006; Lee Ann Womack, email correspondence with author, Feb. 27, 2006; Carlin, *Country Music*, pp. 437–38; Bufwack and Oermann, *Finding Her Voice*, pp. 494–95.

108. Elster, *International Who's Who in Popular Music 2004*, p. 54; Geoffrey Himes, "Clint Black," in Kingsbury, *Encyclopedia of Country Music*, pp. 35–36.

109. Malone, *Country Music, U.S.A.*, pp. 438–41; Carlin, *Country Music*, pp. 49, 64.

110. Richards and Shestack, *New Country Music Encyclopedia*, pp. 55–56, 132; Carlin, *Country Music*, pp. 49, 64; Janet E. Williams, "Tracy Lawrence," in Kingsbury, *Encyclopedia of Country Music*, pp. 291–92.

111. Clark Parsons, "Lee Roy Parnell," in Kingsbury, *Encyclopedia of Country Music*, pp. 404–405. See also Guy Clark, interview by Tamara Saviano, Apr. 1, 2000, TSTMA.

112. Jo Sgammato, *Dreams Come True: The Le Ann Rimes Story*; Bufwack and Oermann, *Finding Her Voice*, pp. 486–87; Marjie McGraw, in Kingsbury, *Encyclopedia of Country Music*, pp. 446–47.

113. Herzhaft and Brémond, *Guide de la Country Music et du Folk*, p. 160; Carlin, *Country Music*, pp. 107–108; Bufwack and Oermann, *Finding Her Voice*, pp. 495–99; Kennedy, *Music from the Heart*, p. 332.

114. Hartman, "From Yellow Roses to Dixie Chicks"; Chris Willman, "Stars and Strife," *Entertainment Weekly* 708 (May 2, 2003), p. 22; Van Sickel, Robert W. "A World without Citizenship: On (the Absence of) Politics and Ideology in Country Music Lyrics, 1960–2000," *Popular Music and Society* 28, no. 3 (July 2005): 313–31.

115. One of the more popular offshoots of the newer Americana singer-songwriter tradition is the "Texas/Red Dirt" movement. Represented largely by Oklahoma artists who either have relocated to Texas or perform frequently throughout Texas (including Cross Canadian Ragweed, Stoney LaRue, Jason Boland, and others), the Texas/Red Dirt movement reflects the long-standing tradition of musical cross-pollination between Texas and Oklahoma within the larger cultural context of the Southwest. For more on the Texas/Red Dirt music see John Wooley, "Cross Canadian Ragweed: Establishing Roots for Healthy Growth," *Mavrik* (Jan.–Feb. 2007), pp. 20–24.

116. For more on the local songwriting culture in Texas see Andrews, "It's the Music"; Kennedy, *Music from the Heart*; and Rod Kennedy, interview by Chris Lehman, May 26, 2005, TMOHP.

117. For a brief overview of folk music in Texas see Francis E. Abernethy, "Folk Music," in Barkley et al., *Handbook of Texas Music*, pp. 105–107; Koster, *Texas Music*, p. 192. The woman commonly referred to as Emily Morgan, the "Yellow Rose of Texas," most likely was a free-born black named Emily D. West, who came to Texas in 1835 to work on Colonel James Morgan's plantation near modern-day Morgan's Point. For a variety of perspectives on this song see James Lutzweiler, "Emily D. West and the Yellow Prose of Texas: A Primer on Some Primary Documents and Their Doctoring"; Frances E. Abernethy, "The Elusive Emily D. West, Folksong's Fabled 'Yellow Rose of Texas,'" in Abernethy, *2001: A Texas Folklore Odyssey*, pp. 294–329; and Martha Ann Turner, *The Yellow Rose of Texas: The Story of a Song*. See also Hartman, "From Yellow Roses to Dixie Chicks"

regarding the social and cultural implications of the mythology surrounding "The Yellow Rose of Texas."

118. Steve Buchanan, "David Wendell Fentress Guion," in Hitchcock and Sadie, *New Grove Dictionary of American Music*, vol. 2, p. 296; James Dick, "David Wendel Guion," in Barkley et al., *Handbook of Texas Music*, pp. 128–29. For a more complete collection of primary materials on Guion see the David Wendell Guion Collection at the Harry Ransom Center, University of Texas–Austin.

119. See Woody Guthrie, *Bound for Glory*; Richard B. Hughes, "Woody Guthrie," in Barkley et al., *Handbook of Texas Music*, pp. 129–30; Malone, *Don't Get above Your Raisin'*, pp. 233–35; and Joe Klein, *Woody Guthrie: A Life*.

120. Cindy Walker, telephone conversation with author, Apr. 17, 2005; Bufwack and Oermann, *Finding Her Voice*, pp. 486–87; Robert K. Oermann, "Cindy Walker," in Kingsbury, *Encyclopedia of Country Music*, pp. 567–68; Malone, *Country Music, U.S.A.*, pp. 212–13; Michael Corcoran, "Cindy Walker, Prolific Country Songwriter, Dies at 87," *Austin American-Statesman* (Mar. 24, 2006), www.Austin360.com (accessed Mar. 27, 2006).

121. Carolyn Hester and Rod Kennedy, conversations with author, June 2, 2006; Kennedy, *Music from the Heart*, pp. 23–25, 129–33; Carolyn Hester, email interview by author, July 29, 2006; Hudson, *Telling Stories, Writing Songs*, pp. 182–86; Bufwack and Oermann, *Finding Her Voice*, p. 417; Romanowski and George-Warren, *New Rolling Stone Encyclopedia*, pp. 256–57.

122. Elster, *International Who's Who in Popular Music 2004*, p. 450; Carlin, *Country Music*, p. 103; Bobby Bridger, email correspondence with author, Dec. 18, 2005; Koster, *Texas Music*, p. 195; Kennedy, *Music from the Heart*, pp. 210–12.

123. Billy Joe Shaver, interview by author, May 2, 2004; Billy Joe Shaver, assisted by Brad Reagan, *Honky Tonk Hero*, pp. 2–6, 29–35; Jimmy Guterman, "Billy Joe Shaver," in Kingsbury, *Encyclopedia of Country Music*, pp. 477–78.

124. Guy Clark, conversation with author, Jan. 8, 2004; Guy Clark, interview by Tamara Saviano, Apr. 1, 2000, TSTMA; Richards and Shestack, *New Country Music Encyclopedia*, p. 57; "Kris Kristofferson," in Dellar, Cackett, and Thompson, *Harmony Illustrated Encyclopedia of Country Music*, p. 32; Hudson, *Telling Stories, Writing Songs*, pp. 54–64; Carlin, *Country Music*, pp. 65–66.

125. John McVey, "John Townes Van Zandt," in Barkley et al., *Handbook of Texas Music*, pp. 338–40; John Lomax III, "Townes Van Zandt," in Kingsbury, *Encyclopedia of Country Music*, p. 562; Hudson, *Telling Stories, Writing Songs*, pp. 65–76; Margaret Brown's 2005 documentary "Be Here to Love Me" is a very revealing look at Van Zandt's life and legacy.

126. Daniel Cooper, "Whitey Shafer" and Jay Orr, "Sonny Throckmorton," in Kingsbury, *Encyclopedia of Country Music*, pp. 476–77, 538; Hudson, *Telling Stories, Writing Songs*, pp. 22–28, 194–98.

127. Reid, *Improbable Rise of Redneck Rock*, pp. 324–30; Carlin, *Country Music*, p. 103; Hudson, *Telling Stories, Writing Songs*, pp. 266–70; Robert K. Oermann, "Lyle Lovett," in Kingsbury, *Encyclopedia of Country Music*, p. 307; Hinton, *South by Southwest*, pp. 100–10; Malone, *Country Music, U.S.A.*, pp. 443–49.

128. Robert Earl Keen, conversations with author, Jan. 6 and 7, 2006; Rick Mitchell, "Robert Earl Keen," in Kingsbury, *Encyclopedia of Country Music*, p. 276; Hudson, *Telling Stories, Writing Songs*, pp. 271–75; Reid, *Improbable Rise of Redneck Rock*, pp. 318–24.

129. For a behind-the-scenes look at Griffith's life and career see Nanci Griffith and Joe Jackson, *Nanci Griffith's Other Voices: A Personal History of Folk Music*. See also Koster, *Texas Music*, p. 200, and Carlin, *Country Music*, pp. 161–62.

130. Malone, *Country Music, U.S.A.*, p. 449; Tish Hinojosa, conversations with author, Feb. 26, 2002, and Dec. 15, 2005; Tish Hinojosa, email correspondence with author, Jan. 2, 2006; Friskics-Warren, "Tish Hinojosa," in Kingsbury, *Encyclopedia of Country Music*, p. 242; Hudson, *Telling Stories, Writing Songs*, pp. 158–61.

131. Lauren St. John, *Hardcore Troubadour: The Life and Near Death of Steve Earle*, pp. 9–11, 44–49, 134–37; Herzhaft and Brémond, *Guide de la Country Music et du Folk*, pp. 171–74; Carlin, *Country Music*, pp. 120–21.

132. Cheryl Simon, "Walter Hyatt," in Barkley et al., *Handbook of Texas Music*, pp. 148–149; Champ Hood, conversation with author, Mar. 19, 2002; Reid, *Improbable Rise of Redneck Rock*, p. 328.

133. Joe Ely, conversation with author, Feb. 26, 2002; Joe Ely, interview by Tamara Saviano, Mar. 23, 2000, TSTMA; Hinton, *South by Southwest*, pp. 106–10; Malone, *Country Music, U.S.A.*, pp. 443–44; Rick Mitchell, "Joe Ely," Ben Sandmel, "Jimmie Dale Gilmore," and Don McLeese, "Butch Hancock," in Kingsbury, *Encyclopedia of Country Music*, pp. 163–64, 202–203, 226–27.

134. Hinton, *South by Southwest*, pp. 106–10; www.kimmierhodes.com; Radney Foster, conversation with author, Mar. 21, 2006; Carlin, *Country Music*, p. 141.

135. Romanowski and George-Warren, *New Rolling Stone Encyclopedia*, pp. 893–94; Kennedy, *Music from the Heart*, pp. 297, 308; Herzhaft and Brémond, *Guide de la Country Music et du Folk*, p. 336.

136. Terri Hendrix and Lloyd Maines, conversations with author, Mar. 21, 2006, and Oct. 12, 2006; Ruthie Foster, conversation with author, Apr. 12, 2005.

137. Shawn Colvin, conversation with author, Apr. 10, 2005; Bufwack and Oermann, *Finding Her Voice*, pp. 253, 500; Romanowski and George-Warren, *New Rolling Stone Encyclopedia*, pp. 204–205, 1079–80; Carlin, *Country Music*, p. 433; Eliza Gilkyson, conversation with author, June 12, 2005; Richard Skanske, "Eliza Gilkyson," *Texas Music* 24 (Fall 2005): 40–47.

CHAPTER 7

1. For a concise overview of Texas rock & roll and pop see Laurie E. Jasinski, "Rock & Roll," in Barkley et al., *Handbook of Texas Music*, pp. 270–75.

2. Wyman, *Blues Odyssey*, pp. 159–61, 234, 269; Nick Tosches, *Unsung Heroes of Rock 'n' Roll: The Birth of Rock in the Wild Years before Elvis*, pp. 39–53, 103–108. See especially James M.

Salem, *The Late Great Johnny Ace and the Transition from R&B to Rock 'n' Roll*, for a discussion of how black entertainers paved the way for white rock-and-roll artists. Although Johnny Ace was from Memphis, he achieved national fame through his recordings with Houston-based Duke Records, owned by Don Robey, who aggressively promoted Ace throughout the country. Ace also often used Texas-based blues singer Big Mama Thornton as his opening act. In fact, Thornton was present when Johnny Ace killed himself in the backstage dressing room at the Houston City Auditorium in 1954 at the age of twenty-five.

3. Starr and Waterman, *American Popular Music*, pp. 53–58; Appell and Hemphill, *American Popular Music*, pp. 281–98.

4. John Swenson, *Bill Haley: The Daddy of Rock & roll*, pp. 15–31, 162–63. For a more sympathetic yet still informative look at Haley's life see John W. Haley and John von Hoelle, *Sound and Glory: The Incredible Story of Bill Haley, the Father of Rock 'n' Roll and the Music That Shook the World*; Romanowski and George-Warren, *New Rolling Stone Encyclopedia*, pp. 408–409.

5. Philip Norman, *Buddy: The Biography*, pp. 27–35. Holly dropped the "e" from his last name early in his career after signing with Decca Records. Ellis Amburn, *Buddy Holly: A Biography*, pp. 3, 10–14, 20–25. See also Philip Norman, *Rave On: The Biography of Buddy Holly*.

6. Specht, "I Forgot to Remember to Forget," p. 10; Martin Donell Kohout, "Buddy Holly," in Barkley et al., *Handbook of Texas Music*, pp. 139–41. See also Matthew Tippens, "Norman Petty," in Barkley et al., *Handbook of Texas Music*, p. 243, for a brief discussion of the personal and professional relationship between Holly and Petty.

7. Ted Fox, *Showtime at the Apollo*, pp. 206–207; Philip Norman, *Shout! The Beatles in Their Generation*, pp. 51–53.

8. Amburn, *Buddy Holly*, pp. 251–61.

9. Gillian G. Garr, *She's a Rebel: The History of Women in Rock & Roll*, 2d exp. ed., pp. 158–59; Romanowski and George-Warren, *New Rolling Stone Encyclopedia*, pp. 851–52; Amburn, *Buddy Holly*, pp. 302–303.

10. Norman, *Shout!*, pp. 51, 53, 59, 73–74. According to Norman, Lennon, McCartney, Harrison, and Stuart Sutcliffe, the bass player at the time, had been performing under the name Johnny and the Moondogs when they decided it was time for a change. "What they needed was something spry and catchy, like Buddy Holly's Crickets. Stu Sutcliffe, half-jokingly, wrote down 'beetles' in his sketchbook, such a silly idea that the others said, why not? John, unable to leave any word alone, changed it to 'beat-les,' as a pun on beat"; Norman, *Buddy*, pp. 5, 13–17, 331; Ambrun, *Buddy Holly*, pp. 263–64, 295–305.

11. Dafydd Rees and Luke Crampton, *Rock Movers & Shakers*, p. 440; Ambrun, *Buddy Holly*, pp. 298–99; Romanowski and George-Warren, *New Rolling Stone Encyclopedia*, p. 846.

12. Alan Lee Haworth, "Big Bopper," in Barkley et al., *Handbook of Texas Music*, p. 20;

Rees and Crampton, *Rock Movers & Shakers*, p. 50. For a more complete look at Richardson's life and career see Tim Knight, *Chantilly Lace: The Life and Times of J. P. Richardson.*

13. Johnny Preston, interview by Chava Sanderson, May 25, 2005, TMOHP; Romanowsk and George-Warren, *New Rolling Stone Encyclopedia of Rock & Roll*, p. 787.

14. Alan Clayson, *Only the Lonely: Roy Orbison's Life and Legacy*, pp. 2, 6–13, 33–34; George B. Ward, "Roy Kelton Orbison," in *Handbook of Texas Music*, pp. 236–37.

15. Romanowski and George-Warren, *New Rolling Stone Encyclopedia*, pp. 729–30. See also Ellis Amburn, *Dark Star: The Roy Orbison Story.* Orbison had recorded an earlier version of "Ooby Dooby" with the Teen Kings in Clovis, New Mexico, and released it on Je-Wel Records, a small Texas label.

16. Rees and Crampton, *Rock Movers & Shakers*, pp. 371–73; Ward, "Roy Kelton Orbison," in Barkley et al., *Handbook of Texas Music*, pp. 236–37; Romanowski and George-Warren, *New Rolling Stone Encyclopedia of Rock & Roll*, p. 1014. See also Peter Lehman, *Roy Orbison: The Invention of an Alternative Rock Masculinity*, especially pp. 21–22, 25–27, for a discussion of the unique timbre of Orbison's voice and the way in which his overall public persona ran counter to the more macho image of so many of his contemporaries.

17. H. Allen Anderson, "Buddy Wayne Knox," in Barkley et al., *Handbook of Texas Music*, pp. 179–80; Elster, *International Who's Who in Popular Music 2004*, p. 343; Don Cusic, "B. J. Thomas," in Kingsbury, *Encyclopedia of Country Music*, p. 535.

18. Koster, *Texas Music*, p. 86; Romanowski and George-Warren, *New Rolling Stone Encyclopedia*, pp. 247, 641–42, 752, 763–64; Norman, *Shout!*, p. 165; Robert M. Blunt, "Bobby Fuller," in Barkley et al., *Handbook of Texas Music*, p. 113.

19. Romanowski and George-Warren, *New Rolling Stone Encyclopedia*, pp. 163, 879–80; Rees and Crampton, *Rock Movers & Shakers*, pp. 460–61.

20. Norman, *Shout!*, pp. 202–204, 218–28.

21. Patoski, "Uno, Dos, One, Two, Tres, Quatro," pp. 12–14; Romanowski and George-Warren, *New Rolling Stone Encyclopedia*, pp. 806–807, 872.

22. James Head, "Douglas Wayne Sahm," in Barkley et al., *Handbook of Texas Music*, pp. 280–81.

23. Olsen, "San Antonio's West Side Sound," pp. 26–39.

24. Huey P. Meaux, correspondence with author, Dec. 5, 2005; Rees and Crampton, *Rock Movers & Shakers*, pp. 479–80; Romanowski and George-Warren, *New Rolling Stone Encyclopedia*, pp. 903–904; Patoski, "Uno, Dos, One, Two, Tres, Quatro," p. 14.

25. Joel Selvin, "At the Crossroads: The Psychedelic Sounds of Texans in the Summer of Love," *Texas Music* 11 (Summer 2002): 58–65.

26. Thomas Goldsmith, "Kenny Rogers," in Kingsbury, *Encyclopedia of Country Music*, pp. 453–56; Rees and Crampton, *Rock Movers & Shakers*, pp. 437–39.

27. Laura Joplin, *Love, Janis*, pp. 26–27, 53–62. Of the several monographs available on Janis Joplin, this one, written by her younger sister, gives the most balanced account without focusing inordinately on the singer's personal afflictions. Richard B. Hughes, "Janis Lyn Joplin," in Barkley et al., *Handbook of Texas Music*, p. 167.

28. Alice Echols, *Scars of Sweet Paradise: The Life and Times of Janis Joplin*, pp. 53–59; Joplin, *Love, Janis*, pp. 97–104. See also Claude Mathews Collection, Center for American History, University of Texas–Austin, Box 4, folder titled "Singing the Yodeling Blues: Final Narration," from a documentary film by Claude Mathews about Threadgills. On pp. 1–2 and 13–14 of this transcript, Joplin says she played in this "hillbilly" band (the Waller Creek Boys) mainly because it was a way to spend more time with her friends. Also in Box 4, in a folder titled "Transcripts: Audio Tape Interviews," Juli Paul says that she was the one who took Joplin to Threadgill's for the first time in 1962, after meeting Joplin, St. John, and Wiggins walking near the University of Texas campus. Paul says she remained close to Joplin until her death in 1970 and states that most biographers have exaggerated how wild and out of control Joplin was.

29. Myra Friedman, *Buried Alive: The Biography of Janis Joplin*, pp. 63–65; Joplin, *Love, Janis*, pp. 137–43.

30. Ellis Amburn, *Pearl: The Obsessions and Passions of Janis Joplin*, pp. 121–31; Hughes, "Janis Lyn Joplin," p. 168.

31. Rees and Crampton, *Rock Movers & Shakers*, pp. 281–82.

32. Eyerman and Jamison, *Music and Social Movements*, pp. 130–39.

33. Jerry Rodnitzky, "Janis Joplin: The Hippie Blues Singer as Feminist Heroine," *Journal of Texas Music History* 2, no. 1 (Spring 2002): 7–15; Echols, *Scars of Sweet Paradise*, pp. 305–309; Garr, *She's a Rebel*, pp. 94–98.

34. Casey Monahan, ed., *Openers II: The Lyrics of Roky Erickson*, pp. 296–304; Joplin, *Love, Janis*, p. 142; Romanowski and George-Warren, *New Rolling Stone Encyclopedia*, pp. 312–13.

35. Elster, *International Who's Who in Popular Music 2004*, pp. 413–14; Koster, *Texas Music*, p. 90; Romanowski and George-Warren, *New Rolling Stone Encyclopedia*, pp. 675–76, 701–702; Rees and Crampton, *Rock Movers & Shakers*, pp. 345–47.

36. Stephen Holden, "Stephen Stills," in Hitchcock and Sadie, *New Grove Dictionary of American Music*, vol. 1, p. 548; Romanowski and George-Warren, *New Rolling Stone Encyclopedia*, pp. 129–30, 227–28, 676; Rees and Crampton, *Rock Movers & Shakers*, pp. 345–47.

37. Richard Bowden, conversation with author, Sept. 22, 2005; Laurie Jasinski, "Rock & roll," in Barkley et al., *Handbook of Texas Music*, p. 272; Rees and Crampton, *Rock Movers & Shakers*, pp. 168–69, 238–39, 449; Romanowski and George-Warren, *New Rolling Stone Encyclopedia*, pp. 293–95, 851; Debbie Kruger, "J. D. Souther Interview, October 2, 1997," at www.debbiekruger.com (accessed Oct. 8, 2005); Stacia Proefrock, "J. D. Souther," at www.allmusic.com (accessed Oct. 8, 2005).

38. John Rockwell, "Steve Miller," in Hitchcock and Sadie, *New Grove Dictionary of American Music*, vol. 3, p. 233; Rees and Crampton, *Rock Movers & Shakers*, pp. 341–42; www.stevemillerband.com/ppda/Steve-Miller-Bio (accessed Oct. 8, 2005).

39. Elster, *International Who's Who in Popular Music 2004*, p. 503; Stephen Holden, "Boz Scaggs," in Hitchcock and Sadie, *New Grove Dictionary of American Music*, vol. 4, pp. 146–47; Romanowski and George-Warren, *New Rolling Stone Encyclopedia*, pp. 875–76.

40. Romanowski and George-Warren, *New Rolling Stone Encyclopedia*, pp. 912–13; www.rockhall.com/hof/inductee (accessed Oct. 8, 2005).

41. Wyman, *Blues Odyssey*, p. 373; Rees and Crampton, *Rock Movers & Shakers*, pp. 570–71; Romanowski and George-Warren, *New Rolling Stone Encyclopedia*, pp. 1087–88.

42. David Blaney, *Sharp Dressed Men: ZZ Top behind the Scenes, from Blues to Boogie to Beards*, pp. 8–11; Deborah Frost, *ZZ Top: Bad and Worldwide*, pp. 16–18.

43. Jasinski, "Rock & Roll," in Barkley et al., *Handbook of Texas Music*, pp. 272–73; www.rockhall.com/hof/inductee; Frost, *ZZ Top*, pp. 49–58; Blaney, *Sharp Dressed Men*, pp. 19, 23, 129–46.

44. Elster, *International Who's Who in Popular Music 2004*, pp. 129, 382; Romanowski and George-Warren, *New Rolling Stone Encyclopedia*, pp. 228–29, 648–49; Rees and Crampton, *Rock Movers & Shakers*, pp. 132, 336–37. All three sources list different birth years for Meatloaf, including 1947, 1948, and 1951.

45. Ira A. Robbins, ed., *The Trouser Press Guide to '90s Rock*, pp. 427, 543–44; Jasinski, "Rock & Roll," pp. 273–75; Romanowski and George-Warren, *New Rolling Stone Encyclopedia*, pp. 116–17, 137–38, 153–54, 886–87; Corcoran, *All Over the Map*, pp. 98–102; Garr, *She's a Rebel*, pp. 412–14; Elster, *International Who's Who in Popular Music 2004*, p. 341.

46. Andy Langer, "Spotlights: Norah Jones," *Austin Chronicle* (Mar. 15, 2002); BBC News (Feb. 13, 2006), at www.news.bbc.co.uk; "Norah Jones," *Wikipedia: The Free Encyclopedia*, www.wikipedia.org.

Bibliography

* * * * * * * * * * * * * * * * * * * *

PRIMARY SOURCES

Country Music Hall of Fame and Museum, Nashville, Tennessee
    Frist Library and Archive.
    Country Music Foundation Oral History Project (CMFOHP).

Marcelo H. Tafoya Archives, Austin, Texas
    Scott, Ramon. "Rudy Tee Gonzales & The Reno Bops: Biography and Fact Sheet."

Texas Music Museum Archives, Austin, Texas

Texas State University–San Marcos
    Center for Texas Music History.
    Saviano, Tamara, Texas Music Archives (TSTMA).
    Texas Music Oral History Program Archives (TMOHP).

Southwestern Writers Collection
Crawford, Bill, and Joe Nick Patoski: Stevie Ray Vaughan Biography Papers.
Daily, Harold W. "Pappy," Collection.
de Vaca, Cabeza. *La Relación y Comentarios*. Also available online in both English and the original Spanish at the Southwestern Writers Collection website: www.library.txstate. edu/swwc.
Nelson, Willie, Collection.
Patoski, Joe Nick: Selena Quintanilla Pérez Biography Papers (SQPBP).

University of Mississippi–Oxford
    J. D. Williams Library Special Collections.

University of Texas at Austin
Center for American History
    Lipscomb, Mance, and Glen Alyn, Collection.
    Lomax, John A., Family Papers (JALFP).
    Mathews, Claude, Collection.
    Turner, Allan, Oral History Collection (ATOHC).
    Venth, Carl, Papers.

Harry Ransom Center
   Guion, David Wendell, Collection.

Author's Interviews, Conversations, and Correspondence with the following:
   Antone, Clifford
   Ball, Marcia
   Benson, Ray
   Bowden, Richard
   Bridger, Bobby
   Cashdollar, Cindy
   Clark, Guy
   Colvin, Shawn
   Cuviello, Johnny
   Daily, Mike
   Durham, Marcia
   Elders, Gene
   Ely, Joe
   Foster, Radney
   Foster, Ruthie
   Gilkyson, Eliza
   Gimble, Johnny
   Glasse, Paul
   Hauschild, Henry
   Hendrix, Terri
   Hester, Carolyn
   Hinojosa, Tish
   Jiménez, Flaco
   Keen, Robert Earl
   Kennedy, Rod
   Kurtz, Gene
   Maines, Lloyd
   McRae, Rick
   Meaux, Huey P.
   Murphey, Michael Martin
   Naylor, Jerry
   Richey, Slim
   Saldivar, Mingo
   San Miguel, Guadalupe, Jr.
   Shaver, Billy Joe
   Tafoya, Marcelo H.
   Walker, Cindy

Wexler, Jerry

Willing, Sharon

Womack, Lee Ann

Wood, Roger

SECONDARY SOURCES: BOOKS, ARTICLES, CHAPTERS, AND REPORTS

Abernethy, Francis E. "The Elusive Emily D. West, Folksong's Fabled 'Yellow Rose of Texas.'" In Abernethy, 2001, 318–29.

———. "Folk Music." In Barkley et al., *Handbook of Texas Music*, 105–107.

———. *Singin' Texas*. Dallas: E-Heart Press, 1983.

———. *2001: A Texas Folklore Odyssey*. Denton: University of North Texas Press, 2001.

Acosta, Teresa Palomo. "Armando Marroquín." In Barkley et al., *Handbook of Texas Music*, 203–204.

———. "Hauschild Music Company." In Barkley et al., *Handbook of Texas Music*, 134–35.

———. "Narciso Martínez." In Barkley et al., *Handbook of Texas Music*, 205–207.

———. "Robert Shaw." In Barkley et al., *Handbook of Texas Music*, 287–88.

———. "Tejano Conjunto Festival." In Barkley et al., *Handbook of Texas Music*, 308–10.

———. "Texas Mexican Conjunto." In Barkley et al., *Handbook of Texas Music*, 315.

Addis, Cameron. "The Baptist Beat in Modern Jazz: Texan Gene Ramey in Kansas City and New York." *Journal of Texas Music History* 4, no. 2 (Fall 2004): 8–21.

Ahr, Wayne M. "Henri Castro and Castroville: Alsatian History and Heritage." In Lagarde, *French in Texas*, 128–41.

Albrecht, Theodore. "Carl Beck." In Barkley et al., *Handbook of Texas Music*, 17.

———. "German Music." In Barkley et al., *Handbook of Texas Music*, 118–19.

———. "Scott Joplin." In Barkley et al., *Handbook of Texas Music*, 168–71.

———. "Wilhelm Carl August Thielepape." In Barkley et al., *Handbook of Texas Music*, 319.

Allen, Bob. "George Jones." In Kingsbury, *Encyclopedia of Country Music*, 268–69.

———. "Tanya Tucker." In Russell D. Barnard, ed., *The Comprehensive Country Music Encyclopedia*. New York: Random House, 1994.

———. "Willie Nelson." In Kingsbury, *Encyclopedia of Country Music*, 374–76.

Allen, Tommy, as told to Jack Lane. *The Texas Honky-tonk Trail*. Bloomington, Ind.: 1st Books, 2004.

Alyn, Glen. *I Say Me for a Parable: The Oral Autobiography of Mance Lipscomb, Texas Bluesman*. New York: Norton, 1993.

Amburn, Ellis. *Buddy Holly: A Biography*. New York: St. Martin's, 1995.

———. *Dark Star: The Roy Orbison Story*. New York: Lyle Stewart, 1990.

———. *Pearl: The Obsessions and Passions of Janis Joplin*. New York: Warner, 1992.

Ancelet, Barry Jean. *The Makers of Cajun Music.* Austin: University of Texas Press, 1984.

Anderson, H. Allen. "Buddy Wayne Knox." In Barkley et al., *Handbook of Texas Music,* 179–80.

Andrews, Gregg. "It's the Music: Kent Finlay's Cheatham Street Warehouse in San Marcos, Texas." *Journal of Texas Music History* 5, no. 1 (Spring 2005): 8–25.

Antone, Susan. *Picture the Blues.* Austin: Blues Press, 1986.

Appell, Glenn, and David Hemphill. *American Popular Music: A Multicultural History.* Belmont, Calif.: Thomson Higher Education, 2006.

Arteaga, Alfred, ed. *An Other Tongue: Nation and Ethnicity in the Linguistic Borderlands.* Durham: Duke University Press, 1994.

———. *Chicano Poetics: Heterotexts and Hybridities.* New York: Cambridge University Press, 1997.

Asch, Moses, and Alan Lomax, eds. *The Leadbelly Songbook.* New York: Oak, 1962.

Aubrey, Elizabeth. *The Music of the Troubadours.* Bloomington, Ind.: Indiana University Press, 1996.

Bailey, Joe. "'The Texas Shuffle': Lone Star Underpinnings of the Kansas City Jazz Sound." *Journal of Texas Music History* (2006): 8–29.

Bane, Michael. *The Outlaws: Revolution in Country Music.* New York: Country Music Magazine Press, 1978.

Banfield, Stephen. "Popular Song and Popular Music on Stage and Film." In Nicholls, *Cambridge History of American Music,* 322–37.

Barbash, Louis, and Frederick P. Close. "Lydia Mendoza: The Voice of the People." In *Texas Humanist* 6 (November–December, 1983): 18–20.

Barkley, Roy, Douglas E. Barnett, Cathy Brigham, Gary Hartman, Casey Monahan, Dave Oliphant, and George B. Ward, eds. *The Handbook of Texas Music.* Austin: Texas State Historical Association, 2003.

Barnard, Russell D., ed. *The Comprehensive Country Music Encyclopedia.* New York: Random House, 1994.

Barr, Alwyn. *Black Texans: A History of African Americans in Texas, 1528–1995.* Norman: University of Oklahoma Press, 1996.

Bauman, Richard, and Roger D. Abrahams, eds. *And Other Neighborly Names: Social Process and Cultural Image in Texas Folklore.* Austin: University of Texas Press, 1981.

Bego, Mark. *The Story of Country's Living Legend: George Strait.* New York: Kensington, 1997.

Béhague, Gerard H. "Hispanic-American Music." In Hitchcock and Sadie, eds., *New Grove Dictionary of American Music,* vol. 2, 395–99.

———. *Music in Latin America: An Introduction.* Englewood Cliffs, N.J.: Prentice-Hall, 1979.

Berlin, Edward A. *King of Ragtime: Scott Joplin and His Era.* New York: Oxford University Press, 1994.

———. *Slaves without Masters: The Free Negro in the Antebellum South.* New York: Pantheon, 1975.

Bernard, Shane K. *Swamp Pop: Cajun and Creole Rhythm and Blues.* Jackson: University Press of Mississippi, 1996.

Biesele, Rudolph L. "Heinrich Guenther." In Barkley et al., *Handbook of Texas Music,* 127–28.

———. *The History of the German Settlements in Texas.* San Marcos: German-Texan Heritage Society, 1987.

Blaney, David. *Sharp Dressed Men: ZZ Top behind the Scenes, from Blues to Boogie to Beards.* New York: Hyperion, 1994.

Blood, Anne J., and Robert J. Zatorre. "Intensely Pleasurable Responses to Music Correlate with Activity in Brain Regions Implicated in Reward and Emotion." Montreal Neurological Institute, McGill University, Montreal, Quebec, H3A 2B4. http://www.pnas.org/cgi/doi/10.1073/pnas.191355898 (accessed March 24, 2007).

Boatright, Mody C. *Mexican Border Ballads and Other Lore.* Dallas: Southern Methodist University Press, 1967.

Bohlman, Philip V. "Immigrant, Folk, and Regional Musics in the Twentieth Century." In Nicholls, *Cambridge History of American Music,* 276–308.

Boyd, Jean. *The Jazz of the Southwest: An Oral History of Western Swing.* Austin: University of Texas Press, 1998.

———. *"We're the Light Crust Doughboys from Burrus Mill": An Oral History.* Austin: University of Texas Press, 2003.

Brackett, David, ed. *The Pop, Rock, and Soul Reader: Histories and Debates.* New York: Oxford University Press, 2005.

Brigham, Cathy. "Waylon Jennings." In Barkley et al., *Handbook of Texas Music,* 161–62.

Brooks, William. "Music in America: An Overview (Part 1)." In Nicholls, *Cambridge History of American Music,* 30–48.

Brown, Andrew. "Ba ova eska Kapela: A Visit with Clarence Baca." In *Taking Off: Musical Journeys in the Southwest and Beyond,* ed. Andrew Brown, 42–51, no. 1 (Spring). Carthage, Tex.: Pine Grove Press, 2005.

———. "Texas Rancher: The Tony Sepolio Interview." In Brown, ed., *Taking Off,* 2–29.

Brown, Jarad. "Gene Autry." In Barkley et al., *Handbook of Texas Music,* 12–13.

———. "Ivory Joe Hunter." In Barkley et al., *Handbook of Texas Music,* 147.

Broyles, Michael. "Immigrant, Folk, and Regional Musics in the Nineteenth Century." In Nicholls, *Cambridge History of American Music,* 135–57.

Bufwack Mary A., and Robert K. Oermann. *Finding Her Voice: Women in Country Music, 1800–2000.* Nashville: Country Music Foundation Press and Vanderbilt University Press, 2003.

Burr, Ramiro. "The Accordion: Passion, Emotion, Musicianship." In Tejeda and Valdez, *Puro Conjunto,* 121–26.

———. *The Billboard Guide to Tejano and Regional Mexican Music.* New York: Billboard, 1999.

Bynum, Victoria E. *The Free State of Jones: Mississippi's Longest Civil War.* Chapel Hill: University of North Carolina Press, 2001.

Cabal, Ron. *A Honky Tonk Odyssey: My Eight Years with George Strait.* Austin: Author, 1990.

Calvert, Robert A., and Arnoldo De León. *The History of Texas.* Arlington Heights, Ill.: Harlan Davidson, 1990.

Campbell, Randolph B. *Gone to Texas: A History of the Lone Star State.* New York: Oxford University Press, 2003.

Candelaria, Cordelia Chávez. "*Différance* and the Discourse of 'Community' in Writings by and about the Ethnic Other(s)." In Arteaga, ed., *Other Tongue,* 185–202.

Carlin, Richard. *Country Music: A Biographical Dictionary.* New York: Routledge, 2003.

Carner, Mosco. *The Waltz.* New York: Chanticleer, 1948.

Carr, Joe, and Alan Munde. *Prairie Nights to Neon Lights: The Story of Country Music in West Texas.* Lubbock: Texas Tech University Press, 1995.

Carter, Cecile Elkins. *Caddo Indians: Where We Come From.* Norman: University of Oklahoma Press, 1995.

Clayson, Alan. *Only the Lonely: Roy Orbison's Life and Legacy.* New York: St. Martin's, 1989.

Clayton, Lawrence, and Joe Specht, eds. *The Roots of Texas Music.* College Station: Texas A&M University Press, 2003.

Cockrell, Dale. "Nineteenth-century Popular Music." In Nicholls, *Cambridge History of American Music,* 158–85.

Coffey, Kevin. *Cliff Bruner and His Texas Wanderers.* CD liner notes, Bear Family Records, 1996.

———. "New Riders of the Purple Sage." In Kingsbury, ed. *Encyclopedia of Country Music,* 377.

———. "Steel Colossus: The Bob Dunn Story." *Journal of Country Music* 17, no. 2 (1996): 90–109.

———. "The Story of the Big 'D' Jamboree." CD liner notes for *The Big "D" Jamboree Live!* vols. 1–2, 2000, Dragon Street Records.

———. "The Tony Sepolio Discography." In Brown, ed., *Taking Off,* 23–29.

Cohen, Ronald D., ed. *Alan Lomax: Selected Writings, 1934–1997.* New York: Routledge, 2003.

Conn, Charles Paul. *The Barbara Mandrell Story.* New York: Berkley Books, 1989.

Conway, Cecilia. *African Banjo Echoes in Appalachia: A Study of Folk Traditions.* Knoxville: University of Tennessee Press, 1995.

Cook, Pansy. *The Saga of Jim Reeves: Country and Western Singer and Musician.* Los Angeles: Crescent, 1977.

Cooper, Daniel. "Jerry Jeff Walker." In Kingsbury, *Encyclopedia of Country Music,* 569.

———. "Lefty Frizzell." In Kingsbury, *Encyclopedia of Country Music,* 184–86.

———. *Lefty Frizzell: The Honky Tonk Life of Country Music's Greatest Singer.* Boston: Little, Brown, 1995.

———. "Ray Price." In Kingsbury, *Encyclopedia of Country Music,* 422–23.

———. "Tanya Tucker." In Kingsbury, *Encyclopedia of Country Music,* 549–50.

Copeland, Carlyn. "Amos Milburn." In Barkley et al., *Handbook of Texas Music,* 209–10.

Corcoran, Michael. *All over the Map: True Heroes of Texas Music.* Austin: University of Texas Press, 2005.

———. "Cindy Walker, Prolific Country Songwriter, Dies at 87," *Austin American-Statesman* (March 24, 2006), http://www.Austin360.com (accessed March 24, 2007).

———. "The Invisible Genius: Steve Jordan." *Journal of Texas Music History* 3, no. 1 (Spring 2003): 24–28.

———. "Remembering Gatemouth Brown: This Guitar Genius Went Far, So Far beyond the Blues." *Austin-American Statesman* (September 13, 2005), http://www.statesman.com/life/content/life/stories/09/13gatemouth.

Curry, Leonard. *The Free Black in Urban America, 1800–1850.* Chicago: University of Chicago Press, 1981.

Curtis, Susan. *Dancing to a Black Man's Tune: A Life of Scott Joplin.* Columbia: University of Missouri Press, 1994.

Cusic, Don. "B. J. Thomas." In Kingsbury, *Encyclopedia of Country Music,* 535.

———. "Riders in the Sky." In Kingsbury, *Encyclopedia of Country Music,* 444–45.

Cutrer, Thomas W. *The English Texans.* San Antonio: University of Texas Institute of Texan Cultures at San Antonio, 1985.

Dance, Helen Oakley. "T-Bone Walker." In Barkley et al., *Handbook of Texas Music,* 348–49.

———. *Stormy Monday: The T-Bone Walker Story.* New York: Da Capo, 1987.

Davis, Charles G. "Jack Teagarden." In Barkley et al., *Handbook of Texas Music,* 306–307.

Davis, Francis. *The History of the Blues.* New York: Hyperion, 1995.

De León, Arnoldo. *They Called Them Greasers: Anglo Attitudes toward Mexicans in Texas, 1821–1900.* Austin: University of Texas Press, 1983.

DeKunder, David. "Joe Patek." In Barkley et al., *Handbook of Texas Music,* 239–41.

Dellar, Fred, Alan Cackett, and Roy Thompson. *The Harmony Illustrated Encyclopedia of Country Music.* London: Salamander, 1986.

Dempsey, John Mark. *The Light Crust Doughboys Are on the Air: Celebrating Seventy Years of Texas Music.* Denton: University of North Texas Press, 2002.

———. "Marvin 'Smokey' Montgomery: A Life in Texas Music." *Journal of Texas Music History* 1, no. 2 (Fall 2001): 45–57.

Denisoff, R. Serge. *Waylon: A Biography.* Knoxville: University of Tennessee Press, 1983.

Deutsch, Sarah. *No Separate Refuge: Culture, Class, and Gender on an Anglo-Hispanic Frontier in the American Southwest, 1880–1940.* New York: Oxford University Press, 1987.

Dick, James. "David Wendel Guion." In Barkley et al., *Handbook of Texas Music,* 128–29.

Dickey, Dan W. "Corridos." In Barkley et al., *Handbook of Texas Music,* 63–65.

———. *The Kennedy Corridos: A Study of the Ballads of a Mexican American Hero.* Austin: Center for Mexican American Studies, University of Texas, 1978.

———. "Música Norteña." In Barkley et al., *Handbook of Texas Music,* 220–22.

Dickinson, Chris. "George Strait." In Kingsbury, *Encyclopedia of Country Music,* 513–14.

Djedje, Jacqueline Cogdell. "African American Music to 1900." In Nicholls, *Cambridge History of American Music,* 103–34.

Dunbar, Bob. *From Bob Wills to Ray Benson: A History of Western Swing Music.* Austin: Term Publications, 1988.

Dutton, Robin. "Stevie Ray Vaughan." In Barkley et al., *Handbook of Texas Music,* 340–41.

Dyer, John. *Conjunto: Voice of the People, Songs from the Heart.* Austin: University of Texas Press, 2005.

Echols, Alice. *Scars of Sweet Paradise: The Life and Times of Janis Joplin*. New York: Metropolitan, 1999.

Ermarth, Michael. "Hyphenation and Hyper-Americanization: Germans of the Wilhelmine Reich View German-Americans, 1890–1914." *Journal of American Ethnic History* 21, no. 2 (Winter 2002): 33–58.

Erny, Janine. "Grounds for Emigration: Alsace at the Time of Henri Castro." In Lagarde, *French in Texas*, 124–27.

Esparza, Jesse J. "D. J. Screw." In Barkley et al., *Handbook of Texas Music*, 74.

Espinosa, Aurelio M. In *The Folklore of Spain in the American Southwest: Traditional Spanish Folk Literature in Northern New Mexico and Southern Colorado*, ed. J. Manuel Espinosa, 120–33. Norman: University of Oklahoma Press, 1985.

Evans, Rush. "Bob Wills: The King of Western Swing." *Journal of Texas Music History* 2, no. 2 (Fall 2002): 16–29.

Everett, Dianna. *The Texas Cherokees: A People between Two Fires, 1819–1840*. Norman: University of Oklahoma Press, 1990.

Eyerman, Ron, and Andrew Jamison. *Music and Social Movements: Mobilizing Traditions in the Twentieth Century*. New York: Cambridge University Press, 1998.

Fenster, Mark. "Buck Owens." In Kingsbury, *Encyclopedia of Country Music*, 399–400.

Filene, Benjamin. "Our Singing Country: John and Alan Lomax, Leadbelly, and the Construction of the American Past." *American Quarterly* 43, no. 4 (December 1991): 602–24.

Flannery, John Brendan. *The Irish Texans*. San Antonio: University of Texas Institute of Texan Cultures at San Antonio, 1980.

Flippo, Chet. "Mac Davis." In Kingsbury, *Encyclopedia of Country Music*, 137.

———. "Waylon Jennings." In Kingsbury, *Encyclopedia of Country Music*, 263–64.

Flores, Carlos Jesús Gómez. "The Accordion on Both Sides of the Border." In Tejeda and Valdez, *Puro Conjunto*, 71–80.

Foley, Neil. *The White Scourge: Mexicans, Blacks, and Poor Whites in Texas Cotton Culture*. Berkeley: University of California Press, 1997.

Folkins, Gail. "Texas Dance Halls: History, Culture, and Community." *Journal of Texas Music History* (2006): 54–62.

Fontenot, Kevin S. "Henry Clay Gilliland." In Barkley et al., *Handbook of Texas Music*, 120.

Fowler, Gene, and Bill Crawford. *Border Radio: Quacks, Yodelers, Pitchmen, Psychics, and Other Amazing Broadcasters of the American Airwaves*. Austin: University of Texas Press, 2002.

Fox, Aaron A. *Real Country: Music and Language in Working-class Culture*. Durham: Duke University Press, 2004.

Fox, Ted. *Showtime at the Apollo*. Rhinebeck, N.Y.: Mill Road Enterprises, 2003.

Frantz, Joe B. "Charles Christian." In Barkley et al., *Handbook of Texas Music*, 50–51.

Friedman, Myra. *Buried Alive: The Biography of Janis Joplin*. New York: Morrow, 1973.

Frisbie, Charlotte J., ed. *Explorations in Ethnomusicology: Essays in Honor of David P. McAllester*. Detroit: Information Coordinators, 1986.

Friskics-Warren, Bill. "Tish Hinojosa." In Kingsbury, *Encyclopedia of Country Music*, 242.

Frost, Deborah. *ZZ Top: Bad and Worldwide*. New York: Rolling Stone Press, 1985.

Fry, Phillip L. "Ernest Dale Tubb." In Barkley et al., *Handbook of Texas Music*, 329–30.

———. "Lefty Frizzell." In Barkley et al., *Handbook of Texas Music*, 112.

———. "Roger Dean Miller." In Barkley et al., *Handbook of Texas Music*, 210–11.

Fulbrook, Mary. *A Concise History of Germany*. New York: Cambridge University Press, 1990.

Galán, Hector. *Accordion Dreams* (documentary film). Austin: Hector Galán Productions, 2001.

———. *Los Lonely Boys: Cottonfields and Crossroads* (documentary film). Austin: Hector Galán Productions, 2006.

———. *Songs of the Homeland* (documentary film). Austin: Hector Galán Productions, 1995.

———. *Tish Hinojosa: My Heart, My Life* (documentary film). Austin: Hector Galán Productions, 2005.

Gardner, Charles. "The Origins of the Texas Style of Traditional Old-time Fiddling." In *2001: A Texas Folklore Odyssey*, ed. Frances Edward Abernethy, 54–73. Denton: University of North Texas Press, 2001.

Garr, Gillian G. *She's a Rebel: The History of Women in Rock & Roll*, 2d ed., expanded. New York: Seal, 1992.

Gazsi, Mélina. "A Tribute to Victor Schoelcher: Down with Slavery!" *Label France*, no. 56 (October–December 2004). http://www.france.diplomatie.gouv.fr/label_france/56 (accessed on May 6, 2005).

Genovese, Eugene. *Roll, Jordan, Roll: The World the Slaves Made*. New York: Pantheon, 1974.

Giesenschlag, N. D. "Virgil Oliver Stamps." In Barkley et al., *Handbook of Texas Music*, 296.

Gil, Carlos B. "Lydia Mendoza: Houstonian and First Lady of Mexican American Song." In *Houston Review* 3 (Summer 1981): 249–57.

Ginell, Cary. "Milton Brown." In Kingsbury, *Encyclopedia of Country Music*, 58–59.

———, with special assistance from Roy Lee Brown. *Milton Brown and the Founding of Western Swing*. Urbana: University of Illinois Press, 1994.

———, and Kevin Coffey. *Discography of Western Swing and Hot String Bands, 1928–1942*. Westport, Conn.: Greenwood, 2001.

Gish, Theodore, ed. *Travels in Texas (Texas Fahrten)*. Austin: Nortex, 1985.

Gjerde, Jon, ed. *Major Problems in American Immigration and Ethnic History*. Boston: Houghton Mifflin, 1998.

Goldsmith, Thomas. "Kenny Rogers." In Kingsbury, *Encyclopedia of Country Music*, 455–56.

Gorbatov, Andrei. *Wanted: Country Music in Russia and the Ex-USSR*. Moscow: InterMedia News Agency, 1993.

Govenar, Alan B. *African American Frontiers: Slave Narratives and Oral Histories*. Santa Barbara, Calif.: ABC-CLIO, 2000.

———. "Blind Lemon Jefferson." In Barkley et al., *Handbook of Texas Music*, 159–61.

———. "Clifton Chenier: African-American Zydeco Accordionist (Creole)." In Govenar, *Masters of Traditional Arts*, vol. 1, 126–28.

———. "Dewey Balfa: Cajun Fiddler." In Govenar, *Masters of Traditional Arts*, vol. 1, 53–55.

———. "Dixie Hummingbirds: African-American Gospel Singers." In Govenar, *Masters of Traditional Arts*, vol. 1, 170–72.

———. *Living Texas Blues*. Dallas: Dallas Museum of Art, 1985.

———. *Masters of Traditional Arts: A Biographical Dictionary*, vols. 1–2. Santa Barbara, Calif.: ABC-CLIO, 2001.

———, and Jay F. Brakefield. *Deep Ellum and Central Track: Where the Black and White Worlds of Dallas Converged*. Denton: University of North Texas Press, 1998.

Green, Archie. "Austin's Cosmic Cowboys: Words in Collision." In *And Other Neighborly Names: Social Process and Cultural Image in Texas Folklore*, ed. Richard Bauman and Roger D. Abrahams, 153–62. Austin: University of Texas Press, 1981.

Green, Douglas B. *Singing in the Saddle: The History of the Singing Cowboy*. Nashville: Country Music Foundation Press and Vanderbilt University Press, 2002.

Green, Jared, ed. *Rap and Hip Hop: Examining Pop Culture*. Farmington Hills, Mich.: Greenhaven, 2003.

Greene, Victor. *A Passion for Polka: Old-time Ethnic Music in America*. Berkeley: University of California Press, 1992.

Gregory, James N. *American Exodus: The Dust Bowl Migration and Okie Culture in California*. New York: Oxford University Press, 1989.

Griffis, Ken. "The Ken Maynard Story." *John Edwards Memorial Foundation Quarterly* 9, no. 30, Part 2 (Summer 1973): 67–70.

Griffith, Carolyn F. "Czech and Polish Music in Texas before World War II." In Clayton and Specht, eds., *The Roots of Texas Music*, 175–91.

Griffith, Nanci, and Joe Jackson. *Nanci Griffith's Other Voices: A Personal History of Folk Music*. New York: Three Rivers, 1998.

Guerra, Carlos. "Accordion Menace . . . Just Say Mo'!" In Tejeda and Valdez, *Puro Conjunto*, 115–20.

———. "The Unofficial Conjunto Primer for the Uninitiated Music Lover." In Tejeda and Valdez, *Puro Conjunto*, 3–9.

Guterman, Jimmy. "Billy Joe Shaver." In Kingsbury, *Encyclopedia of Country Music*, 477–78.

Guthrie, Woody. *Bound for Glory*. New York: New American Library, 1983.

Gutiérrez, José Angel. "Chicano Music: Evolution and Politics to 1950." In Clayton and Specht, eds., *Roots of Texas Music*, 146–74.

Gutiérrez, Ramón A. *When Jesus Came, the Corn Mothers Went Away: Marriage, Sexuality, and Power in New Mexico, 1500–1846*. Stanford: Stanford University Press, 1991.

Haggard, Merle, with Peggy Russell. *Sing Me Back Home: My Story*. New York: Pocket Books, 1981.

Haley, John W., and John von Hoelle. *Sound and Glory: The Incredible Story of Bill Haley, the Father of Rock 'n' Roll and the Music That Shook the World.* Wilmington, Del.: Dyne-American, 1990.

Hamm, Christine. "Huddie Ledbetter." In Barkley et al., *Handbook of Texas Music,* 183.

Hardman, Peggy. "Blind Willie Johnson." In Barkley et al., *Handbook of Texas Music,* 164–65.

Harris, Sheldon. *The Blues Who's Who: A Biographical Dictionary of Blues Singers.* New York: Da Capo, 1989.

Hartman, Gary. "The Bob Bullock Museum Celebrates Texas Country Music." *Journal of Texas Music History* 2, no. 2 (Fall 2002): 7–15.

———. "Building the Ideal Immigrant: Reconciling Lithuanianism and 100 Percent Americanism to Create a Respectable Nationalist Movement, 1870–1922." *Journal of American Ethnic History* 18, no. 1 (Fall 1998): 36–76.

———. "Foy Willing." In Barkley et al., *Handbook of Texas Music,* 355–56.

———. "From Yellow Roses to Dixie Chicks: Women and Gender in Texas Music History." In John Storey and Mary Kelley, eds., *Twentieth-century Texas: A Social and Cultural History.* Denton: University of North Texas Press, 2008.

———. "Ideal Records." In Barkley et al., *Handbook of Texas Music,* 150.

———. "Texas Music in Europe." *Journal of Texas Music History* 4, no. 1 (Spring 2004): 33–41.

Haslam, Gerald. *Working Man Blues: Country Music in California.* Berkeley: University of California Press, 1999.

Hauschild, Henry J. *A Musical Chronicle from the Historical Scrapbooks.* Victoria, Tex.: Author, 1999.

Haworth, Alan Lee. "Big Bopper." In Barkley et al., *Handbook of Texas Music,* 20.

———. "Lightnin' Hopkins." In Barkley et al., *Handbook of Texas Music,* 142.

———. "Willie Mae Thornton." In Barkley et al., *Handbook of Texas Music,* 324–25.

Head, James. "Douglas Wayne Sahm." In Barkley et al., *Handbook of Texas Music,* 280–81.

———. "Esther Mae Phillips." In Barkley et al., *Handbook of Texas Music,* 243–44.

———. "George Washington Thomas Jr." In Barkley et al., *Handbook of Texas Music,* 320–21.

———. "Hersal Thomas." In Barkley et al., *Handbook of Texas Music,* 323.

———. "Hot Lips Page." In Barkley et al., *Handbook of Texas Music,* 239.

———. "Johnny Watson." In Barkley et al., *Handbook of Texas Music,* 350–51.

———. "King Curtis." In Barkley et al., *Handbook of Texas Music,* 178–79.

———. "Texas Alexander." In Barkley et al., *Handbook of Texas Music,* 2.

Heide, Jean. "Celebrating das Deutsche Lied in Texas." *Journal of Texas Music History* 3, no. 2 (Fall 2003): 29–38.

Henderson, Clayton W. "Minstrelsy." In Hitchcock and Sadie, *New Grove Dictionary of American Music,* vol. 3, 245–47.

Henry, Jacques. "From *Acadien* to *Cajun* to *Cadien*: Ethnic Labelization and Construction of Identity." *Journal of American Ethnic History* 17, no. 4 (Summer 1998): 29–62.

Hentoff, Nat. *Listen to the Stories: Nat Hentoff on Jazz and Country Music.* New York: Harper Collins, 1995.

Hernández, Ramón, Jr. "Three of the Greatest Bajo Sexto Players in the History of Conjunto." In Tejeda and Valdez, *Puro Conjunto*, 81–84.

Hernandez, Raoul. "Equality: Harmolodicizing with Ornette Coleman." *Austin Chronicle* (November 12, 2004). http://www.austinchronicle.com/issues/dispatch/2004–11–12/music.

Herzhaft, Gérard, and Jacques Brémond, eds. *Guide de la Country Music et du Folk.* Paris: Librairie Arthème Fayard, 1999.

Hickinbotham, Gary. "B. W. Stevenson." In Barkley et al., *Handbook of Texas Music*, 297–98.

———. "A History of the Texas Recording Industry." *Journal of Texas Music History* 4, no. 1 (Spring 2004): 18–32.

Hillis, Craig. "Cowboys and Indians: The International Stage." *Journal of Texas Music History* 2, no. 1 (Spring 2002): 17–30.

———. *Texas Trilogy: Life in a Small Texas Town*, with photos by Bruce F. Jordan. Austin: University of Texas Press, 2002.

Himes, Geoffrey. "Clint Black." In Kingsbury, *Encyclopedia of Country Music*, 35–36.

Hinton, Brian. *South by Southwest: A Road Map to Alternative Country.* London: Sanctuary, 2003.

Hitchcock, H. Wiley, and Stanley Sadie, eds. *The New Grove Dictionary of American Music*, vols. 1–4. London: Macmillan, 1986.

Holmesly, Sterlin. "Texas Jazz Veterans: A Collection of Oral Histories." *Journal of Texas Music History* 10 (2006): 30–53.

Hook, Jonathan B. *The Alabama-Coushatta Indians.* College Station: Texas A&M University Press, 1997.

Hoyt, Cathryn A. "Riches, Religion, and Politics: Early Exploration in Texas." In Simons and Hoyt, *Hispanic Texas*, 13–23.

Hudson, Kathleen. *Telling Stories, Writing Songs.* Austin: University of Texas Press, 2001.

Hughes, Richard B. "The Czech Texans." Booklet. Institute of Texan Cultures, University of Texas–San Antonio, 1972.

———. "The French Texans." Booklet. Institute of Texan Cultures, University of Texas–San Antonio, 1973.

———. "The German Texans." Booklet. Institute of Texan Cultures, University of Texas–San Antonio, 1987.

———. "Janis Lyn Joplin." In Barkley et al., *Handbook of Texas Music*, 167–69.

———. "The Jewish Texans." Booklet. Institute of Texan Cultures, University of Texas–San Antonio, 1974.

———. "The Mexican Texans." Booklet. Institute of Texan Cultures, University of Texas–San Antonio, 1986.

———. "The Polish Texans." Booklet. Institute of Texan Cultures, University of Texas–San Antonio, 1972.

———. "Woody Guthrie." In Barkley et al., *Handbook of Texas Music*, 129–30.

Jackson, Bruce. *Wake Up, Dead Man: Afro-American Work Songs of Texas Prisons.* Cambridge, Mass.: Harvard University Press, 1972.

James-Reed, Mint O. *Music in Austin, 1900–1956.* Austin: Von Boeckmann–Jones, 1957.

Jasinski, Laurie. "Rock and Roll." In Barkley et al., *Handbook of Texas Music*, 270–75.

"Jimmie Rodgers." In Barkley et al., *Handbook of Texas Music*, 275–76.

Johnson, John G. "Albert Collins." In Barkley et al., *Handbook of Texas Music*, 62.

Jones, George, with Tom Carter. *I Lived to Tell It All.* New York: Villard, 1996.

Jones, Hettie. *Big Star Fallin' Mama: Five Women in Black Music.* New York: Viking, 1974.

Jones, Margaret. "Jimmy Dean." In Kingsbury, *Encyclopedia of Country Music*, 140.

Joplin, Laura. *Love, Janis.* New York: Villard, 1992.

Jordan, Terry G. *German Seed in Texas Soil: Immigrant Farmers in Nineteenth-century Texas.* Austin: University of Texas Press, 1966.

Kamen, Henry. *Spain 1469–1714: A Society of Conflict.* New York: Longman, 1983.

Karlok, Dan. *Antones: Home of the Blues.* (Documentary film.) Austin: Silver Star Entertainment Group, 2005.

Kashanipour, Ryan A. "Tiny Moore." In Barkley et al., *Handbook of Texas Music*, 215–16.

Keller, Kate Van Winkle, with John Koegel. "Secular Music to 1800." In Nicholls, *Cambridge History of American Music*, 49–77.

Kennedy, Rod. *Music from the Heart: The Fifty-year Chronicle of His Life in Music (with a Few Sidetrips!).* Austin: Eakin, 1998.

Kingsbury, Paul, ed. *The Encyclopedia of Country Music: The Ultimate Guide to the Music.* New York: Oxford University Press, 1998.

———. "Willis Alan Ramsey." In Kingsbury, *Encyclopedia of Country Music*, 428.

Klein, Joe. *Woody Guthrie: A Life.* New York: Knopf, 1980.

Knight, Tim. *Chantilly Lace: The Life and Times of J. P. Richardson.* Port Arthur, Tex.: Port Arthur Historical Society, 1989.

Koegel, John. "Crossing Borders: Mexicana, Tejana, and Chicana Musicians in the United States and Mexico." In *From Tejano to Tango: Latin American Popular Music*, ed. Walter Aaron Clark, 97–125. New York: Routledge, 2002.

Kohout, Martin Donell. "Adolph Hofner." In Barkley et al., *Handbook of Texas Music*, 137.

———. "Buddy Holly." In Barkley et al., *Handbook of Texas Music*, 139–42.

———. "Dale Evans." In Barkley et al., *Handbook of Texas Music*, 95–97.

Kolar, Roger H. *Early Czech Dance Halls in Texas.* Austin: Roger H. Kolar, 1975.

Kostelanetz, Richard, ed. *The B. B. King Companion: Five Decades of Commentary.* New York: Schirmer, 1997.

Koster, Rick. *Texas Music.* New York: St. Martin's, 1998.

Kownslar, Allan O. *The European Texans.* College Station: Texas A&M University Press, 2004.

Kruger, Debbie. "J. D. Souther Interview, October 2, 1997." http://www.DebbieKruger.com (accessed October 8, 2005).

La Vere, David. *Life among the Texas Indians: The W.P.A. Narratives.* College Station: Texas A&M University Press, 1998.

Lagarde, François. "Diplomacy, Commerce, and Colonization: Saligny and the Republic." In *The French in Texas: History, Migration, Culture*, ed. François Lagarde, 107–23. Austin: University of Texas Press, 2003.

Lange, Jeffrey J. *Smile When You Call Me Hillbilly: Country Music's Struggle for Respectability, 1939–1954*. Athens: University of Georgia Press, 2004.

Laubin, Reginald, and Gladys Laubin. *Indian Dances of North America: Their Importance to Indian Life*. Norman: University of Oklahoma Press, 1977.

Lehman, Peter. *Roy Orbison: The Invention of an Alternative Rock Masculinity*. Philadelphia: Temple University Press, 2003.

Leifeste, Linc. "Ted Daffan." In Barkley et al., *Handbook of Texas Music*, 74–75.

Leigh, Keri. *Stevie Ray: Soul to Soul*. Dallas: Taylor, 1993.

Levine, Lindsay. "American Indian Music, Past and Present." In Nicholls, *Cambridge History of American Music*, 3–29.

LeVine, Michael. *Johnny Horton: Your Singing Fisherman*. New York: Vantage, 1982.

Lich, Glen E. *The Federal Republic of Germany and Texas: A Sesquicentennial Tribute*. Bonn, Germany: Inter Nationes, 1986.

———, and Dona B. Reeves, eds. *German Culture in Texas: A Free Earth; Essays from the 1978 Southwest Symposium*. Boston: Twayne, 1980.

Lich, Glen E., and Brandy Schnautz. "Luckenbach, Texas." In Barkley et al., *Handbook of Texas Music*, 193–94.

Lightfoot, John. "Early Texas Bluesmen." In Clayton and Specht, eds., *Roots of Texas Music*, 95–118.

Limerick, Patricia Nelson. *Legacy of Conquest: The Unbroken Past of the American West*. New York: Norton, 1988.

Lindaman, Matthew. "Heimat in the Heartland: The Significance of an Ethnic Newspaper." *Journal of American Ethnic History* 23, no. 3 (Spring 2004): 78–98.

Linn, Karen Elizabeth. "The 'Elevation' of the Banjo in Late Nineteenth-century America." *American Music* 8, no. 4 (Winter 1990): 441–64.

Litweiler, John. *Ornette Coleman: A Harmolodic Life*. New York: Morrow, 1992.

Lloyd, David. "Adulteration and the Nation: Monologic Nationalism and the Colonial Hybrid." In Arteaga, ed., *Other Tongue*, 53–92.

Lock, Cory. "Counterculture Cowboys: Progressive Texas Country of the 1970s and 1980s." *Journal of Texas Music History* 3, no. 1 (Spring 2003): 14–23.

Lomax, Alan. *The Land Where the Blues Began*. New York: New Press, 2002.

Lomax, John A. *Cowboy Songs and Other Frontier Ballads*. New York: Sturgis and Walton, 1910.

———. *Songs of the Cattle Trail and Cow Camp*. New York: Duell, Sloan, and Pearce, 1947.

Lomax, John, III. "Don Williams." In Kingsbury, *Encyclopedia of Country Music*, 589.

———. "Townes Van Zandt." In Kingsbury, *Encyclopedia of Country Music*, 562.

Lornell, Kip, and Anne K. Rasmussen, eds. *Musics of Multicultural America: A Study of Twelve Musical Communities*. New York: Schirmer, 1997.

Lucko, Paul M. "Harry H. Choates." In Barkley et al., *Handbook of Texas Music*, 49–50.

———. "Moon Mullican." In Barkley et al., *Handbook of Texas Music*, 218–19.

Lutzweiler, James. "Emily D. West and the Yellow Prose of Texas: A Primer on Some Primary Documents and their Doctoring." In Abernethy, 2001, 294–317.

Machann, Clinton, and James W. Mendl, Jr., eds. *Czech Voices: Stories from Texas in the Amerikán Národní Kalendár.* College Station: Texas A&M University Press, 1991.

———. *Krásná Amerika: A Study of the Texas Czechs, 1851–1939.* Austin: Eakin, 1983.

Magee, Jeffrey. "Ragtime and Early Jazz." In Nicholls, *Cambridge History of American Music*, 388–417.

Malone, Bill C. *Country Music, U.S.A.,* 2d rev. ed., Austin: University of Texas Press, 2002.

———. "Jim Reeves." In Barkley et al., *Handbook of Texas Music*, 262–63.

———. "Jukeboxes." In Kingsbury, *Encyclopedia of Country Music*, 273–74.

———. "Orvon Gene Autry." In Hitchcock and Sadie, *New Grove Dictionary of American Music*, vol. 1, 93–94.

———. *Singing Cowboys and Musical Mountaineers: Southern Culture and the Roots of Country Music.* Athens: University of Georgia Press, 1993.

———. *Southern Music/American Music.* Lexington: University Press of Kentucky, 1979.

———. "Texas Myth/Texas Music." *Journal of Texas Music History* 1, no. 1 (Spring 2001): 4–11.

Martínez, Max. "El Conjunto Bernal: Style and Legacy." In Tejeda and Valdez, *Puro Conjunto*, 97–105.

Mason, Richard J. "Gospel Music." In Barkley et al., *Handbook of Texas Music*, 122–24.

Maxwell, Lisa C. "Red Garland." In Barkley et al., *Handbook of Texas Music*, 114–15.

Mayhall, Mildred P. *The Kiowas.* Norman: University of Oklahoma Press, 1971.

McCormick, Mack. "Mance Lipscomb: Texas Sharecropper and Songster." *American Folk Music Occasional*, Berkeley, Calif., no. 1 (1964), 61–73.

McDowell, John Holmes. "The Corridos of Greater Mexico as Discourse, Music, and Event." In *And Other Neighborly Names: Social Process and Cultural Image in Texas Folklore*, ed. Richard Bauman and Roger D. Abrahams, 45–75. Austin: University of Texas Press, 1981.

McGraw, Marjie. "Le Ann Rimes." In Kingsbury, *Encyclopedia of Country Music*, 446–47.

McLean, Duncan. *Lone Star Swing: On the Trail of Bob Wills and His Texas Playboys.* New York: Norton, 1997.

McLeese, Don. "Butch Hancock." In Kingsbury, *Encyclopedia of Country Music*, 226–27.

McVey, John. "John Townes Van Zandt." In Barkley et al., *Handbook of Texas Music*, 338–40.

Millard, Bob. "Charley Pride." In Kingsbury, *Encyclopedia of Country Music*, 423–24.

Minton, John. "Mance Lipscomb." In Barkley et al., *Handbook of Texas Music*, 185–87.

Mitchell, Rick. "Joe Ely." In Kingsbury, *Encyclopedia of Country Music*, 163–64.

———. "Robert Earl Keen." In Kingsbury, *Encyclopedia of Country Music*, 276.

Moag, Rod. "The History of Early Bluegrass in Texas." *Journal of Texas Music History* 4, no. 2 (Fall 2004): 22–48.

Monahan, Casey, ed. *Openers II: The Lyrics of Roky Erickson*. Los Angeles: 2.13.61 Press, 1995.

Monge, Luigi, and David Evans. "New Songs of Blind Lemon Jefferson." *Journal of Texas Music History* 3, no. 2 (Fall 2003): 8–28.

Monsho, Kharen. "Gene Ramey." In Barkley et al., *Handbook of Texas Music*, 251–52.

Montejano, David. *Anglos and Mexicans in the Making of Texas, 1836–1986*. Austin: University of Texas Press, 1987.

Mooney, Kevin. "Texas Centennial 1936: African-American Texans and the Third National Folk Festival." *Journal of Texas Music History* 1, no. 1 (Spring 2001): 36–43.

Moore, Allan, ed. *The Cambridge Companion to Blues and Gospel Music*. New York: Cambridge University Press, 2002.

Moore, Matthew Douglas. "Jesse Ashlock." In Barkley et al., *Handbook of Texas Music*, 10.

Morris, Desmond. *The Naked Ape*. New York: Dell, 1984.

Morris, Nick A. *A History of the S.P.J.S.T.: A Texas Chronicle, 1897–1980*. Temple, Tex.: Slavonic Benevolent Order of the State of Texas, 1984.

Mulroy, Kevin. *Freedom on the Border: The Seminole Maroons in Florida, the Indian Territory, Coahuila, and Texas*. Lubbock: Texas Tech University Press, 1993.

Nelson, Willie, with Bud Shrake. *Willie: An Autobiography*. New York: Simon and Schuster, 1988.

Nettl, Bruno, Charlotte Heth, and Gertrude Prokosch Kurath. "Indians, American." In Hitchcock and Sadie, eds., *New Grove Dictionary of American Music*, vol. 2, 460–79.

Nicholls, David, ed. *The Cambridge History of American Music*. New York: Cambridge University Press, 1998.

Norman, Philip. *Buddy: The Biography*. London: Macmillan, 1996.

———. *Rave On: The Biography of Buddy Holly*. New York: Simon and Schuster, 1996.

———. *Shout! The Beatles in Their Generation*. New York: Fireside, 1996.

Oermann, Robert K. *America's Music: The Roots of Country*. Atlanta: Turner, 1996.

———. "Cindy Walker." In Kingsbury, *Encyclopedia of Country Music*, 567–68.

———. "Lyle Lovett." In Kingsbury, *Encyclopedia of Country Music*, 307.

Oliphant, Dave. "Bebop Messengers to the World: Kenny Dorham and Leo Wright." *Journal of Texas Music History* 1, no. 1 (Spring 2001): 15–23.

———. *The Early Swing Era, 1930 to 1941*. Westport, Conn.: Greenwood, 2002.

———. "Eddie Durham." In Barkley et al., *Handbook of Texas Music*, 86–87.

———. "Eddie Durham and the Texas Contribution to Jazz History." *Southwestern Historical Quarterly* (April 1993): 491–525.

———. "Emilio Caceres" In Barkley et al., *Handbook of Texas Music*, 43.

———. "Ernesto Caceres." In Barkley et al., *Handbook of Texas Music*, 43.

———. "Henry Thomas." In Barkley et al., *Handbook of Texas Music*, 321–23.

———. "Oscar Frederic Moore." In Barkley et al., *Handbook of Texas Music*, 215.

———. *Texan Jazz*. Austin: University of Texas Press, 1996.

———. "The Wisconsin-Texas Jazz Nexus." *Journal of Texas Music History* 4, no. 1 (Spring 2004): 8–17.

Oliver, Paul. "Clifton Chenier." In Hitchcock and Sadie, eds., *New Grove Dictionary of American Music*, vol. 1, 414.

Olivier, Rick, and Ben Sandmel. *Zydeco!* Jackson: University of Mississippi Press, 1999.

Olsen, Allen. "San Antonio's West Side Sound." *Journal of Texas Music History* 5, no. 1 (Spring 2005): 26–39.

Olsen, Dale A., and Daniel E. Sheehy, eds. *The Garland Handbook of Latin American Music*. New York: Garland, 2000.

Opdyke, Steven. *Willie Nelson Sings America*. Austin: Eakin, 1998.

Oster, Harry. "The Louisiana Acadians." In Strachwitz and Welding, *American Folk Music Occasional*, 18–21.

Owens, William A. *Tell Me a Story, Sing Me a Song: A Texas Chronicle*. Austin: University of Texas Press, 1983.

Palmer, Jack. "Vernon Dalhart." In Barkley et al., *Handbook of Texas Music*, 75–77.

———. *Vernon Dalhart: The First Star of Country Music*. Denver: Mainspring, 2005.

Pappas, Theodore, ed. *Britannica Precise Encyclopedia*. Chicago: Encyclopaedia Britannica, 2002.

Paredes, Améric. *A Texas-Mexican Cancionero: Folksongs of the Lower Border*. Urbana: University of Illinois Press, 1976.

———. *With His Pistol in His Hand*. Austin: University of Texas Press, 1976.

Parker, Donna P. "Sippie Wallace." In Barkley et al., *Handbook of Texas Music*, 349–50.

Patoski, Joe Nick. *Selena: Como la Flor*. Boston: Little, Brown, 1996.

———. "Uno, Dos, One, Two, Tres, Quatro." *Journal of Texas Music History* 1, no. 1 (Spring 2001): 12–14.

———, and Bill Crawford. *Stevie Ray Vaughan: Caught in the Crossfire*. Boston: Little, Brown, 1993.

Peña, Manuel. "Conjunto Music: The First Fifty Years." In Tejeda and Valdez, *Puro Conjunto*, 61–69.

———. "The Emergence of Conjunto Music, 1935–1955." In Tejeda and Valdez, *Puro Conjunto*, 13–30.

———. *The Mexican American Orquesta: Music, Culture, and the Dialectic of Conflict*. Austin: University of Texas Press, 1999.

———. *Música Tejana: The Cultural Economy of Artistic Transformation*. College Station: Texas A&M University Press, 1999.

———. *The Texas-Mexican Conjunto: History of a Working-class Music*. Austin: University of Texas Press, 1985.

Pérez-Torres, Rafael. "Mestizaje in the Mix: Chicano Identity, Cultural Politics, and Postmodern Music." In Radano and Bohlman, *Music and the Racial Imagination*, 206–30.

Perkins, John E., Jr. *Leon Rausch: The Voice of the Texas Playboys*. Arlington, Tex.: Swing, 1996.

Perry, Ann. "Tejano Festivals: Celebrations of History and Community." In Simons and Hoyt, *Hispanic Texas*, 120–29.

Peterson, Richard A. *Creating Country Music: Fabricating Authenticity*. Chicago: University of Chicago Press, 1997.

Petrie, Paul. "The History of Gospel Music." http://www.afgen.com/gospel (accessed December 13, 2004).

Phillips, Stacey. *Western Swing Fiddle.* New York: Oak, 1994.

Plater, Ormonde, Cynthia Speyrer, and Rand Speyrer. *Cajun Dancing.* Gretna, La.: Pelican, 1993.

Porterfield, Bill. *The Greatest Honky Tonks in Texas.* Dallas: Taylor, 1983.

Porterfield, Nolan. *Jimmie Rodgers: The Life and Times of America's Blue Yodeler.* Urbana: University of Illinois Press, 1992.

Pride, Charley, with Jim Henderson. *The Charley Pride Story.* New York: Morrow, 1994.

Proefrock, Stacia. "J. D. Souther." http://www.AllMusic.com (accessed October 8, 2005).

Proulx, E. Annie. *Accordion Crimes.* New York: Scribner, 1996.

Pugh, Ronnie. "Ernest Tubb." In Kingsbury, *Encyclopedia of Country Music,* 547–49.

———. *Ernest Tubb: The Texas Troubadour.* Durham: Duke University Press, 1996.

Radano, Ronald, and Philip V. Bohlman, eds. *Music and the Racial Imagination.* Chicago: University of Chicago Press, 2000.

Ragland, Cathy. "La Voz del Pueblo Tejano: Conjunto Music and the Construction of Tejano Identity in Texas." In Tejeda and Valdez, *Puro Conjunto,* 211–27.

Ramsey, Guthrie P., Jr. *Race Music: Black Cultures from Bebop to Hip-Hop.* Berkeley: University of California Press, 2003.

Rees, Dafydd, and Luke Crampton. *Rock Movers & Shakers.* New York: Billboard, 1991.

Reich, Howard. *Van Cliburn.* Nashville: Thomas Nelson, 1993.

Reid, Jan. *The Improbable Rise of Redneck Rock.* Austin: University of Texas Press, 2004.

Reyna, José R. "Notes on Tejano Music." *Aztlán: International Journal of Chicano Studies Research* 13, nos. 1 and 2 (Spring and Fall 1982): 82–83.

———. "Tejano Music as an Expression of Cultural Nationalism" In Tejeda and Valdez, *Puro Conjunto,* 191–98.

Rhodes, Don. "Jeannie C. Riley." In Kingsbury, *Encyclopedia of Country Music,* 446.

Rice, James. *Texas Honky-tonk Music.* Austin: Eakin, 1985.

Richards, Tad, and Melvin B. Shestack. *The New Country Music Encyclopedia.* New York: Fireside, 1993.

Richardson, Rupert N., Adrian Anderson, Cary D. Wintz, and Ernest Wallace. *Texas: The Lone Star State.* Upper Saddle River, N.J.: Prentice Hall, 2001.

Risling, Greg. "Country Music Superstar Buck Owens Dies at 76," Associated Press (March 25, 2006).

Robbins, Ira A., ed. *The Trouser Press Guide to '90s' Rock.* New York: Fireside, 1997.

Rodnitzky, Jerry. "Janis Joplin: The Hippie Blues Singer as Feminist Heroine." *Journal of Texas Music History* 2, no. 1 (Spring 2002): 7–15.

Rodríguez, Juan Carlos. "Beto Villa." In Barkley et al., *Handbook of Texas Music,* 342–43.

———. "Bob Dunn." In Barkley et al., *Handbook of Texas Music,* 86.

———. "Chelo Silva." In Barkley et al., *Handbook of Texas Music,* 288.

———. "Valerio Longoria." In Barkley et al., *Handbook of Texas Music,* 190–91.

Roeckle, Charles A. "Fritz Oberdoerffer." In Barkley et al., *Handbook of Texas Music,* 232.

Romanowski, Patricia, and Holly George-Warren, eds. *The New Rolling Stone Encyclopedia of Rock & Roll.* New York: Rolling Stone Press, 1995.

Romero, Brenda M. "Cultural Interaction in New Mexico as Illustrated in the Matachines." In *Musics of Multicultural America: A Study of Twelve Musical Communities,* ed. Kip Lornell and Anne K. Rasmussen, 155–85. New York: Schirmer, 1997.

Romero, Yolanda. "Trini Gámez, the Texas Farm Workers, and Mexican American Community Empowerment: Toil and Trouble on the South Texas Plains." In Zamora, Orozco, and Rocha, *Mexican Americans in Texas History,* 143–55.

Rosenberg, Neil V. *Bluegrass: A History.* Urbana: University of Illinois Press, 1985.

Rumble, John. "Floyd Tillman." In Kingsbury, *Encyclopedia of Country Music,* 540.

———. "Hank Thompson." In Kingsbury, *Encyclopedia of Country Music,* 536–37.

———. "Jim Reeves." In Kingsbury, *Encyclopedia of Country Music,* 435–36.

Salem, James M. *The Late Great Johnny Ace and the Transition from R&B to Rock 'n' Roll.* Urbana: University of Illinois Press, 1999.

San Miguel, Guadalupe, Jr. "Música Tejana: Nuestra Música." *Journal of Texas Music History* 1, no. 1 (Spring 2001): 24–35.

———. *Tejano Proud: Tex-Mex Music in the Twentieth Century.* College Station: Texas A&M University Press, 2002.

Sandmel, Ben. "Jimmie Dale Gilmore." In Kingsbury, *Encyclopedia of Country Music,* 202–203.

Santelli, Robert. *The Big Book of Blues: A Biographical Encyclopedia.* New York: Penguin, 1993.

Savage, William W., Jr. *Singing Cowboys and All That Jazz: A Short History of Popular Music in Oklahoma.* Norman: University of Oklahoma Press, 1983.

Schilz, Thomas F. *Lipan Apaches in Texas.* El Paso: Texas Western Press/University of Texas–El Paso, 1987.

Schnautz, Brandy. "Bacas of Fayetteville." In Barkley et al., *Handbook of Texas Music,* 14.

———. "Gruene Hall." In Barkley et al., *Handbook of Texas Music,* 126.

Scudday, Roy G. "Tex Beneke." In Barkley et al., *Handbook of Texas Music,* 19–20.

Seeber, Jill S. "Eck Robertson." In Barkley et al., *Handbook of Texas Music,* 268–69.

———. "Johnny Horton." In Barkley et al., *Handbook of Texas Music,* 142–43.

———. "Santiago Jiménez, Sr." In Barkley et al., *Handbook of Texas Music,* 163–64.

Seemann, Charlie. "Carl T. Sprague." In Kingsbury, *Encyclopedia of Country Music,* 499.

Self, Greg. "Stamps-Baxter Music and Printing Company." In Barkley et al., *Handbook of Texas Music,* 296–97.

Selvin, Joel. "At the Crossroads: The Psychedelic Sounds of Texans in the Summer of Love." *Texas Music* 11 (Summer 2002): 58–65.

Sgammato, Jo. *Dreams Come True: The Le Ann Rimes Story.* New York: Ballantine, 1997.

Shaver, Billy Joe, assisted by Brad Reagan. *Honky Tonk Hero.* Austin: University of Texas Press, 2005.

Sheehy, Daniel. "Mexican Mariachi Music: Made in the U.S.A." In Lornell and Rasmussen, *Musics of Multicultural America,* 131–54.

Shelemay, Kay Kaufman, ed. *The Garland Library of Readings in Ethnomusicology,* vol. 1: *History, Definitions, and Scope of Ethnomusicology.* New York: Garland, 1990.

Shreve, Bradley. "Blind Arizona Dranes." In Barkley et al., *Handbook of Texas Music*, 83.

Simon, Cheryl. "Euday Louis Bowman." In Barkley et al., *Handbook of Texas Music*, 32.

———. "Walter Hyatt." In Barkley et al., *Handbook of Texas Music*, 148–49.

Simons, Helen, and Cathryn A. Hoyt, eds. *Hispanic Texas: A Historical Guide*. Austin: University of Texas Press, 1992.

Skanske, Richard. "Eliza Gilkyson." *Texas Music* 24 (Fall 2005): 40–47.

Skrabanek, Robert L. *We're Czechs*. College Station: Texas A&M University Press, 1988.

Smith, Richard D. *Can't You Hear Me Callin': The Life of Bill Monroe, Father of Bluegrass*. Boston: Little, Brown, 2000.

Smyrl, Vivian Elizabeth. "Teddy Wilson." In Barkley et al., *Handbook of Texas Music*, 359.

Specht, Joe W. "The Blue Yodeler Is Coming to Town: A Week with Jimmie Rodgers in West Texas." *Journal of Texas Music History* 1, no. 2 (Fall 2001): 17–22.

———. "Hoyle Nix." In Barkley et al., *Handbook of Texas Music*, 231.

———. "I Forgot to Remember to Forget: Elvis Presley in Texas, 1955." *Journal of Texas Music History* 3, no. 1 (Spring 2003): 7–13.

———. "Put a Nickel in the Jukebox: The Texas Tradition in Country Music, 1922– 1950." In Clayton and Specht, eds., *Roots of Texas Music*, 66–94.

Spell, Lota M. "Adolph Fuchs." In Barkley et al., *Handbook of Texas Music*, 112–13.

———. "The Early German Contribution to Music in Texas." *American-German Review* 12, no. 4 (April 1946): 8–10.

———. *Music in Texas: A Survey of One Aspect of Cultural Progress*. Austin, 1936.

Spottswood, Dick. "Hawaiian Music." In Kingsbury, ed. *Encyclopedia of Country Music*, 231–32.

St. John, Lauren. *Hardcore Troubadour: The Life and Near Death of Steve Earle*. New York: Fourth Estate, Harper Collins, 2003.

Stambler, Irwin, and Grelun Landon, eds. *Country Music: The Encyclopedia*. New York: St. Martin's, 1997.

Stancell, Steven. *Rap Whoz Who: The World of Rap Music, Performers, Producers, Promoters*. New York: Schirmer, 1996.

Star, Larry, and Christopher Waterman. *American Popular Music: The Rock Years*. New York: Oxford University Press, 2006.

Stevenson, Robert. *Music in Mexico*. New York: Crowell, 1971.

Stewart, Kenneth L., and Arnoldo De León. "Literacy among Immigrantes in Texas, 1850– 1900." *Latin American Research Review* 20, no. 3 (1985): 180–87.

Stivale, Charles J. *Disenchanting les Bons Temps: Identity and Authenticity in Cajun Music and Dance*. Durham: Duke University Press, 2003.

Stokes, Martin. "Introduction: Ethnicity, Identity, and Music." In Martin Stokes, ed., *Ethnicity, Identity, and Music: The Musical Construction of Place*, 1–27. Providence, R.I.: Berg, 1994.

Strachwitz, Chris. "Cajun Country." In *The American Folk Music Occasional*, ed. Chris Strachwitz and Pete Welding, 13–17. New York: Oak, 1970.

———. "Texas Polka Music: Interview with Joe Patek." In Strachwitz and Welding, *American Folk Music Occasional*, 73–75.

———. "Zydeco Music, i.e., French Blues." In Strachwitz and Welding, *American Folk Music Occasional*, 22–24.

———, with James Nicolopulos. *Lydia Mendoza: A Family Autobiography*. Houston: Arte Público, 1993.

Stricklin, Al, with Jon McConal. *My Years with Bob Wills*. Austin: Eakin, 1980.

Style, Lyle E. *Ain't Got No Cigarettes: Memories of Music Legend Roger Miller*. Winnipeg, Manitoba: Great Plains, 2005.

Sutton, Randi. "Alexander Herman Moore." In Barkley et al., *Handbook of Texas Music*, 213–14.

Swenson, John. *Bill Haley: The Daddy of Rock and Roll*. New York: Stein and Day, 1982.

Tate, Paul. "The Cajuns of Louisiana." In Strachwitz and Welding, *American Folk Music Occasional*, 8–12.

Teja, Jesús F. de la, Paula Marks, and Ron Tyler. *Texas: Crossroads of North America*. New York: Houghton Mifflin, 2004.

Tejeda, Juan. "¡Conjunto! Estilo y Clase: Narciso Martínez, Valerio Longoria, Tony de la Rosa, Paulino Bernal, Flaco Jiménez y Esteban Jordán." In Tejeda and Valdez, *Puro Conjunto*, 315–51.

———. "Eva Ybarra." In Tejeda and Valdez, *Puro Conjunto*, 295–300.

———. "An Odyssey through the Magical Land of Conjunto, el Movimiento Xicano, and the Tejano Conjunto Festival." In Tejeda and Valdez, *Puro Conjunto*, 359–77.

———. "Santiago Jiménez, Sr." In Tejeda and Valdez, *Puro Conjunto*, 255–78.

———, and Avelardo Valdez, eds. *Puro Conjunto: An Album in Words and Pictures*. Austin: University of Texas Press, 2001.

Texas Music Museum. "Música Tejana: History and Development of Tejano Music." Booklet. Texas Music Museum, Austin, 1996.

———. "Musikfest: German Contributions to Texas Music." Booklet. Texas Music Museum, Austin, 1992.

———. "Muziky, Muziky: Czech Contributions to Texas Music." Booklet. Texas Music Museum, Austin, 1995.

———. "Our Native Spirit." Booklet. Texas Music Museum, Austin, 1998.

———. "Rags to Rap: African-American Contributions to Texas Music." Booklet. Texas Music Museum, Austin, 1997.

"Tex Ritter." In Barkley et al., *Handbook of Texas Music*, 267.

Texanische Lieder: Aus mündlicher und schriftlicher Mitteilung deutscher Texaner. San Felipe de Austin, Tex.: Adolph Fuchs, 1834.

Thorp, N. Howard. *Songs of the Cowboys*. Boston: Houghton Mifflin, 1908.

Tichi, Cecilia. *High Lonesome: The American Culture of Country Music*. Chapel Hill: University of North Carolina Press, 1994.

Tillis, Kirvin. "Joseph Arrington, Jr." In Barkley et al., *Handbook of Texas Music*, 8.

Tippens, Matthew. "Norman Petty." In Barkley et al., *Handbook of Texas Music*, 243.

Tisserand, Michael. *The Kingdom of Zydeco.* New York: Arcade, 1998.

Tosches, Nick. *Unsung Heroes of Rock 'n' Roll: The Birth of Rock in the Wild Years before Elvis.* New York: Da Capo, 1999.

Townsend, Charles. "Bob Wills." In Barkley et al., *Handbook of Texas Music*, 356–57.

———. *San Antonio Rose: The Life and Music of Bob Wills.* Urbana: University of Illinois Press, 1986.

———. "Tommy Duncan." In Barkley et al., *Handbook of Texas Music*, 85–86.

———. "Western Swing." In Kingsbury, *Encyclopedia of Country Music*, 579–80.

Trachtenberg, Jay. "Dream Story: Eli's Coming, Hide Your Horn, Man." *Austin Chronicle* 26, no. 5 (October 6, 2006): 70.

Treviño, Geronimo. *Dance Halls and Last Calls: A History of Texas Country Music.* Plano: Republic of Texas Press, 2002.

Tucker, Stephen R. "Kinky Friedman." In Kingsbury, *Encyclopedia of Country Music*, 184.

Tucker, Tanya, and Patsi Bale Cox. *Nickel Dreams: My Life.* New York: Hyperion, 1997.

Turner, Martha Anne. *The Yellow Rose of Texas: The Story of a Song.* El Paso: Texas Western Press, University of Texas–El Paso, 1971.

Turpin, Solveig A. "Native American Music." In Barkley et al., *Handbook of Texas Music*, 225–28.

Uhler, David. "University Researchers Are Trying to Record State's Unique, and Dying, German Language." *San Antonio Express-News* (January 30, 2005).

Utterback, Martha. "French Artists in Texas." In Lagarde, *French in Texas*, 178–91.

Valdez, Avelardo, and Jeffrey A. Halley. "The Popular in *Conjunto Tejano* Music: Changes in Chicano Class and Identity." In Tejeda and Valdez, *Puro Conjunto*, 199–209.

Van Beveren, Amy. "Freddie King." In Barkley et al., *Handbook of Texas Music*, 177–78.

Van Sickel, Robert W. "A World without Citizenship: On (the Absence of) Politics and Ideology in Country Music Lyrics, 1960–2000." *Popular Music and Society* 28, no. 3 (July 2005): 313–31.

Wade, Maria F. *The Native Americans of the Texas Edwards Plateau, 1582–1799.* Austin: University of Texas Press, 2003.

Wald, Elijah. *Narcocorrido: A Journey into the Music of Drugs, Guns, and Guerillas.* New York: Harper Collins, 2001.

Walker, Mack. *Germany and the Emigration, 1816–1885.* Cambridge, Mass.: Harvard University Press, 1964.

Ward, George B. "Roy Kelton Orbison." In Barkley et al., *Handbook of Texas Music*, 236–37.

Waterman, Christopher A. "Race Music: Bo Chatmon, 'Corrine, Corrina,' and the Excluded Middle." In Radano and Bohlman, *Music and the Racial Imagination*, 167–205.

Weddle, Robert S. "Cross and Crown: The Spanish Missions in Texas." In Simons and Hoyt, *Hispanic Texas*, 25–35.

West, Sarah Ann. *Deep Down Hard Blues: A Tribute to Lightnin' Hopkins.* Lawrenceville, Va.: Brunswick, 1995.

Wheat, John. "Armadillo World Headquarters." In Barkley et al., *Handbook of Texas Music*, 6–7.

White, Raymond E. *King of the Cowboys, Queen of the West: Roy Rogers and Dale Evans*. Madison: University of Wisconsin Press, 2005.

Whiteside, Jonny. "Spade Cooley." In Kingsbury, *Encyclopedia of Country Music*, 109.

Williams, Janet E. "Tracy Lawrence." In Kingsbury, *Encyclopedia of Country Music*, 291–92.

Williams, Stephen G., and Kharen Monsho. "Arnett Cobb." In Barkley et al., *Handbook of Texas Music*, 58.

Willing, Sharon Lee. *No One to Cry to: A Long, Hard Ride into the Sunset with Foy Willing of the Riders of the Purple Sage*. Tucson: Wheatmark, 2006.

Willman, Chris. "Stars and Strife." *Entertainment Weekly* 708 (May 2, 2003), 22.

Willoughby, Larry. *Texas Rhythm, Texas Rhyme: A Pictorial History of Texas Music*. Austin: Texas Monthly Press, 1984.

Wills, Rosetta. *The King of Western Swing: Bob Wills Remembered*. New York: Billboard, 1998.

Wilson, Burton, with Jack Ortman. *The Austin Music Scene through the Lens of Burton Wilson, 1965–1994*. Austin: Eakin, 2001.

Winans, Robert B. "The Folk, the Stage, and the Five-string Banjo in the Nineteenth Century." *Journal of American Folklore* 89, no. 354 (October 1976): 407–37.

Wolfe, Charles K. *The Devil's Box: Masters of Southern Fiddling*. Nashville: Country Music Foundation Press and Vanderbilt University Press, 1997.

———. "Eck Robertson." In Kingsbury, *Encyclopedia of Country Music*, 450–51.

———, and Kip Lornell. *The Life and Legend of Leadbelly*. New York: Harper Collins, 1992.

Wolz, Larry. "Roots of Classical Music in Texas: The German Contribution." In Clayton and Specht, eds., *The Roots of Texas Music*, 119–37.

Wood, Roger. "Black Creoles and the Evolution of Zydeco in Southeast Texas: The Beginnings to 1950." In Clayton and Specht, eds., *The Roots of Texas Music*, 192–216.

———. *Down in Houston: Bayou City Blues*. Austin: University of Texas Press, 2003, 245.

———. "Southeast Texas: Hothouse of Zydeco." *Journal of Texas Music History* 1, no. 2 (Fall 2001): 23–44.

———. *Texas Zydeco*. Austin: University of Texas Press, 2006.

———. "Zydeco." In Barkley et al., *Handbook of Texas Music*, 365–66.

Wyman, Bill. *Blues Odyssey: A Journey to Music's Heart and Soul*. New York: DK Publishing, 2001.

Zamora, Emilio, Cynthia Orozco, and Rodolfo Rocha. *Mexican Americans in Texas History: Selected Essays*. Austin: Texas State Historical Association, 2000.

Zolten, Jerry. *Great God A'Mighty! The Dixie Hummingbirds: Celebrating the Rise of Soul Gospel Music*. New York: Oxford University Press, 2003.

Index

Italicized page numbers indicate illustrations.

"96 Tears" (song), 50, 207

? and the Mysterians (group), 50, 207

accordion: Anglo adoption of, 131; in country music, 135; cultural origin of, 28, 30, 248n24 (110); in French music, 120, 121; in música tejana, 23, 27, 28–29, 30, 38, 42, 44, 45, 50, 51; in onda chicana, 46; for orquesta-conjunto blends, 32
Ace in the Hole Band, 95, 177
African American music: African traditions, 22; Anglos influenced by, 131–32; Europeans influenced by, 77; German influences, 105; influences on, 222; market for, 4, 69, 223; recording of, 40; slavery period, 60–61
African Americans: assimilation of, 62–63; civil rights for, 26, 81; cowboy movies, 143; demographics, 59–60; discrimination against, 24, 56, 59, 62, 197–98; economic opportunities for, 26; impact of, 56–57, 98; religion of, 61–62; stereotypes of, 71; Texas migration of, 58, 59; Texas music influenced by, 2–3, 56
Alexander, Alger "Texas," 72–73, 77
Americana (musical genre), 129, 170, 179, 186, 188
American immigrants to Texas, 9, 133–34
American music, Texas influence on, 2–4, 6
"American Pie" (song), 201
amplifiers, 44, 75

Anglo-Tejano relations in music, 34, 35–36
Anglo (term), 130
Anglo Texans, 9, 10
Antone, Clifford, 84, 87–88
"Arkansas Traveler" (song), 137, 184
Armadillo World Headquarters, 165, 166, 167, 168, 172, 217
Armstrong, Louis, 74, 75, 89, 90, 93, 94
Arthur, Charline (born Charline Highsmith), 159–60, 203
Asian immigrants to Texas, 10
Asleep at the Wheel (group), 112, 146, 147, 166
assimilation by ethnic minorities: Anglo group, absorption into, 130; baby boomers, 47; class differences, 37, 38–39; German views on, 110, 246nn5–6 (102); pressure for, 235n41 (37); resistance to, 34. *See also term* assimilation of *under specific ethnic group, e.g.*: African Americans: assimilation of
Atkins, Chet, 156, 158, 175
Atlantic Records, 74, 168
audience participation in music, 60–61, 67, 68, 92, 234n33 (34), 250n55 (121)
Austin, Moses and Stephen, 9, 58, 133
Austin (city), 165–66, 230n1 (15)
Austin City Limits (PBS program), 5, 166, 170, 190, 224
Austin Lounge Lizards, 154–55
Autry, Orvon "Gene," 3, 129, 139, 140, 141, 142, 153, 157, 199, 222

Baĉa band, 113–14, 116
Baez, Joan, 184, 210
bajo sexto (twelve-string guitar), 27–28, 29, 38, 45